Our Gonce Ancestors

Covering the first two generations of the Gonce family in what is now the United States, as well as the next six generations in the direct line from Justice Gonce, who died in Delaware shortly after the American Revolution, to his 5th great-granddaughter (my mother), who lived from 1919 to 2013.

Appendices summarize, among other subjects, the migration of the southern branch of the Gonce family to Tennessee and beyond, information on Gonces known to have taken part in the American Civil War on both the Union and Confederate sides, and provide evidence for various birth and death dates chosen (where these are doubtful).

Also covered in a more limited manner are various families that have married into the mid-Atlantic line (primarily in Maryland) over the generations, including our Clautice, Comegys, Farring, Hedney, Hulshoff, Kerchner, Lowery, O'Brien, Sullivan, and Vansant ancestors.

Frank Oberle

Our Gonce Ancestors

Revision II: Copyright © 2013 by Frank Oberle

Cover Painting: Watercolor by my first cousin JoAnn Iglehart, daughter of Mary Regina Gonce and one of Justice and Magdalen Gonce's 6th great-granddaughters.

ISBN-10: 0615923143
ISBN-13: 978-0615923147

PREFACE

There have been a number of books published about the genealogy of various segments of the Gonce family, although all of those that I'm aware of deal with portions of what I refer to as the family's "Southern Branch". Since I haven't encountered any publications that discuss my Mother's "mid-Atlantic" branch, one aim of this book is to remedy that lack.

Another aim is to provide an earlier history of the Gonce family that will permit readers to connect the various Gonce genealogy and history books, and make the relationships across the various branches of the family more clear. In several of the published works, the authors have only speculated on the earliest Gonce settlers in this country and, in most cases, later information has shown some of those speculations to be incorrect.

This book therefore covers the arrival of the first Gonce settlers in this country, and follows the three brothers, sons of Justice and Magdalen Gonce, through the American Revolution and the departure of the "Southern Branch" founders to Tennessee after the American Revolution. It then continues by focusing on my direct line – the descendants of the youngest of the three immigrant brothers: my 5th great-grandfather Daniel Gonce.

Although intended for my own descendants, this book will likely be of interest to others of my relatives, many of whom obviously share much of the same ancestry.

Publications Related to the "Southern Branch" of the Gonce Family

Other publications that may be of interest to members of the Gonce family, particularly those in the much larger "Southern Branch" (including early settlers of Tennessee, Alabama, Missouri, and Texas) are:

"The Gonce & Wynne Genealogy"; Barbara Gonce-Clepper; first published in 1986, but now out of print, although available from some libraries that specialize in genealogy. A copy is contained as Item 4 on Microfilm 1320567 from the Church of Jesus Christ of Latter Day Saints; Family History Library. This is the best researched of the published material, although limited to the author's own line.

"Leaves from our Family Tree"; Mettie Marie Taylor Barton; first published in 1990, but now out of print, although available from some genealogical libraries. This book likewise focuses on the author's own line, of which the Gonce clan is a side branch, and contains some interesting anecdotes.

"The Roots and Branches of Jacob (Jake) Newton Williams and Sallie Elizabeth Allison" by Betty Williams Houston; specifically pages 97 & 98 "The Gonce Family" contributed by Eliza B. Woodall; 1984 (out of print, available from some genealogical libraries)

"The Family of Benjamin Hutchisson 1765-1852, 2nd Edition"; Elmer Hutchisson, published in September 1976, but now out of print, although available from some libraries that specialize in genealogy.

"Abraham Rudolph Gonce – Missouri Pioneer"; Frank Oberle. ISBN: 978-06159-12448. This covers the most infamous member of the Gonce family, and follows several of his descendants who were equally well known for their exploits – such as the Colorado "Baby Bandits" and the Nevada "Senior Citizen" robbers.

"Descendants of Matthew Russell and Related Families of Jackson County"; Walter A. Russell; ISBN: 1438924275. Part Seven of this book (page 333 &ff) covers the Gonce family in Jackson County but, since the author used "The Gonce & Wynne Genealogy" as a primary source, there is little new information on the Gonce family. For Gonce readers, its main advantage is that it remains in print.

"Descendants of Hezekiah Davis I" Arch O. Heck; Columbus Ohio, 1965. Out of print, but available for loan from the Abraham Lincoln Presidential Library, 112 N Sixth St, Springfield IL 62701. Dr. Heck's book seems to be a comprehensive history of the Davis family, although his discussions of the Gonces connected to that line contain some significant errors.

Letter dated 16 September 1899 from William H. Watterson of Glen Ash TN to his cousin Flora V. Pounds; William was a grandson of Benjamin Hutchisson [ID 2591] and keeper of the Hutchisson family bible.

Letters dated 15 July 1922 and 8 March 1923 from William Leroy Rogers, then of Cleburne, Texas, to some of his grandchildren regarding their early family history in Tennessee and Alabama.

Some members of the "Southern Branch" of the Gonce family are also mentioned in the appendix "Gonces in the American Civil War" on page 175 of this book, and the section "Gonce Reverse Migrations" on page 149.

Revision II Notes

This revision, in addition to correcting various errors and adding some new names to our Gonce lineage, includes considerably more coverage of the mid-Atlantic branch's Comegys, Vansant, Farring and Clautice ancestors, as well as expanded coverage of my Gonce grandparents Charles and Gertrude. I have also added an improved (easier-to-follow) ancestry chart as well as more than sixty-five new photographs throughout the book and in an appendix.

Table of Contents

PREFACE..iii
   Publications Related to the "Southern Branch" of the Gonce Family.....................iii
   Revision II Notes...iv
Table of Contents...v
Our Gonce Ancestors..1
The Gonces Arrive in America..3
   Pre-American Origins..4
   1st Generation in America: Justice & Magdalen Gonce..4
      The Death of Justice Gonce..6
   2nd Generation: The Three Colonial Gonce Brothers: Rudolph, Abraham, and
      Daniel..9
      Rudolph Gonce – the oldest brother..10
      Children and Grandchildren of Rudolph Gonce & Polly McDade........................11
      Abraham Gonce – the middle brother..14
      My fifth great-grandfather Daniel Gonce – the youngest brother (an introduction)........14
      Revolutionary War Service of the Three Gonce Brothers....................................15
      Delaware Census of 1782..18
   2nd Generation: Daniel Gonce – the youngest brother (cont.) & Mary Lowery....20
      My fifth great-grandmother Mary Lowery & Our Lowery Ancestors...................20
      Daniel Gonce & Mary Lowery..20
      Children of Daniel Gonce & Mary Lowery...21
Our Direct-Line Gonce-Side Ancestors...22
   3rd Generation: Rudolph Gonce & Elizabeth Hedney...22
      My 4th great-grandmother Elizabeth Hedney Gonce & Our Hedney Ancestors..............22
      Rudolph Gonce & Elizabeth Hedney..22
      Children and Grandchildren of Rudolph Gonce & Elizabeth Hedney.................24
      Ann Cox & the Cox Family..24
      Rudolph Gonce & Nancy Ann Cox...25
      Origins of Our Dutch Ancestors – Map of Modern Holland...............................28
      My 4th great-grandmother Rachel Vansant Comegys & Our Vansant Ancestors..............29
      Garrett Vansant & Elizabeth Gerritse..33
      Children of Garrett Vansant & Elizabeth Gerritse...36
      Christoffel Vansant & Rachel Courson...37
      Children of Christoffel Vansant & Rachel Courson..40
      Joshua Vansant & Catherine Johnston...41
      Children of Joshua Vansant & Catherine Johnston...41
      John R. Vansant...43
      John R. Vansant, Jr. & his daughter Rachel...44
      My 3rd great-grandmother Catherine "Kitty" Comegys & Our Comegys Ancestors........45
      Children of Cornelius Comegys & Rebecca Smith..46
      Edward Comegys & Mary Harwood..47
      Children of Edward Comegys & Mary Harwood..47
      Edward Comegys [II] & Mary Thraul...48
      Children of Edward Comegys [II] & Mary Thraul..48
      Jesse Comegys & his wife Mary [unknown surname]...49

Table of Contents

Children of Jesse Comegys & his wife Mary...49
Samuel Comegys & Rachel Vansant...51
George Gonce's Childhood..55
4th Generation: George Gonce & Kitty Comegys..55
George's Final Two Years..63
Children and Grandchildren of George Gonce & Catherine Comegys......64
5th Generation: John Thomas Gonce & Catharine Ann Sullivan................66
Catharine Ann Sullivan – Our Sullivan & O'Brien Ancestors....................66
John Thomas Gonce & Catharine Ann Sullivan – before the Civil War...69
John Thomas Gonce & Catharine Ann Sullivan – the Civil War Years.....72
The Battle of Opequon..75
Details of John's Wound..79
John Thomas Gonce & Catharine Ann Sullivan – after the Civil War......80
Children and Grandchildren of John Thomas Gonce & Catharine Ann Sullivan.....88
6th Generation: William Henry Gonce & Alice Elizabeth Clautice...........89
My second great-grandmother Laura Ann Farring & Our Farring Ancestors.....89
Children and Grandchildren of John & Eliza Farring................................91
Augustus H. Farring & Ellen Clouse..91
Children and Grandchildren of Augustus H. Farring & Ellen Clouse......92
My great-grandmother Alice Elizabeth Clautice & our Clautice Ancestors.....94
John Peter & Anne Marie Clautice...94
Children and grandchildren of John Peter & Anne Marie Clautice..........94
John W. Clautice & Elizabeth Goodwin..97
Children and grandchildren of John W. Clautice & Elizabeth Goodwin..98
John W. Clautice & Laura Ann Farring...99
Children of John W. Clautice & Laura Ann Farring................................101
William Henry Gonce & Alice Elizabeth Clautice...................................101
Children and Grandchildren of William Henry Gonce & Alice Clautice....107
7th Generation: Charles Richard Gonce & Anna Gertrude Hulshoff.......109
My great-grandmother Mary Regina Kerchner & Our Kerchner Ancestors....109
Anna Gertrude Hulshoff & Her Family...110
Charles Gonce & Gertrude Hulshoff – The Great War (World War I)...111
Charles Gonce & Gertrude Hulshoff – After the Great War....................123
The 1929 Stock Market Crash...127
Charles and Gertrude's Separation...128
8th Generation: Children of Charles Richard Gonce & Anna Gertrude Hulshoff
....137
9th Generation:...137
10th Generation:...138

Appendix I...139
The Gonce Family Southern Migrations...141
The "Southern Branch" of the Gonce Family...141
The Tennessee Migration..141
The Alabama Migration..146
Gonce Reverse Migrations..149
Earl "Woodie" Gonce..149
Hugh Bernard Gonce; Pilot Officer of the Royal Air Force....................150
Hezekiah Davis Gonce..150

Appendix II...153

Location of Samuel Comegys in 1820 155
   Pros and Cons for Selecting the Samuel Comegys in Kent County 156
   Pros and Cons for Selecting the Samuel Comegys in Cecil County 156

Appendix III 159
Birth Year of George Gonce 161
   Synopsis of Sources for George Gonce's Date of Birth 161

Appendix IV 163
Birth Year of Catherine Comegys 165
   Synopsis of Sources for her Date of Birth 165

Appendix V 167
Birth Year of Catharine Ann Sullivan 169
   Synopsis of Sources for Catharine Ann Sullivan's Date of Birth 169
   Catharine's Age at Marriage Based on Suspected Years of Birth 171

Appendix VI 173
Gonces in the American Civil War 175
   Other Gonces in the American Civil War 175
   Civil War Miscellany – George Gonce's Sons 178
   Memorial to the 6th Maryland Infantry Regiment 180

Appendix VII 181
Cemetery Mysteries – Section T Lot 295 183
   The Occupants of Lot 295 187
   Reburials at New Cathedral Cemetery (in alphabetical order) 187
   "New" Burials at the cemetery (in chronological order by burial date) 189
   Other Mysteries to be Unraveled 191
   Locating the Grave Site at New Cathedral Cemetery 193
Gonce Cemeteries of Interest 195
   Gonce Cemetery – Gonce Hollow Road – Gonce Hollow (Eidson), Tennessee. 195
   Gonce Cemetery, Franklin County, Tennessee 196

Appendix VIII 197
Descendants of Justice Gonce 199

Appendix IX 231
Ancestors of Rosalie Gonce & her Siblings 233
   Five Generations of Comegys from Cornelius to Samuel 236
   Five Generations of Vansants from Harmens to Joshua 237
   Four Generations of Vansants from Joshua to Rachel 238
   Five Generations of Gonces from Justice to John Thomas 239
   Four Generations of Clautices from John P. to Alice E. (with Farrings &
      Goodwins) 240
   Four Generations of Gonces from John Thomas to Rosalie, Jean, Charles &
      George 241

Appendix X 243
Gonce Ancestors Photo Album 243

Appendix XI 261
Suggestions for Further Research 263

TABLE OF CONTENTS

    Notes on Research ID #56 – Location of John Thomas Gonce and Family in 1860.....268
    Possibility 1: They could have been living with John or Catharine's parents in 1860.......269
    Possibility 2: They could have been living with John's grandparents in 1860...................270
    Possibility 3: They could have been living with Catharine's grandparents in 1860...........271
    Possibility 4: They could have been living with one of John's siblings in 1860................271
    Possibility 5: They could have been living with one of Catharine's siblings in 1860........273

Appendix XII..**275**
Possible Gonce Family Origins..277
  Part I – Likely Timing of Gonce Immigration..278
    Maryland Records...278
    Delaware (and Pennsylvania) Records..280
    Conclusion...282
  Part II – North American Entry Point...282
  Part III – Suggested Countries of Origin...282
    Germany..284
    Holland – The Netherlands...287
    Alsace / Alsace-Lorraine...289
    American Colonies (other)..291
    … The Gonces and the Rockefellers in the New Jersey Colonies?..........................291
    American Indian – Native American...294
    Belgium..294
    Canada...295
    Croatia...296
    Cuba..296
    England / Great Britain...297
    France..299
    Hungary...302
    Ireland...302
    Italy...303
    Mexico...303
    Panama..304
    Puerto Rico..304
    Scotland...306
    Spain..306
    Sweden...307
    Switzerland..308
    And: Beware of False Gonces!..309
    CONCLUSION...310
  Part IV – Name Etymology..310
    The Surname "Gonce"..310
    The Given Name "Justice"..311
    The Given Name "Magdalen"...311
    The Given Names Rudolph, Daniel and Abraham..312
  Part V – Tentative Conclusions..312
  Part VI – Distribution of Gonce Births in Twentieth Century France........................315
  Part VII – Time Lines for Delaware, Scotland/Ireland, Puerto Rico, and France
    related to Gonce Family Events..316

Appendix XIII..**325**
Family Group Sheets: Extending the Line...325

Photo # NH 44755 USS Northern Pacific stranded off Fire Island, N.Y., January 1919

Photos from the United States Naval Archives of the U.S.S. Northern Pacific after it ran aground on 1 January 1919. See the story of my grandfather Charles R. Gonce and more photos on page 118.

Photo # NH 44759 USS Northern Pacific stranded off Fire Island, N.Y., January 1919

OUR GONCE ANCESTORS

The Gonce Family in America

John. T. Gonce

Signature of John Thomas Gonce, my 2nd great-grandfather, from his letter dated 16 January 1865 (see page 77)

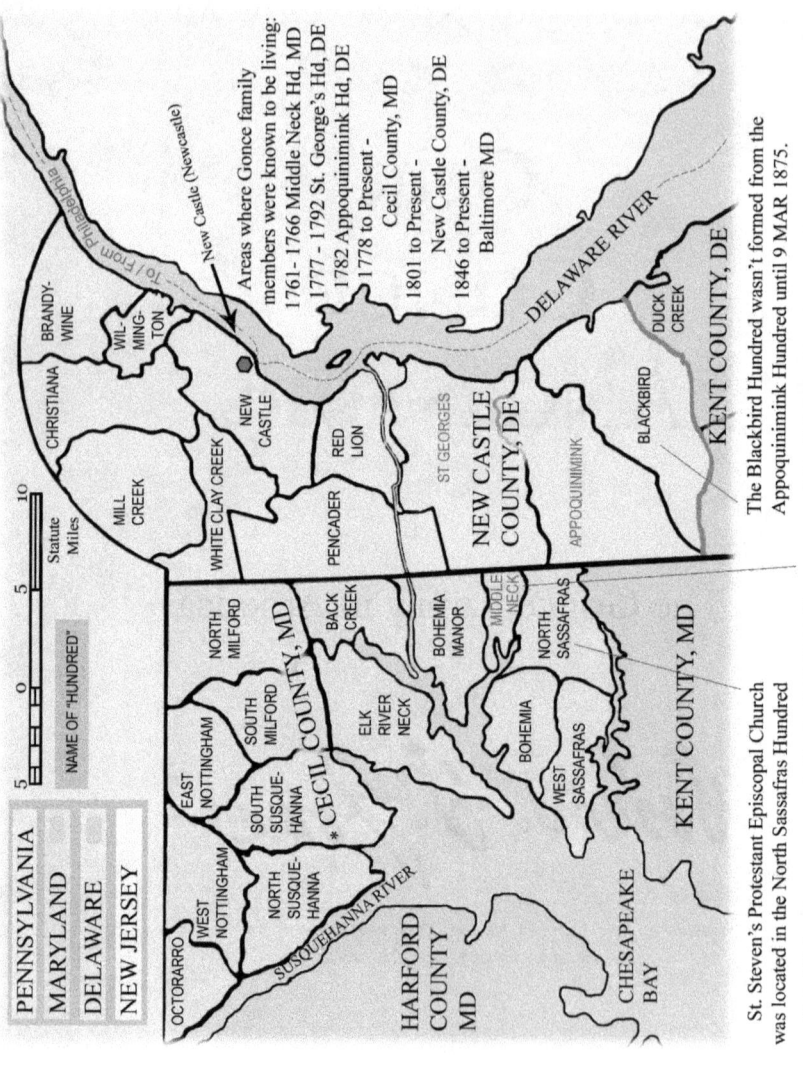

The Gonces Arrive in America

In the late seventeenth and early eighteenth centuries, Philadelphia was the busiest port for both commerce and immigration to the North American Colonies. Although this preeminence developed naturally, mainly due to the marketing skills of William Penn and his successors, it was later reinforced by the infamous English "Navigation Acts," a series of rules and taxes[1] intended to protect English industry from competition. One of these required that any vessel carrying salt had to be landed first at a northern port. Thus, even some settlers who had originally intended to land in the southern colonies[2] were first rerouted up the Delaware River to Philadelphia.

What isn't as well known is that all vessels headed to or departing from Philadelphia were obliged by English law to stop at Newcastle (in what is now Delaware[3]) as well. Until 1707, when the Fort there was completed, this edict wasn't very strictly observed[4], but the result, nevertheless, was that a notable number of immigrants took advantage of this early opportunity to disembark. The Scotch-Irish immigration at Newcastle during this period, for instance, was described as "impressive."[5]

The reasons for disembarking at Newcastle varied from a simple wish to return to dry land as soon as possible, to avoid a "big city" environment, or to a desire to enter the colonies at a point where there was somewhat less of a government presence and therefore fewer questions regarding who or what was coming ashore.

Thus it happened that, for whatever reason, Justice Gonce $^{\text{ID 2577}}$ [6], his wife Magdalen $^{\text{ID 2858}}$, and their three sons Rudolph $^{\text{ID 2578}}$, Abraham $^{\text{ID 2579}}$, and Daniel $^{\text{ID 2580}}$ came ashore at Newcastle in about 1759[7], and settled inland to the southwest in Cecil County, Maryland very shortly thereafter (see a map of this area on the previous page). At the time they arrived, I estimate the ages of the sons to be about sixteen, eleven and one year old respectively.

Virtually all of the Gonces in the United States today are descended from this family.

---

[1] This is the very same group of taxes that were referred to in the phrase "taxation without representation," and which eventually helped precipitate the American Revolution.
[2] According to "Colonial Records of North Carolina," VI, pp 1030-1031, for instance, the Governor of that colony complained publicly that his settlements were being deprived of new settlers by this edict.
[3] What is now Delaware was then known as the three "Delaware Counties" of Pennsylvania.
[4] "A History of Delaware;" Powell, pp 88 and 96.
[5] "Population Distribution in Colonial America," Stella H. Sutherland, Columbia University Press, NY, 1936; reprinted 1966 by AMS Press, NY. Northwestern University Library reference 312.73/S966p.
[6] The ID numbers are from my genealogy database and are provided to permit correlation with various different reference material and other publications and documents I have created.
[7] … or at least sometime between 1755 and 1760.

Pre-American Origins

To date, I have uncovered no compelling evidence to suggest where Justice and his family may have originated. Among those doing genealogical research on this extended family, there is a wide variety of speculation concerning the origins of the first Gonce(s) to arrive in the new world. A discussion of all these theories would take many pages and be a distraction at this point, so I've included an appendix[8] that outlines each theory and source I've run across, and comments on each of them in turn.

1st Generation in America: Justice & Magdalen Gonce

We know almost nothing of Justice and his wife Magdalen. It should be noted, however, that there are gaps between the estimated birth dates for their three known sons, so it is possible that the couple had other children – quite possibly even some females, who tend not to be as well represented in records from this era as males. None of the colonial (i.e. pre-revolutionary) marriage records I've examined have Gonce brides, however.

The first mention of the name Gonce[9] in any American source I am aware of is in the 1761 "List of Taxables for Middle Neck Hundred,"[10] where "Justis Gonce" and "Radalph Gonce" are mentioned. These are assumed to be Justice Gonce and his oldest son Rudolph Gonce, who would then have been about twenty-two years old.

Abraham, the second of the sons, joined "Justis" and Rudolph on the list for 1766[11], which is consistent with the view that Abraham was born a few years after Rudolph; a birth year of 1748 would make Abraham about 18 at the time of the 1766 list.

Seal of Cecil County, MD

When he was about twenty-six, Rudolph ID 2578, the oldest known son of Justice and Magdalen, married the widow Polly McDade ID 2581 in Middletown[12], Delaware in early 1769, and seems to be the first of the Gonces to relocate to the Delaware side of the border.

---

[8] See the appendix "Possible Gonce Family Origins" beginning on page 277.

[9] Well – at least related to our family line. See an earlier reference to another "Justice Gonce" on page 291.

[10] The tax lists are recorded in the book "Inhabitants of Cecil County Maryland. 1639-1774"; Family Line Publications; Westminster, MD, 1993; University of Baltimore; Baltimore MD; F187. LoC Catalog Number C3 P135 1993 (S138 – S indicates the Source Number from my database); page 48.

[11] ibid; page 80. This is the next extant list of taxables; no lists between 1761 and 1766 are known to exist.

[12] Family of Benjamin Hutchisson 1765-1852, 2nd Edition; Elmer Hutchisson; September 1976, page 25. Also recorded in "Maryland Marriages 1667-1899" compiled by Jordan Dodd of Liahona Research. (S56)

Justice appears again on the list of persons owing Cecil County, Maryland, court costs in 1774.[13]

The areas of Delaware and Maryland where the Gonce family lived in the decades after their arrival stretched no more than ten miles between the Chesapeake Bay on the west and the Delaware River on the east. Because of this environment, the land was mostly a light, sandy loam, suitable for growing corn, wheat, and various types of fruit, including tomatoes, potatoes, onions, melons, strawberries, as well as a variety of green vegetables. Truck farming[14] was the most common occupation in the area, so rather than specializing in a single crop, it's likely that our ancestors grew a variety of crops. A network of shallow, slow-moving streams permitted relatively easy transport of their harvests to ports on the Delaware River for further transport to Philadelphia[15]. Payment for the crops would primarily have been in commodities or manufactured goods from Philadelphia or even England.

Like Rudolph, the other Gonces also moved back across the border into New Castle County Delaware before the American Revolution, since the names of all three sons appear in Revolutionary War era records of Delaware; these records and their service will be discussed in more detail below.

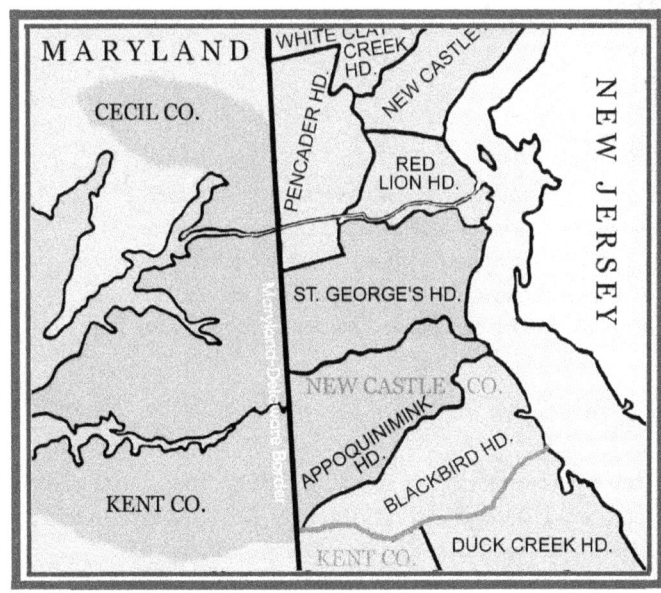

Areas where the Gonce family originally settled are highlighted in the map on the left. Many Gonces still live in this area.

See the map on page 2 as well as the one on page 314 for context.

---

[13] From "List of Amerciaments in 1774" provided in "Inhabitants of Cecil County Maryland. 1649-1774", page 62

[14] "Truck Farming" has nothing whatever to do with "Trucks" as we know them today. The term derives from the Middle English word "truck," which meant the bartering or exchange of commodities.

[15] Baltimore was relatively close as well, but it was more easily supplied from farms on the outskirts of that city. Also, there was not as much ship traffic going between Baltimore and the Cecil County area.

1759 – 1983 History

The Death of Justice Gonce

Justice Gonce died in New Castle County, apparently in the fall of 1782. A handwritten entry dated 4 November 1782 referring to Justice and Magdalen Gonce can be found in the New Castle County (Delaware) Will Book L, page 302. This is illustrated below; a transcription follows:

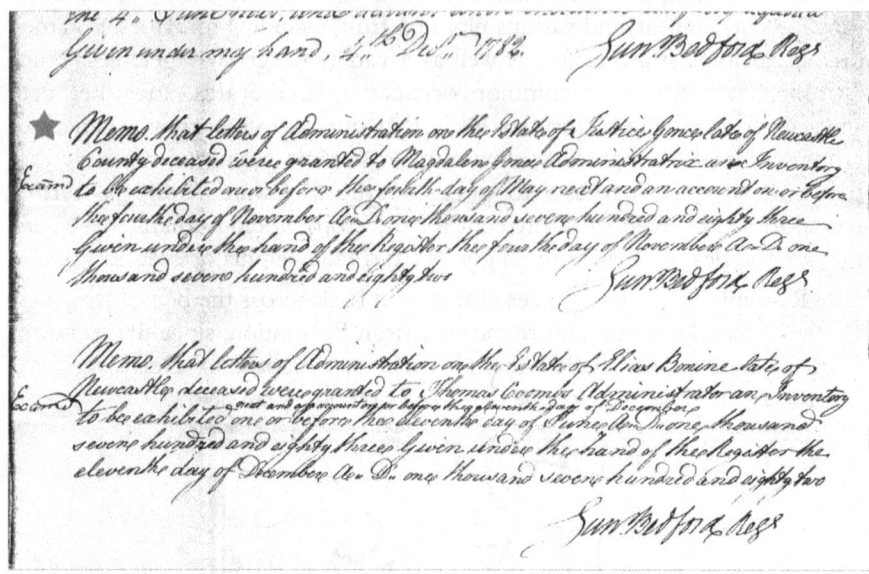

Memo that letters of Administration on the Estate of Justice Gonce late of Newcastle County deceased were granted to Magdalene Gonce Administratrix an Inventory to be exhibited on or before the fourth day of May next and an account on or before the fourth day of November A.D. one thousand seven hundred and eighty three. Given under the hand of the Register the fourth day of November A.D. one thousand seven hundred eighty two.

Sam'l Bedford, Regt.

In accordance with the provisions of the above, the document illustrated on the next page, a Delaware Estate Bond, appears in the Delaware Archives (marked there as a "mutilated document") dated 4 November 1783.

KNOW all Men by these Presents, That WE ~~Magdalin Gonce Widow and Rudolphe~~ *Gonce* & *Peter Hunt* of the County of *New-castle*, are held and firmly bound unto the *Delaware State*, in the Sum of *Three hundred pounds* current Money of the said State; unto which Payment well and truly to be made unto the said State, We do bind ourselves, our Heirs, Executors and Administrators, firmly by these Presents. Sealed with our Seals, and dated at *New-castle*, in *New-castle* County aforesaid, this ____ Day of ____ in the Year of our Lord One Thousand Seven Hundred and Eighty- ____

>> "Magdalin and Rudolphe"

THE Condition of this Obligation is such, That if the above bounden *Magdalin Gonce Widow* *Gonce*

>> "Magdalin Gonce, Widow"

Administrat___ of all and singular the Goods and Chattels, Rights and Credits of *_____* deceased, do make, or cause to be made, a true and perfect Inventory of all and singular the Goods and Chattels, Rights and Credits, of the said Deceased, which have or shall come to the Hands, Possession or Knowledge of the said *Magdalin* or unto the Hands or Possession of any Person or Persons, for *her* and the same so made, do exhibit, or cause to be exhibited, unto the Register's Office of the County of *New-castle* aforesaid, at or before the *fourth* Day of *May* next ensuing the Date hereof, and the same Goods and Chattels, Rights and Credits of the said deceased at the Time of *his* Death, or which at any Time after shall come to the Hands or Possession of the aforesaid *Magdalin* or into the Hands or Possession of any other Person or Persons, for *her* do well and truly administer according to Law; and further do make, or cause to be made, a true and just Account of *her* Administration, at or before the *fourth* Day of *May* which shall fall in the Year of our Lord One Thousand Seven Hundred and *eighty three* and all the Rest and Residue of the said Goods and Chattels, Rights and Credits, which shall be found remaining upon the said Administrat___ Account, the same being first examined and allowed of by the Orphans Court of *New-castle* County aforesaid, shall deliver and pay unto such Person or Persons respectively, as the said Orphans Court, by their Decree or Sentence, pursuant to the true Intent and Meaning of this Act, shall limit and appoint. And if it shall hereafter appear, that any last Will and Testament was made by the Deceased, and the Executor or Executors therein named, do exhibit the same in the Register's Office, making Request to have it allowed and approved accordingly; if the said *Magdalin* within Bounden, being thereunto required, do surrender and deliver up the said Letters of Administration, (Approbation of such Testament being first had and made in the Register's Office) then this Obligation to be void, and of none Effect; or else to remain in full Force and Virtue.

>> <<
>> <<
>> <<

Signed, Sealed and Delivered in the Presence of us

Magdalin M Gonce mark

>> "her mark"

Rud Gonce

>> (Signature)
[Jacob Vanhorn, who witnessed the document, is mentioned later.]

Jacob Vanhorn

A transcription of this printed form is given below with handwritten entries underlined to distinguish them from the printed boilerplate.

KNOW all Men by these Presents, That WE <u>Magdalin Gonce, Widow and Rudolphe Gonce</u>[16], <u>of St.Geo</u>[17] <u>Hundred</u> of the County of New-castle, are held and firmly bound unto the Delaware State, in the sum of <u>Three hundred pounds</u> current Money of the said State; unto which Payment well and truly to be made unto the said State, We do bind ourselves, our Heirs, Executors and Administrators, firmly by these Presents. Sealed with our Seals, and dated at New-castle, in the New-castle County aforesaid, this <u>4th</u> Day of <u>Nov</u> in the Year of our Lord One Thousand Seven Hundred and <u>Eighty Three</u>.

The Condition of this Obligation is such, That if the above bounden

<u>Magdalin Gonce Widow</u>[18], [illegible word follows]

Administratrix of all and singular the Goods and Chattels, Rights and Credits of <u>Justice Gonce late of the Hundred Appominink</u>[19] deceased, do make, or cause to be made, a true and perfect Inventory of all and singular the Goods and Chattels, Rights and Credits, of the said Deceased, which have or shall come to the Hands, Possession or Knowledge of the said <u>Magdalin</u> or unto the Hands or Possession of any Person or Persons, for [illegible] and the same so made, do exhibit, or cause to be exhibited, unto the Register's Office of the County of New-castle aforesaid, at or before the <u>fourth</u> day of <u>May</u> next ensuing the Date hereof, and the same Goods, Chattels, Rights, and Credits of the said [blacked out] the time of <u>his</u> Death, or which at any Time after shall come to the Hands or Possession of the aforesaid <u>Magdalin</u> or into the Hands or Possession of any Person or Persons, for <u>her</u> do well and truly administer according to Law; and further do make, or cause to be made, a true and just Account of <u>her</u> Administration, at or before the <u>fourth</u> Day of <u>Novr</u> which shall fall in the Year of our Lord One Thousand Seven Hundred and <u>eighty three</u> and all the Rest and Residue of the said Goods and Chattels, Rights and Credits, which shall be found remaining upon the said Administratr<u>ixes</u> Account, the same being first examined and allowed of by the Orphans Court of New-castle County aforesaid, shall deliver and pay unto such Person or Persons respectively, as the said Orphans Court, by their Decree or Sentence, pursuant to the true Intent and Meaning of this Act, shall limit and appoint. And if it shall hereafter appear, that any last Will and Testament was made by the Deceased, and the Executor or Executors therein named, do exhibit the same in the Register's Office, making

---

[16] This assignment is consistent with Rudolph being the oldest son.

[17] To me, this looks like "St. Cyr", but other records indicate that her son Rudolph lived in St. George Hundred. Since there is no St. Cyr Hundred and never has been as far as I can determine, I assume this is actually "St. Geo."

[18] The previous document only implies that Magdalen was Justice's wife; this confirms it.

[19] The spelling reflects that of the original document; this is obviously the "Appoquinimink" Hundred.

request to have it allowed and approved accordingly; if the said __Magdalin__ within Bounden, being thereunto required, do surrender and deliver up the said letters of Administration, (Approbation of such Testament being first had and made in the Register's Office) then this Obligation to be void, and of none Effect; or else to remain in Full Force and Virtue.

There are no extant references to Magdalen Gonce after the settlement of her husband's estate, nor does there appear to be any other information that would suggest when she died. Likewise, I have found no information suggesting where Justice and Magdalen Gonce are buried, although I presume this would have been in New Castle County, Delaware, possibly on a family plot on their farm or in a pre-revolutionary churchyard.

2nd Generation: The Three Colonial Gonce Brothers: Rudolph, Abraham, and Daniel

Family traditions[20] have long related that three Gonce brothers were our first ancestors in this country, although the names in the stories vary, and none of the legends mention their parents. Records indicate that the actual names of these three brothers, sons of Justice and Magdalen, were Rudolph [ID 2578], Abraham [ID 2579], and Daniel [ID 2580], although it isn't absolutely certain if that is the correct birth order. The order I've given seems most likely, however. As seen from the 1783 estate bond shown above, Rudolph became co-executor of Justice's estate, a responsibility almost always delegated to the eldest son.

Two of these sons of Justice and Magdalen Gonce, Rudolph and Daniel, are the progenitors of the main branches of the Gonce family in the United States. Rudolph's five children became the original "Southern branch" that eventually spread across Tennessee, Alabama, Georgia, Missouri and Texas, while Daniel's became the "Mid-Atlantic branch," which largely remains in the Delaware/Maryland area even today.

Although I am aware of no published histories for my own "Mid-Atlantic branch" of the Gonce family, there are several that discuss selected portions of the "Southern branch", and these are outlined in the preface to this book (see page 3). Since the primary intent of this book is to concentrate on the direct line between my 6th great-grandfather Justice Gonce and my mother Rosalie Gonce Oberle, I will only touch briefly on ancestors outside that line – specifically on Daniel's older brothers Rudolph and Abraham. This will establish a connection point to the "Southern Branch" histories for those who wish to pursue them.

---

[20] …and these stories are similar in both the mid-Atlantic and southern branches of the Gonce family.

Rudolph Gonce – the oldest brother

As mentioned earlier, Justice and Magdalen's oldest son Rudolph [ID 2578], who was born in about 1745[21], married the widow Polly McDade[22] [ID 2581] in Middletown, Delaware in 1768/69[23]. Polly had two sons from her first marriage[24]: Jeremiah McDade, known as Jerry, and Hugh McDade. Several web postings suggest that Jeremiah and Hugh McDade may have been twins, but none of the postings provide any source for this belief, and I have been unable to confirm it one way or another. Rudolph and Polly had six known children together, including their first two sons, the twins Isaac [ID 2583] (known as "Ikie") and Abraham [ID 2584] (known as "Abie"[25]).

New Castle County Tax Rolls for St. George's Hundred in Delaware show the following assessments for Rudolph Gonce in the years from 1777 to 1782[26]:

Name as recorded	Amount (in Pounds)	Assessment Date
Rudolph Gaunce (sic)	6	1777
Rudolph Gaunce (sic)	9	1778
Rudulph Gaunce (sic)	25	16 Aug 1779
Rodalph (sic) Gonce	25	23 Nov 1779
Rudolph Gonce	25	25 Nov 1780
Rudolph Gonce	25	Dec 1781
Rudolph Gonce	25	Nov 1782

Note the significant jump in his taxes for 1779[27], likely indicating he was becoming quite successful.

---

[21] 1745 seems to be a consensus guess among all the sources I have looked at, but I haven't yet located any evidence to support this. It doesn't conflict with any other known facts, however, so I am accepting it for the moment.

[22] Barbara Gonce-Clepper, author of one of the books listed in the preface q.v., suggests that Polly's original name was Vance, but provides no other details. Abraham [ID 2584], one of Rudolph and Polly's twin sons, also married a woman named Polly Vance [ID 2590].

[23] See "Maryland Marriages 1667-1899" compiled by Jordan Dodd of Liahona Research. (S56) "1768/69" is probably an old/new style year designation. The British changed from the Gregorian to the Julian calendar when 3 September 1752 became 14 September 1752; New Year's Day in 1752 was 25 March, while New Year's Day 1753 was 1 January. The colonies also officially adopted the new calendar then, but the transition wasn't immediate. If this assumption is correct, it would indicate that their marriage took place between January 1 and March 25, 1769.

[24] I suspect that her first husband was the John McDade who appears in the 1761 list of taxables for the South Susquehanna Hundred in Cecil County (Inhabitants of Cecil County 1639-1774, page 42) (S138), but have no evidence to confirm this.

[25] Barbara Gonce-Clepper documents the use of these nicknames in her book mentioned earlier.

[26] "New Castle Co, DE tax lists 1738 – 1783: A list of the taxable persons and estates in the new acquired part of St. George's Hundred." I have been unable to locate any similar listings for the period between 1783 and 1790.

[27] I have found no explanation for this. It doesn't seem to have come from his marriage, which was in 1768. The tax rate didn't change (see his brothers' taxes), and any inheritance from his father wouldn't have come until 1782.

An Aside:

In this and subsequent tables showing early American tax assessments, the amounts are shown in Pounds because that was the currency most commonly used in this period. The use of the Dollar was not even approved in principle by Congress until 8 August 1786. Alexander Hamilton wasn't able to have the Dollar established as the preferred unit of currency until 1792 and, even after that, other currencies were still commonly used until 1863. It wasn't until then that the Dollar became the only "official" currency for the United States.

Rudolph is the only one of Justice's sons known to have owned slaves, having purchased "a Negro boy Samuel, about seven years old and a Negro girl, Juliet, 18 months old for 30 pounds" on 16 May 1788 [28].

Rudolph died in St. George's Hundred, New Castle County, Delaware, on 29 April 1790[29], but I have yet to locate any information regarding his place of burial. Some time after this, in about 1797, Rudolph and Polly's children migrated to the southern part of the country[30]. Because all of Polly's children left for what at the time was the frontier in Tennessee, I believe it is safe to assume that Polly died between 1791 and 1796, and that she is likely buried in the same location as Rudolph, but this is uncertain[31].

Children and Grandchildren of Rudolph Gonce & Polly McDade

This information is provided to permit the reader to correlate this history of my specific Mid-Atlantic branch of the Gonce family with the various histories that have been published about the Southern branches.

- Isaac (Ikie) Gonce ^{ID 2583}, born Thursday 26 July 1770, and his wife Frances "Frankie" Wilson ^{ID 2589}, had at least ten children:

  Elizabeth (Bettie) Gonce ^{ID 2658}, born 10 May 1798, married William Leroy Rogers and, after his death in 1816, James Matthews

  Randolph Gonce ^{ID 2659}, born 11 June 1800, married Elizabeth Talley

---

[28] New Castle County, DE, land records, book 16, page 345. These slaves were purchased from Henry Robinson of Cecil County, MD

[29] "DAR Patriot Index - Volume II (G-O)"; National Society Daughters of the American Revolution (referred to later as "DAR"); Gateway Press, Inc.; Baltimore, MD, 2003 (S70); page 1082.

[30] See the appendix "The Gonce Family Southern Migrations" on page 141 for further details of the migration to Tennessee and later to Alabama.

[31] Polly may have predeceased him. On 7 October 1790, Jacob Van Horn (presumably related to their daughter Margaret's mother-in-law Mary Van Horn Hutchisson) became the court-appointed guardian for all of Rudolph and Polly's children mentioned in the listing above except for Mary. At that time, though, assignment of a guardian would not necessarily have indicated that Polly was deceased, since women could not legally serve as guardians.

Margaret (Peggy) Gonce ^{ID 2660}, born 5 February 1802, who married twice

Frances (Fannie) Gonce ^{ID 2661}, born 1804, married Thomas Reid Shipp

Ann Gonce ^{ID 2662}, born 1806, married Robert McKinney

Sarah Gonce ^{ID 2663}, born 1808, married Roland Childs

Wilson Gonce ^{ID 2664}, born 1810, married Malinda Rice

Mary Gonce ^{ID 2665}, born 1812, married John R. Wilkinson

Lydia C. Gonce ^{ID 2666}, born about 1820, married her sister Margaret's stepson.

Kiziah Gonce ^{ID 2667}, born 1822, married John B. (Preacher Jack) Rogers

♦ Abraham (Abie) Gonce ^{ID 2584}, born 26 July 1770, and his wife Polly Vance ^{ID 2590}, had at least four children, and possibly five:

Margaret E. Gonce ^{ID 3557}, born about 1798, married John T. Mendanall (now usually spelled Mendenhall).

Abraham Gonce ^{ID 3117}, lived from 8 November 1800 to 3 June 1851. He and his wife Celia raised at least seven children in Indiana.

Isaac Gonce, reported by some sources to be a twin of Abraham, but I've found no evidence that he actually existed.

Vance [32] Gonce ^{ID 2881}, born 1802, married Martha Patsy Davis

John Rudolph Gonce ^{ID 2880}, born 1805, married twice and had twenty children

♦ Lydia Gonce ^{ID 2586}, born about 1771, and her husband Thomas Sprowl ^{ID 2592}, had at least two children:

Thomas Sprowl, Jr. ^{ID 3863}, born 1798

John Sprowl ^{ID 3864}, born 1800

♦ Margaret Gonce ^{ID 2585}, born Saturday 15 February 1772, and her husband Benjamin Hutchisson ^{ID 2591} had at least thirteen children[33]:

Jemima Hutchisson ^{ID 3593}, born 13 April 1792

Keziah Hutchisson ^{ID 3594}, born 13 April 1792

Elizabeth Hutchisson ^{ID 3595}, born 24 September 1793

Sarah Hutchisson ^{ID 3597}, born 6 May 1795

Joseph Hutchisson ^{ID 3766}, born 22 April 1797

---

[32] One of Vance Gonce's sons, Doctor Abraham Rudolph Gonce, is one of the more colorful characters in the Gonce line. I have written a book titled "Abraham R. Gonce – Missouri Pioneer" (ISBN 978-06159-12448) giving a brief history of his life as well as transcripts of his trials for bigamy and murder.

[33] Benjamin had a child with his first wife, who died in 1789; see the Hutchisson book referenced earlier.

Lydia Hutchisson [ID 3767], born 22 July 1799

Benjamin Hutchisson [ID 3782], born 26 October 1801

Rebecca (Becca) Hutchisson [ID 3783], born 18 October 1803

John [34] Hutchisson [ID 3852], born 6 December 1805

William Hutchisson [ID 3784], born 11 December 1808

Rudolph Hutchisson [ID 2872], born 29 November 1810

Eleanor Ingram Hutchisson [ID 3785], born 25 December 1812

Margaret Hutchisson [ID 3786], born 16 May 1815

- Mary Vance (Polly) Gonce [ID 2587], born about 1774, and her husband James C. Larkin had no children that I am aware of. Although she is listed in several places[35] as a child of Rudolph and Polly, she was not listed as a minor child when Jacob Van Horn became the guardian of Rudolph's children in 1790[36], nor was she listed as one of the children who eventually migrated to Tennessee[37]. Also note that there are only three minor females in Rudolph's household in the 1782 Delaware Census discussed later on page 18. It therefore seems questionable to me that she is actually their child.

- Sarah Gonce [ID 2588], born 1777, and her husband Aaron Wells had at least two children:

Jeremiah Wells [ID 3861], born 1794

Isaac Wells [ID 3862], born 1798

None of the published sources I've encountered suggest any particular reasons for the migration of *all* Rudolph's children to the south at the same time. Based on the tax assessments above, Rudolph seems to have been fairly well off, so it doesn't seem likely that his children left simply for better economic opportunities. They were all minors when their father died, however, so it is possible that all the land and assets went to their (by then adult) McDade half-brothers, or that any inheritance they anticipated may have been squandered or withheld by their guardian Jacob Vanhorn.

The New Castle County Tax Rolls for St. George's Hundred in Delaware show the following assessments for Rudolph Gonce's *Land* [38], which would seem to indicate that, at least through 1793, its disposition had not been settled.

---

[34] John is the great-grandfather of Elmer Hutchisson, author of one of the previously referenced books.
[35] Although none of these provides any source references.
[36] See earlier footnote 31 on page 11.
[37] See the appendix "The Gonce Family Southern Migrations" beginning on page 141.
[38] I was unable to locate any tax listings for Rudolph, Abraham and Daniel between 1783 and 1790.

Name as recorded	Amount (in Pounds)	Assessment Date
Rudolph Gaunce Land	20	1791
Rudolph Gaunce's Land	20	22 Nov 1791
Rudolph Gaunce's Land	17	27 Nov 1792
Rudolph Gaunce's Land	17	24 Nov 1793

Abraham Gonce – the middle brother

Based on my belief that Justice' son Abraham is the same Abraham Gonce who served in Dunmore's War of 1774[39] in Virginia, I am estimating that he was born between 1750 and 1759. In addition to the references discussed under "Another Abraham Gonce?" below, the only other extant references to Abraham [ID 2579] in the Delaware/Maryland area seem to be the following Delaware tax assessments:

Name as recorded	Amount (in Pounds)	Assessment Date
Abraham Gonce	6	Dec 1781
Abraham Gonce	6	Nov 1782

I suspect that Abraham may have gone back to Virginia in the 1780s. He may be the ancestor of some Gonces that appear to have been in Virginia and North Carolina in the very late eighteenth and early nineteenth centuries, and eventually seemed to have relocated to Kentucky (by the 1820 Census, several Gonce families[40] began appearing in Jefferson County there). Unfortunately, I haven't been able to locate enough records from those areas to confirm this suspicion. Also see the comments on page 17. Many other Kentucky Gonces, however, were Rudolph's descendants who moved northwest from Tennessee).

My fifth great-grandfather Daniel Gonce – the youngest brother (an introduction)

My 5th great-grandfather Daniel, the youngest of the brothers, appears to have been born in about 1758. Before continuing with the history of Justice and Magdalen's third son and his descendants, the focus of this book, a short discussion of the Gonce brothers' military service during the Revolutionary War, as well as the migration of some of the family to Tennessee after the war, seems warranted.

---

[39] See the sidebar "Another Abraham Gonce?" on page 15.
[40] Those of Samuel, John, George and Philip Gonce.

Revolutionary War Service of the Three Gonce Brothers

At least one published book[41] and a few correspondents have suggested that the Gonce brothers may have declined military service during the Revolutionary War but, since this may be somewhat misleading, a few comments are in order.

The following quotes appear in existing records; both were given on 18 June 1777: "Could not go at this present time." (Rudolph Gonce), and "Being ailing, I can't bear the fatigue." (Daniel Gonce). Taken as individual responses, these suggest a wish to avoid military service. A closer, more thorough examination of the record summaries, however, suggests that these may have been contrived responses. Daniel's is not only a common response, but in the actual roll it is shown merely as "ditto[44]." Is it possible the brothers were declining *British* Service, as Barbara Gonce Clepper surmises in her book? I believe this is a reasonable conclusion, though it might be difficult to prove.

In point of fact, there are indications that the Gonce sons did participate in the Revolutionary War on the Colonial side. On August 17, 1778, all three of the

Another Abraham Gonce?

There was a man known variously as Abraham Gaunce or Abram Gonce, who served in the Virginia Militia under British Captain James Morrison in "Dunmore's War of 1774" although, along with 14 others of the 58 men in the company, he is said to have deserted. It seems reasonable to assume that he must have been at least fifteen years old at this time, making his birth year no later than 1759, and more likely closer to 1750. Thus, he would have been in the same generation as our Rudolph, Abraham and Daniel.

He was also on a list of those paid off in 1775 at Romney, Virginia[42] after this conflict, and the author of one book states: "most of these troops joined the Army of the Revolution after they were paid off.[43]" This leads me to the conclusion that the term "desertion" may simply represent a British perspective on someone who decided to join (or not oppose) the rebellion.

It seems reasonable that this Abraham Gonce may be related to Justice and our family, but I have been unable to locate enough information to confirm or refute this.

It is interesting to note, however, that, although his brothers appear in Delaware records earlier, Abraham doesn't appear until August of 1778. In fact, I could find no overlaps between the Delaware and Virginia records. It therefore seems likely to me that this could very well be the same Abraham that is the middle son of Justice and Magdalen Gonce.

---

[41] This is on page 31 of the Clepper book mentioned.
[42] See pages 137 and 140 of "Historical Register of Virginians in the Revolution 1775-1783" by John H. Gwathmey; Genealogical Publishing Company; Baltimore, MD. 1938, 1979. Copyright © 1938 John H. Gwathmey (renewed 1966) (S73)
[43] ibid; page 314
[44] "Delaware Archives: Military and Naval Records Volume II"; The Public Archives Commission of Delaware; Mercantile Printing Company, 1912, page 812, a copy of which is reproduced on the following page.

brothers took an oath of allegiance[45] to the State of Delaware and further swore that they no longer had any allegiance to the King.

812   DELAWARE ARCHIVES.

Persons Names	Reasons for Non-Attendence.
Rudolph Gonce	Could not go at this present time.
John Vernor	Could not leave his farm or would go.
Isaac Vanhorn	Promised but proved delinquent.
William Rice	his father could not spare him.
Joseph McLan	Lying in the small-pox.
George Rice	I think it my duty to take care of my crap.
Alexander Patterson	Cant go by any means
Garret Vanzant	being ailing I cant bear the fatigue.
Daniel Gonce	ditto
Matthias Cazier	his father says he is under age.
Joshua Eliason	If I go my crap is lost.
John Henderson	I will go if all the rest will.
Ephraim Weily	Promised but proved delinquent.
William Chick	I will go if all the rest goes.
Abraham Eliason	Swears he will not go.
Nicholas Harras	I have a boil under my arm, & cant go.
Cornelius Eliason	I have my Harvest to mind, & none but myself.
James Stuart	his father would not let him go, being under his tuition.
Benjamin Touland	not known.
Richd Reynolds Sergt	Cant go without loosing my crap, which I dont choose.

(Captain Ellis's Company)

Nath. Silsbie	A substitute during war.
George Ramsey	his wife expected to ly in.
Matthew Farris	A substitute during war.
William Good	a substitute for the first call & would not now turn out.
Jacob Cannon	A substitute during war.
George Clark	ditto & is not in health.
John McKanna	says he cannot leave his shallop.
William Camel	took with the small-pox on the road & was oblidg'd to return home.

                       ABRAHAM STAATS, Captain.

     A Return of those persons names that were notified and did not attend of Captn Thomas Wattsons Class.

Shem James	has got a substitute since notified.
Robert McCoobery	would not come.
John Grimes?	Run out of the way.

Of Captn Isaac Lewis's Class

William Robeson	would not come.
Jacob Morgan	not permitted by his Uncle.

Of Captn Isaac Alexander's Class............none.

                     THOS. WATTSON Capt.
June 24th 1777.

Capt. Watsons return the persons notified and refusal June 19 1777. (This on the back.)

Delaware Archives, page 812. Index of those declining service in 1777 during the Revolutionary War, indicating that several responses were "token" at best (Daniel's is given simply as "ditto"). Note that Sgt Richard Reynolds "crap" in "Can't go without loosing [sic] my crap" is simply an archaic spelling of "crop." Rudolph and Daniel both fought on the side of the Americans in the Revolutionary War.

Garret Vansant, a distant relative of ours listed immediately above Daniel Gonce, is mentioned under his grandfather Albert Vansant in the section "Garrett Vansant & Elizabeth Gerritse" that begins on page 36.

---

[45] ibid;; pages 994, 996 and 998

Beginning on 8 July 1780, Abraham served in the 6th Company (under Captain John Crawford) of the 3rd Regiment (under Colonel Henry Neill). There are actually records of two Gonces with very similar names in the rolls of Henry Neill's Regiment during this period. An Abram Gonce is shown on the payroll of Captain McClement's Company on 31 October of 1780[46], and it seems likely this was not simply a misspelling of "Abraham." Abraham himself is still on Captain Crawford's rolls on 5 July 1781[47], and a document dated 19 January 1791 indicates that Abram had back pay (9 pounds) still due from service with Captain McClement's Company[48]. I have been unable to determine who Abram was, although the only other use of the spelling Abram is in the Virginia records alluded to in the sidebar above.

> 76   THE STREETS FAMILY.
>
> Copies of papers relating to the military services of Jacob and Robert Streets, from the office of the Secretary of State, at Dover, Delaware, are herewith appended."
>
> "These are therefore to certify that I have Enlisted three effective able bodied Men out of my Company of the Militia [3rd Regiment], namely: James Lyle, Jacob Street & John Reid, agreeable to a late Act of Assembly of the Delaware State, in order to re-inforce the Continental Army, under command of the Commander in Chief of the United forces of America.
>
> "Given under my hand this 8th day of July, 1780.
>
> THOS WITHERSPOON, Capt."
> "To Capt SAML SMITH, Esq.
> Lieut. of New Castle Co."
>
> "This is to certify that I have inlisted for the Battalion now to be raised agreeable to an Act of the General Assembly for my Quota the men hereafter named—to wit: Robert Craig, Joseph Hawks,
>
> October, of the same year. It was designated the "Continental Regiment, No. 38." It was stationed for duty in Kent county, Maryland, and served there for the period stated. (Publications of the Delaware Historical Society. "Historical and Biographical Papers." Volume II.)
>
> "Published in 1912, in volumes I and II of "Delaware Archives."
>
> THE STREETS FAMILY.   77
>
> Abraham Gonce and *Robert Streets*, as witness my hand this 8th day of July, 1780.
>
> JNO CRAWFORD."
>
> "New Castle County, } SS
> The Delaware State. }
>
> "The Deposition of Jacob Streets. Taken before me, Wm Alfree, one of the Justices of the peace for the said County, this 27th Day of April, 1787.
>
> "This Deponent on his oath saith that he was Listed under Hugh McCracking, Captain, in Caronel Henry Neal's Redgment for four months and that He had a Regularly Discharge from General Pikren, and by order of his Exlency Gen'l Washington, and he fetch'd nothing with him Excepting his Napsack & Haversack which to the Best of his knowledge was Either Give to him or settled for Before he left the Army, as there was no demand made of them when he Came Away; And further he saith that he Did not fetch Anything Belonging to the Continental Stores.
>
> "And further, that his Brother Robert Streets was Listed as Above Described and Discharged as Above who is sence Dead and that he fetched nothing with him only his napsack & haversack which this Deponent understood was Allso Give or settled for as Above when Discharged and that he the said

Letters from "The Descendants of Thomas Hale of Delaware" (T.H. Streets, Philadelphia, 1913 – out of print) showing John Crawford's recruitment of Abraham Gonce into his unit.

It isn't clear to me what became of Abraham Gonce or his descendants or, indeed, if he had any descendants. After the Delaware tax assessments for 1781 and 1782 listed above, and the Delaware census of 1782, I have found no credible trace of him. As mentioned earlier, I suspect he may be the forebear of the Gonces/Gaunces living in the Carolinas after the

---

[46] ibid; page 642
[47] ibid; page 656
[48] ibid; page 694

Revolutionary War[49] and who later, like a few of the Tennessee Gonces, migrated to Kentucky, but I have so far not had the opportunity to research this as much as I would like.

Delaware Census of 1782

A census of the new State of Delaware[50] was taken on 10 June 1782, and shows the two heads-of-household of the Gonce family at the time – the "Widow Gonse" and "Rudolph Gonse", along with the number of persons in selected age groupings within their households. The tables below show the age groupings recorded, along with my guesses as to their likely identities.

Reconstructed Delaware State Census of 1782: Listing for "Widow Gonse" (St. George's Hundred)	
1782 Census counts	Comments (my assumptions)
1 of 2 Males above 18:	born bef 1770 – Abraham Gonce [2579], son, born about 1748
2 of 2 Males above 18:	born bef 1770 – Daniel Gonce [2580], son, born about 1758 **Our Direct Ancestor**
1 of 1 Males below 18:	born bef 1770 – Rudolph Gonce [2596], grandson (son of Daniel), born about 1779 **Our Direct Ancestor**
1 of 2 Females above 18:	born bef 1770 – Magdalen Gonce [2858], Head of Household, Justice [2577] Gonce's widow **Our Direct Ancestor**
2 of 2 Females above 18:	born bef 1770 – Mary (Lowery) Gonce [2582], who married Daniel Gonce 9 Dec 1778 **Our Direct Ancestor**

As seen in the table above, Magdalen, her second and third sons Abraham and Daniel, along with Daniel's wife Mary and three year old son Rudolph, appear to be living together in the same household. The "above 18" and "below 18" categories represent birth years before and after the year 1764, so the assignment of known names to the counts given seems to be justified.

Rudolph's household is rather large, consisting of eleven persons, making the assignment of names to the counts less certain. Nonetheless, I believe that the identification of all but two of these seems fairly certain. Because Rudolph's wife Polly was a widow with at least two children[51] at the time he married her, we also need to keep in mind that this is likely a combined household with remnants of Polly's original family as well as her children with Rudolph.

---

[49] A discussion of the reasons for my suspicions is out of scope here, but is touched on briefly in the "Gonce Tennessee Migration" document referred to earlier.

[50] The Reconstructed Delaware State Census of 1782 (10 June 1782); Harold Bell Hancock, Editor; The Delaware Genealogical Society, 1983. (S135). The odd headings are as shown on the original, and I am assuming first that 18 year olds were not meant to be excluded from the census and, second, that the "above 18" categories exclude any eighteen year olds, but this can't be certain from the headings. (i.e. I am interpreting the categories as follows: "above 18" means 19 and above; "below 18" means 0 through 18 inclusive).

[51] Jeremiah and Hugh McDade, who were mentioned earlier. Speculation they are part of Rudolph's household is supported by the fact that there seem to be no other McDade households reported in the 1782 or 1790 censuses.

Reconstructed Delaware State Census of 1782: Listing for "Rudolph Gonse" (St. George's Hundred)	
1782 Census counts	**Comments (my assumptions)**
1 of 3 Males above 18:	Rudolph Gonce [2578], born about 1743 (ergo age about 39 in 1782) Head of Household, son of Justice and Magdalen
2 of 3 Males above 18:	Jeremiah[52] McDade, born about 1759, ergo about age 23, son of Polly by her first marriage.
3 of 3 Males above 18:	Hugh McDade, born about 1759, ergo about age 23, son of Polly by her first marriage.
1 of 3 Males below 18:	Abraham [2583], son, born 26 Jul 1770, ergo about age 12 in 1782.
2 of 3 Males below 18:	Isaac [2584], son, born 26 Jul 1770 (twin brother of Abraham above)
3 of 3 Males below 18:	Unknown (possibly another son of Polly by her first marriage, or a grandson, i.e. a son of Jeremiah or Hugh McDade). The only grandson I know of, however, another Hugh McDade, lived between 1785 and 1794.
1 of 2 Females above 18:	Polly (McDade) Gonce [2581], wife, married Rudolph Gonce in early 1769
2 of 2 Females above 18:	Unknown (possibly Polly's mother, a wife of one of the McDade sons, or a live-in housekeeper/maid)
1 of 3 Females below 18:	Lydia Gonce [2586], daughter, born about 1771 (ergo age about 11)
2 of 3 Females below 18:	Margaret Gonce [2585], daughter, born 15 Feb 1772 (ergo age about 10) – could this be the reported daughter "Mary" (see below)?
3 of 3 Females below 18:	Sarah Gonce ID 2588, daughter, born about 1777 (ergo age about 5)

Mary Gonce [ID 2587], supposedly born about 1774 and mentioned earlier as a reported daughter of Rudolph and Polly, would therefore have been about age 8 at the time of this census, but is not accounted for, reinforcing my belief that, whoever she might be, she is not Rudolph and Polly's daughter.

---

[52] Another Jeremiah McDade, whom I cannot identify, is reported to have been born in Delaware in about 1750.

2nd Generation: Daniel Gonce – the youngest brother (cont.) & Mary Lowery

My fifth great-grandmother Mary Lowery & Our Lowery Ancestors

John Lowery [ID 3516], who died in March 1780, and his wife[53] Ann [ID 3592], my 6th great-grandparents, had at least eight children[54]:

- John Lowery, who died in 1781
- William Lowery, who married Sarah Aldridge on 24 May 1785. William died in 1791
- James Lowery, who married Catharine Elliott on 10 March 1792
- Elijah Lowery, who married Ann Savin on 13 July 1785
- Robert Lowery, who was listed on page 79 of "1766 Taxables in Back Creek Hundred."
- Stephen Lowery, who died in 1794
- Ann Lowery, who married a man named Foster
- Mary Lowery [ID 2582], my 5th great-grandmother, who was probably born about 1760.

John and his family lived in the Back Creek Hundred of Cecil County, Maryland, just across the border from New Castle County, Delaware.

Daniel Gonce & Mary Lowery

Justice and Magdalen's third known son, my 5th great-grandfather Daniel Gonce [ID 2580], was born some time between 1753 and 1760, most likely in 1758 – a year or so before his parents brought him to this country. He married[55] Mary Lowery [ID 2582] in Cecil County Maryland shortly after their license was issued on Wednesday 9 December 1778. Daniel was about twenty years old at the time of their marriage; Mary's age is uncertain, but she was likely about eighteen years old. It isn't clear whether they ever lived in Cecil County, though, since Daniel continued to own land in New Castle County

---

[53] I'm not certain that Ann is his wife. John's brother James, who died in 1778, was also married. Their wives were named Ann and Jane, but it isn't clear which wife went with which husband. Since John had a daughter named Ann, that seemed to be the most likely of the two. James had previously been married to Mary Vezey on 27 April 1748 in St. Mary Ann's parish in North Elk Township of Cecil County. (Maryland Marriages 1634-1777; Barnes; page 112)

[54] John's children were listed in his estate records: Cecil County Accounts Book 5, pp 111 & 116, referenced in "1766 Taxables in Back Creek Hundred", Cecil County, page 79 (S138). These and other Lowerys are listed in "Inhabitants of Cecil County Maryland. 1774-1800" compiled by Henry C. Peden, page 161. (S140)

[55] See "Maryland Marriages 1667-1899" compiled by Jordan Dodd of Liahona Research (S56). Also referenced in "Inhabitants of Cecil County Maryland. 1774-1800" compiled by Henry C. Peden, page 103 (S140) and "Cecil County, Maryland Marriage Licenses 1777-1840" page 2 (S157). The Reverend William Thomson presided.

until at least December 1781 as indicated by the Delaware tax roll entry below[56]:

Name as recorded	Amount (in Pounds)	Assessment Date	Daniel's Age
Daniel Gonce	6	Dec 1781	about 23

Until the early twentieth century, all of the Gonces living in the mid-Atlantic region were descendants of Daniel and Mary. This remained true until Hezekiah Davis (Car) Gonce [ID 3038] relocated his wife and nine children from Tennessee to Howard County, Maryland in 1920[57]. Much later in the twentieth century, one of my own first cousins moved to Alabama, albeit to the other end of the State from our distant Gonce cousins.

Children of Daniel Gonce & Mary Lowery

The only known child of Daniel and Mary Gonce was one of my 4th great-grandfathers – another Rudolph Gonce [ID 2596], who was born in about 1777. Rudolph was only about four years old when his father Daniel died in 1782 at about age 24; I have been unable to locate any information (other than his seemingly contrived 1777 statement "being ailing, I can't bear the fatigue") to suggest why Daniel died at such a young age or where he is buried.

Other than the marriage, military and tax records alluded to earlier, there is no known documentation of Daniel's life; he seems to have died in New Castle County, Delaware, but I've found no records that would confirm this.

On 25 Jun 1783[58], Daniel's widow Mary Lowery Gonce married a man named Noble Boulden. Some speculations concerning Mr. Boulden will be discussed under "Rudolph and Elizabeth" below.

From here on, we leave the southern branch of the Gonce family, and this narrative will concentrate on the direct line of ancestors from Daniel's son (my 4th great-grandfather) Rudolph Gonce [ID 2596] to Rosalie Gonce [ID 242] and her siblings, with some discussions of various families that have married into this "mid-Atlantic" line of Gonces.

---

[56] I haven't been able to locate Daniel on any earlier or later tax rolls for Delaware.
[57] See "Gonce Reverse Migrations" on page 149 for further details.
[58] "Inhabitants of Cecil County Maryland. 1774-1800" compiled by Henry C. Peden, page 161 (S140). This marriage, by the way, is why we can assume that Rudolph died between the 1782 Delaware census and before Mary remarried.

Our Direct-Line Gonce-Side Ancestors

3rd Generation: Rudolph Gonce & Elizabeth Hedney

My 4th great-grandmother Elizabeth Hedney Gonce & Our Hedney Ancestors

The only one of Elizabeth [ID 2597] Hedney's ancestors I've been able to identify is her father (and my 5th great-grandfather) George Hedney [ID 2595]. George was probably born somewhere around 1760, and died in late 1824 or very early 1825. Mr. Hedney's Will[59] lists George Gonce [ID 2511], my 3rd great-grandfather, as his grandson.

I have been unable to locate any name resembling George Hedney in any Colonial records, including the 1790 or 1800 censuses for Maryland[60], so it is difficult to guess whether Elizabeth had any siblings. The 1810 census for "Geo. Hedney", the only record that could reasonably be considered relating to our ancestor, is discussed on page 26, although another record that could possibly be him is discussed on page 157.

George's daughter Elizabeth [ID 2597] was probably born in about 1780.

Rudolph Gonce & Elizabeth Hedney

My 4th great-grandfather Rudolph Gonce was about four years old when his mother Mary remarried following his father Daniel's death. Lacking any further information, I can only speculate that Rudolph must have been raised in the Boulden household. In the 1790 U.S. Census, there is a listing for a Noble Bolding, who is most likely[61] the same person. His household in Cecil County was composed of the following:

1790 United States Census Listing for "Noble Bolding" in Back Creek Township, Cecil County MD	
1790 Census counts	Comments (my assumptions)
1 of 2 Free White Males 16 or over:	born in or before 1774; assumed to be Noble Boulden
2 of 2 Free White Males 16 or over:	born in or before 1774
1 of 3 Free White Males under 16:	born after 1774 (son of Noble Boulden's from an earlier marriage?)

---

[59] Cecil County MD Probate Records, Vol. 15 - 1825, page 406 (Located in Maryland Archives in Annapolis). His grandson George received his final distribution on 7 March 1825.

[60] There is a reconstructed census for Delaware for 1790, but there is no George Hedney listed there either. There is an 1820 Census (National Archives Series m033, roll 45, page 143) for a "George Hadley" in Cecil County MD, but the counts on that entry are not a good fit. The 1820 census entry for Mr. Hadley is discussed in the appendix beginning on page 157.

[61] National Archives Series m637, Roll 3, page 548. (S76) On the actual document the name looks more like "Beedle" to me, but the listing is in alphabetical order and the name appears between Richard Boulden and John Boulden; given the unusual first name Noble, I think my use of the phrase "most likely" is justified.

2 of 3 Free White Males under 16:	born after 1774 (son of Noble Boulden's from an earlier marriage?)
3 of 3 Free White Males under 16:	Born after 1774 (possibly Rudolph [2596], who would have been about 13) **Our Direct Ancestor?**
1 of 2 Free White Females:	Possibly Mary Lowery Gonce Boulden [2582] **Our Direct Ancestor?**
2 of 2 Free White Females:	(daughter of Noble's from earlier marriage?)
No Other Free Persons nor Indians	
6 Slaves	(the 1790 census provided no indication of the gender or age or the slaves – simply a total count)

The Tax Rolls for the 1st District of Cecil County, Maryland[62] show the following assessments for this Rudolph Gonce, which seem to indicate that Rudolph may possibly have inherited land[63] belonging to his father Daniel, who died in 1782:

Name as recorded	Amount	Assessment Date	Rudolph's Age
Rudulph Gonce	£13	1793	16
Rudulph Gonce	£13	1794	17
Rhudolph Gonce Junr[64]	£13	1795	18

Rudolph married Elizabeth Hedney[65] [ID 2597] on 26 October 1796 in Cecil County, very shortly after the birth of their first son and my 3rd great-grandfather George Gonce [ID 2511] on 12 October 1796[66].

Rudolph and Elizabeth had at least one more child, a second son, John T. Gonce[67] [ID 2628], who was born in about 1800[68]. Although his parents remained

---

[62] Cecil County, Maryland Tax Assessments 1793-1795 (S159)

[63] If this were the case, however, the land would likely have been held in trust for him between 1783 and 1793. I was unable to locate any tax payments that would seem to match this land. The most likely trustee for this would have been his mother and, after her marriage, Noble Boulden, but I found no listings for either of them in extant tax records. Not all such records have survived, however.

[64] This is Daniel's son, not Daniel's brother Rudolph. Use of the term "Junior" was often used to distinguish between relatives such as uncles and nephews rather than just between fathers and sons as it is now. In any case, the older Rudolph died in 1790 and his land was in Delaware.

[65] See Maryland Marriages 1667-1899; Jordan Dodd, Liahona Research, Compiler. (S56).; Elizabeth's actual last name was Hedney, but the transcriber either read this as Headner, or it was printed incorrectly in the original newspaper. (S56) Another reference is "Cecil County, Maryland Marriage Licenses 1777-1840" page 16 (S157), which lists the presiding minister as William Duke.

[66] There is a bit of uncertainty concerning George's birth year. I have outlined why I believe 12 October 1796 is the most likely and credible date in the appendix "Birth Year of George Gonce" beginning on page 161.

[67] George's younger brother is *not* the John T. Gonce in our direct line. The name John T. Gonce appears in several generations, and care should be taken to distinguish among these.

[68] The six-year gap between the two sons would have been fairly unusual for the time, so it is possible that there were other children who died young, or who simply never appeared in any records.

in Cecil County, John resettled in Delaware and, on 1 April 1825[69], married a woman named Susan ID 2629 and had at least two children (shown below).

My 4th great-grandmother Elizabeth Hedney Gonce died in early 1800, quite possibly during or after the birth of her son John. George would have been no more than four years old when his mother died. To date, I've located no information that would confirm her date of death or where she is buried.

Children and Grandchildren of Rudolph Gonce & Elizabeth Hedney

Rudolph and Elizabeth had only two children that I have been able to discover:

- George Gonce ID 1576, our direct ancestor, will be discussed in more detail below.

- John T. Gonce ID 2628, born in 1800, and his wife Susan (1803-1852) had only two children that I could locate.
  John R. Gonce ID 2612, born in 1831, married Sarah Elizabeth Alrich ID 2613 in 1858 and had a son John Eugene Gonce ID 2617 in 1859 and a daughter Mary Alrich Gonce ID 2621 in 1861. John died in 1870.
  Susannah Gonce ID 2630, born in 1835. Susannah married W. L. Thompson on 3 January 1865.

Except for the relatively few descendants of John R. Gonce ID 2612, and those Gonces who returned to Maryland after the southern migration (see page 149), the remainder of the Gonces now living in the mid-Atlantic States are all descendants of our ancestor George Gonce ID 1576, who is discussed in more detail beginning on page 55. Rudolph soon married for a second time.

Ann Cox & the Cox Family

Nancy Ann[70] Cox ID 2598, who is listed in the records we are concerned with only as "Ann Cox," was born in 1784[71]. The surname Cox is quite common in the available contemporary records of Cecil County, so it is difficult to determine who Ann's parents were, but the most likely candidate is John C. Cox, since he was a close neighbor, later appears in Ohio where Ann and her second husband relocated.

---

[69] Delaware Bible Records, Volume 2; Donald O. Virdin; page 6. (S57) John and Susan are there listed as the parents of John R. Gonce.

[70] Since Ann is not actually in our lineage, a full explanation of how we know this seems beyond the scope of this document, but essentially it is based on later records from her second marriage and subsequent life in Ohio. If anyone is interested, I will be happy to send the explanation as provided to me by one of her descendants.

[71] Ann's year of birth is given in her son (by her second marriage) George Washington Owens' bible.

Rudolph Gonce & Nancy Ann Cox

On 24 January 1801, when my 3rd great-grandfather George was probably about four years old, his father Rudolph married for the second time[72] to Nancy Ann Cox [ID 2598]. Ann, as she was known, would have been about sixteen years old at the time of this marriage, and Rudolph about twenty-two.

Rudolph and Ann had at least one daughter, Elizabeth (known as "Bets") [ID 4751], who was born in the latter part of 1802, although the 1810 Census record for Rudolph's first father-in-law George Hedney of Cecil County, discussed below, might be interpreted to suggest they had another daughter sometime in 1803 or 1804. If so, there is no evidence of her in records I've looked at, although she could well have been married by the time of the 1820 census.

Rudolph was killed by a falling tree[73] shortly after this marriage, probably in late 1803 or early 1804. He was about twenty-four years old at the time of his death[74], but I have found no record of burial location, which presumably is in Cecil County. Elizabeth's sons George (my 4th great-grandfather) and John would have been seven and three years old respectively at that time; they and Ann's daughter Elizabeth were now orphans.

Ann seems to have become a housekeeper and babysitter for Stephen Owens, a neighbor whose second wife had recently died in childbirth, leaving him with an infant daughter named Harriet. On 1 November 1804, Ann became Stephen's third wife[75]. After May 1810, when Stephen purchased land in Zanesville, Muskingon (now Perry) County, Ohio, the couple permanently relocated there with Elizabeth (Rudolph's child) and Harriet. They remained in Ohio and eventually had another eight children there. Stephen died first, in 1837[76], followed by Ann in 1866.

It is clear that neither George nor John Gonce moved with their stepmother and her new husband to Ohio[77]. All indications suggest that the boys were raised by either their Hedney grandparents or possibly by their paternal

---

[72] See "Maryland Marriages 1667-1899" referenced above (S56). Another reference is "Cecil County, Maryland Marriage Licenses 1777-1840" page 20 (S157), which lists the presiding minister as Rev. William Cosden.

[73] This according to handwritten notes of George Washington Williams (1861-1933), great-grandson of Steven and Nancy (aka Ann) Gonce Owens, transcribed by Virgil Owens. Unfortunately, I've been unable to locate any further details of the incident.

[74] ... coincidentally about the same age as his father Daniel was when he died in 1782.

[75] Maryland Marriages 1667-1899; Jordan Dodd, Liahona Research, Compiler. (S56). Stephen had been married twice before: to Elizabeth Harwood on 18 January 1785, and to Charlott (sic) Edenor on 4 December 1799. The Harwood name also appears when discussing my 7th great-grandfather Edward Comegys [ID 2443], who married Mary [ID 2458], the widow of John Harwood..

[76] Interestingly, in Stephen's Will, Rudolph's daughter Elizabeth, who eventually married Frank Wilkins, was given half of the amount given to his other children, most likely because she was not his biological daughter. This was not uncommon at the time.

[77] This was confirmed by my correspondence and exchange of information with one of Stephen Owens' descendants.

1759 – 1983 History

grandmother Mary and her husband. Mary Lowery Gonce Boulden would have been about forty-three years old at the time of her son Rudolph's death, and would have been living with her second husband Noble for about twenty years, so she seems the less likely candidate[78].

As for their Hedney grandparents, the only George Hedney listed in the 1810 census[79] for Cecil County, Maryland has no age-appropriate count there for a George who could be Elizabeth's father. In fact, there doesn't appear to be any adult male in the household (which may simply be an oversight[80]). The following segment of the census form shows the counts from the line labeled "Geo. Hedney" in 1810, followed by my transcription and assumptions.

1810 United States Census Listing for "Geo Hedney" in Cecil County, MD	
1810 Census counts	Comments (my assumptions)
1 Free White Female, age 26-44:	born 1766-1784 – likely George Hedney's wife (my 5th great-grandmother) **Our Direct Ancestor**
1 Free White Male, age 10-15:	born 1795-1800 – likely the Hedneys' grandson George Gonce, age 14 **Our Direct Ancestor**
1 Free White Male, age <10:	born 1801-1810 – likely the Hedneys' grandson John T. Gonce, age 9
1 of 2 Free White Females, age <10:	born 1801-1810 – likely Elizabeth (Bets) Gonce, daughter of son-in-law Rudolph Gonce and his second wife Ann, and half-sister of the Hedneys' grandsons George and John.
2 of 2 Free White Females, age <10:	born 1801-1810 – possibly a second child of Rudolph Gonce and his second wife Ann.
4 Other Free Persons not Indians	Steven Owens[81], Nancy Ann Cox-Gonce-Owens, and their new daughter Rebecca might be three of the four listed here. Stephen's daughter Harriet by his first wife might be the fourth.
1 Slave	(the 1810 census provided no indication of the gender or age or the slaves – simply a total count)

---

[78] I haven't been able to locate any records of Noble Boulden or similar name in this period; headcounts in the 1800 to 1820 censuses in particular would likely be helpful.

[79] National Archives Microfilm Series m252, Roll 15, Page 235.

[80] The only way George would have been listed as Head of Household without an age-appropriate count would be if he had recently died, but he lived until at least 1824 when he wrote his Will.

[81] The presence of Stephen's family with the Hedneys, unrelated but for the fact that Ann was previously married to their deceased son-in-law Rudolph, and particularly given that Stephen had his own household, might not be so unusual. Owens family stories suggest that Stephen and his brother had gone to Ohio a few years earlier to locate land. In May of 1810, Stephen purchased land in Ohio. If he had left his family with the Hedneys while he was away, he likely would have been listed in the Census with the Hedneys whether he had already returned or not. In any case, this isn't relevant to our Gonce history.

The only males counted were in the "under 10" and "10-15" columns, and if this were indeed the household of our Hedney ancestors, we would expect a count in the fourth or fifth column. If George and John Gonce were living in this household, it still isn't clear whether the grandsons moved in with the Hedneys after their mother Elizabeth's death in about 1800, after their father Rudolph's death in about 1803, or when Ann (their stepmother) and her new husband Stephen Owens married on 1 November 1804 and later moved to Ohio. If the younger of the two male children is indeed John Thomas Gonce, however, and he was born around the cut-off for the census counts, it supports the possibility that Elizabeth may have died in childbirth with him.

There is also the presence of a second female under the age of ten to account for, however. She could not be a daughter of Rudolph and Elizabeth, since she must have been born after John Gonce was (i.e. and therefore after Elizabeth had died). As mentioned earlier, it is possible that Rudolph may have had two daughters with Ann Cox prior to his death, and that these were being cared for by the Hedneys with their half-siblings until Ann moved to Ohio. Ann and her new husband had 2 daughters born between 1801 and 1804 with them at the time of the 1820 Census[82]., but one of them is known to be Stephen's daughter Harriet from his marriage to Charlott Edenor.

It is certainly possible that this "Geo. Hedney" may not be the George Hedney who is our ancestor, although I've been unable to locate another George Hedney in earlier or later records of Maryland or its adjoining states.

My 3rd great-grandfather George Gonce eventually married Catharine Comegys [ID 2510], the daughter of Samuel Comegys [ID 2508] and Rachel Vansant [ID 2509]. Before continuing with the Gonce line, therefore, the following pages will discuss the history of our Vansant and Comegys ancestors, both of which had arrived in America over a century[83] before Justice and Magdalen Gonce.

The map on the following page will serve as a reference for the discussions of our Vansant and Comegys ancestors that follow:

---

[82] i.e. born before the move to Ohio. National Archives Microfilm Series m033, Roll 95, Page 16a.
[83] Garret Stoffelse Vansant arrived in 1651, and Cornelius Comegys arrived in 1654.

1759 – 1983 History

Origins of Our Dutch Ancestors – Map of Modern Holland

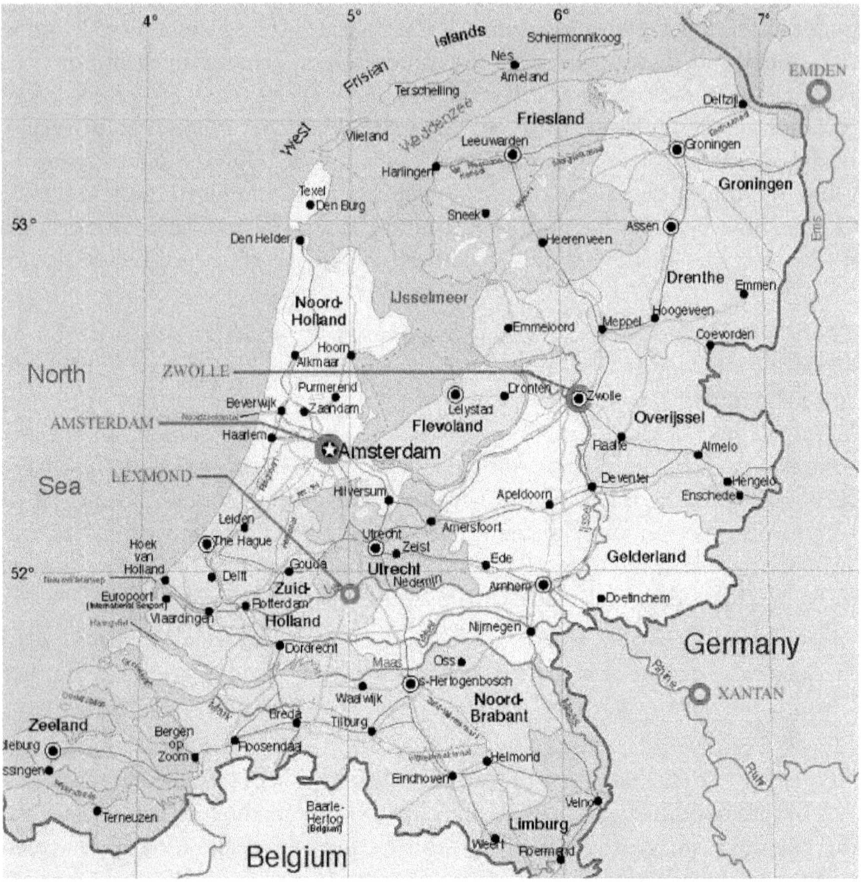

Zwolle: origin of my 11th great-grandfather Gerrit Janszen, born there in 1592.

Amsterdam: where our Comegys and Vansant ancestors departed for the "New World."

Lexmond: origin of my 9th great-grandfather Cornelius Comegys, baptized there in 1630.

> Xantan: early origin of the Vansants (i.e. "from Xantan"), who later migrated to Kleverins (near Jever, Germany, east of Emden), and then to Amsterdam.

"Nieuw Jorck" in 1673, where our Vansant & Comegys forebears had arrived in 1651 & 1654

My 4th great-grandmother Rachel Vansant Comegys & Our Vansant Ancestors

The earliest of our Vansant ancestors[84] I have identified are three of Rachel's 6th great-grandparents (my 11th great-grandparents):

Van Zandt Coat of Arms

♦ Harmens Vansant [ID 4568], about whom I have found no information other than that he lived in Kleverins, a town near Jever[85], Germany, and died before 1643.

In about 1618, in Kleverins, Harmens had a son named Christoffel Harmenszen[86] Vansant [ID 4563], who was generally known as "Stoffel," the common abbreviation for the Dutch version of "Christopher." The name of Harmens' wife is so far unidentified. Harmans eventually migrated northwest to the town of Amsterdam with at least his son[87] and lived on the Hoochstraet in Amsterdam.

♦ Gerrit Janszen [ID 4566] was born in 1592 in Zwolle, Overijssel, Holland, and died in about 1634. His name suggests his father's name is Jan, but having no further information, I can't guess his surname.

♦ Vroutgen (Vroutie) Pieters [ID 4567], who died after 1643.

Gerrit and Vroutie were married on 13 November 1616 in the New Church in Amsterdam, Holland, and had at least one daughter, named Moedertien Gerrits[88] Janszen, who was baptized on November 2, 1623. She also appears in records of the time as "Moeder Gers." Gerritt died in 1634 when his daughter was about 11 years old, but Vroutie and Moeder were known to be living on Breestraet in Amsterdam in 1643.

---

[84] … and the earliest of any of our Gonce-side ancestors that I've identified.

[85] Jever is about 190 miles east-northeast of Amsterdam in Ostfriesland, and about 45 miles along the way, the route passes a few miles south of Emden, from which my Kiwiet ancestors (Oberle-side) emigrated in the late nineteenth century (see my book "Our Oberle Ancestors"; ISBN 978-1-61600-291-6)

[86] "Harmenszen," or just "Harmens," of course, means he is Harmens' son. The Dutch had the concept of family names (what we call surnames) by this time, but their use in records of the period was sporadic. The spelling of this particular family name, which seems to mean that they had come "from Xantan", a town about 100 miles southeast of Amsterdam, appears in many forms: Van Zandt, Van Sandt, Van Zant, Van Sant, and so forth. I will be using the spelling "Vansant" exclusively, since that is the spelling used by our most recent ancestor from that family, George Gonce's mother-in-law Rachel Vansant Comegys. The actual meaning of the town name Xantan (the possible significance of this will become clear later – see the box titled "Purchasing Manhattan" on page 31) seems to have something to do with a prominent mound of rock, or perhaps a mound of dirt.

[87] There is insufficient information to guess whether Stoffel's wife (my 11th great-grandmother) had died before or after the move to Amsterdam, but she definitely predeceased Harmens.

[88] Meaning "Gerrit's daughter." See the earlier footnote about the name "Harmenszen."

My 10th great-grandfather Stoffel Vansant met Moeder Gerrits in Amsterdam, and on June 13, 1643, their wedding banns were announced.

> *Christoffel Harmens, from Jever, journeyman tailor*[89] *living on the Hoochstraet, having no living parents, age 25, and Moederke Gerrits, from Amsterdam, living on the Breestraet, attended by her mother, Vroutie Pieters.*

Two weeks later, on June 28th, Stoffel and Moeder, then almost 22, were married in Amsterdam's old church. The couple "signed" the wedding register by "placing their marks," indicating that neither of them could write, which was not unusual at all for this time.

In July of 1644, a little over a year after their marriage, Moeder gave birth to my 9th great-grandfather Garrett Stoffelse[90] Vansant $^{ID\ 4545}$, but Moeder died during or due to her son's birth, and was buried at St. Anthonius Church in Amsterdam on July 17th.

A little over a year later, on September 9, 1645, Stoffel again announced his intention to marry – this time to Trijntje Claesen Pieterz $^{ID\ 4565}$, a daughter of Claes Pieterz $^{ID\ 4560}$ and Giertje Heeren $^{ID\ 4577}$. It seems likely, although unconfirmed, that Claes was a brother of my 11th great-grandmother Vroutie, and that Trijntje was therefore Moeder's first cousin.

Trijntje and Stoffel's first and only son was born on September 16, 1646 and, as custom would dictate, was named Claestien Stoffelszen Vansant $^{ID\ 4573}$. Unfortunately, Claestien died in early childhood.

At this point in Stoffel's life, it had only been a few years since the famous explorer Henry Hudson had returned in 1609 from the Dutch colony of New Amsterdam. Because of the apparent opportunities, there was much discussion in Holland about the benefits of migrating to the colony. We can only assume that such talk, coupled with the couple's recent losses, contributed to their decision to contemplate a move to New Amsterdam.

On July 10, 1649, Judicq van de Vin notarized Stoffel's Testament[91] and it was registered in Amsterdam on 18 July 1649. Stoffel arranged to have his family's passage to New Amsterdam paid by making an agreement to enter the service of Cornelis de Potter there. In 1651, Stoffel, Trijntje, and their son Garrett arrived in New Amsterdam, making them the earliest of our Gonce-side ancestors to come to this continent[92]. The details of this indenture, filed by Mr. de Potter's representative after the family began their

---

[89] In Dutch, literally, a "cloth worker."

[90] In the tradition of the time, he was named after his maternal grandfather. Stoffelse, of course, meant that he was Stoffel's son.

[91] What we would today call a Will.

[92] My 9th great-grandfather Cornelius Comegys didn't arrive until 1654, and Justice Gonce likely didn't arrive until about a century later. There is a possibility that another relative of the Vansant family may have arrived a quarter century earlier – see the sidebar "Purchasing Manhattan" above.

service in New Amsterdam, can be found in the Notarial Archives of Amsterdam:

> *Nord Amerika Chronologie, 1598-1750: "1652 April 16. Abraham de Wijs. Merchant in Amsterdam, in the name of Cornelis de Potter, his brother-in-law, who lives in the Manhattans in New Netherland. He takes into service for him: Christoffel Harmens and Trijinje Claes to work there for de Potter. Also their son Gerrit Christoffels, 8 years old, shall work with them. This is for a time period of three years, at 200 Carolus guilders per year. Free board and room."*

Whether Stoffel was still in Cornelis de Potter's service in 1655 is unclear, but it is possible he had become a member of the Burgher Guards (the local militia) by then, which might provide one explanation of how he came to be killed.

On September 15th of that year, a nearby Manhattan farmer and administrator for the Dutch West India Company named Hendrick Thomasse Van Dyck caught a young Wappinger Indian woman named Tachiniki taking a peach from one of the trees in his orchard. Peaches were relatively new to the area, having been brought to the Virginia area by English settlers in the early 1600s and only recently introduced to the Dutch colonists in New Amsterdam. It isn't clear, therefore, if Tachiniki was "stealing[93]" a peach or merely attempting to sample something new and unfamiliar.

Purchasing Manhattan

Everyone seems to remember the story from their early school years of the purchase of Manhattan from the Indians in 1626 by Peter Minuet for $24. What isn't so well known is that these negotiations were actually conducted on Minuet's behalf by a group led by Oloffe Van Kortlandt – the three others in the group were named Abraham Harden Broeck, Jacobus Van Zandt, and Winant Ten Broeck.

Jacobus Van Zandt had left Amsterdam for the Americas in 1613 on the ship Goode Vrow (The Good Wife). Based on his origins, it is possible that he and my 11th great-grandfather Harmens Vansant could be brothers, although there isn't any proof of this. In his rather humorous history of the period, Washington Irving describes Jacobus as follows:

"Had I the benefit of mythology and classic fable above alluded to, I should have furnished the first of the trio with a pedigree equal to that of the proudest hero of antiquity. His name, Van Zandt--that is to say, from the dirt--gave reasons to suppose that, like Triptolemus, Themis, the Cyclops, and the Titans, he had sprung from Dame Terra or the Earth! This supposition is strongly corroborated by his size, for it is well known that all the progeny of Mother Earth were of a gigantic stature; and Van Zandt, we are told, was a tall, raw-boned man, above six feet high, with an astonishingly hard head. Nor is this origin of the illustrious Van Zandt a whit more improbable or repugnant to belief than what is related and universally admitted of certain of our greatest, or rather richest, men, who we are told with the utmost gravity did originally spring from a dunghill!"

Nonetheless, Van Dyck shot and killed her for this offense. The Wappinger tribe, who by this time were serving as "enforcers" for several other tribes in

---

[93] "Stealing," when discussing eating fruit from a tree, was not a concept the Indians would likely have had much exposure to.

the region, took offense at this and sent a war party of over 200 canoes from their camp several miles north on the west side of the Hudson River.

Their objective was, of course, to seek revenge and, although they managed to wound Van Dyck with an arrow, they encountered a group of the Burgher Guards and were driven off the island after a battle with them. The details of this skirmish are spotty, but what is known is that one of those killed in this attack was my 10th great-grandfather Stoffel. In history books that deal with the obscure, this incident, along with the subsequent raids by the escaping Wappinger on Staten Island and Pavonia[94] is often referred to by the rather pretentious name of "the Peach War."

Based on Stoffel's earlier Testament bequeathing half his estate to his only son, the Orphanmaster's Court appointed John Nevius and Jacques Corteljou as guardians of Garrett's share, since he was only about eleven years old[95]. The guardians were instructed by the court to secure Garrett's share "by mortgage on the lands or other real estate." Garret remained living with his stepmother, Trijntje, however.

Trijntje soon married another immigrant from Amsterdam – a bachelor named Rutger Joosten van Brunt[ID 4592] who had arrived in New Utrecht in about 1653[96]. Trijntje and Garrett moved around this time to Rutger's property in the area of New Utrecht in Brooklyn[97]. Later records of English censuses and tax assessments show that the couple had at least two sons of their own (Cornelis and Joost).

Although some of his assets were the result of his new wife's inheritance, Rutger seemed to be reasonably well off. The tax assessment of 1675[98] showed that he owned 5 horses, 16 cows and calves, 13 sheep, 1 hog, and 72

---

[94] Pavonia is present day Jersey City, New Jersey.

[95] The "Minutes of the Orphanmaster of New Amsterdam, 1655-1663" says that he was 12 at the time. But this is based on the European style of computing age, which is ordinal (you are in your first year as soon as you are born) rather than our custom of using cardinal ages (i.e. you aren't one year old until the first anniversary of your birth.) That I'm following. This two-volume source is edited by Berthold Fernow, and can be found on LDS Microfilm 497643, available from any LDS Family History Center.

[96] When Rut Joosten took the English Oath of Allegiance in 1687, he stated that he had been living in the colony for "34 Jeare." A Documentary History of the State of New York; E.B. O'Callaghan, M.D.; Weed, Parsons & Co.; Albany; 1850 Volume II, page 36. [S174]

[97] This was called Brooklyn after the Dutch town of Breuckelen (meaning "marsh land"). New Utrecht was founded in 1657. New Utrecht was combined in with other towns in that part of Long Island in about 1667, 3 years after British rule began. As late as 1698, the non-native population of New Utrecht and its surrounds was only 259 – a figure that included 39 men, 38 women, 134 children and 48 slaves (over 20% of the population). A Documentary History of the State of New York; E.B. O'Callaghan, M.D.; Weed, Parsons & Co.; Albany; 1850 Volume III, page 89. [S174]

[98] A Documentary History of the State of New York; E.B. O'Callaghan, M.D.; Weed, Parsons & Co.; Albany; 1850 Volume IV, page 103. [S174]

morgens[99] of land (equivalent then to a little over 152 acres). In 1676[100], he had 4 horses, 6 cows, 9 oxen, 12 sheep, and an estate of 100 morgens (about 212 acres).

Garrett Vansant & Elizabeth Gerritse

My 9th great-grandfather Garrett continued living with his stepparents for many years, even after his eventual marriage. By 1668, he had married my 9th great-grandmother Elizabeth Gerritse [ID 4562] there.

Elizabeth, who had been born in Middleburg, Zeeland, Holland in 1647, was the daughter of my 10th great-grandparents Cornelis Gerrits van Westen [ID 4571] and Josyntje ver Hagen [ID 4572].

In 1670, Elizabeth gave birth to their first known child, my 8th great-grandfather Christoffel. Over the years between then and 1692, Garrett and Elizabeth had nine more children. Records for the baptisms of at least five of these children at the Dutch Reformed Church of New Netherlands survive.

In 1664, when Garrett was about twenty years old, the English first captured New Amsterdam, renaming it New York. By 1674, English rule of the area became permanent. The Dutch had briefly recaptured the area about a year after the first English conquest, but were eventually forced to formally cede all of New Amsterdam to England in that year.

Although it isn't clear how long he held the post, there is a record that Garrett was a Magistrate of the King's Court[101] in New Utrecht in 1681, indicating that he wasn't completely uncomfortable with British control.

When the Roman Catholic King James II came to the throne in early 1685, the local political environment began to slowly change: not only were the Dutch settlers under English rule, but they were under English *Catholic* rule. The new monarch decreed that all of his adult subjects must swear loyalty to him, and this edict was soon being carried out in the colonies as well. Thus, Garrett took the Oath of Allegiance in New Utrecht in September 1687[102]. Acceptance of English rule by many of the Dutch in the New York area was becoming less enthusiastic. Coincidentally, the English themselves (at least those in positions of power) were less than enthusiastic about having a Catholic monarch. James' daughter Mary, a committed Protestant, was

---

[99] "Morgen" came from the German word for Morning, and the term originally meant the amount of land that a farmer could plow from sunup to midday. As a result of this lack of precision, the term came to represent a widely divergent amount of land in places such as South Africa, Taiwan, etc. In this time and place, though, a Dutch morgen seemed to be equivalent to 2.1167 English acres.

[100] A Documentary History of the State of New York; E.B. O'Callaghan, M.D.; Weed, Parsons & Co.; Albany; 1850 Volume II, page 282. [S174]

[101] This was, of course, the English King's Court, specifically the court of the restored Stuart King Charles II (known as the "Merrie Monarch" – his father Charles I had been beheaded on 30 January 1649); Charles II ruled from 1660 to 1685, but was then deposed and replaced by his brother James II.

[102] Garrett listed his age then at 43. A Documentary History of the State of New York; E.B. O'Callaghan, M.D.; Weed, Parsons & Co.; Albany; 1850 Volume I, page 431. [S174]

beginning to be viewed as a favorable alternative. Mary, who was married to William of Orange, was tacitly invited to have her husband "invade" England. This took place on 13 February 1689 was largely unopposed, at least publicly; Mary II was now Queen, with her husband William III as co-regent[103].

The Dutch in the colonies viewed this favorably, since they now at least had a Protestant queen and – even better – a Dutch Protestant King.

As late as 1685, Garrett was known to still be a tenant on his stepparents' farm, even though he and Elizabeth had seven children. In 1686, however, he appears as one of fourteen original landowners mentioned in the 13 May, 1686 Patent for the "Commons of New Utrecht" by then Governor Thomas Dongan, suggesting that he had acquired land of his own. Then, on February 1st 1691, he purchased two "half lots" of land from a neighboring farmer named Denys Teunisse.

Garrett was reported in at least one source to be a Magistrate of the King's Court in New Utrecht in 1691, but since I can find no confirmation of this, it may simply be a typographical error[104].

As the seventeenth century was ending, the New York area was becoming quite Anglicized. In spite of having a Dutch co-regent on the English throne, Dutch customs were increasingly becoming marginalized and, in the spirit of many succeeding waves of immigrants, the Dutch were growing concerned that their culture and language would disappear before too long, exemplified nicely by the following petition[105] submitted to New York's Governor:

> *Petition of the Elders of the Dutch Churches in Kings Co.*
>
> *To his Excellency Edward Lord Viscount Cornbury her[106] Majesty's Capt General and Governor in Chiefe of the Province of New Yorke and territoryes depending thereon in America &c. and Vice admiral of the same &c. The humble petition of the Elders of four dutch Churches in Kings County Brookland, fflatbush, fflatlands and New Utrecht whose names are underwritten*
>
> HUMBLY SHEWETH
>
> *Vnto your Excellency that your petitioners of late were impowered by the people of their several townes to call and send for a minister either out of this province or out of Holland to instruct them in their mothers tongue in the place of their late Minister Mr Lupardus deceased and accordingly had severall meetings about said matter, and at last concluded to address y^r Excellency ffor leave to send ffor and call one Mr Bernardus ffreeman Minister of Schenechida to be their Minister,*

---

[103] This couple is the famous "William and Mary."
[104] Recall that an earlier record lists him as a magistrate in 1681.
[105] A Documentary History of the State of New York; E.B. O'Callaghan, M.D.; Weed, Parsons & Co.; Albany; 1850 Volume III, page 89. [S174]
[106] Queen Mary II was the actual titular monarch; her husband William was King by virtue of his marriage to her, even though, like Mary, he was also a grandchild of the previously beheaded Charles I.

whereupon may it please your Excellency a petition was prepared by y^r Petitioners ffor that end and sent by Coll Gerardus Beekman to y^r Excellency who promised the delivery of it, but ffailed in his …

In 1692, my 9th great-grandmother Elizabeth gave birth to the couple's last child, Garrett[107]. Circumstantial evidence suggests that Elizabeth may have died during or as a result of her last son's birth. She doesn't appear in any later records in either New York or Pennsylvania that I am aware of.

On July 31, 1695, Garrett sold at least the two half lots he had purchased in 1691 to Derick Janse van Zutphen[108], and seems to have left the New Utrecht area by at least 1698, since he was not listed in the New Utrecht census[109]. His third son Harmen is listed in that census with a wife, but no children[110].

With the exception of Harmen, none of our Vansant ancestors or their families appears in any New Utrecht records I could locate between the end of July 1695 and February 1699, a period of three and a half years[111]. It is evident however, that by 1699, Garrett and at least part of his family had relocated to Bucks County, Pennsylvania.

Coincidentally by this time, the Englishman[112] William Penn was actively recruiting both Europeans as well as those in other New World colonies to come live in his new settlements, promising a greater degree of religious and political freedoms than were the norm in America. Pennsylvania may have seemed attractive to my 9th great-grandfather, although it isn't known for certain if Penn's marketing campaigns influenced his decision to relocate.

Once there, Garrett purchased 150 acres of farmland just outside of the town of Bensalem[113] on 10 February 1699[114] from Joseph Growdon.

---

[107] There is a birth record for a Garrett Vansant on 4 May 1695, but this is Elizabeth's grandson – the second child of our ancestor Christoffel – and not her last child.

[108] "Dirck," as he was also known, had a wife, eight children, and three slaves at this time, and already owned land in the area.

[109] I was also unable to locate him in any other records until his later appearance in Pennsylvania.

[110] Harmen had married his first wife Elizabeth Brouwers, daughter of William Brouwers and Elizabeth Simpson, before this 1698 census; their first son Garrett wasn't born until after the census. A Documentary History of the State of New York; E.B. O'Callaghan, M.D.; Weed, Parsons & Co.; Albany; 1850 Volume III, page 88. [S174]

[111] Garret's oldest son Stoffel had relocated to Staten Island, and that will be discussed in the next section, and although I didn't encounter any evidence that his father or brothers were with him then, that has to be considered a possibility.

[112] Strictly speaking, he was an Englishman, but see footnote Error: Reference source not found on page 300.

[113] Bensalem is just outside Philadelphia and is today located off one of the first suburban exits north of Philadelphia on Interstate 95.

[114] Some sources give this as 10 December 1698, but that is an incorrect interpretation of the "10th day of the 12th month 1698." At this time, the English and its colonies had not yet made the transition from the Julian to the Gregorian calendar, and the twelfth month of the year 1698 was what we now know as February 1699 (explaining why the names September, October, November and December are based on the Latin words for seven, eight, nine and ten). The switch was eventually made on September 2,

Garrett's oldest son, our ancestor Christoffel, certainly wasn't with the family at this time, but Garrett's second son Cornelius purchased another 150 acres adjoining his father's plot from Mr. Growdon as well[115]. What is important about this purchase is that Garrett identified himself solely as "Garret Van Sandt," his first use of a fully "Americanized" surname with no reference to his being "Stoffelszen."

Unlike his father, Garrett never made a Will and, when he died in early 1706, he died intestate. The result of this was that his property and household passed in equal shares to his six living adult sons. In June, Johannes and Jacobus, together with their two living younger siblings, purchased their older brothers' shares of this property for £150. This transaction is recorded in the Bucks County, Pennsylvania Grantor Book, p. 3-256, #23671:

> "Deed of Jun. 20, 1706. Stophell Vansand, Cornelius Vansand, Harman Vansand, Albert Vansand, Johanes Vansand, all of Bucks Co., sons of Garret Vansand, late of Bucks Co., dec'd., and Jezina Vansand and Garret Vansand, younger children of said Garret Vansand, dec'd., for £150 paid by Jacobus Vansand and George Vansand, a tract beginning at a birch tree by Nesahminy[116] River and against the house formerly belonging to Edward Carter - 150 acres which is part of a tract of 5000 acres granted to Joseph Growdon on 24/25 Oct 1681 and the 150 acres was granted by Joseph Growdon to Garrat Vansand by deed dated 10 Feb 1698 and Garrat Vansant dying intestate the land descended to all his children. Rec: 26 Jul 1706."

Because she isn't mentioned in this transaction, it seems certain that my 9th great-grandmother Elizabeth[117] must have died prior to 1706 if not, as suggested earlier, prior to the move from New Utrecht to Pennsylvania.

Children of Garrett Vansant & Elizabeth Gerritse

The children of my 9th great-grandparents Garret Stoffelse Vansant [ID 4545] and his wife Elizabeth Gerritse [ID 4562], all born in the New York area, are:

- **Christoffel (Stoffel) Vansant** [ID 4552] was born in 1670 and died in 1749. Stoffel is our direct ancestor and will be discussed below.

- Cornelius Vansant [ID 4553] was born in 1672 and died on 9 May 1734. Cornelius married twice, had at least three children and eventually settled in Maryland.

1752, resulting in the "loss" of eleven days, since the next day was September 14th. From that time on, the New Year began on January 1st, rather than March 25th.

[115] Cornelius paid £28.15 for his plot. Bucks County Grantee Book, Vol 2, page 266.

[116] This was also known as the "River Nehamiah."

[117] Some genealogies show that Garrett had a second wife named Lysbeth Cornelis, but this is almost certainly the same person using the Dutch form of her name with her father's name.

- Harman Vansant [ID 4554] was baptized on 10 June 1674 and died on 9 May 1759. Harman married three times, had at least five children — more likely nine — and remained in Pennsylvania.

- Josius Vansant [ID 4555] was born on 29 October 1676 and died shortly thereafter.

- Albertus (Albert) Vansant [ID 4556] was born on 17 May 1681 and died on 16 December 1751. Albert married twice, had nine children, and eventually settled in Delaware. Interestingly, Albert's grandson Garret Vansant was a neighbor of the Gonce brothers in Delaware, and appears directly above my 5th great-grandfather Daniel Gonce in the Delaware Archives sheet where Garret also declined military service with the excuse "being ailing I can't bear the fatigue." Garret later moved to North Carolina and became a Captain in the Revolutionary Army[118].

- Johannes (John) Vansant [ID 4557] was born in 1683 and died on 30 October 1714. John married Leah Groesbeck in 1702 and remained in Pennsylvania, but I am not aware of any children.

- Jacobus (James) Vansant [ID 4558] was born on 15 February 1685 and died on December 1744. James married Rebecca Vandegrift in 1707 and had seven children.

- Joris (George) Gerritse Vansant [ID 3732] was baptized on 24 April 1687 and died on 22 March 1755. George married Maike Van de Grift in 1706 and had at least twelve children. George's son John [ID 3738] is mentioned later.

- Tryntje (Jesina) Vansant [ID 4559] was born on 20 October 1689 and died shortly thereafter.

- Garrett Vansant, Jr. [ID 4561] was born in 1692 and died in 1746. Garrett married a woman whose first name was Claubchy (possibly Claetie), and had at least one and possibly two daughters.

Christoffel Vansant & Rachel Courson

Like his father, my 8th great-grandfather Christoffel Vansant [ID 4552], known as Stoffel, took the Oath of Allegiance in New Utrecht in 1687; he was about seventeen years old at the time. In about 1692, he married his first wife (not our ancestor) Annetje Jansz Duyts [ID 4589], daughter of Jan Duyts [ID 4595] and Jannetje Jeuriaens [ID 4596] in New Utrecht.

---

[118] Garret and his younger brother Jacob eventually settled in Kentucky, where Jacob's Will was witnessed by Davy Crockett. Their father's Will of 10 December 1751, gave his second wife Sarah the use of his land, with the stipulation that she was forbidden to ever rent any of it to an Irishman. The Will further stipulated that she would forfeit her entire inheritance if she married "an Irishman or any of that Extraction." None of this is relevant to our family's history, but just seemed too interesting to ignore.

The children of my 8th great-grandfather Christoffel Vansant [ID 4552] and his first wife Annetje Jansz [ID 4589] are:

- Jannitje Vansant [ID 4574] was baptized on 3 September 1693 and married Willem Renbergh in 1711.

- Gerrit Vansant [ID 4575] was baptized on 4 May 1695 and died the same year. His mother Annetje Jansz[119] seems to have died around the time he was born.

A few years later, in about 1696, Stoffel married for a second time to Hannah Risley[120] [ID 4586].

The only child of my 8th great-grandfather Christoffel Vansant [ID 4552] and his second wife Hannah Risley [ID 4586] is:

- John Vansant [ID 4578], born and died in 1697. His mother Hannah seems to have died around the time he was born, suggesting that she may have died in childbirth, but this isn't known for certain.

In about 1698, Stoffel married for the third and last time, to my 8th great-grandmother Raeghel (Rachel) Courson [ID 4590], daughter of Hendrick Courson[121] [ID 4593] and Aeltje Gerritsen [ID 4594]. My 9th great-grandfather Hendrick was known to be living in "Brauchelen" in September 1676[122], where his property, consisting of 3 horses, 3 cows, and "12 morg. land & valley," was valued at £90.10. His daughter Raeghel seems to have been born in about 1674.

It is clear from surviving records that both Stoffel and Rachel were born and lived in New Utrecht. It isn't clear though where they were married, nor is it clear when they left the New Utrecht area[123]. What is known is that on 22 May 1699, Stoffel, under the anglicized name Christopher Garretson, purchased 78 acres on Staten Island at the settlement of New Dorp[124] for £120 from Josiah and Jane Marlet.

---

[119] Annetje is recorded in the baptismal records of the Dutch Reformed Church of Brooklyn as "Annetje Stoffels," but this use of the husband's given name as a family identifier/surname was fairly common.

[120] Her surname is possibly "Ridley," but I haven't been able to locate any information about her.

[121] This surname appears in several forms, e.g. Corson, Coursen, etc.; Rachel's father's name is given in one source as Joshua, but I don't believe the evidence supports that.

[122] A Documentary History of the State of New York; E.B. O'Callaghan, M.D.; Weed, Parsons & Co.; Albany; 1850 Volume II, page 275. [S174]

[123] A Genealogical and Personal History of Bucks County, Pennsylvania; William W. H. Davis; 1975; Genealogical Publishing Co., Inc. Baltimore, MD; ISBN: 0-8063-0641-6; page 24 says "He [Stoffel] probably removed to Bucks county at the same time as his father, in 1699," but this is clearly incorrect.

[124] Richmond County Deeds B:348, recorded 23 September 1699. By an interesting coincidence, my parents lived very close to this area in the mid-1960s and often shopped there; my sister attended school in New Dorp for a period. New Dorp is the next Staten Island Commuter Railroad station north of the Oakwood Heights station near our home there.

Stoffel's fourth child Jacobus (James), and his first with Rachel, was born in New Dorp in 1699 as well, as were the couple's next four children. On 5 March 1702, bought another 78 acres of land there.

In 1703, the same year in which his sixth child – my 7th great-grandfather Joshua – was born, Stoffel was first elected a Supervisor for the Southern Division of Richmond County (Staten Island). He was by now 35 years old.

Records from 1705 show that Stoffel was re-elected to the Supervisor position and had registered his cattle brand[125].

While the reasons for his move from New Utrecht to New Dorp aren't clear, Stoffel's relocation of his family to Bensalem in 1706 is almost certainly related to his father's death as well as the inheritance of a part ownership of his father's estate[126] there, and appears to have been made quite quickly.

On May 2nd 1706 Stoffel, again as Christopher Garretson, sold the 156 acres he owned[127] in New Dorp to Aries Janson for £300. It seems safe to assume that he also resigned as a county supervisor then as well.

There is no record of his presence in Pennsylvania until after his father's death in 1706, when he inherited part ownership of his father's estate[128], and he appears frequently in the records after that date. My suspicion, therefore, is that, since he married Rachel at about the time his father Garret relocated, he and Rachel likely remained in New York until his inheritance prompted their family to move as well. One source suggests that Rachel was one of the Corsons of Staten Island, and that Stoffel and his father's family may have lived there during the three and one half years between their last appearance in New Utrecht and there first appearance in Pennsylvania. As far as I can determine, Rachel's father is not related to the Staten Island group, and in the few records of Richmond (Staten Island) I have been able to locate, the name Vansant or similar doesn't appear at all.

As mentioned earlier, Stoffel sold his portion of his father's estate that he inherited to some of his younger siblings. Shortly thereafter, on 23 May 1706, he purchased 300 acres in Middletown[129] from Henry Pawlus for £350. He would eventually transfer ownership of 100 acres each to his younger sons Garret and John.

On 20 May 1710, the Reformed Low Dutch Church of Neshaminy and Bensalem was established, and its first pastor, the Reverend Paulus Van Vlecq established his church council, which included Stoffel, by now age 40, as one of his two Deacons. Rachel, of course, was inducted as a member as well at

---

[125] "Historical and Genealogical Miscellany"; John E. Stillwell, editor; 1903; 1:30, 50, and 51.

[126] He is the "Stophell Vansand" mentioned in the 1706 deed quoted above.

[127] Richmond County Deeds B:539, recorded 4 May 1706.

[128] He is the "Stophell Vansand" mentioned in the 1706 deed quoted above.

[129] "Abstracts of Bucks County Land Records 1684-1723"; Charlotte D. Meldrum, editor; pages 115 & 116. Variously called Middleton, Middle Town, etc. in this period; it is located close to Bensalem.

this time. Interestingly, however, an older gentleman named Hendrick Van Dyck[130] was appointed as one of the two Elders of the church when it was established.

In that same year, Stoffel first became a representative to the Pennsylvania Colonial Assembly, and was also a representative to the subsequent 1712, 1714, and 1719 sessions.

In 1714, he became a founding member of the Abington Presbyterian Church. In the following year, Stoffel served his first term as a Justice; he held this position from 1715 through 1718, and again from 1723 through 1727.

On 3 May 1730, Stoffel was established as an Elder of the Bensalem Dutch Reformed Church.[131]

My 8th great-grandfather Christoffel Vansant ID 4552 died in Middleton in 1749; his third wife (my 8th great-grandmother) Rachel's year of death is unknown.

Children of Christoffel Vansant & Rachel Courson

The children of my 8th great-grandparents Christoffel Vansant ID 4552 and Rachel Courson ID 4590 are:

- Jacobus (or "James") Vansant ID 4584, born in 1699, married Margaret Brice in Philadelphia on 1 October 1732 and had at least four children.
- Elizabeth Vansant ID 4576, born in 1700, seems to have been married twice. Her second marriage in Philadelphia on 6 September 1718 to John Enoch produced several children. Elizabeth died in 1749.
- Joshua Vansant ID 3751 was born in 1703. Joshua is our direct ancestor and will be discussed below.
- Cornelius Vansant ID 4580 was born in 1704.
- John Vansant ID 4581 was born in 1705 and married Robina Cox in New Jersey on 19 August 1728, with whom he had five daughters and a son. John died in 1749.
- Aaltje (or Olshe; "Alice" would be the American form of this name) Vansant ID 4587 was born in 1708, married Samuel LaRue in Churchville, Pennsylvania on 27 March 1746 and had several children.
- Garret Vansant ID 4583 was born in 1709; he married Leah Nixon on 15 April 1747 and had seven children. Garret died in July 1789.

---

[130] If this name seems familiar, recall that it was Hendryk Thomasse Van Dyck who shot and killed the Indian girl Tachiniki back in 1655. That Hendryk would have been in his eighties in 1710, so it seems unlikely this is the same person, although many Dutch from New Amsterdam came to Bensalem.

[131] Records of the Dutch Reformed Church, Bensalem, Bucks County, Pennsylvania; pg 120 [S175]

- Rachel Vansant ^{ID 4585} was born in 1710, married Lewis LaRue in Philadelphia on 24 March 1736 and had several children..

- Jesainah (equivalent to the Germanic "Gesina") Vansant ^{ID 4582} was born in 1711 and died in 1766, but I have encountered no evidence that she ever married.

Joshua Vansant & Catherine Johnston

My 7th great-grandfather Joshua Vansant ^{ID 3751} was the third child of Christoffel[132] Vansant ^{ID 4552} and Rachel Courson ^{ID 4590} and was born in about 1703 in New Dorp on Staten Island (Richmond County), New York. Joshua was therefore about three years old when his family moved to Bensalem.

Joshua married my 7th great-grandmother Catherine Johnston ^{ID 4579} on 20 February 1728 when he would have been about 24 years old. Although he and Catherine were both residents of Bucks County, Pennsylvania at the time, their marriage took place in New Jersey[133]. Shortly thereafter, on 28 October 1728, Joshua's father Stoffel purchased land in Kent County, Maryland, which he immediately transferred to Joshua, presumably as a wedding gift.

Up to this point, our Vansant ancestors had belonged to the Dutch Reformed Church in New York and Pennsylvania and, in fact, had been quite active in church activities. For whatever reason, however, the Vansants who settled in Maryland and the part of Pennsylvania that was eventually to become Delaware quickly became just as active in the Society of Friends[134].

In 1738, Joshua and John Browning were appointed to purchase land and manage the building of a new Meeting House at the confluence of Swan Creek and the Sassafras River; they successfully completed this project by June 13th of 1739.

My 7th great-grandmother Catherine Johnston ^{ID 4579} evidently died at some point between the birth of her last child in 1742 and her husband Joshua's second marriage, but I haven't located any record of her death.

Children of Joshua Vansant & Catherine Johnston

The children of my 7th great-grandparents Joshua Vansant ^{ID 3751} and Catherine Johnston ^{ID 4579} are:

---

[132] Joshua was Christoffel's sixth child, but the third from his marriage to Rachel Courson.

[133] New Jersey Marriage Records 1665-1800, page 416; William Nelson; Genealogical Publishing Company; 1973. Joshua's younger brother John ^{ID 4581} married Robina Cox in New Jersey even though both of them lived in Pennsylvania as well.

[134] ...more commonly known, of course, as the Quakers, a group formed in the mid-1600s in England and which began appearing in Barbados shortly afterwards. From there, the movement quickly spread to the eastern shore areas of Virginia and Maryland.

- Christopher Vansant [ID 3763] was born about 1726, and died relatively young in December 1759.

- Rachel Vansant [ID 3761] was born in about 1728, and married Gersham Mott, Jr. [ID 3764] on 8 June 1750 at the Chester Meeting House[135]. Rachel died after 20 April 1762 (I believe her date of death is 27 March 1775, but given the common name, can't be certain.)

- Sarah Vansant [ID 3762] was born in about 1730, and married Writson Browning [ID 3765] on 9 May 1753 at the Cecil Meeting House[136]. Writson seems to have been the nephew of the John Browning mentioned above. Sarah died in June 1775.

- John R. Vansant [ID 2498], born about 1731, is our direct ancestor, and will be discussed below.

- Joshua Vansant, Jr. [ID 3760] was born in about 1732 and died after 27 March 1775. Our ancestor John R. Vansant's younger brother Joshua had both a son [ID 4548] and grandson [ID 4550] named Joshua. The grandson, who married Mary Ann Menzies [ID 4551] of Boston, was the postmaster of Baltimore from 1839 to 1841 and, in addition to a variety of local and national political offices, was later Mayor of Baltimore from 6 November 1871 to 1 November 1875. He is mentioned later in this book when discussing the Comegys family.

On 10 November 1749[137], when he was about 46, Joshua married for a second time to Isabella Bowers [ID 3758], fourth of eight children of Thomas Bowers [ID 3755], a yeoman[138] who died in November of 1771[139]. I found no record of any children from Joshua's second marriage.

There is at least one source[140] reporting that Isabella was also married to Joshua's younger first cousin John[141] Vansant [ID 3738], who lived from 18 December 1724 to 10 August 1773. I found no records to support this, but it seems possible.

---

[135] "Quakerism on the Eastern Shore"; Kenneth Carroll; Garemond/Pridemark Press for Maryland Historical Soc., 1970), page 276.

[136] "Quakerism on the Eastern Shore"; Kenneth Carroll; Garemond/Pridemark Press for Maryland Historical Soc., 1970), page 276.

[137] Maryland Marriages 1634-1777; page 84; Robert Barnes, Compiler; 1975; Genealogical Publishing Co., Inc. Baltimore, MD; ISBN: 0-8063-0700-5. [S123]

[138] At the time, a yeoman was a farmer who cultivated his own land as opposed to farming on land belonging to someone else.

[139] In addition to my seventh great-grandmother Isabella, her father Thomas' Will of 6 December 1768 mentions sons Pearce, William, and Thomas, as well as daughters Ann Gilbert (husband's name not given); Martha Jordan (husband's name not given); Mary Corse (married to David) and her three children James, Thomas and Ann; Hannah Bradley or Bordley (married to Stephen) and her son William. Thomas' Will can be found in the Maryland Will Book 38, Part II 1771-1772, page 425.

[140] The S.M. Lawson Genealogy.

[141] John was the eleventh child of Joshua's younger brother Joris (George) Vansant [ID 3732] and Maike Vandegrift [ID 3733].

Joshua's sons John R. and Joshua Jr. were named as co-administrators of his will[142], and when he died in 1770, his son John (my 6th great-grandfather) disputed the validity of the Will. According to notes in the probate file, dated 1 January 1771: "Son John refuses to administer his father's estate claiming the testator had not regarded the writing as a Will for years."

This was apparently resolved by January 10 1772[143], although in this record only John Vansant is listed as the executor, and the only next of kin listed were "Isabella Vansant (widow) and Sarah Browning."[144] Although not certain, it appears that one possible reason for the younger Joshua not being listed in the final settlement is that he may have relocated to Baltimore by that time. Our ancestor Joshua's estate was valued at £271.5.9, and included tracts of land named "Difficulty," "The Endeavor," and "Bordley's Gift." It isn't clear why his daughter Rachel Mott wasn't listed at this time, since she doesn't seem to have died until 1775.

I have been unable to locate any information concerning Isabella after her husband's death. If she did indeed marry her husband's cousin John, as mentioned earlier, he would have been about 48 and Isabella would have been about 39.

John R. Vansant

My 6th great-grandfather John R. Vansant [ID 2498] doesn't appear in any records I could locate until his Will[145] of 17 February 1773 refers to a "daughter Rachel[146] and the child my wife is pregnant with." I have found nothing, including a marriage record, regarding the identity of his wife who, although obviously still living at the time, isn't mentioned by name in the Will. To his daughter Rachel and the unborn child, John left the "right of my father's dwelling plantation."

John must have died between the writing of his Will and the probate that took place on March 15th of the same year, and would have been only about 32 years old at the time of his death. My 6th great-grandmother, whatever her name, seemed to still be living at the time of the 1790 and 1800 Censuses (see my transcriptions below), but I've located no death record for her.

---

[142] His oldest son, Christopher, had died in December 1759 before his father's Will was written. Kent County Maryland Calendar of Wills, 1767-1772, Volume 14, page 159 (S34).

[143] Kent County Maryland Prerogative Court Abstracts 1769-1772, 107.279B.

[144] Joshua and Isabella's third child Sarah Vansant [ID 3762] married Writson Browning [ID 3765] in June 1750.

[145] Kent County Maryland Calendar of Wills, 1772-1774, Volume 15, page 40 (S34). Probated 15 March 1773.

[146] This Rachel [ID 4173], was born in about 1771.

John R. Vansant, Jr. & his daughter Rachel

The unborn, unnamed child my 6th great-grandfather referred to in his Will was my 5th great-grandfather John R. Vansant, Jr. [ID 3769], probably born in July or August 1773, shortly after his father's early death.

Although I haven't located a marriage record, and thus have been unable to determine the name of John, Jr.'s wife [ID 4177], the couple was likely married in about 1788 when John was fairly young, since the 1790 U.S. Census[147] suggests that John and his wife had two daughters before the census was taken. The table below gives my tentative interpretation of John's record:

1790 United States Census Listing for "John Vansant" in Kent County, MD	
1790 Census Counts	Comments (my assumptions)
1 Free White Male, age 16 & over:	born before 1775 – John R. Vansant, Jr. [3769], born in July or August 1773 **Our Direct Ancestor**
1 of 5 Free White Females, any age:	Wife (name unknown) [4177] **Our Direct Ancestor**
2 of 5 Free White Females, any age:	Sister Rachel Vansant [4173], born about 1771
3 of 5 Free White Females, any age:	Unknown Daughter, born between 1788 and 1790
4 of 5 Free White Females, any age:	Unknown Daughter, born between 1788 and 1790
5 of 5 Free White Females, any age:	Mother (name unknown) [2499] **Our Direct Ancestor**
No other entries on line	

If these are indeed two daughters, and we assume that John was married earlier, he could have been as young as 15 when he was married (if the daughters were born in, say, 1789 and 1790 before the census) or no older than 17 (if the girls were twins and both born in 1790 before the census).

John's next two children were my 4th great-grandmother Rachel [ID 2509] (not to be confused with her Aunt Rachel mentioned above), born in about 1791, and an as yet unidentified son, born probably after 1792 and before the 1800 U.S. Census[148], shown below:

1800 United States Census Listing for "John Vansant" in Kent County, MD	
1800 Census Counts	Comments (my assumptions)
1 Free White Male, age 27-45:	born 1755-1773 – John R. Vansant, Jr. [3769], likely born July or August 1773 **Our Direct Ancestor**
1 of 2 Free White Females, age 11-16:	born 1784-1789 – Unknown Daughter, born between 1788 and 1790
2 of 2 Free White Females, age 11-16:	born 1784-1789 – Unknown Daughter, born between 1788 and 1790

---

[147] National Archives Microfilm Series m637, roll 3, page 563.
[148] National Archives Microfilm Series m032, roll 10, page 235

1 Free White Female, age <10:	born 1790-1800 – Rachel Vansant [2509], born about 1791 **Our Direct Ancestor**
1 Free White Male, age <10:	born 1790-1800 – Unknown Son, born 1792 or later
1 Free White Female, age > 46:	Mother Unknown Name [2499] **Our Direct Ancestor**
4 Slaves	

As is evident from studying the census listing, John's mother was still living[149], but his wife had died by this time. The most common explanation for this would have been, of course, death associated with the birth of her last son. Unfortunately, I have located no records that might add more detail to this.

I have located no record of my 5th great-grandfather John R. Vansant Jr. after the 1800 census. Although it seems likely, therefore, that he must have died before 1810, I have found no confirmation of that.

A two page diagram of our Vansant lineage begins on page 237.

In about 1807, when she would have been about 16 years old, my 4th great-grandmother Rachel Vansant [ID 2509] married Samuel Comegys[150], whose family history is discussed next. My 4th great-grandparents Samuel and Rachel Vansant Comegys eventually had two daughters, the first of which was our ancestor "Kitty" Comegys [ID 2510]. Rachel outlived her husband Samuel and will be revisited in a later section; her Will is presented on page 53.

My 3rd great-grandmother Catherine "Kitty" Comegys & Our Comegys Ancestors

Kitty's 3rd great-grandfather (my 9th great-grandfather) Cornelius Comegys [ID 2431] was baptized on 10 October 1630 in Lexmond, Holland[151], the son of Cornelius Comen Ghysen [ID 4546] and Jannegan Jans [ID 4547] of that town. He came to New Amsterdam in 1654, about three years after our earliest Vansant ancestor did[152], and married his first wife (not our ancestor) Willimentze Gysbert [ID 2432] there on 29 March 1658. For reasons that are a mystery to me, the couple initially settled in the English village of Jamestown[153], Virginia,

---

[149] Unless the older woman was John's mother-in-law instead of his mother; in either case though, she would still be our direct ancestor and one of my 6th great-grandmothers.

[150] "Descendants of Cornelius Comegys in Maryland and Delaware," compiled by Guy Wallis, dated 25 August 2003. Mr. Wallis agrees they were married, but guesses on page 126 that this took place in 1820. I suspect that 1820 is too late to be possible, however. In fairness, he wasn't focused on the Vansant relationships.

[151] The location of Lexmond can be seen in the map on page 28Error: Reference source not found. See our direct Comegys ancestors listed in the chart on page 236. Much information on the Comegys family is summarized in the aforementioned document "Descendants of Cornelius Comegys in Maryland and Delaware," and so will not be repeated here. Another good discussion of the Comegys family is found in the book "Cornelius Comegys of Kent County, Maryland," written by Ernestine Parke Moss, dated 1982, and also with no copyright notice.

[152] See page 29.

[153] This is interesting because, except for a token attempt in 1614, the English did not make their first serious bid to take over New Amsterdam until 1664. Cornelius and Willimentze were **not**, however, original Jamestown settlers, all of whom had been dead or missing for over forty-five years by this time. Their move came after the settlement had been rebuilt and finally begun prospering.

but then relocated to Kent County, Maryland after the birth of their first child (Cornelius II [ID 2437]). Cornelius (the elder) was naturalized as a Maryland citizen on 20 October 1671[154]. Many members of the Comegys family are listed in DAR registers, and a large number of Cornelius' descendants still live in the Northern Maryland and Delaware[155] areas although, as with our colonial Gonce ancestors, a contingent of them migrated to the southern part of the country after the Revolutionary War. Willimentze died in about 1671 after she and Cornelius had four children.

During the time that Cornelius was living in New Amsterdam, Quakerism was beginning to appear in Maryland and Virginia, but I've seen no indication that it had yet had any impact in the Dutch colonies of the new world[156], where the Dutch Reformed Church was still in effect the "official" religion for the immigrants from Holland. Whether Cornelius left with his family because of a "conversion" to Quakerism (which seems unlikely to me), or became a Quaker while living in Jamestown, it is clear that he and the rest of his family had become Quakers by the time they settled in Kent County, Maryland.

On December 7, 1675, at *"a Court holden for ye County of Kent,"* Cornelius was appointed *"Overseer for ye highways of Langford's Bay Hundred and yt he make cleare a road from Richard Joanes his house to Swan Creeke road* [157]*, according to Act of Assembly, which road is to bee ten (10) foot wide & yt sufficient bridges to be made in ye sd Roade, passable for horse & foot, if need require."* This would seem to indicate that he was held in fairly high esteem at the time.

Nonetheless, Cornelius was "encouraged" by his Quaker community to marry again in about 1678 after having a child out of wedlock with one of his servants (Mary Browne [ID 2435]); Mary died sometime after June of 1685. She and Cornelius had only one son, Nathaniel, that I am aware of.

Cornelius married his third wife, the widow Rebecca Smith [ID 2436] (this was her third marriage[158] as well), in about 1688. Cornelius and Rebecca are my 8th great-grandparents. They had six children together, who were the sixth through eleventh of Cornelius' children.

Children of Cornelius Comegys & Rebecca Smith

♦ Rebecca Comegys [ID 2442], born about 1688, who was married to John Taylor after her first husband (name unknown) died. Rebecca died before 10 May 1735 when her mother's Will was written.

---

[154] Colonial Maryland Naturalizations; Jeffry A. Wyland; 1975; volume 2, page 331. Baltimore MD.

[155] According to a researcher at the Delaware Historic Society, current members of the family, several of whom she knows personally, pronounce the name Cómma-Jeez (", ggg"), so it is assumed that this is how Cornelius pronounced it.

[156] Several early Quaker preachers were quite active in Amsterdam itself, however, so it's not impossible.

[157] I assume this is the ancestor of the Swan Creek Road that runs through present day Rock Hall, Md.

[158] Her first marriage was to John Campbell and the second to Benjamin Smith; I haven't been able to determine her birth name. After Cornelius' death, she again married to John Evans on 7 July 1713.

- Edward Comegys ID 2443 is our direct ancestor and will be discussed below.
- Gysbartus Comegys ID 2543 was born about 1691.
- Martha Comegys ID 2544, born about 1693, who married James Piner ID 2549.
- Mary Ann Comegys ID 2545, born about 1695, who married Thomas Wilkins ID 2550.
- Sarah Comegys ID 2546, born about 1697, who first married George Skirven, then later (after 1736) Thomas Crow ID 2551.

Cornelius seems to have died in 1708, although he must have been deceased by August 2, 1709 when his estate was probated[159]. After Cornelius' death, my 8th great-grandmother Rebecca married for the fourth time to John Evans; she died after 10 May 1735 when her Will was written[160], although I haven't been able to locate any record of her death.

Edward Comegys & Mary Harwood

My 7th great-grandfather and the oldest male of the family, Edward Comegys ID 2443, was born in late 1689[161] and died in April 1761. In the 1715 census[162] of Maryland, he was recorded as living in Cattle Marks Township, Kent County; he would have been about twenty-six years old at the time. I have found no evidence that he was previously married, but on 17 November 1717, he married Mary Harwood ID 2548, widow of John Harwood[163].

Children of Edward Comegys & Mary Harwood

Edward and Mary Harwood Comegys had at least eight children:

- Edward Comegys II ID 2552, born about 1718, was our direct ancestor and will be discussed in more detail below[164].
- Mary Comegys ID 2553 was born in about 1720.
- Martha Comegys ID 2554 was born in about 1724.
- Bartus Comegys ID 2555 was born in about 1725.

---

[159] His Will was dated 20 November 1707, and was proven 22 June 1708. Maryland Calendar of Wills, Volume 3, page 105; Jane Baldwin & F. Edward Wright; Kohn & Pollock, 1904.

[160] My 8th great-grandmother Rebecca's Will was proven on 11 December 1736. Maryland Calendar of Wills, Volume 6, page 208; Jane Baldwin & F. Edward Wright; Kohn & Pollock, 1904. Her Will, in the name of Rebecca Evans, was probated on 18 November 1738 by her son Edward.

[161] A deposition he made in 1739, recorded in Kent County Maryland Land Records, Liber JS22, Folio 523, stated that he was 50 years old, tending to support this year of birth.

[162] Maryland Census 1772-1890; Ron V. Jackson; Accelerated Indexing Systems.

[163] The Harwood name also appears when discussing my 4th great-grandfather Rudolph Gonce's second wife Ann, whose second husband Stephen's first wife was Elizabeth Harwood.

[164] The designators Edward I, Edward II, etc. were not used by our ancestors (at least as far as I have been able to determine), but are used for my own convenience to more easily distinguish among them.

- Gideon Comegys ID 2556 was born in about 1726.
- Rebecca Comegys ID 2557 was born in about 1728.
- Joseph Comegys ID 2558 was born in about 1730.
- Jesse Comegys ID 2559 was born in about 1732.

Edward likely died in April 1761[165]. His wife, our ancestor Mary (the "Widow Harwood"), presumably died before 8 November 1756, because she wasn't mentioned in the Will Edward composed on that date.

Edward Comegys [II] & Mary Thraul

Their first child, our ancestor Edward Comegys II ID 2552, married my 6th great-grandmother Mary Thraul ID 2560 on 15 December 1737 in Kent County, Maryland[166]. When his father died in April 1761, Edward II, being the oldest male, inherited his father's land, an estate known as "Utrick," as well as two slaves. Edward II and Mary Thraul had a total of at least seven children between 1738 and 1755, and each of them received a £10 bequest in their father's Will. The bulk of his estate, valued at £639.4.8[167], passed to his oldest son Edward III.

Children of Edward Comegys [II] & Mary Thraul

- Edward Comegys III ID 2561, born 8 September 1738 and died 14 June 1803; married Mary Trew ID 2568 and had at least six children.
- Mary Comegys ID 2562 was born on 15 June 1740 and died before 14 November 1804; she never married as far as I can determine.
- Martha Comegys ID 2563 was born on 7 December 1742; she married Samuel Wales but I haven't attempted to locate any children of theirs
- Jesse Comegys ID 2564 was born on 10 June 1747. He is our direct ancestor and will be discussed in more detail below.
- Gideon Comegys ID 2565, born 27 February 1749 and died in 1799. Gideon married Elizabeth Lorain ID 2571 and they had at least six children.
- Rebecca Comegys ID 2566, born 23 August 1752.
- Joseph Comegys ID 2567, born 15 September 1755 and died before 31 December 1799.

---

[165] Maryland Calendar of Wills, Volume 12, page 38; Jane Baldwin & F. Edward Wright; Kohn & Pollock, 1904.

[166] "Quakerism on the Eastern Shore"; Kenneth Carroll; Garemond/Pridemark Press for Maryland Historical Soc., 1970), page 276.

[167] Maryland Prerogative Court Extracts 1755-1763; Liber 3, folio 152.

Jesse Comegys & his wife Mary [unknown surname]

My 5th great-grandfather Jesse Comegys [ID 2564], the fourth of Edward II's children, was born on 10 June 1747. There are surviving records of an interesting incident in his life.

On 13 March 1776, the Cecil Monthly Meeting (convened in Kent County) registered a formal complaint against my 5th great-grandfather Jesse and his younger brother Gideon for "neglecting attendance of meetings and bearing arms to learn the art of War[168]," something that was not in keeping with the sect's beliefs. At the time, Jesse was about 28 years old. How this incident was resolved is unclear, but I was unable to locate any evidence that either of the brothers actually served in the military during the revolution[169], so I would assume that the church elders prevailed.

This line of the Comegys family, although Quakers, were also slave owners, which was becoming an issue as the American Revolution began to unfold. In the early years of the eighteenth century, the general view began spreading among the Quaker community that slavery was inconsistent with their religious beliefs. Since many Quakers owned slaves, this presented financial difficulties for many of them.

In about 1781, when he was about 34 years old[170], Jesse married a woman named Mary [ID 2570], whose surname I've been unable to ascertain. In this same year, he freed the two slaves that he owned, and his siblings Edward III [ID 2561], Mary [ID 2562], and Joseph [ID 2567] together freed a total of sixteen slaves.

By 1787, the Society of Friends had decided to insure that the remainder of their members would also manumit any slaves they owned and, further, that none of their members would continue employment as overseers on farms that kept slaves. To that end, they set up a committee to "have under care and notice, the State and Situation of the Negroes." Their purpose was two-fold: to visit those who still owned or worked with slaves and persuade them of the moral necessity of choosing their conscience over their economic desires; their other task was to review earlier manumissions to insure that these had been accomplished in a way that was legally enforceable. Jesse's older brother Edward III [ID 2561] was on this committee with Joshua Vansant [ID 3760], son of my 7th great-grandfather Joshua Vansant [ID 3751] and younger brother of my 6th great-grandfather John R. Vansant [ID 2498].

Children of Jesse Comegys & his wife Mary

Jesse and his wife Mary had five children[171]:

---

[168] Quaker Minutes of the Eastern Shore of Maryland, 1676-1779, page 116; F. Edward Wright.

[169] Our ancestor Jesse Comegys is NOT the Lieutenant Jesse Comegys (30 Oct 1749-20 May 1803, married 8 December 1777 to Mary Everyt), whose military records from that conflict still exist. That Jesse was a second great-grandson of Willimentze Gysbert, first wife of our ancestor Cornelius [ID 2431].

[170] Given his age, it seems possible that he may have been married earlier, but I found no record to indicate that.

- **Samuel Comegys** [ID 2508], born about 1784, is our direct ancestor, and will be discussed in more detail below.
- **Martha Comegys** [ID 2575], born about 1790. There is an interesting gap of six years between Martha and her brother Samuel, which may indicate the possibility that were other children, but I haven't found any records to support this.
- **Jesse Comegys** [ID 2573], born about 1791.
- **Bartus Comegys** [ID 2574], born on 12 March 1793. Bartus married Susan Yearly on 23 March 1826 in Baltimore and had three daughters.
- **Mary Comegys** [ID 2576], born about 1795.

My transcription of line 239 from page 332 of the 1790 (first) U.S. Census[172] is shown below with my assumptions as to the identities of the counts:

1790 United States Census Listing for "Jessee Comegys" in Kent County, MD	
1790 Census Counts	Comments (my assumptions)
1 of 2 Free White Males, age 16 & over:	born before 1775 – Jesse Comegys [2564], born 10 June 1747 **Our Direct Ancestor**
1 Free White Female, any age:	Mary UnkF Comegys [2570], **Our Direct Ancestor**
2 of 2 Free White Males, age 16 & over:	born before 1775 – Jesse's unmarried brother Joseph [2567], born 15 September 1755
1 Free White Male, age below 16:	born in or after 1775 – Samuel Comegys [2508], born about 1788 **Our Direct Ancestor**
Other Free Persons	None
4 Slaves	

On 31 December 1799, Jesse's oldest brother Edward III wrote a Will[173] leaving his house and four acres of land to Jesse. Since Edward didn't die until 14 June 1803, however, he outlived Jesse by more than three years.

Jesse does seem to have survived long enough to appear in the next U.S. Census for 1800[174] however. Since Jesse's Will was probated on 9 January 1801[175], it seems very likely that he died between the time the census was taken (officially, as of 1 June 1800 but, like today, the actual counts were obtained over a several week period) and the late fall of 1800.

The following counts from the 1800 census are interesting:

---

[171] These five children are listed in the Orphan's Court Record of 1801: Kent County Probate Records, Guardian Bonds 1798-1802 folio 281-3.
[172] National Archives Microfilm Series m637 Roll 3 Page 332. His name appears as "Jessee" on the form.
[173] Kent County MD Probate Records; Wills Liber 8 folio 195.
[174] National Archives Microfilm Series m032 Roll 10 Page 237. As with the 1790 Census, his name seems to be spelled "Jessee."
[175] Kent County MD Probate Records; Guardian Bonds 1798-1802 folio 281-3.

1800 United States Census Listing for "Jessee Comegys" in Kent County, MD	
1800 Census Counts	**Comments (my assumptions)**
1 Free White Male, age 45 & over:	born before 1755 – Jesse Comegys [2564], born 10 June 1747 **Our Direct Ancestor**
1 Free White Female, age 17-26:	born 1774-1783 – Mary UnkF Comegys [2570], **Our Direct Ancestor**
1 Free White Male, age 17-26:	born 1774-1783 – Samuel Comegys [2508], born in about 1783 **Our Direct Ancestor**
1 Free White Female, age 11-16:	born 1784-1789 – Martha Comegys [2575], born about 1790
8 Slaves	

Jesse's Will names all five of his children, but it is clear from the table above that the three youngest, Jesse, Bartus, and Mary, all born before 1800, are not living in the household when the census was taken.

It could be speculated that Jesse may have been ill enough when he wrote his Will that his wife Mary sent the youngest children to live with a relative during this period but, not knowing her surname, it is impossible to search for likely households in which the children may have been living. It does seem clear, though, that there were no suitable counts of children born in the last decade of the eighteenth century in any of Jesse's male siblings' households. I've found no record of his sisters Mary [ID 2562] or Rebecca [ID 2566] having married; his sister Martha [ID 2563] married a man named Samuel Wales, but I haven't located that couple in 1800[176] to determine where they lived or whether there were children of the appropriate ages to be Jesse's.

All we know about my 5th great-grandmother Mary's death is that it must have been after Jesse's Will was probated in early 1801.

Samuel Comegys & Rachel Vansant

As mentioned earlier my 4th great-grandfather Samuel Comegys married Rachel Vansant in about 1807 when he was about 19 and she was about 16. Their first child, my 3rd great-grandmother Catharine Comegys, was born on 15 August 1808[177].

In the 1810 U.S. Census[178] for Kent County, his name is abbreviated, as was the custom at the time, and it is difficult to determine whether or not Samuel has a middle initial – and, if so, whether that initial is J, L, or S – so the name as written by the census taker is reproduced below.

---

[176] There were heads-of-household named Samuel Wales in Massachusetts and North Carolina, but it didn't seem plausible that this would be the same person.

[177] As with her husband George, there is a bit of uncertainty concerning Catharine's birth year, but I have discussed why I believe 15 August 1808 is the most likely and credible date in the appendix "Birth Year of Catherine Comegys" on page 165.

[178] National Archives Microfilm Series m252 Roll 14 Page 906

1759 – 1983 History

Extract of 1810 US Census Sheet m252r0014p906 (Kent County MD) showing Samuel Comegys

The counts in this census are shown in the table below:

1810 United States Census Listing for "Sam'l L Comegys" in Kent County, MD	
1810 Census Counts	Comments (my assumptions)
1 Free White Male, age 26-44:	born 1766-1784 – Samuel Comegys [2508], born about 1783 **Our Direct Ancestor**
1 Free White Female, age 16-25:	born 1785-1794 – Rachel Vansant Comegys [2509], born about 1791 **Our Direct Ancestor**
1 Free White Female, age <10:	born 1801-1810 – Catharine Comegys [2510], born 1808 **Our Direct Ancestor**
No Other Entries on Line:	(no slave ownership)

Sometime between the 1810 and 1820 (shown below)[179] censuses, Samuel and Rachel had a second daughter[180], but I've been unable to determine anything about her.

1820 United States Census Listing for "Sam'l Comegys" in Kent County, MD	
1820 Census Counts	Comments (my assumptions)
1 Free White Male, age 26-44:	born 1776-1794 – Samuel Comegys [2508], born about 1784 **Our Direct Ancestor**
1 Free White Female, age 18-26:	born 1794-1802 – Rachel Vansant Comegys [2509], born about 1791 **Our Direct Ancestor**
1 Free White Female, age 10-15:	born 1805-1810 – Catharine Comegys [2510], born 1808 **Our Direct Ancestor**
1 Free White Female, age <10:	born 1811-1820 – An unknown younger daughter
No Other Entries on Line:	(no slave ownership)

I haven't located Samuel and Rachel's family at the time of the 1830 census, nor have I located any report of Samuel's death.

Rachel filed her will in Baltimore County Maryland on 13 April 1841, shortly before her death on May 2nd of that same year[181]. This Will, shown below, is referred to again in later sections.

---

[179] National Archives Microfilm Series m033 Roll 44 page 126.

[180] There is a possibility that they may have had two sons rather than one daughter, but I doubt it. My arguments for this are presented in the appendix that begins on page 155.

[181] Baltimore Sun Death Notices of 4 May 1841. (S66)

Baltimore Will Book 18: Bottom of Page 269

Baltimore Will Book 18: Top of Page 270

Will of Rachel Vansant Comegys dated 30 April 1841 – Extracts from the Baltimore County Maryland Wills, Book 18, 1840-42, Pages 269 and 270. This will is available on LDS Microfilm FHL-13598. My transcription is provided on the next page.

Because the page in the Baltimore County Will Book shown on the previous page is very washed out and difficult to interpret, particularly in a printed reproduction of this sort, I've transcribed each individual line in the original below with the line endings intact, so that a line-by-line comparison with the reproduction can easily be made. Rachel's Will was filed on 13 April 1841 and she died less than a month later on 2 May.

Rachel Comegys Last Will & Testament	*I Rachel Comegys of the City of Baltimore, State of Maryland, do bequeath after all legal claims which may be against me shall be paid by my executor, all of my personal estate consisting of monies*	Transcribed from bottom of page 269: Baltimore County Maryland Wills, Book 18, 1840-42

	on deposit in the Savings Bank of Baltimore and household furniture to John Thomas Gonse, my grandson and son of George and Kitty Gonse now living in Cecil County, Maryland and I do hereby appoint Joshua Vansant of the City of Baltimore my Executor who will appropriate the bequest to the education of said John Thomas Gonse or such portion thereof as may be necessary for the object specified and if a balance of monies should remain thereafter said balance to be paid to John Thomas Gonse when he shall arrive at twenty-one years of age, or if said John Thomas Gonse should die before he arrives at the age of twenty-one years then all monies which may be in the hands of my Executor at my bequest at the time of the death of said John Thomas Gonse to be appropriated to the education of the children of the aforesaid <u>John</u> and Kitty Gonse.
	 In testimony of which I herewith offer my hand and seal the thirtieth of April eighteen hundred and forty-one.
	     her
	 Rachel (x) Comegys
	     mark
	 Benjamin W. Quinlan
	 Isaac M. Denson } *Witnesses*
		1
		 2
		 3
		 4
		
		 Transcribed from top of page 270: Baltimore County Maryland Wills, Book 18, 1840-42
		
		 5
		
		 6

<u>NOTES ON RACHEL'S WILL</u>

1. <u>John Thomas Gonce</u> [ID 1576], born to George and Kitty on 22 December 1823, and aged 17 yrs, 4 months at the time of this Will. John and Catharine Sullivan had just gotten married on 12 January 1841. John's father <u>George Gonce</u> [ID 2511] was the husband of Rachel's daughter <u>Catherine "Kitty" Comegys</u> [ID 2510].

2. It isn't clear whether "now living in Cecil County" refers to John or to George and Kitty, but it seems unlikely that John was living there, since he would have to have been living in Baltimore in order to meet Catharine Ann Sullivan, whom he had just married on January 12th.

3. <u>Joshua Vansant</u> is not likely Rachel's uncle – the younger brother [ID 3760] of Rachel Comegys' father John R. Vansant [ID 2498], because he seems to have died young. The only candidate I can find seems to be the Baltimore Postmaster Joshua Vansant who later became Mayor of Baltimore, but I can't prove this.

4. Rachel apparently was illiterate (see the line numbered 6, where she signed with a mark), but recognized the value of an education. George and Rachel's daughter Kitty had seven children at this time ranging from the oldest, John Thomas, aged 17, to Thomas Allibone, aged 2.

5. The name "John" is underlined in the original of the Will book, apparently not by the transcriber. It is almost certainly an error by the clerk, and should say "George and Kitty" rather than "John and Kitty."

George Gonce's Childhood

George's mother Elizabeth died when he was less than four years old, and his father Rudolph remarried very shortly thereafter. Rudolph then died when George was only seven. George presumably lived with his stepmother Ann Cox Gonce, who would have been less than twenty when Rudolph died. After Ann's second marriage to Stephen Owens in 1804, it isn't clear where George or his brother were living.

Ann and Stephen moved away to Ohio when George was between ten and fourteen years old, and it is clear that neither George nor his younger brother John went with them. The boys' paternal grandfather (Daniel Gonce) had died before either of them were born; their paternal grandmother had been remarried for 13 years when George was born, so it doesn't seem likely that they were raised by any of their Gonce relatives. Their maternal Hedney grandparents didn't die until much later, when George was about 30; coupled with George Hedney's mention of his grandson George Gonce in his Will, it seems likely that George and John were both raised for most of their childhood with the Hedney family, although I have located nothing to substantiate this supposition.

4th Generation: George Gonce & Kitty Comegys

My 3rd great-grandparents George Gonce [ID 2511] and Catherine (known as Kitty[182]) Comegys [ID 2510] were married on 2 April 1823 at St. Steven's Church, North Sassafras, in Cecil County, Maryland[183]. George was twenty-six and Kitty fifteen at the time of their marriage. Eight months and twenty days later, on Monday 22 December 1823, John Thomas Gonce [ID 1576], their first son and my 2nd great-grandfather, was born.

Over the next six years, George and Kitty had at least three more children: a daughter Margaret Ann [ID 2519] on 23 December 1825, a son George

---

[182] We know she was called Kitty because, in the will mentioned above, Rachel refers to: "a grandson, John T. Gonse [sic], son of George and Kitty Gonce".

[183] Maryland Marriages 1667-1899; Jordan Dodd, Liahona Research, Compiler. (S56). Minister Wilton and "G. Miller" presided at their wedding. Also listed in "Cecil County, Maryland Marriage Licenses 1777-1840", (S157) page 47 and in "Marriages, Births & Deaths - St. Stephen's Parish, Cecil County, Maryland 1687-1837," (S158) which simply says "Gonce to Comegys" without mentioning any first names.

Washington [ID 2520] on 30 June 1828, and a daughter Mary Matilda [ID 2601] on 16 October 1829.

The Fifth U.S. Census of 1830[184] shows George Gonce (second line from bottom). Note that their Cecil County neighbor Cornelius Vansant is living just three households away. A transcription in given on the following page:

1830 United States Census Listing for "George Gonce" in Cecil County, MD	
1830 Census Counts	**Comments (my assumptions)**
1 Free White Male, age 30-39:	born 1791-1800 – George Gonce [2511], born October 1796, age 34 **Our Direct Ancestor**
1 Free White Female, age 20-29:	born 1801-1810 – Catharine Comegys [2510], born 1808, age 22 **Our Direct Ancestor**

---

[184] National Archives Series m019, Roll 56, page 5.

1 Free White Female, age 10-14:	born 1816-1820 – Unknown, possibly Catharine's younger sister
1 Free White Male, age 5-9:	born 1821-1825 – John Thomas Gonce [1576], born 1823, age ~7 **Our Direct Ancestor**
1 of 2 Free White Females, age < 5:	born 1826-1830 – Margaret Ann Gonce [2519], born 1825, age ~4
1 Free White Male, age < 5:	born 1826-1830 – George W. Gonce [2520], born 1828, age ~2
2 of 2 Free White Females, age < 5:	born 1826-1830 – Mary Matilda Gonce [2601], born 1829, age ~1
No Other Entries on Line:	(specifically, no slaves were listed)

The unknown female in the household certainly can't be Kitty's child, since she is only eight to twelve years younger than Kitty, and thus would have been somewhere between three and seven years old when George and Kitty were married. It is possible that she might have been George's child from an earlier marriage[185], but I haven't found any other marriage record for him. The unknown girl is unlikely to be a younger sibling of George's, since his father died in about 1803. If she is Kitty's younger sister (see the 1820 census transcribed earlier), this raises a few questions, since Kitty's mother Rachel was still alive at this time.

During the next ten years, George and Kitty had at least three more children: Augusta [ID 2605], born on 6 March 1834, Benedict Rudolph [ID 2602], born on 3 March 1836, and Thomas Allibone Robaris [ID 2602], born on 21 December 1839.

As with most residents of Cecil County at the time, George and Kitty were farmers, but George does not appear to have been a landowner himself, at least initially. We know that he rented property known as the "Red House Farm" during the period from 1 January to 31 December 1836. This land at the time belonged to Julianna Donaldson and was located in the Village of Cecilton[186].

George later entered into a lease to rent a farm for a period of twenty years, from 1 January 1837 until 31 December 1856. The area is described in the following transcription from Land Records now located at the Maryland Archives in Annapolis:

"Agreement between Alfred C Nowland, Merchant of Village of Cecilton and George Gaunce farmer of Sassafras Neck, Cecil Co

The land was described as being[187]

---

[185] George would have been between about 20 and 24 years old when this girl was born, so the possibility that he may have previously been married can't be discounted, although there is no evidence of this.

[186] Articles of agreement between Alfred C Nowland and George Gaunce 26 October 1835 to occupy and cultivate the "Red House Farm" for one year from Jan 1 - Dec 31, 1836. Witnessed by Jos W. Wroth; recorded 8 Dec 1836

[187] Transcription of Land Records from the originals in Annapolis, Maryland.

> "in Cecil County upon the north side of the Grove Neck bounded on the north by a branch, or rivulet, emptying into Ponds Creed, on the west by lands of John Serverson's heirs, on south by lands of John Wroth's heirs, and on east by a public road, leading from the grove to the ponds neck and continuing 275 acres of land to be divided in 5 fields ...
>
> Witnessed by George A. Ford."

In his capacity as a surveyor, the poet James McCauley, while traveling through Cecil County to inspect George's "bounty land", made the following notation in his diary, dated 19 October 1837:[188]

> "19 Sunday ...went to see George Gonce – the old man was complaining ..."

Life as a farmer was apparently not very easy in those days, since the "old man" Mr. McCauley was describing had just turned forty-one years old[189]. Perhaps George was just a curmudgeonly sort.[190]

Among some researchers, there is a question as to whether George had moved his family for a period of time to Charles County, located near Washington D.C. in south central Maryland. The source of this confusion was apparently that Ancestry.com had categorized a number of the Cecil County pages from the 1840 census, which had no page headers, as being from Charles County. There is no doubt that the pages are from Cecil County, however, since the presence of Thomas A. Roberts (on the ninth line below George) and other neighbors are mostly all the same as those shown in the 1830 and 1850 Censuses.

The Sixth U.S. Census of 1840[191] is shown on the following page, with a transcription on the next page.

---

[188] "The James McCauley Diaries" located in the archives of the Historical Society of Cecil County. At the time of this diary entry James McCauley was acting as a surveyor. He later served in local and state government in several capacities, and was a well-known author and poet.

[189] The year in the diary could be read as either 1837 or 1857 but, since the 19th was not a Sunday in 1857 but was a Sunday in 1837, the year seems certain. I am unaware what "bounty land" in this context meant. On Sunday, 19 October 1837, George would have been just seven days beyond his 41st birthday.

[190] I inherited that trait from somewhere – it could be...

[191] National Archives Series m704, Roll 163, page 206.

Page from the Sixth U.S. Census of 1840 showing George Gonce's Family (m704, r163, p206)

The right hand side of the census form showing slave holdings is not reproduced here, but George had by this time acquired one male slave.

1759 – 1983 History

1840 United States Census Listing for "George Gonce" in Cecil County, MD	
1840 Census Counts	**Comments (my assumptions)**
1 Free White Male, age 40-49:	born 1791-1800 – George Gonce [2511], born October 1796, age 44 **Our Direct Ancestor**
1 Free White Female, age 30-39:	born 1801-1810 – Catharine Comegys [2510], born 1808, age 32 **Our Direct Ancestor**
1 Free White Female, age 10-14:	born 1816-1820 – Unknown, possibly Catharine's younger sister
1 Free White Male, age 15-19:	born 1821-1825 – John Thomas Gonce [1576], born 1823, age ~17 **Our Direct Ancestor**
1 of 2 Free White Females, age 10-14:	born 1826-1830 – Margaret Ann Gonce [2519], born 1825, age ~14
1 Free White Male, age 10-14:	born 1826-1830 – George W. Gonce [2520], born 1828, age ~12
2 of 2 Free White Females, age 10-14:	born 1826-1830 – Mary Matilda Gonce [2601], born 1829, age ~10
1 Free White Female, age 5-9:	born 1831-1835 – Augusta Gonce [2605], born 1834, age ~7
1 of 2 Free White Males, age < 5:	born 1836-1840 – Benedict R. Gonce [2602], born 1836, age 3
2 of 2 Free White Males, age < 5:	born 1836-1840 – Thomas A. Gonce [2604], born 1839, age 1
1 Male Slave, age 10-24	born 1816-1830 – not on 1830 Census

Kitty's mother Rachel Vansant Comegys died in Baltimore, where she had relocated after the death of her husband, on 2 May 1841, shortly after this census was taken.

One of her Baltimore cousins, Joshua Vansant, was by this time a Maryland Senate Elector, and would later become a Director of the Mechanics Bank[192]. He was eventually a member of the Maryland House of Delegates and served as both Mayor and Comptroller of Baltimore.

In Rachel's 13 April 1841 Will mentioned earlier, she writes about "a grandson, John T. Gonse [sic], son of George and Kitty Gonse now living in Cecil County, Maryland."

Circumstantial evidence suggests that George's son John Thomas Gonce likely relocated to Baltimore very shortly after the 1840 census was taken, and certainly before 1846.

Joshua Vansant

---

[192] He became a Director in 1843. This eventually became the National Mechanics Bank, which in 1916 acquired the assets of the original First National Bank of Baltimore. Citizen's National Bank, where my paternal grandfather Joseph Oberle was Vice-President and Cashier, merged with Mechanics in 1928, and adopted the earlier name of First National Bank of Baltimore for the new entity.

Between the 1840 and 1850 censuses, George and Kitty had their last two (their eighth and ninth) children: Laura Ellen ID 2606, born on 17 March 1843, and James Allibone ID 2607, born on 7 October 1844. The 1850 U.S. Census is illustrated below.

SCHEDULE I. —Free Inhabitants in The 1st Election District 1st Vot in the County of Cecil State of Maryland enumerated by me, on the 21st day of August 1850. Jacob H. Mahon Ass't Marshal.

Dwelling-houses numbered in the order of visitation.	Families numbered in the order of visitation.	The Name of every Person whose usual place of abode on the first day of June, 1850, was in this family.	Age.	Sex.	Color, White, black, or mulatto.	Profession, Occupation, or Trade of each Male Person over 15 years of age.	Value of Real Estate owned.	Place of Birth. Naming the State, Territory, or Country.	Married within the year.	Attended School within the year.	Persons over 20 y'rs of age who cannot read & write.	Whether deaf and dumb, blind, insane, idiotic, pauper, or convict.
		James	12	M				"				
131	131	George Gunce	56	M		Farmer	7000	"				
		Catharine "	46	F				"				
		Mary "	21	F				"				
		George "	23	M		Farmer		"				
		Augusta "	17	F				"				
		Benidict "	15	M				"				
		Ababora "	11	M				"				
		Laura "	7	F				"				
		James "	5	M				"				
		Emily "	22	F				"				
		Charles Roberts	20	M		Labour		"				
		Edward Lee	23	M		"		"				

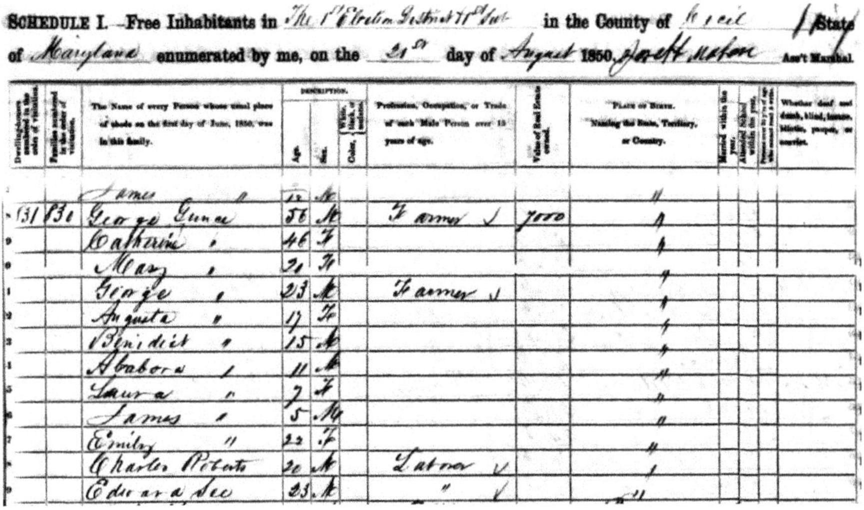

Extract from 1850 U.S. Census page (National Archives Series m432, Roll 290, page 59) for my 3rd great-grandfather George Gonce (transcribed as "Gunce" in some indexes) and his family.

As reported in that census, George's land holdings are valued at $7,000[193], a medium sum for the time, although he still had leased land that he was farming. George and Kitty also have two laborers boarding with them; one of these, Charles Roberts, is most likely the Roberts who married their daughter Mary[194]. Edward Lee, the other laborer, was or would become Augusta's husband.

Note that George and Kitty's first son, my 2nd great-grandfather John T. Gonce, had already moved out of Cecil County and south to the city of Baltimore. Margaret Ann Gonce is no longer present in the 1850 Census; she had married George Moore on 7 January 1846[195].

The eleven-year-old fifth child listed above appears to be named "Ababora" or "Alabora," but I believe this is likely "Alibone," since the name Thomas A. Gonce ID 2504 appears in George's will as a son, and the name Thomas Alibone Gonce appears in later generations of Gonces living in Cecil County.

---

193 Looking at the eighth column the illustration above, this might be read as $1,000, but a comparison of the "1" and "7" digits as written in the age columns (e.g. Augusta's age) makes it fairly clear that the entry is actually $7,000. According to the inflation calculators at http://www.westegg.com/inflation, and http://www.measuringworth.com/uscompare/, $7,000 in 1850 was equivalent to something between $190,000 and $212,000 in 2012.

194 Charles' and Mary's identical ages lend credence to this, but I have been unable to prove this suspicion.

195 Maryland Marriages 1667-1899; Jordan Dodd, Liahona Research, Compiler. (S56).

An Aside

The name Alibone or Allibone shows up in connection with the Gonce family as both a surname and a given name into the twentieth century, but the connection, which must date from at least before Thomas Allibone [ID 2604] Gonce's birth in 1839, is unclear to me. The earliest appearance of the surname Allibone I could locate was Edward Allibone. Edward owned 52 acres, called "Allibone's Addition," in Kent County in 7 Nov 1709[196].

World War II Draft Card for Thomas Allibone Gonce[ID 2711].

The name appears as a farm hand for George W. Gonce in the 1860 census (which is almost certainly George W's brother Thomas A.- see illustration on page 63), and Thos Allibone, age 3, and Margaret Allibone, age 1, are living with George's son Benedict Gonce and his wife Margaret in 1860[197]. In this case, "Allibone" appears to be a surname (Mary Roberts[198], George's widowed daughter, is also living with them). As late as the 1920 census[199] we find a widower Thomas M. Allibone living in Bel Air, MD with George C. Moore, son of George Moore, one of George W. Gonce's other farmhands and the widower of Margaret Ann Gonce [ID 2519] shown in the 1860 census (see below). George Moore is listed as Thomas M. Allibone's brother-in-law in that census. Thomas M. Allibone's age is listed as 68 there, which would make his birth year around 1852. George and Catharine's last son James [ID 2607] also had the middle name Allibone.

Another Thomas Allibone Gonce [ID 2711], part of the Gonce family in North East, Maryland, was born in Earleville, Maryland on 6 January 1882, and appears in the Censuses from 1900 through 1920. His World War II draft card can be seen in the illustration above.

---

[196] Settlers of Maryland 1679-1783; Peter Wilson Coldham; published by Genealogical Publishing Co. Inc., Baltimore, MD. ISBN 0-8063-1693-4; R929.3752 (S121). Edward Allibone appears on page 10.

[197] National Archives Microfilm Series m653 Roll 472 Page 51 (S17). It is possible that these names are intended to be Thomas Allibone Gonce and Margaret Gonce, but if the usual conventions for showing surnames on the census listings is being followed, their surname would be Allibone.

[198] So whether or not Charles Roberts was the man she married, the marriage was evidently quite short. We know Mary Roberts was George's daughter, because she is listed under that name in his will.

[199] National Archives Microfilm Series t625 Roll 675 Page 12a (S21).

The Emily Gonce, age 22, shown on the 1850 census above, is George's daughter-in-law – his son George Washington's wife as of January 2nd that year[200] – and whose full birth name was Emmaline Cox.

Catherine "Kitty" Comegys Gonce passed away in 1858. The inscription on her tombstone was transcribed as "In memory of Catharine A. wife of George Gonce who departed this life July 26, 1858 Aged 19 Yrs. 11 mos. & 11 days."[201] She is buried in St. Stephens Protestant Episcopal Church Cemetery in Earleville, Maryland (see photo on page 166).

George's Final Two Years

The 1860 census shows that George, now a widower, is living in the household[202] headed by his 36-year-old son George Washington Gonce and his daughter-in-law Emmaline [ID 2522] (known as Emily). A segment of this census is shown below.

Extracted from 1860 U.S. Census page (National Archives Series m653, Roll 472, Page 44). George Gonce is now living with his son George W. and daughter-in-law Emily. Note that George W. (the son) has a farm hand known simply as Allibone (and so we assume his surname is Gonce), which is probably his brother Thomas Allibone Gonce. See footnote Error: Reference source not found regarding the "insane" notation for Samuel in the last column.

Because of the conventions for name entry on the census forms, it would appear that George, William, and Samuel were all named Moore, and were not children of George W. and Emily. I believe these were sons of the George Moore [ID 2521] who married Margaret Ann Gonce [ID 2519] on 7 January

---

[200] Maryland Marriages 1667-1899; Jordan Dodd, Liahona Research, Compiler. (S56)

[201] Yes, the book really says "19 Yrs" and is obviously incorrect. The tombstone transcription is from "Tombstone and Family Records of Cecil County, Maryland; Volume II" (S156); compiled by Leone R. (Mrs. W. H.) Terrell, Chapter Chair, Daughters of the American Revolution; Elk Chapter. I discuss the implications of her tombstone inscription in the appendix "Birth Year of Catherine Comegys" on page 165. St. Stephen's Protestant Episcopal Church Cemetery is located at 14 Glebe Road in Earleville, Maryland just north of the intersection with Crystal Beach Road.

[202] This is most likely his father's farm, where he was known to be working in 1850.

1846 in Cecil County[203]. What the notation "insane" [204] meant as applied to Samuel Moore is unknown, but since neither the Moores nor the Allibones are in our direct family line, these matters will be left for someone else to pursue. Margaret Ann must have died prior to June 15th, the date this census was taken.

My 3rd Great-Grandfather George Gonce died on 26 June 1860, very shortly after the previously illustrated census was taken. His Will was entered into probate on 9 September 1861[205], and each of his children at the time was given a 1/8 share of his then $4,199.52 estate (slightly over $100,000 in 2010 currency), a sum which amounted to $524.94 each. His married daughter Margaret Ann Gonce Moore was not named in the Will, tending to confirm that she had died prior to the 1860 census.

Children and Grandchildren of George Gonce & Catherine Comegys

In order to retain a focus on our direct line, the following section will provide only a brief commentary on each of George and Kitty's children.

- ♦ John Thomas Gonce [ID 1576], our direct ancestor, will be discussed in more detail below. John was the first of the Gonces to move to Baltimore, thus creating the "Baltimore Branch" of the "mid-Atlantic" Gonce clan.

- ♦ Margaret Ann Gonce [ID 2519] (23 December 1825 –) and her husband George Moore [ID 2521] had at least three sons. Margaret likely died shortly after the 1860 census.

    George Moore [ID 2523] (born about 1846). The George G. Moore born in 1861 who is living with Thomas M. Allibone in Belair on the 1920 census is probably his son, but I have been unable to identify his wife.
    William Moore [possibly ID 2524], born about 1852.
    Samuel Moore [possibly ID 2525], born about 1855.

- ♦ George Washington Gonce [ID 2520] (30 June 1828 – 15 August 1902) and his wife Emily raised at least three children:

    George Rudolphus Gonce [ID 2709] (11 June 1852 – 26 July 1913) and his wife Susan, adopted some of the Pope children after their mother Laura (George's aunt; see below) died in 1875, and also had at least eight children of their own (the first named Thomas Allibone

---

[203] Maryland Marriages 1667-1899; Jordan Dodd, Liahona Research, Compiler. (S56). I suspect that Margaret Ann Gonce is either a daughter or niece of George Gonce, but have no evidence to support this. She is not mentioned in George's will of 1861, but if she died before the 1860 census, she would not have been mentioned.

[204] See the column on the far right. According to the instructions for the 1880 supplemental schedules, the term "insane" at that time included "mania, melancholia, paresis (general paralysis), dementia, epilepsy and dipsomania," and generalized the description as "defective, dependent, and delinquent individuals." In short, it seemed to have meant "not normal" in some fashion.

[205] Information supplied by one of my distant cousins, but I haven't yet been able to obtain a copy.

Gonce). For unknown reasons, he is listed as P. George Gonce in some Ancestry indexes.

William T. Gonce ^{ID 2524}, born in January 1856, married Henrietta in about 1885 and had at least two children, James and Emily. Unlike Samuel below, William is listed in George W. Gonce's bible, but I suspect that he, too, was the adopted son of George's older sister Margaret Ann and her husband George Moore.

Unknown An unknown child, who died at age 11, is listed in George W. Gonce's bible.

Samuel Gonce ^{ID 2525}, born about 1855. This birth date, given on the 1900 Census, suggests the possibility that this may be the same person as Samuel Moore above, indicating that he may have been adopted or taken his mother's surname for some other reason. He is not listed in George W. Gonce's bible.

- Mary Matilda Gonce ^{ID 2601}, born 16 October 1829, married Charles Roberts but, as far as I know, had no children. Charles was one of her father's farmhands and is shown on the 1850 census[206] with the Gonce family. This appears to be the Mary Roberts who is buried in the Sullivan-Gonce plot T-295 at New Cathedral Cemetery in Baltimore, but when, why, or how she moved to Baltimore or converted to Catholicism is unknown. See the appendix on page 183.

- Augusta Gonce ^{ID 2605}, born 6 March 1834, married Edward Lee ^{ID 2656}. Edward was one of her father's farmhands and is shown on the 1850 census[207] with the Gonce family. Augusta was mentioned in her father's will as "Augusta Lee," so they were married before September of 1861.

    Ann Lee ^{ID 3834}, born about 1853
    Charles Lee ^{ID 3835}, born about 1855
    Edward Lee ^{ID 3836}, born about 1858

- Benedict Rudolph Gonce ^{ID 2602}, born 3 March 1836, married Margaret and had seven children:

    Frank R. Gonce ^{ID 2614}, born in October 1863, and his wife Annie, had at least one child, Benedict Jones Gonce.

    Benjamin F. Gonce ^{ID 2648}, born in May 1864, and his wife Annie, had four girls.

    William Gonce ^{ID 2879}, born in about 1864, never married as far as I could determine.

    Mary E. Gonce ^{ID 2704}, born in about 1866, and her husband James Baley, had three girls and a boy.

---

[206] See the illustration on page 61.
[207] ibid.

Georgiana Gonce [ID 2874], born in about 1867, never married as far as I can determine.

Martina Gonce [ID 2875], born in about 1869, never married as far as I can determine.

Walter Gonce [ID 2876], born in about 1875, appears to have married twice and had two or three sons by his first marriage, and two sons and a daughter by his second marriage.

Additionally, the 1860 Census[208] shows two other children, Thomas Allibone [ID 4151], age 3, and Margaret Allibone [ID 2644], living with Benedict and Margaret. It is possible that the child Margaret, age 1, may actually be a Gonce, since the form is hard to interpret.

♦ Thomas Allibone Robaris Gonce [ID 2604], born 21 December 1839 was named in his father's will, so must have died after 1861, but I can find no further references to him.

♦ Laura Ellen Gonce [ID 2606], born 12 March 1843, and her husband Charles Pope had at least six children, including a set of boy-girl twins, Susan and Dennis, born in 1875. The available information seems to imply that Laura died in childbirth while delivering the twins.

♦ James Allibone Gonce [ID 2607], born 7 October 1844, and his wife Sarah had at least four children including a set of boy-girl twins, Benjamin and Sarah.

5th Generation: John Thomas Gonce & Catharine Ann Sullivan

Catharine Ann Sullivan – Our Sullivan & O'Brien Ancestors

According to their responses to the 1850 U.S. Census (see below), my 3rd great-grandfather Eugean [sic] Sullivan [ID 2599] and his wife Mary Ann O'Brien [209] [ID 2600] were immigrants from Killarney, County Kerry, Ireland. They must therefore have arrived in this country[210] sometime between 1805 (their year of birth) and 1830 (the year before their daughter Catharine [sic] [ID 1577] was born in Pennsylvania[211]). We know Eugean had a brother Daniel [ID 2970], since

---

[208] National Archives Microfilm Series m653 Roll 472 Page 52.

[209] Catharine Gonce's death certificate lists her parents' names as Eugene Sullivan and Mary O'Brien. The information was supplied by her daughter Catharine Gonce Linzey. He consistently used the spelling "Eugean" however.

[210] Either separately or together – whether they were married prior to immigrating is also unknown. We know about Eugean's Killarney origin from his brother Daniel's 1850 Baltimore Sun obituary.

[211] According to Eugean and Mary on the 1850 U.S. Census illustrated here. On the 1900 U.S. Census (see page 102) my great-grandfather William Henry Gonce says that his mother Catharine was born in Virginia. I am assuming he was simply mistaken, since there seems to be no other evidence that she was ever in Virginia. Catharine's name, by the way, is consistently spelled with two "A"s.

when Daniel died on 19 April 1850, Eugean was listed as his surviving brother[212].

The 1880 Census[213] on which my 2nd great-grandmother Catharine Ann Sullivan Gonce (Eugean's daughter) ID 1577 appeared indicated that her parents Eugean and Mary were both from Pennsylvania but on the 1900 U.S. Census[214] she indicated that they were both from Ireland. I suspect that Catharine simply misunderstood the intent of the question in 1880.

Eugean and Mary were probably married in the 1825 to 1829 time frame, but I have not located any record of their marriage. Whether this indicates they were married before arriving in this country is an open question; they may have been the Eugene and Maria Sullivan who arrived in New York from Ireland and England on the ship Jubilee on 12 May 1828[215].

The Fifth U.S. Census of 1830[216] shows Eugean living in the Walnut Ward of Philadelphia, Pennsylvania with the following household:

1830 United States Census Listing for "Eugine Sullivan" in Philadelphia, Pennsylvania	
1830 Census Counts	Comments (my assumptions)
1 Free White Male, age 20-29:	born 1801-1810 – Eugean Sullivan [2599], born ~1805, age ~25 **Our Direct Ancestor**
1 Free White Female, age 20-29:	born 1801-1810 – Mary Ann O'Brien [2600], born ~1805, age ~25 **Our Direct Ancestor**
1 Free White Female, age < 5:	born 1826-1830 – Catharine Sullivan [1577], newborn
No Other Entries on Line:	

---

[212] Baltimore Sun Obituaries of 20 April 1850. (S66) According to the obituary, Daniel was a coach maker.
[213] Church of Latter Day Saints Series mdt9, Roll 505, page 480. (S26) See a segment of this on page 84.
[214] National Archives Microfilm Series t623, Roll 616, Page 179. (S19) See a segment of this on page 85.
[215] NARC Microfilm Series m237 Roll 11 List 204: the name "Maria" is very clear, and her age is shown as 21, so this isn't a perfect match (Mary would have been about 23 in 1828). There are other, even less likely arrivals under the name Eugene Sullivan; see the notes that appear in the Appendix "Suggestions for Further Research" on page 263, specifically item #50.
[216] National Archives Series m019, Roll 159, page 465. (S80)

After Catharine's birth in 1829, and before James' birth in about 1838, the family moved to Baltimore, where Eugean was working as a watchman in 1850. I haven't located the Sullivans in the 1840 census, which might provide more details on Catharine's siblings, particularly on whether she had an older brother Samuel (see later discussion). He certainly isn't in the 1830 listing above, however.

Extract from 1850 U.S. Census page (National Archives Series m432, Roll 284, page 189) for my 3rd great-grandfather Eugean Sullivan (here spelled Eugine) and his family. The name appearing to be "Gonly" in the seventh line is "Gonce." George and John "Gonley" are the Sullivan's daughter Catharine's son and husband respectively. Also see the 1850 census listing for Catharine and John on page 70.

In addition to Catharine, born on 7 November 1829[217], we know of only three other Sullivan children for certain, although the appendix "Cemetery Mysteries – Section T Lot 295" on page 183 discusses the possibility that there may have been more. James was born in Maryland in about 1838. Mary Ann, the daughter mentioned in the previous paragraph, was born in about 1840 in Maryland, and a son Eugean [ID 3552] was born there in about 1842.

By the time of the 1850 census, taken in Baltimore on 7 October, their daughter Catharine Ann, then aged twenty, was already married to John T. Gonce and had her first child George [ID 2609]. George and John are shown at the end of the list with the name "Gonly," showing that they were living with the Sullivans at this time[218]. As can be seen, John still listed his profession as Farmer.

My 3rd great-grandmother Mary A. O'Brien Sullivan likely died before 1859[219], since she was not listed with Eugean as a parent when their younger

---

[217] On the 1900 census (see page 85), she gives "November 1834", and her tombstone (see page 86) says "1832." See "Birth Year of Catharine Ann Sullivan" on page 169 for a discussion of her birth year.

[218] John and Catharine appear twice in the 1850 census; this is discussed on page 70.

[219] ... but obviously after the 1850 Census.

■ 68 ■

daughter Mary Ann ID 2865 married T. James McKenna ID 2866 on 24 November 1859[220].

Eugean, Mary, their daughters and sons-in-law are all buried in New Cathedral Cemetery in Lot T-295. There is also a Samuel Sullivan buried in the same lot, and it is possible that he is another, earlier, child of Eugean and Mary's. If he was born between 1826 and Catharine's birth in 1831, he may have been out of the household at the time of the 1850 census[221].

John Thomas Gonce & Catharine Ann Sullivan – before the Civil War

My 2nd great-grandfather John Thomas Gonce was born on 22 December 1823[222]. Little is known about his early life in Cecil County, but he listed his profession as "farmer" in all the records I have found.

I have found nothing to suggest what prompted John's move to Baltimore, or when exactly he moved there, but he was certainly there before 1846, since that is where his future wife Catharine was living. It is possible that the move was prompted by his grandmother Rachel Vansant Comegys's move to Baltimore and her push for his education, leading to the suspicion that she might have taken him with her when she relocated to Baltimore, presumably after her husband Samuel's death[223]. Rachel died on 2 May 1841, and left John her account[224] at the Savings Bank of Baltimore as well as her household furniture – both actions clear indications that he was then living in Baltimore.

On Tuesday 12 January 1847, in the Bishop's house of the Baltimore Cathedral[225], John converted to Catholicism, was baptized, and was married to Catharine Ann Sullivan, who had just turned 17. Their first child, George E.[226] Gonce ID 2609, was born seven months later, on 30 September 1847.

---

[220] Baltimore Sun Marriage Announcements of 26 November 1859. (S67)

[221] There was a Samuel Sullivan (although not necessarily this one) who married Mary Renn on 16 January 1851 (reported in the Baltimore Sun on 10 March). I also found a record for a Samuel S. Sullivan, born 1828, who served in the Union Navy in the Civil War. These two and the Samuel in Lot T-295 may be the same, but it isn't certain.

[222] The 1900 census, shown on page 85, gives this as December 1824, and his tombstone (see page 86) says "1822," but the 1823 year seems supported by most available documentation. In the appendix "Cemetery Mysteries – Section T Lot 295" on page 183, I mention that the tombstone seemed to have been placed well after his and Catharine's death, which may account for the discrepancy. Until my daughter and I located it, New Cathedral Cemetery had no record that there was any tombstone on the plot and has no record of when or by whom it was placed.

[223] The timing would be rather tight if this were the case, however. John appears to have still been in his father's household at the time of the 1840 census, and I haven't found a record of Samuel's death date or location.

[224] Since John was not yet twenty-one years old, the money was left in the control of Joshua Vansant (see page 60). See an image of the Will Book and my transcription of the Will beginning on page 53.

[225] See National Archives Military Records; the presiding priest was Fr. Hickey.

[226] The middle initial E. probably stands for "Eugene," both because Catharine would have used her father's name for one of her children at least once, and because the name George Eugene was often used in later generations.

On the 1900 U.S. Census[227], Catharine states that she was a mother of 10, of whom 6 were living. I believe it is safe to infer that at least two of the unidentified children, who would be their second and third, were born in the period between July 1848 and March of 1850, and that both likely died before the summer of 1850 when the 1850 census below was taken. Based on the sequence of names in the New Cathedral Cemetery records, these were likely James F. [ID 2973] and Joseph R. [ID 2639]. Mary E. Gonce [ID 2610], born on 15 September 1852, would then be the fourth child.

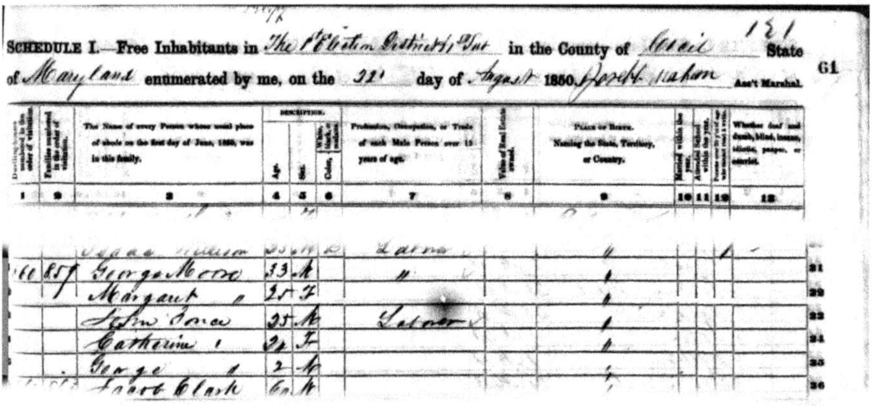

Above: Extract from 1850 U.S. Census page (National Archives Series m432, Roll 290, Page 61)

This page shows John and Catharine Gonce living with John's sister Margaret and her husband George Moore in Cecil County on August 22, 1850. On October 7th, John and Catharine are residing with Catharine's parents in Baltimore (see page 68). Since John and Catharine were married in Baltimore in 1847, it is assumed that John must have relocated there by that time, and that he and Catharine were simply visiting John's relatives in Cecil County when the census was taken there in August.

Their first son George is the only child shown on the two 1850 census entries for John and Catharine.

In 1853, John was known to be living on Chase Street near Decker in Baltimore City; he is shown as "John Gonse, laborer" in the Baltimore City Directory for 1853-54 illustrated below.

---

[227] National Archives Microfilm Series t623 Roll 616, Page 179. See illustration on page 85.

GOD	120	
GODWIN & BROWNE grocers, 4 Bowley's whf	Goli James B. gentleman, 77 Peirce	
Godwin Wm. B. grocer, 50 Lee	Goman George, trader, Pennsylvania av ex…	
Godwin Wm. jr. firm G. & Brown, dw 50 Lee	Gommell Walter, helper at depot, 167 Raborg	
Goers Wesley, carpenter, Gibson n of Preston	Gomph Fredk. paver, 58 n Amity	
Goetleib Charles, tailor, 30 Low	Gonse John, laborer, Chase near Decker	
Goertler Francis, beer brewer, cor Canton av and Choptank st	Gontz A. 47 Lancaster	
Goff Wm. cake man, next 27 C. Market	Good Wm B. F. tavern keeper, n w cor Cowpen and Liberty st. dw Frederick st	
Goforth George W. bacon dealer, 407 n Gay	Goodacre Daniel, stone cutter, cor President and Stiles, dw 93 Albemarle	
Gogel Chas. C. butter & ice cream dealer, 375 n Gay		
Goh Henry, locksmith, 19 Arch	Goodall Matthew, Hollins st w Republican	
Goh Philip, locksmith. 19 Arch	Goode John B. furniture dealer, 37 Harrison	
Going A. machinist, 106 st Mary	Goode Patrick, wheelwright, 199 Chesnut	
Gold Abraham, dry goods dealer, 649 Baltimore	Goodhand John, clerk, 15 Fremont	
Gold Columbus, printer, 68 French	Goodimut John, paver, 67 n Schroeder	
Gold Frederick, baker, 22 Park	Goodman A. clothier, 38 Pratt, dw 37 Fawn	
Gold Mary, 65 s Charles	Goodman Edward C. boot & shoemaker, 150 n Gay	
Gold Samuel, printer, Bond s of Mullikin	Goodman H. & Bro. clothiers, 10 C. Market	
Goldbroke Wm. cabinet maker, 320 s Bond	Goodman Isaac, second hand furniture dealer, … Harrison	
Goldbury Wm. J. clerk, F.P. Sav. Inst. 100 Aisquith		
Golden Bernard, shoemaker, 72 C. Market	Goodman Jacob, whitesmith, 451 w Lombard	
Golden Michl. laborer, 111 n Paca	Goodman John Geo. grocer, s e cor Fayette & Arch	
Golden Michl. 8 Raborg	Goodman John, wagoner, 108 Franklin	
Goldenberg Levi, dry goods dealer, 55 Baltimore, dw 137 Aisquith	Goodman Lewis, furn. & glass dealer, 60 Harrison	
	Goodman Samuel, cooper, 478 w Baltimore, shop Raborg	
Goldenburg Reuben, firm Hecht & G. 653 Balt. st		
GOLDER A. & SON, importers and manufacturers of paper hangings, 33 and 35 Hanover st. dw A. G. 113 Fayette	Goodmanson Capt. James H. 88 n Eden	
	Goodmanson Samuel, tailor, 194 n Eden	
	GOODRICH & BEAN, grocers and commission merchants, 104 Dugan's wharf	
Golder James C. firm A. G. & Son, dw 81 Park	Goodrich Geo. carpenter, 58 Second, shop Fredk.	
Goldinghurst George, tavern, 15 Commerce	Goodrich Geo. W. proprietor Coach House tavern, 23 s Frederick	
Goldsborough Aex. W. dry goods dealer, 168 n Gay & 7 Ensor, dw 37 s Eutaw		
Goldsborough John, 186 Eastern av	Goodrich Henry, firm G. & Bean, 16 Exeter	
Goldsborough N. W. firm R. M. Lockwood & Co. dw 5 McCulloch	GOODRICH THOMAS T. carpenter, 10 s Frederick, dw. 32 e Baltimore	
Goldsmith & Co. dry goods and trimming dealers, 150 1-2 Lexington, dw 168	Goodwalt Michl. laborer, 56 Bank	
	Goodwin Charles, of Merchants' Bank, dw 239 w Lombard	
Goldschmidt Sol. shoemaker, 195 Alice Anna		
Goldsmith Edward, cigar maker, 26 s Charles, dw 123 s Paca	Goodwin George D. omnibus driver, 115 Preston	
	Goodwin John, blacksmith and shoer, 403 Balt.	
Goldsmith Eliza, 171 Park	Goodwin M. P. 181 Hanover	
Goldsmith Hartz, dealer, 37 Lancaster	Goodwin Misses, 223 Aisquith	
Goldsmith, Jonas, clothier, 80 East	Goodwin Richard B. firm Goodwin & Stephens, dw 29 Stiles	
Goldsmith Lewis, at custom house, 21 Orchard		
Goldsmith Reuben S. dry goods dealer, 188 Alice Anna	Goodwin & Stephens, ship builders, City Block	
	Goodwin Thomas, 62 s Eutaw	
Goldsmith Samuel H. 85 n Calvert	Goodwin Wm. J. carpenter, 165 n Canal	
Goldstein Aaron, store keeper, 225 n Canal	Goose H. rear Fountain st w Castle al	
Goldstone B. dry goods dealer, 165 e Baltimore	Goosman Phil. Durham n Thames	
Golibart R. Simon, lumber merchant, Washington st s of Pratt	Gooson John, laborer, 146 Eastern av	
	Gootsberger John, laborer 84 Albemarle	

Page 120 from the Baltimore City Directory of 1853-54 showing John Gonse, laborer, living on Chase near Decker, and A. Gontz of 47 Lancaster. John Gonse is probably John T. Gonce. The following name, "A. Gontz," has so far been unidentified, but doesn't seem to be one of "our" Gonces. He is likely one of the original Baltimore "Gantz" family from Germany that is unrelated to our Gonce family. See page 284.

John and Catharine's fifth child, Benny M. Gonce [ID 2974], was born in about 1854.

I believe it is safe to infer once again that the last of John and Catharine's unidentified children, who would be their sixth child, was born in the period between mid-1855 and early 1856. This would have been Emma Gonce ID 3596. Obviously, of course, my inferences regarding the four unidentified children are arbitrary. Sometime before 1858, John and Catharine moved to 12 Tyson in Baltimore, as can be seen in the city directory shown below.

```
                    GOO           133           GOR

Goll James B., prop. Gen Wayne's hotel, W   Goodwin Richard, shipwright, Patterson's wharf,
   Baltimore cor Paca, h do                    Fell's point, h 27 Stiles
Goll Elizabeth, wid William, seamstress, h 229  GOODWIN R. R. & CO. (Richard B. Goodwin
   Hollins                                     and William Stevens), shipwrights, Patter-
Golric Henry, plumber, h 119 S Register        son's wharf, Fell's point
Goman Bryan, grocery, 79 Richmond, h do     Goodwin Thomas, bootmaker, h 90 Holliday
Gompf Peter, boots and shoes, 76 Pearl, h do Goodwin Thomas, dry-goods com., 1 and 3 Ger-
Gonce John T., farmer, h 12 Tyson              man, h 29 Hollins
Gonder Jacob, stonecutter, bds 60 N Eutaw    Goold William (col'd), laborer, h 211 S Dallas
Gondy Susanna, wid Jonathan, h 386 W Lom-   Gootee George S., com. mer., h 99 S Washington
   bard                                     Gootee Henry P., salesman, h 99 S Washington
Gontrum Conradt, bootcutter, h 229 N Caroline Goppart George, gunsmith, 468 Penn. av, h do
Gontrum Peter, shoemaker, h 455 N Gay       Gordon Alice (col.), washerwoman, h 35 N Sharp
Good William, grocer, h 180 Pearl           Gordon Bridget, coffee house, 29 S Paca, h do
```

Top of page 133 from The Baltimore City Directory: 1858; compiled by William H. Boyd; Richard Edwards and William H. Boyd, Publishers. In this directory, John again listed his profession as a farmer.

By 1860, John and Catharine had their seventh and eighth children: my great-grandfather William Henry Gonce [ID 32], born on Thursday 15 January 1857, and Thomas S. Gonce [ID 1579], born on 15 April 1859.

The 1860 U.S. Census might help answer some of the questions about John and Catharine's children and their years of birth but, unfortunately, I have been unable to locate John and his family in that census. See the notes beginning on page 269.

John Thomas Gonce & Catharine Ann Sullivan – the Civil War Years

South Carolina seceded from the Union in December 1860 and by mid-1861, the situation had degenerated into declared war. John enlisted in Baltimore as a Union soldier on 11 August 1862[228], and on 21 August was assigned to Company B of the 6th Regiment of the Maryland Infantry[229]. Company B was primarily made up of volunteers from Cecil County, where he had originally come from, but it is assumed that John joined this unit because Companies F and I, recruited from Baltimore City, weren't formed until later.

---

[228] The muster roll shown on the next page erroneously shows his assignment date as his enlistment date, but seems to confirm that he enlisted in Baltimore rather than in Cecil County.

[229] John's younger brother George Washington Gonce [ID 2520] was in Company H of the 6th Regiment, a unit comprised primarily of those recruited from Washington County, although it isn't clear where he lived at the time; as far as I can tell, George's service was apparently uneventful.

In his military records, John was described as having blue eyes and dark hair and, most interestingly, was only 5 feet 3 inches tall as a forty-one year old adult. See the document to the right, completed near the end of his service in the Civil War – service that not only delayed the growth of his family, but also altered his life and physical condition considerably.

Standard of the 6th Regt, Maryland Infantry

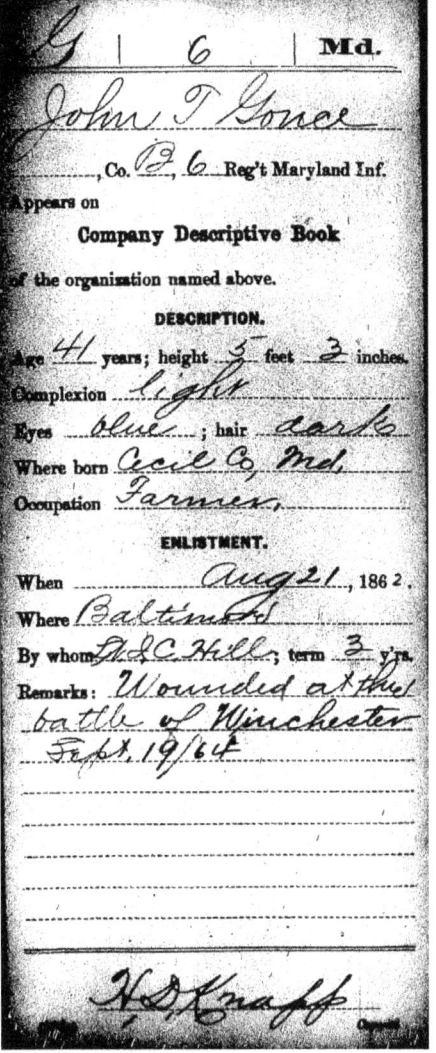

The only known physical description of my ancestor John T. Gonce - from 1864

Once the new companies were formed into the 6th Regiment and given minimal (less than a month) training, they left Baltimore City on September 20, 1862, to join the Maryland Brigade of the 8th Army Corps (part of the Army of the Potomac) in Western Maryland. Although it is known that some troops traveled by train during this period, there seems to be no record of how John's initial deployment was made.

The 6th regiment remained with the Maryland Brigade on the upper Potomac until December 1862, when it marched to and encamped on Bolivar Heights at Harper's Ferry, Virginia.

On March 28th 1863, John and the 6th Regiment were detached from the Maryland Brigade and ordered to Berryville, Virginia, where they were assigned to the 2nd Division of McReynolds' (3rd) Brigade[230]. Most of the unit's remaining service during the conflict was to be in Virginia.

On 13 June 1863, the Confederate army attacked the 3rd Brigade at Berryville[231] in Clarke County Virginia. Although the rest of the Brigade

---

[230] ... which was still part of the 8th Army Corps
[231] This was not the more famous Battle of Berryville, which didn't take place until 3-4 September 1864.

managed to retreat towards Winchester, John was wounded slightly and captured along with a number of others by the Confederate forces.

Insignia of the 6th Regt, MD Infantry

During this part of the war, neither the Union nor Confederate Army was prepared to handle significant numbers of prisoners of war, so they were often "paroled" by the capturing field commander after being ordered to take an oath to not perform any further military service until an exchange of prisoners was arranged. John Gonce was paroled in this fashion, and assigned on 13 June 1863 to the recently opened Union holding area at Camp Parole[232] to await exchange. By September 1863, however, he had been returned to active duty with Company B. (Parole oaths were not recognized or considered binding by the Union Army.)

Company B Muster Rolls for July through October of 1863 showing John's absence during his time as a prisoner-of-war. The exact date of his subsequent parole and exchange for a southern prisoner-of-war is unknown.

Note that his back pay for the period he was in Confederate custody or parole was $1.16.

Shown above is the memorial marker for Camp Parole; the location is currently in an Annapolis strip mall.

On 24 March 1864, the 6th Regiment had its last reassignment of the war – to the 2d Brigade, 3rd Division, 6th Army Corps. Once again part of the Army of the Potomac, it fought with great honor in the Battle of the Wilderness on 5 May 1864, as well as in the subsequent battles of Spotsylvania, Cold Harbor and Petersburg. See a photo of the unit's memorial on page 180.

---

[232] Camp Parole was located in what is now part of Annapolis, Maryland.

The Battle of Opequon

In July of 1864, the Confederate General Jubal Early led a large force into Maryland in an attempt to capture Washington, D.C. The 6th Regiment was part of the force sent from Petersburg by General Ulysses S. Grant to repel this invasion. Not only did the force save the capitol, it was also able to drive all of Early's forces out of Maryland and back into Virginia.

Immediately after this, General Philip Sheridan[233] was placed in command and began a drive to completely eliminate the Confederate armies in this part of the country. The first major conflict of this offensive was the battle of Opequon (also called the Third Winchester).

The Third Winchester involved 39,236 Union soldiers in three infantry corps and a cavalry corps, and 15,200 Confederate soldiers in four infantry and two cavalry divisions. This was the largest and most desperately contested battle of the Civil War in the Shenandoah Valley, resulting in close to 9,000 casualties[234]. The battle was a turning point of the war in the Valley, marking the rise of Sheridan and the decline of Confederate power. Details of the battle of Opequon can be found on the Internet[235] so will not be repeated.

The Maryland Regiment would continue on to significant victories in Virginia at Winchester (19 September), Fisher's Hill (22 September), Cedar Creek (19 October), Petersburg (2 April), Sailor's Creek (6 April), and at the final surrender of Lee's army at Appomattox Court House on 9 April, 1865. John's service was effectively ended with the battle of Opequon, however, when he was severely wounded in the right leg on Monday September 19, 1864.

Some idea of the conditions under which wounded soldiers were treated can be imagined from surviving medical instrument kits (example on the right) and contemporary photographs; some of which are shown below.

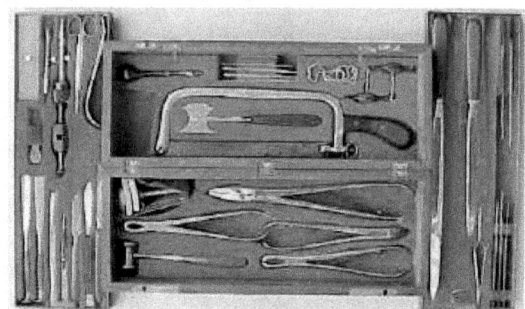

The illustration above shows a Kolbe Surgery Set from 1863, typical of the type that would have been used by the surgeon treating John T. Gonce's leg wounds.

On September 27th, nine days after he was wounded, John finally arrived at the military hospital in Frederick Maryland and was admitted as a patient.

---

[233] For whom Ft. Sheridan, Illinois, is named.
[234] 5,018 Union soldiers and 3,611 Confederate Soldiers were reported as casualties.
[235] One site can be located at http://www2.cr.nps.gov/abpp/shenandoah/svs3-12.html

Photography first began to be widely used in the Civil War. The picture on the left shows wounded soldiers being tended in the field after the Battle of Chancellorsville near Fredericksburg, Virginia on May 2, 1863

This picture is believed to have been taken by the well-known Civil War era photographer Matthew Brady, one of the first of the famous names in photography

There are no known photographs of the Union hospital at Frederick, Maryland, but the photograph to the right will give an idea of field hospital conditions during the Civil War.

This is the Union field hospital at Savage Station, Virginia after the battle of 27 June 1862.

The Photograph was taken by James F. Gibson, born in 1828, and who worked for Matthew Brady. James Gibson also managed Brady's studio in Washington for a period.

After almost four months of treatment, John made the following request for transfer to Baltimore on 16 January 1865:

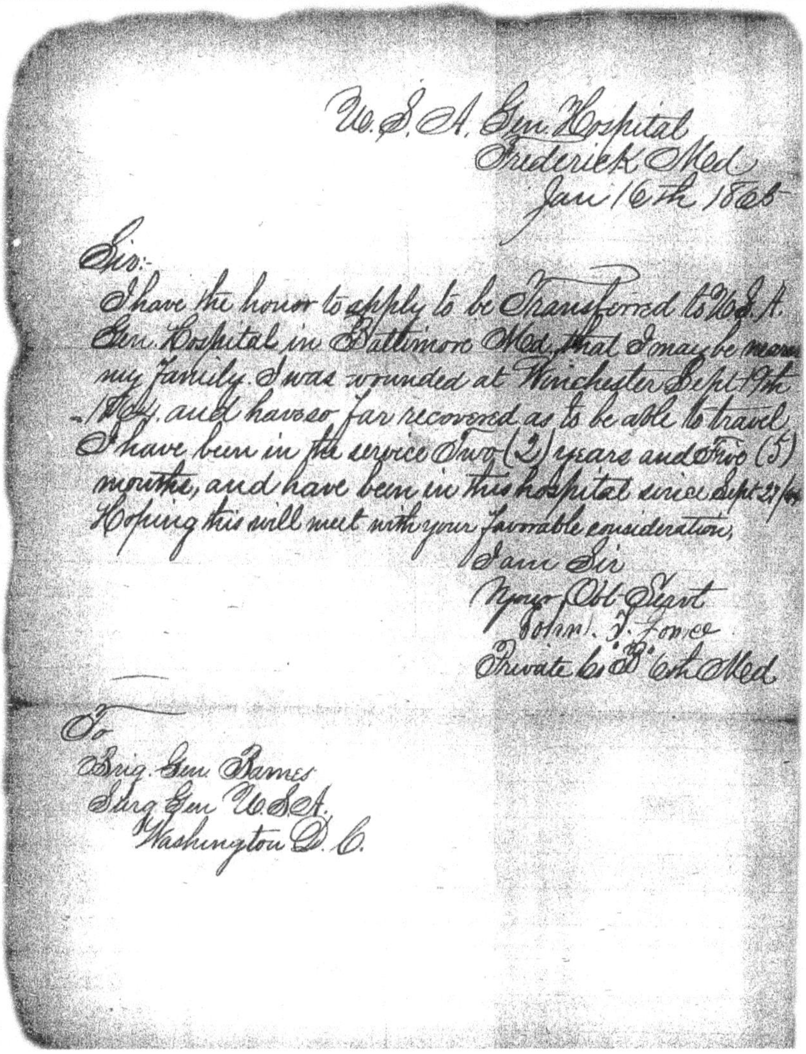

U.S.A. Gen Hospital
Frederick Md
Jan 16th 1865

Sir:-
I have the honor to apply to be Transferred to U.S.A. Gen. Hospital in Baltimore Md, that I may be near my Family. I was wounded at Winchester Sept 19th 1864. and have so far recovered as to be able to travel. I have been in the service Two (2) years and Five (5) months, and have been in this hospital since Sept 27/64 Hoping this will meet with your favorable consideration,
I am Sir
Your Obt Servt
John T. Gonce
Private Co "B" 6th Md.

To
Brig. Gen Barnes
Surg Gen U.S.A.
Washington D.C.

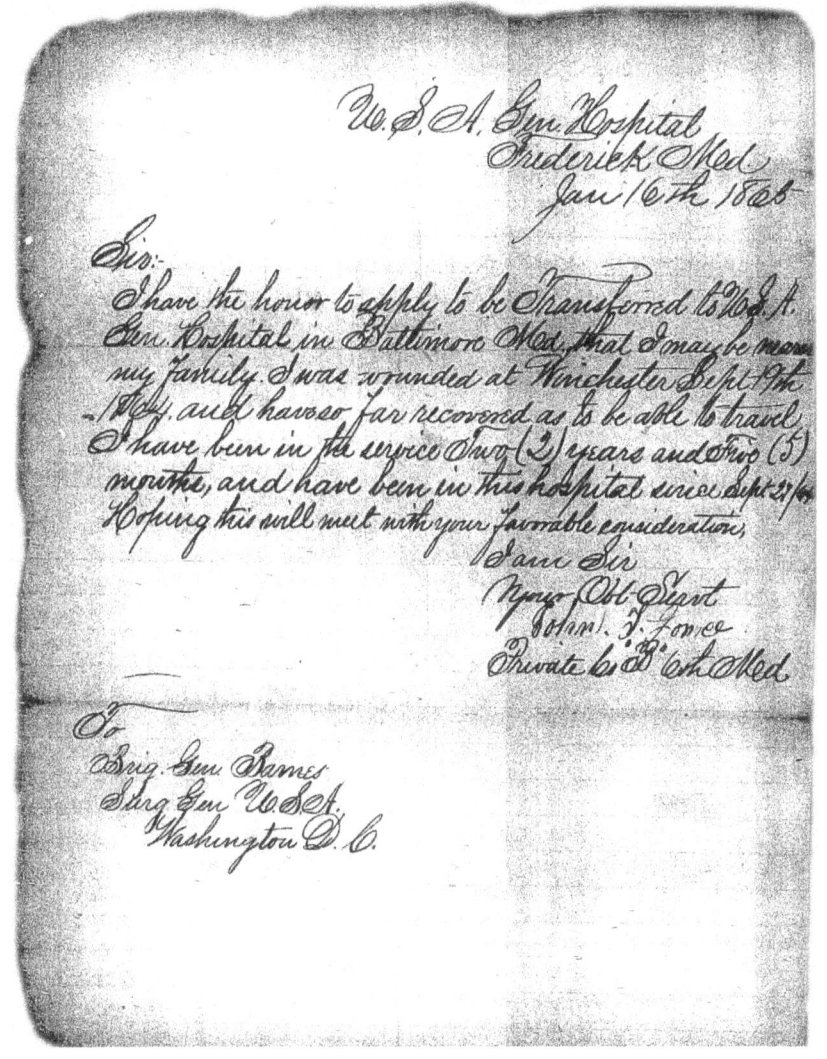

Below is my transcription of the letter:

> *Sir: I have the honor to apply to be transferred to U.S.A. Gen. Hospital in Baltimore Md., that I may be near my Family. I was wounded at Winchester Sept 19th 1864 and have so far recovered as to be able to travel. I have been in the service Two (2) years and Five (5) months, and have been in this hospital since Sept 27/64. Hoping this will meet with your favorable consideration, I am Sir*
>
> *Your Obt. Servt John T. Gonce, Private Co "B" 6th Md."*

Of the usual endorsements that accompany such requests up the military chain of command, the most interesting is the statement of T. E. Mitchell, Jr., his attending physician (again, a transcription follows the image):

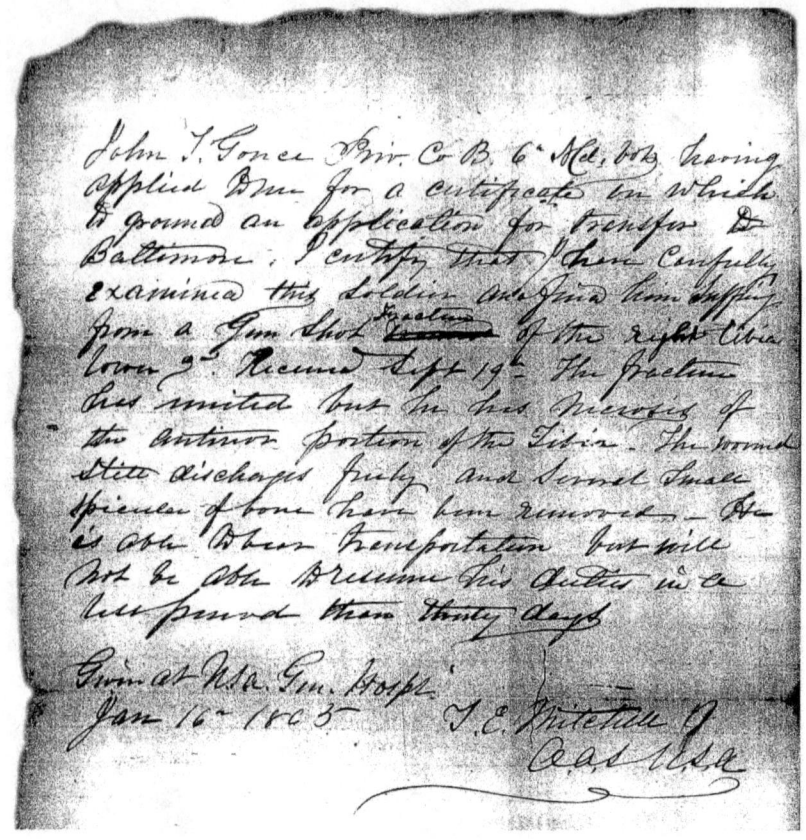

John T. Gonce Priv. Co B. 6th Md Bn, having applied to me for a certificate on which to ground an application for transfer to Baltimore, I certify that I have carefully examined this soldier and find him suffering from a gun shot fracture of the right tibia lower 3rd received Sept. 19th. The fracture has united but he has necrosis of the anterior portion of the tibia. The wound still discharges freely and several small spicules of bone have been removed. He is able to bear transportation[236], but will not be able to resume his duties in a less period than thirty days. Given at USA Gen Hosp Jan 16th 1865

---

[236] Since the surgeon felt compelled to mention that John could "bear transportation" after four months of treatment, one has to wonder how difficult his original move from the battlefield to the hospital must have been.

This request was granted by General Order 77, A.G.O., and on 9 June 1865, John was discharged from the service about two months before his normal enlistment term would have expired.

During the period of the Civil War, the 6th Regiment had lost 8 officers and 120 enlisted men in battle, and 1 officer and 107 men to disease[237]. Over the course of the war, the Regiment had traveled 575 miles by railroad, 577 miles by boat, and 1751 miles on foot, a total distance of 2908 miles.

Details of John's Wound

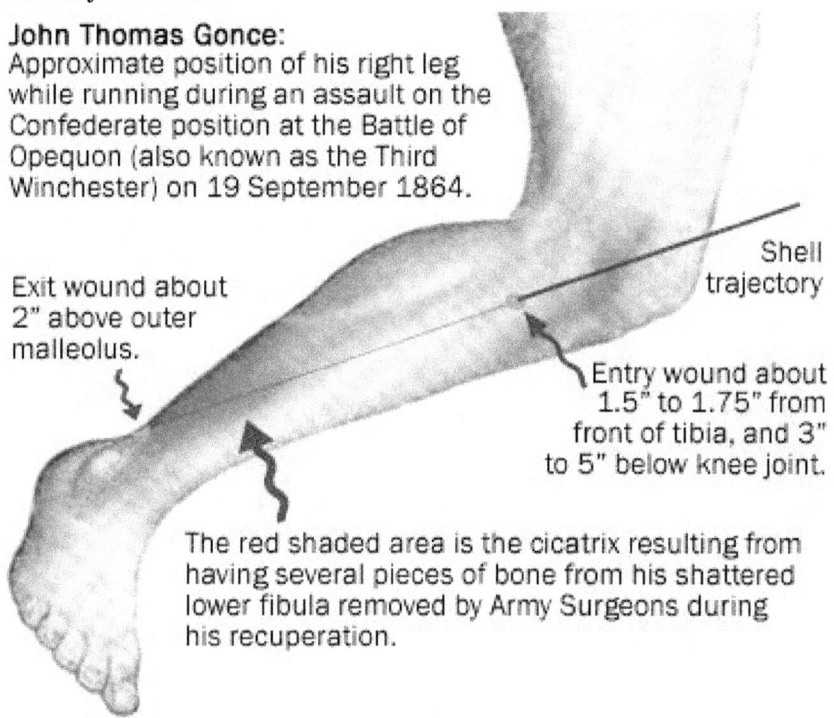

John Thomas Gonce: Approximate position of his right leg while running during an assault on the Confederate position at the Battle of Opequon (also known as the Third Winchester) on 19 September 1864.

Shell trajectory

Exit wound about 2" above outer malleolus.

Entry wound about 1.5" to 1.75" from front of tibia, and 3" to 5" below knee joint.

The red shaded area is the cicatrix resulting from having several pieces of bone from his shattered lower fibula removed by Army Surgeons during his recuperation.

Cicatrix: *contracted tissue at the place where a wound heals.*
Fibula: *the long thin outer bone of the lower leg.*
Malleolus: *lower extremity; the outer malleolus is the portion of the anklebone that protrudes from the side of the foot.*
Tibia: *the inner, thicker bone at the front of the lower leg.*

The wound itself was caused by a musket ball, apparently fired at a slightly downward angle. At the time he was hit in the right leg, John and his compatriots were engaged in a charge against the Confederate lines. He was at a full run, and his leg was more or less at the angle shown in the illustration above when he was hit. The bullet entered the outside of his right leg,

---

[237] ... an interesting comparison of the effects of fighting vs. disease. The number wounded isn't readily available.

approximately 1.5 inches to the side of the tibia and 3 inches below the level of the knee.

The ball traveled through his leg, shattering the lower third of the tibia, and exiting about 2 inches above and a little behind the ankle joint, apparently just to the side of his Achilles tendon. Several pieces of bone were removed from the leg above the ankle, causing the healed tissue in that area to become very tight and inflexible (a cicatrix)[238].

Because he sustained a gunshot wound during the Civil War, my 2nd great-grandfather John Thomas Gonce applied for a disability pension on August 13, 1866. The Army surgeon Thomas Owings, who examined John for his disability claim on 24 October 1866, stated, "the disability may lessen" – a prognosis that turned out to be overly optimistic. Based on this exam, John's disability was originally found to be 50%, and a payment of $6.00 per month was approved in March 1868. He was required to receive periodic medical examinations in order to continue his government disability pension; the majority of these examinations survived and they allow us to see the changes in his health over the years between the Civil War and his death in 1905[239].

John Thomas Gonce & Catharine Ann Sullivan – after the Civil War

During the Civil War, John's family had been living at 24 Ross in Baltimore[240]. When John returned to his family in Baltimore after the war, his son George was almost 17 years old. His daughter Mary was 12, William Henry (my great-grandfather) was 7, and the youngest son Thomas was 6. I have been unable to locate any source that would indicate whether James, Joseph, Benny, or Emma were still alive at this time.

The first mention I could find of John after the Civil War was in the Baltimore City Directory for 1867-68 when he was living at 124 Rose and again listed his occupation as Laborer. It is known that his first employment after the war was for a Mr. S. Fiterman, and that he continued to work for Fiterman at least until 30 July 1866[241] at what must have been a clerical

---

[238] Documents prepared by the surgeons who originally removed the fragments suggest that these slivers of the fibula were as much as two inches in length, but during his examinations in later years, John seems to have begun reporting that they were longer. During his examination on 4 October 1889, he told the examining surgeon that the pieces were as much as four inches long, which the surgeon reported without comment. Despite this effort, his pension was not increased at that time.

[239] All of the examinations referenced can be found in his Civil War Pension Folder at the U.S. National Archives. Quotes from key examinations will be provided through the remainder of this discussion.

[240] John's name appears in the 1864 Baltimore City Directory on page 153 although, as we have seen, he was away fighting until 1865; due to the Civil War, this was the first directory published in Baltimore since 1860. John also had an uncle named John T. Gonce ID 2628 (his father George's older brother). The possibility that this reference is to his Uncle John cannot be completely discounted, but it seems unlikely because of the uncle's known residence in New Castle County Delaware in 1860.

[241] This was the date that Mr. Fiterman wrote him a letter confirming for the Army disability examining board that John's "wound prevented him for some time to care for his family properly." This letter is in John's pension files.

position. When he completed the 1870 census (see the illustration below), John listed his profession as "Clerk," although I haven't been able to determine for what company he worked at that time, or if this was a prelude to his next position.

John and Catharine had at least two more children following the Civil War. Louis (misspelled as "Lewis" in the census below) A. Gonce [ID 1580] was born on 3 October 1866, and Katherine (known as Kate) Gonce [ID 1581] was born on 15 September 1868. Except for Kate, who had only one daughter, all of John and Catharine's children had large families.

Extracted from 1870 U.S. Census - NARC Series m593, Roll 580, Page 565

23	199	1314	Gantz	John	44	m	·	Clerk
24				Cath.	40	F	·	Keeping House
25				Mary E.	17	"	·	
26				Wm H.	15	m	·	
27				Thomas	12	·	·	
28				Lewis	10	·	·	
29				Kate	6	F	·	
30		1315	Butts	Wm	22	m	·	Salesman
31				Mary E	17	F	·	Keeping House

Extracted from 1870 Census – The name is misspelled "Gantz," but this is clearly John T. and Catharine Gonce. John now lists his profession as "Clerk." See remarks about the Butts family on the next page.

My great-grandfather William Henry Gonce (shown as "Wm H.") was 15 at the time of this Census.

William and Mary Butts are a separate family living with John and Catharine. Note that Mary E. Gonce and Mary E. Butts are the same age, but are definitely listed as separate individuals. See the appendix "Cemetery Mysteries – Section T Lot 295" on page 183 for speculation on the relationship of the Butts and Gonce families.

As can be seen in the 1870 census segment above, John and Catharine's oldest son George E. Gonce, a huckster[242], had already moved out (George and his wife Elizabeth had their first son William in March of 1869).

By 1873, John seemed to have settled on a career as a Stove salesman[243] and installer. He continued doing this for many years; the latest mention I have of him in this profession is in 1891[244]. During this period, he and his family lived at 60 Etting Street in Baltimore.

John's difficulties with his right leg apparently became much worse as the years went on. In his periodic examination by the Army Pension Board on 11 September 1875, the examining surgeons, led by Dr. A. W. Dodge, noted: "If he attempts to lift at his work, or to step back, the leg gives way under him." The examiners on 5 September 1877 (whose names are illegible to me) added: "...fibula fails to support leg – gives way especially when lifting even slight weight." This latter report is shown on the following page.

Dr. L. R. Garrett, the surgeon who examined him on 17 March 1880 (John was 56 at this time) made the following observations: "painful in wet weather" and "limps occasionally."

On the 1880 U.S. Census[245], shown on the following page, my 2nd great-grandfather John T. Gonce and his family are shown still living at 60 Etting Street, and we can see that their first two children, George and Mary, had since moved out. The Alice shown as their daughter is actually their daughter-in-law[246], William Henry Gonce's wife. William and Thomas were working as plumbers at this time, but had not yet moved out of the household.

Above John's family on the same census page, and living at 50 Etting Street is the family of another William H. Gonce, a Butcher who I believe to be John T. Gonce's nephew, the son of John's younger brother George W. Gonce.

---

[242] A Huckster was a driver who collected fruits and vegetables in a display truck (the sides and back could be opened up at each stop for housewives to examine the merchandise) and sold them in neighborhoods around the city. This profession survived until the mid-1950s when the spread of supermarkets made it redundant.

[243] In the context of the late nineteenth century, a "Stove" was not primarily something on which one cooked, but rather an "improved" fireplace – an enclosure, usually of metal or ceramic, in which wood or other fuel was burned to heat the outer surface and thus heat the room more efficiently than a fireplace.

[244] Various Baltimore City Directories; See, for example, the 1884 Directory is shown below.

[245] Church of Latter Day Saints Microfilm Series mdt9, Roll 505, page 480. (S26)

[246] My great-grandmother Alice Elizabeth Clautice, who is discussed beginning on page 89.

4   **DUPLICATE.**   4

SURGEON'S CERTIFICATE
OF

Biennial, Annual, or Semi-annual Examination, on which the Pensioner draws his Pension.

State: _Maryland_ County: _____
Post Office: _Balto_ _Sep 5_, 1877.

Pensioner's service. We hereby certify, That we have carefully examined _John T Gonce_, who was a _Pri A_ _6 Md_ in the war _61-5_ and was

Be particular to give Certificate No. granted an Invalid Pension under Certificate No. _89,789_, to be paid now

Agency where to be paid. at the Agency in _Washington_, by reason of alleged disability resulting from _G.S.W. Right leg_

which he states to have been received in the line of duty while he was in the military service of the United States.

State whether disability continues; and, if so, its present degree. In _our_ opinion, the said Pensioner's disability, from the cause aforesaid, continues at _$4/4$ per m_

Particular description. A more particular description of the Pensioner's condition is subjoined:
Height, _5.2_; weight, _123_; complexion, _dark_; age, _56_; respiration, _18_; pulse, _92_.

Ball entered upper 3d of Right leg outside of tibia passed down and out behind external malleolus; fibula was fractured by this ball — ulcerated cicatrix on outer side of lower 3d of leg — alleged spicula, large, have been removed; fibula fails to support, "leg gives way" especially when lifting even slight weight — muscles contracted.

A M Dodge
C W Gaaden
Examining Surgeon.

John Thomas Gonce's periodic medical examination of 5 September 1877

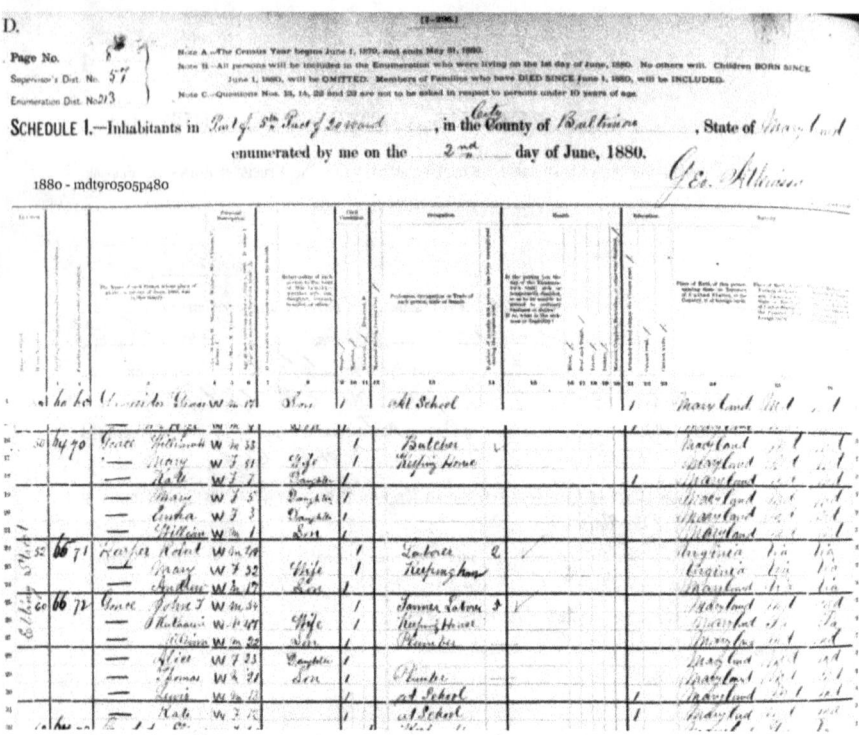

Extract from 1880 census page mdt9, Roll 505, page 480, for Etting Street in Baltimore.

A typical city directory from this period is shown below in which John is shown along with his sons George, Thomas, and Louis.

Page 475 from the 1884 Baltimore City Directory showing the Gonces

The 60 Etting Street address where the family lived in 1880 became 1228 Etting Street when the buildings in Baltimore were renumbered in 1887[247].

On 4 October 1889, John's disability pension was raised to $8 per month.

In early 1890, John and his family moved from Etting Street to 525 Dolphin Street[248]. Although the 1890 Census no longer exists because of a fire, the separate "Veterans Schedules" that were intended to list all veterans and their families are still extant; unfortunately, I have been unable to locate John and his family in these records. Possibly, the family was in transition at the time the census was taken.

By 12 March 1891, when John was 70, the examining surgeons (Drs. Bott, Kerry, and Gorsuch) wrote: "Motion of foot limited – flexion prevented almost entirely …," continuing with a detailed description of the causes for this limitation.

By this time, however, many other problems had appeared. In addition to further deterioration of John's leg, the doctor noted incipient cataracts and excessive secretion from the eyes, hearing problems including partial deafness, and rheumatism. The Board finally ruled that John was completely disabled.

Sometime in the last decade of the century, John began to decline significantly (whether physically, mentally, or both isn't known). By the time of the 1900 census shown below, Catharine, not John, was listed as the head-of-household, and the family was living at 912 Calhoun Street.

Extract from 1900 Census showing Catharine as head-of-household during John's life.

---

[247] Care should be taken when attempting to locate addresses in Baltimore prior to 1887, when all of the buildings and houses were renumbered to reflect their relation to the center of town. The Baltimore City Directory for that year includes a cross reference of old and new street addresses beginning on page 45. See a map showing this location on page 101.

[248] We know from his medical examination records that he was at the Etting Street location on 4 October 1889, and living on Dolphin Street on 10 July 1890, so the move took place between these dates.

The 1900 census has several interesting entries. Catharine's month and year of birth are given as November 1834 (it's actually 1829[249]), while John's is given as December 1824 (it was actually 1823).

The Catherine A. Lindzay (actually Linzey) shown living in the same household is John and Catharine's youngest daughter, married to John Lindzay. Also note that Catharine is shown as a "mother of 10 with 6 living."

John Thomas Gonce died on Wednesday 8 March 1905 at the age of 80. He was buried in his father-in-law Eugean Sullivan's plot (T-295) at New Cathedral Cemetery[250].

Two days later, Catharine applied for a Civil War Veteran widow's benefit. This was approved, and is reflected on the pension card shown on the right, although the amount is unknown.

Note the spelling of her name on the card.

Catharine died a little over six years later, on Saturday 30 September 1911, and was buried with her husband John at New Cathedral Cemetery. A photo of their headstone is shown below. This is the only marker on the plot, which contains twenty-three other presumed relatives in addition to Catharine and John.

Tombstone of John Thomas Gonce and Catharine Ann Sullivan. Note that both birth years are incorrect.

---

[249] See the appendix "Birth Year of Catharine Ann Sullivan" on page 169.

[250] There is a separate appendix regarding the many people buried in this plot beginning on page 183.

OUR GONCE ANCESTORS

No. 41

Received Baltimore, _____ 823292

GEO. R. HEFFNER, Comptroller,

Department of Public Safety,

SUB-DEPARTMENT OF HEALTH,
CITY OF BALTIMORE.

Office of Registrar of Vital Statistics.

A Transcript from the Records of Deaths in the City of Baltimore.

Baltimore, Mar. 15th 1905

NAME OF DECEASED.	DATE OF DEATH.	AGE OF DECEASED.		
		Yrs.	Mos.	Days.
Jno. T. Gonce	Mar. 8, 1905	82	2	14

COLOR, SEX, SOCIAL CONDITION.	OCCUPATION.	NATIVITY OF PARENTS.	
		Father.	Mother.
White, male, married	Retired Store Worker	Md	Md

BIRTHPLACE OF DECEASED.	DURATION OF RESIDENCE IN BALTIMORE.			PLACE OF DEATH.
	Yrs.	Mos.	Days.	
Cecil Co. Md.	not stated			Baltimore

RESIDENCE OF DECEASED.	CAUSE OF DEATH.	DURATION OF LAST SICKNESS.
912 N. Calhoun	Paralysis, superinduced by old age	5 Days

PLACE OF BURIAL.	MEDICAL ATTENDANT.	UNDERTAKER.
New Cathedral Cem	J.S. Raborg, M.D.	Wm Cook

A true copy,

James Bosley M.D.
Commissioner of Health and Registrar,

_____
Clerk to Registrar.

Death Certificate of John Thomas Gonce [ID 1576]

Children and Grandchildren of John Thomas Gonce & Catharine Ann Sullivan

In order to retain a focus on our direct line, the following section will provide only a brief commentary on each of John and Catharine's children.

- George Eugene Gonce ID 2609 (30 September 1847-1926) and his wife Mary Elizabeth ID 2631, had at least three children:

  William H. [251] Gonce ID 2982 (March 1869-1913) married Mary C. ID 2983. They are buried at New Cathedral Cemetery.
  Edna M. Gonce ID 2985, born about 1888, married George H. Smith ID 2984, and had at least one child.
  John Thomas Gonce ID 3458 (22 February 1875 - 30 May 1926) married Julia May Appler ID 3459 and had at least one daughter.
  Albert Gonce ID 2632 was born in 1889. Albert died in 1901 when he was about 12.

- James F. [252] Gonce ID 2973 (born about 1848). James died before summer 1850 and is buried in the Sullivan-Gonce plot Section T – Lot 295 at New Cathedral Cemetery in Baltimore.

- Joseph R. Gonce ID 2639 (born about 1850). Joseph died before summer 1850 and is buried in the Sullivan-Gonce plot Section T – Lot 295 at New Cathedral Cemetery in Baltimore.

- Mary E. Gonce ID 2610, (15 September 1852 – November 1909). I've found no record of any marriage.

- Benny M. Gonce ID 2974 (born about 1854). Benny died as a child and is buried in the Sullivan-Gonce plot Section T – Lot 295 at New Cathedral Cemetery in Baltimore.

- Emma Gonce ID 3596 (born about 1855 and died between 1861 and 1871). Emma is buried in the Sullivan-Gonce plot Section T – Lot 295 at New Cathedral Cemetery in Baltimore.

- William Henry Gonce ID 32, our direct ancestor, will be discussed in more detail below.

- Thomas S. Gonce ID 1579 (born 15 April 1859, died 1931) and his wife Agnes ID 2284 had at least five children:

  William Howard Gonce ID 2285, born 25 June 1886, and his wife Elsie Sudsburg ID 2286, had at least four children.

---

[251] There are several other Gonces named William Henry, so the "H." here likely represents Henry as well, but I have no record stating that explicitly. There is also a William Howard Gonce in the same line (see below).

[252] The order of birth of the children James F., Joseph R., Benny M., and Emma is uncertain, but the years of birth are probably close. This is the order in which they are listed in the New Cathedral Cemetery records (see page 185).

Rae O. Gonce [ID 2291], was born in 1890; I have located no information about her.

Howard Thomas Gonce [ID 2292], born 28 March 1892, married twice: first to Sarah E. Younghein [ID 2768] and second to Anna [ID 3290]. It doesn't appear that he had any children from either marriage.

Mary E. Gonce [ID 2293] was born in 1896; I have located no information about her.

Albert E. Gonce [ID 2294] was born in 1903; I have located no information about him.

Thomas S. Gonce and his wife Agnes are buried in Holy Redeemer Cemetery in Baltimore.

- Louis A. Gonce [ID 1580], born 3 October 1866, and his wife Mary E. [ID2280] had at least six children:

    Catherine M. Gonce [ID 2281], known as Katie, was born 5 May 1891; I have located no information about her.

    Edith Gonce [ID 2282] was born November 1893; I have located no information about her.

    Louis Augustus Gonce [ID 2283], born 2 February 1896, and his wife Pauline [ID 2727] had at least four children. Louis Augustus has the distinction of being counted twice in the 1900 Census since he was a patient at Johns Hopkins Hospital when the census was taken there.

    Ellen Gonce [ID 2734], born about 1899, married Frank Benny [ID 2735]; they had no children that I'm aware of.

    Walter E. Gonce [ID 2732] was born about 1904; I have located no information about him.

    Carl E. Gonce [ID 2733] was born 26 May 1911 and died on 10 August 1992; I have located no information about him.

- Catherine A. Gonce [ID 1581], known as Kate, was born 15 September 1868 and died in late May of 1941. She and her husband John T. Lindsay [ID 2626] had one daughter, Mary, born in October of 1893.

6th Generation: William Henry Gonce & Alice Elizabeth Clautice

My second great-grandmother Laura Ann Farring & Our Farring Ancestors

The Farring surname[253] is most often associated with the many Irish, Scottish and English immigrants who came to this country in the eighteenth and nineteenth centuries, but our own Farring ancestors originated in Hesse, Germany.

---

[253] Some records for our Farring ancestors appear with the names Farrow, Farrel, and other variants, but comparison of name sequences, dates, and the like can be used to determine their connection to our lineage.

My 4th great-grandfather John B. Farring ID 4648 was born sometime between 1766 and 1784²⁵⁴, and most likely between 1772 and 1776. Because the same census tells us that John's oldest son was born in the 1785 to 1794 range, and because his second son Augustus ID 3514, included in the 1795 to 1800 range, was born in 1795, we can be reasonably certain that the oldest son was born closer to 1794 than 1785. It follows, therefore, that John was probably born about twenty years earlier, and that his year of birth was likely close to 1774.

John likely married his wife Eliza ID 4665 in about 1793. I've located no information to suggest when John and Eliza first came to this country, although it seems clear that at least their first two sons accompanied them. Unless there were several other children who didn't survive long enough to be recorded anywhere, the spacing of the children we know of suggests that he may have arrived in the United States in the last few years of the eighteenth century, shortly after the American Revolutionary War.

Because of his origin in Hesse, it is tempting, of course, to wonder if John may have been one of the many Hessian soldiers who remained in this country after the Revolutionary War or the War of 1812²⁵⁵, but the few dates we can establish don't support this and, in any case, names of most of the Hessian troops are seemingly well documented, and there seem to be no Farrings among them.

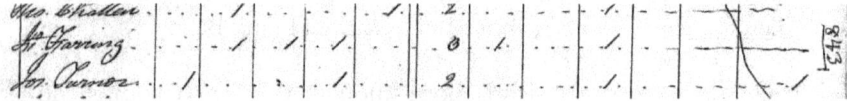

1810 United States Census Listing for "Jno. Farring" in Kent County, MD	
1810 Census counts	Comments (my assumptions)
1 Free White Male, age 26-44:	born 1765-1784 – John B. Farring ID 4648 **Our Direct Ancestor**
1 Free White Female, age 26-44:	born 1765-1784 – John's wife Eliza ID 4665 **Our Direct Ancestor**
1 Free White Male, age 16-26:	born 1785-1794 – John Farring ID 4738
1 Free White Male, age 10-15:	born 1795-1800 – Augustus H. Farring ID 3514 **Our Direct Ancestor**
1 Free White Female, age 10-15:	born 1795-1800 – Unidentified Daughter
2 Free White Females, age <10:	born 1801-1810 – Two Unidentified Daughters
1 Free White Female, age <10:	born 1801-1810 – Susan Farring ID 4711

---

²⁵⁴ His year of birth can only be documented by his being part of the 1765-1784 age bracket in the 1810 U.S. Census (NARC microfilm Series m252, Roll 14, Page 874), taken in Kent County, Maryland, where his neighbors included two Comegys households (George and N.) distantly related to our ancestors. The line for John Farring is transcribed with my interpretation above.

²⁵⁵ At the time, it was not at all unusual for the families of military personnel to accompany them on assignments, even when there was fighting involved.

John and his wife lived in Kent County, Maryland at least through 1810, but likely relocated to Baltimore prior to their son Augustus' 1818 marriage there. Eliza died in Baltimore on 27 August 1839[256], and her husband John passed away very shortly thereafter, on 6 November 1839.

Children and Grandchildren of John & Eliza Farring

My 4th great-grandparents John and Eliza had at least six children:

- John Farring [ID 4738], born between 1785 and 1794, most likely toward the upper end of that 1810 census range. John married a woman named Mary E. [ID 4737], but I haven't located any children. John died on 21 December 1842, and Mary passed away on 23 January 1847.
- Augustus H. Farring [ID 3514] was born in 1795 in Hesse, Germany. Augustus is our direct ancestor, and is discussed below.
- An unidentified female, born between 1795 and 1800.
- Two unidentified females, born between 1801 and 1810.
- Susan Farring [ID 4711], also born between 1801 and 1810. Susan eventually married Daniel Lee [ID 4712], a bricklayer, on 28 August 1836 in Baltimore. Daniel and Susan had at least five children:

  James Lee, born in about 1841.
  Mary I Lee, born in about 1843.
  Susan A Lee, born in about 1845.
  Caroline E Lee, born in about 1848.
  Amanda Lee, born in 1850.

Augustus H. Farring & Ellen Clouse

My 3rd great-grandfather Augustus H. Farring [ID 3514] was born in 1795 in Hesse, Germany, and was a saddler and harness maker by trade.

At some point between the 1810 census, when he was living with his parents in Kent County, and his 1818 marriage, Augustus moved to Baltimore.

I have been unable to locate any history for Ellen Clouse [ID 3515], but she was born in about 1797[257]. She and Augustus were married on 8 December 1818 in Baltimore, Maryland[258].

---

[256] Baltimore Sun; 30 August 1839.. Index to Marriages and Deaths in the Baltimore Sun 1837-1850, page 188; Thomas L. Hollowak, Compiler; Genealogical Publishing Co., Inc., 1978; ISBN: 0-8063-0796-X. [S66, p188]

[257] Based on the 1860 U.S. Census; National Archives Microfilm Series m653, Roll 461, Page 461

[258] Maryland Marriages 1655-1850, Jordan Dodd, Liahona Research, compiler. [S56]

Augustus eventually applied for naturalization when he was about 40 years old, and this was granted on 25 July 1837[259] by the U.S. District Court in Baltimore, Maryland.

Based on census records, Ellen died at some point between 1860 and 1870, and Augustus died between 1870 and 1880, but I haven't located any specific records for either of them, nor have I located their graves.

Children and Grandchildren of Augustus H. Farring & Ellen Clouse

Augustus and his wife Hellen (also listed as Ellen) [ID 3515], had seven children that I've been able to document to some degree:

- Lewis H. Farring [ID 4701], born about 1822, who married a woman named Mary [ID 4702] (born about 1827); they had at least three children:

  Lewis H. Farring [ID 4703], who was born in about 1849.
  Edward Farring [ID 4728], was born on 5 November 1847, and died the following day.
  Elizabeth E. Farring [ID 3816], born about 1852.

- Catherine A. Farring [ID 4709], born in about 1828. Catherine married Henry Herring, Jr. [ID 4713] on 15 January 1840[260]. Catherine and Henry had at least six children:

  Catherine L. Herring, year of birth unknown, who died on 5 June 1847. (also see the death date for George H. Herring below).
  George A. Herring, year of birth unknown, who died on 21 September 1846.
  William E. Herring, born in about 1844.
  Emily N. Herring, born in about 1846
  George H. Herring, year of birth unknown, but likely 1847 based on the entry for George A. Herring above. George H. Herring died on 22 July 1847.
  Mellzina Herring, born in about 1848. The name seems unusual, but that is how it is listed on the 1850 census[261].

- Mary E. Farring [ID 4706], born about 1830, who later married William H. Elliott [ID 4707], with whom she had at least six children:

  William H. Elliott, born about 1847.
  Robert O. Elliott, born about 1850.
  Augustus Elliott, born about 1851.
  Elizabeth Elliott, born about 1852.

---

[259] TS#5, Folio 331-332, which can be found on National Archives Microfilm Series m1168, roll 5.

[260] Baltimore Sun; 20 January 1840. August. Index to Marriages and Deaths in the Baltimore Sun 1837-1850, page 270; Thomas L. Hollowak, Compiler; Genealogical Publishing Co., Inc., 1978; ISBN: 0-8063-0796-X.

[261] National Archives Microfilm Series m432, Roll 282, Page 378b.

Mary Elliott, born about 1854.
Emily (known as Emma) Elliott, born about 1856.

- Rosetta E. (Rose) Farring [ID 4710], born in about 1828. Rose married William A. Thompson [ID 4714] on 8 July 1845[262]. Rose and William had at least three children:

  William A. Thompson, born in about 1847
  Mary E. Thompson, year of birth unknown but presumably between 1846 and 1849, died on 20 February 1849[263].
  Hester A. Thompson, born in 1850.

- An unidentified male, born between 1836 and 1840.

- Laura Ann Farring [ID 2328] was born in about 1839 in Baltimore, Maryland. Laura is our direct ancestor, and is discussed below.

- Emily Jane Farring [ID 3815], born in June 1841. Emily, known as Emma, never married, and eventually moved in with her brother-in-law, my 2nd great-grandfather John W. Clautice [ID 2322], after the death of her older sister Laura Ann[264].

Segment of 1860 Census showing August Farring and his family.[265]
Out ancestor Laura Ann was already married to John W. Clautice by this time.

---

[262] Baltimore Sun; 11 July 1845. Index to Marriages and Deaths in the Baltimore Sun 1837-1850, page 597; Thomas L. Hollowak, Compiler; Genealogical Publishing Co., Inc., 1978; ISBN: 0-8063-0796-X.

[263] Baltimore Sun; 22 February 1849. Index to Marriages and Deaths in the Baltimore Sun 1837-1850, page 596; Thomas L. Hollowak, Compiler; Genealogical Publishing Co., Inc., 1978; ISBN: 0-8063-0796-X.

[264] 1900 U.S. Census; National Archives Microfilm Series t623, Roll 612, Page 103b.

[265] National Archives Series m653, Roll 461, Page 461.

1759 – 1983 History

My great-grandmother Alice Elizabeth Clautice & our Clautice Ancestors

What we know for certain about the Clautice family is spotty, although our direct lineage seems reasonably certain. One difficulty in locating records for the family is that the misspellings of Clautice in nineteenth century records are more imaginative than is usually the case. In the 1860 census[266], for instance, the name is spelled "Colts,"[267] and only a comparison of all the names, dates and the address confirms their identity. There is clear enough evidence, however, to be reasonably certain that our Clautice ancestors arrived in the United States shortly after the American Revolution.

John Peter & Anne Marie Clautice

My 4th great-grandfather John Peter Clautice ID 2330 was born in about 1768 in the Bas-Rhin region of Alsace, France. His wife Anne Marie ID 4647, whose surname is unknown, seems to have been born in about 1774. Although several sources suggest that John Peter, his wife Anne Marie, and their first two children were born in France, this isn't at all clear from extant records. Their oldest known son, Peter Clautice ID 2331, for example, lists his birthplace as "Maryland" on the 1870 census. There is also circumstantial evidence that John Peter may have been married twice, first to Anne Marie, and later to a woman named Elizabeth ID 4743, who is listed in the 1827 Baltimore Directory as a "widow." To date, however, I've been unable to locate any records that would clarify this.

Because of their oldest son's marriage in Baltimore in 1817, we know the family was in the United States at least by then.

Why the Clautice family left Alsace isn't known, but it should be noted that it was in 1787, after many years of increasing unrest, that the French Revolution began in earnest. Although this didn't affect Alsace or the provinces to the east of the Vosges mountain range immediately, the political changes and resulting scrambles for power meant that the results of the severe weather over several subsequent years (and that destroyed much of the crops in the area) was not addressed at all.

My 4th great-grandfather John Peter Clautice died on 12 June 1825 in Baltimore.

Children and grandchildren of John Peter & Anne Marie Clautice

John Peter, father of the first generation American Clautice family, was quite prolific, having fathered at least twelve children between 1796, when he was 28 years old, and 1816, when he was 46. These children are:

---

[266] National Archives Series m653, Roll 462, Page 602.

[267] In addition to Colts, other interesting variants I've encountered for this same family include Claudtice, Clantice, Caritice, Clotis, Caltis, Cloutier and Cloultic.

♦ Peter Clautice [ID 2331], born 26 November 1796, died after 1870. Peter, a blacksmith, married twice – first to Elizabeth Powell [ID 4708] on 22 November 1817 in Baltimore. They seem to have had only two children before Elizabeth's death, which circumstances suggest may have been during the birth of her daughter Elizabeth:

Peter Clautice [ID 4662], born in about 1819. Because a later son was given the same name, it seems likely that Peter died young, but I've found no record of him, including any death notice.

Elizabeth (Liza) Clautice [ID 4663], born in about 1820. This is possibly the Elizabeth Clautice who married George Derenberger on 29 September 1857, although she would have been about thirty-seven years old at the time.

John Peter and Anne Marie Clautice's son Peter's second marriage was to a woman named Mary who was born in about 1811 and died after 1880. Peter and Mary had ten children:

James W. Clautice [ID 2861], born between 1821 and 1825, died on 25 March 1844[268].

Catherine (Kate) Clautice [ID 4664], born about 1824, died presumably before 1860.

Peter Clautice [ID 2860], born about 1826, died on 21 March 1844.

Sarah F. Clautice [ID 2859], born between 1826 and 1830, died on 25 May 1841[269].

Joseph Clautice [ID 2393], born about 1835. Joseph was a Tinner and Can Maker. He registered for the Civil War draft in the June/July 1863 registration period when he gave his age as 28. As far as I could determine, however, he was never called to duty.

An unidentified female who was born between 1831 and 1835, and died before 1860.

Edwin D. Clautice [ID 2395], born in March 1842[270]. Edwin, a plumber, had at least five children with his wife Sarah [ID 4696]. Like his older brother Joseph, Edwin also registered for the Civil War draft, and appears just above his Joseph's on the register. For reasons I can't surmise, Edwin gave his age as 25 instead of his actual age of 21.

An unidentified female who was born between 1836 and 1840, died before 1860.

---

[268] Baltimore Sun; 27 March 1844, where it is explicitly stated that he is the son of Peter and Mary. Index to Marriages and Deaths in the Baltimore Sun 1837-1850, page 107; Thomas L. Hollowak, Compiler; Genealogical Publishing Co., Inc., 1978; ISBN: 0-8063-0796-X.

[269] Baltimore Sun; 28 May 1841, where it is explicitly stated that she is the daughter of Peter and Mary. Index to Marriages and Deaths in the Baltimore Sun 1837-1850, page 107; Thomas L. Hollowak, Compiler; Genealogical Publishing Co., Inc., 1978; ISBN: 0-8063-0796-X.

[270] There is an ancestral file entry (afn MP4T-L2) for an Edward Clautice, born in 1828, but that entry is erroneous. Based on the particulars (e.g. occupation of plumber), that Edward is actually this Edwin.

Elizabeth Clautice ID 2394, born about 1839.
Catherine (Kate) Clautice ID 2396, born about 1842.

- Catherine Clautice ID 4657, born 9 December 1798, died 16 December 1853.

- George Clautice ID 2333, born 3 July 1801, died 24 September 1885. George, a blacksmith, married Katherine Fitzgerald ID 4683; the couple had at least four children:
Mary E. Clautice ID 2397, born about 1830.
George Clautice ID 2398, born about 1832
Alexine Clautice ID 4684, born on 28 November 1833.
William Francis Clautice ID 2399, born on 11 November 1838.

- Anna Mary Clautice ID 4660 was born on 2 January 1803. Because there is a later child with the same name, it is assumed that this Anna Mary died before 1807, when the other was born.

- Elizabeth Clautice ID 4661, born 18 March 1805, died 29 October 1887

- John W. Clautice ID 2320, born about 1806, died before 1870 This, the first of two sequential ancestors named John W. Clautice, is our direct ancestor, and will be discussed below.

- Anna Mary (Ann) Clautice ID 2334, born 28 July 1807, died 5 August 1883

- Mary Clautice ID 2414, born about 1808.

- Joseph Clautice ID 2391, born about 1810, married a woman named Barbara ID 2392. Like his older brothers, he started as a wheelwright, but later in life became a tailor. Joseph and Barbara had at least five children:
Joseph Clautice Jr. ID 2403, born in about 1840, married Annie ID 2404, who was born in about 1846. The couple had at least two children, Austin G. Clautice ID 2409, born in about 1867, and Elmer Clautice ID 4715, born in about 1871.
Mary E. Clautice ID 2405, born in about 1847 -
Teresa (Minnie) Clautice ID 2406, born in about 1850 and married Thomas B. Bryson some time after 1880. Thomas apparently died sometime after their marriage and before 1910.
Laura Clautice ID 2407, born in about 1855 -
John Clautice ID 2408, born in about 1856, became a Cigar Maker.

- Frances Clautice ID 4659, born 23 June 1811

- William Clautice ID 4704, born 27 February 1814, died 11 November 1891, married a woman named Margaret ID 4705, who was born in about 1811. I haven't located any further information about either William or Margaret.

- Francis Clautice [ID 4658], born about 1816, married Sarah Richmond [ID 4694], a German born immigrant, with whom he had at least one child: Ann (Annie) Clautice [ID 4695], born in South Carolina in about 1842[271]. Ann married Cpt. G.W. Cunningham on 12 October 1860.

John W. Clautice & Elizabeth Goodwin

My 3rd great-grandfather John W. Clautice ID 2320 was born in the United States in about 1805, and became a wheelwright[272]. In about 1832, he married Elizabeth (also called Isabella) Goodwin ID 2321, who I suspect, but can't prove, was the daughter of Lloyd Goodwin ID 4656. Elizabeth was approximately ten years younger than John.

Page No. 355 9.

SCHEDULE 1.—Free Inhabitants in 8th Ward Baltimore City in the County of Baltimore State of Maryland enumerated by me, on the 12 day of July 1860. ________ Ass't Marshal.

Post Office Baltimore City.

	Dwelling-houses numbered in the order of visitation.	Families numbered in the order of visitation.	The name of every person whose usual place of abode on the first day of June, 1860, was in this family.	Age.	Sex.	Color, White, black, or mulatto.	Profession, Occupation, or Trade of each person, male and female, over 15 years of age.	Value of Real Estate.	Value of Personal Estate.	Place of Birth, Naming the State, Territory, or Country.	Married within the year.	Attended School within the year.	Persons over 20 y'rs of age who cannot read & write.	Whether deaf and dumb, blind, insane, idiotic, pauper, or convict.	
	1	2	3	4	5	6	7	8	9	10	11	12	13	14	
			Mary [illegible]	46	f					"					
4	2111	2362	John Clautice	55	m		Wheel Wright		250	Md					4
5			Isabella "	45	f					"					5
6			John "	26	m		Huckster			"					6
7			Henry "	24	m		Printer			"					7
8			George "	22	m		Police Officer			"					8
9			Catherine "	20	f					"					9
10			Frances "	17	m		Huckster			"					10
11			Sarah "	15	f					"					11

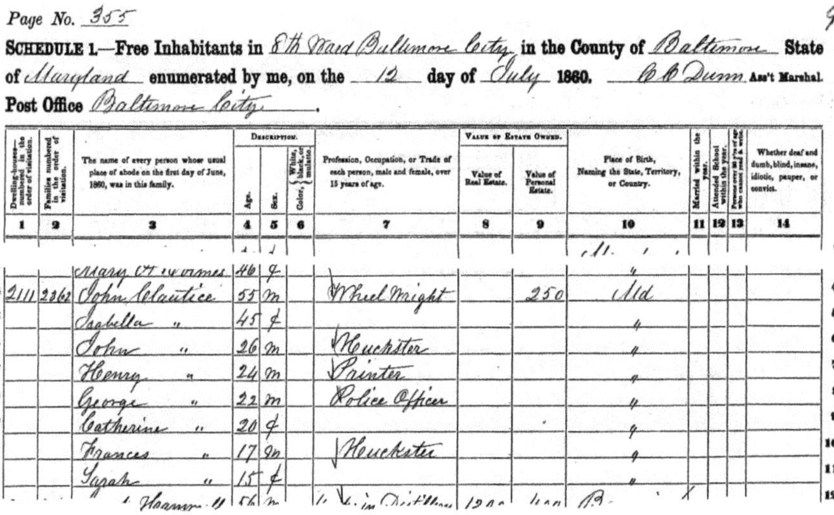

Segment of 1860 Census showing 3rd great-grandfather John W. Clautice and his family [273].

The last record I've located in which John appears was the 1860 census, shown above, where he and my 3rd great-grandmother were living in Baltimore's 8th ward with the youngest five of their six children. Note that, although Elizabeth is called Isabella (line 5), her age, and the names and ages of her children, make it clear that this is our family. John does not appear in the 1870 census, so he likely died between late 1860 and then.

271 This suggests that Francis and Sarah spent some time in that state, but they had returned to Baltimore and appear there in the 1850 census. Ann was married in Maryland.

272 A wheelwright was someone who made or repaired wooden wheels used on wagons and machinery.

273 National Archives Microfilm Series m653, Roll 462, Page 355.

In the 1870 census[274], Elizabeth, listed as age 60, was living with her sister-in-law Ann ID 2334, who was listed as the head of household. In the following census, Elizabeth was living with her youngest daughter Sarah Barlow's family on Aisquith Street in Baltimore in 1880[275], listing her age as 65. I've found no later records to indicate when she died.

Children and grandchildren of John W. Clautice & Elizabeth Goodwin

My 3rd great-grandparents John and Elizabeth had at least six children:

- John W. Clautice, Jr. ID 2322, my 2nd great-grandfather and our direct ancestor, was born in about 1833, and is discussed below.

- Henry C. Clautice ID 2323 was born sometime between 1832 and 1836, probably in 1834, and married Magdalena Burnham ID 2329, daughter of John F. and Susan Burnham. John, a ship rigger, was born in about 1809 and his wife Susan was born in 1805. Henry worked as both a printer and blacksmith during his life. He and Madeline (as she was often referred to) had at least seven children:

  John F. Clautice ID 2335, born in February 1859.
  Susan M. Clautice ID 2336, born about 1860.
  Anna (Annie) Clautice ID 2337, born about 1867.
  Maggie Clautice ID 2338, born about 1869.
  Ella Clautice ID 2339, born about 1872, married and had at least one daughter Annie Balilke (possibly Bahlke) ID 2402, who was born about 1892.
  Ada M. Clautice ID 2340, born about 1875.
  Harry Clautice ID 2341, born about 1879.

- George J. Clautice ID 2324 was born in about 1838, and died on 25 January 1928. George, a Baltimore City policeman, and his first wife Ellen Quinn ID 2342 had at least four sons:

  George Clautice ID 2410, was born in about 1859. George married a woman named Mary, with whom he had three children: Bertha Ellen ID 647, Sarah C. ID 4724, and Joseph L. ID 4725. Being great-grandchildren of George J and Ellen Clautice, they would normally not be mentioned here, but for the fact that Bertha Ellen Clautice also married George Eugene Gonce ID 151, my Grandfather Charles' oldest brother[276].
  John W. Clautice ID 2411, born about 1861.
  Frank Clautice ID 2412, born about 1865.

---

[274] National Archives Microfilm Series m593, Roll 580, Page 489.
[275] U.S. Census for 1880; Church of Latter Day Saints Microfilm 1254500, page 132.
[276] See George Eugene Gonce ID 151 in the section "Children and Grandchildren of William Henry Gonce & Alice Clautice" on page 107.

James Clautice ID 2413 was born in about 1868. His father's second marriage followed within a year of his birth, which might suggest that James and his mother both died in childbirth, but I've found nothing to confirm this.

The name of George's second wife was Mary L. ID 4689, who was born in April of 1851. George and Mary seem to have had only one child:

James B. Clautice ID 4729, born in about 1870. The fact that he was given the name James, lends circumstantial support to the idea that his father's wife Ellen may have died in some manner related to childbirth with the earlier James.

♦ Catherine Clautice ID 2325 was born in about 1840. I've found no further information about her.

♦ Francis (Frank) Clautice ID 2326 lived from May 1843 to 3 March 1932 and never married; he later lived with my great-grandparents William Henry Gonce and Alice Elizabeth Clautice, who was his niece. Like his older brother John, Frank was a huckster by trade.

♦ Sarah Clautice ID 2327 was born in 1845. Sarah married James Barlow and had at least three children:

Katie C. Barlow ID 4691, born about 1869.
Thomas H. Barlow ID 4692, born about 1871.
Laura E. Barlow ID 4693, born about 1873.

John W. Clautice & Laura Ann Farring

As mentioned above, my 2nd great-grandfather John W. Clautice, Jr., a wagon driver and huckster by trade[277], was probably born in about 1833, although I have been unable to locate any record of his birth. The only record I've located that actually gives any birth date for him is the 1900 census[278], which lists him as a 62 year old widower, and lists his month and year of birth as June 1843. Aside from being internally inconsistent (a 62 year old would have been born in 1838), neither of these numbers are consistent with his age as reported on other censuses[279]. John married Laura Ann Farring ID 2328 on 22 October 1854[280] in Baltimore. Although John and his brothers were of the right age to have served in the Civil War, I found no records suggesting that any of them did.

---

[277] National Archives Series m653, Roll 462, Page 355. Footnote Error: Reference source not found on page 82 defines "Huckster."
[278] National Archives Microfilm Series t623, roll 612, page 103b.
[279] He was reported as being age 17 in 1850, age 26 in 1860, and age 48 in 1880.
[280] Baltimore Sun; 25 October 1854. Index to Marriages and Deaths in the Baltimore Sun 1851-1860, page 18; Thomas L. Hollowak, Compiler; Genealogical Publishing Co., Inc., 1978; ISBN: 0-8063-0827-3.

1759 – 1983 History

Segment of 1870 Census showing my 2nd great-grandfather John W. "Clautic" and his family [281].

On 21 September 1883, Laura died at the relatively young age of 44, but none of the records I've been able to locate provide any details. A transcription of her obituary from the Baltimore Sun is shown on the right.

After Laura's death, her younger sister Emma (Emily Jane) Farring [ID 3815] moved in with John[282].

John died on 26 April 1907 at age 74, and was buried in Holy Cross Cemetery[283], although all of the remains there were moved in 1969 to Woodlawn Cemetery, where they were placed in a large lot[284] called "The Holy Cross Section."

Obituary of Laura Ann Farring Clautice

CLAUTICE - On the morning of 21st September, ____, LAURA A. aged 44 years, wife of John W. Clautice and fourth daughter of the late Augustus and Ellen Farring. May she rest in peace.

"None knew her but to love her,
None named her but to praise."

The relatives and friends of the family are respectfully invited to attend the funeral, from her late residence, Boundary avenue, first house east of Harford avenue, tomorrow (Sunday) afternoon at half-past one o'clock.

The Baltimore Sun: 22 SEP 1883

---

[281] National Archives Microfilm Series m593, Roll 575, Page 362a.

[282] See the 1900 U.S. Census, National Archives Series m623, Roll 612, Page 103b.

[283] This was the Catholic cemetery at North Avenue and Broadway in Baltimore, first opened in 1863, and used by St. Patrick, St. Ignatius and St. John the Evangelist parishes. There is another Holy Cross cemetery that was associated with the German community in Baltimore, but these are unrelated.

[284] The Archdiocese of Baltimore's web Page (http://www.stmarys.edu/archives/closed_cemeteries.pdf) indicates that this was a mass burial, with no individual graves or markers.

Children of John W. Clautice & Laura Ann Farring

As far as I could determine, John and Ann (Laura) Clautice had only two children:

- Alice Elizabeth Clautice ID 33, born on Sunday 2 August 1857, was my great-grandmother and is discussed below.

- George Lyman[285] Clautice ID 2400, born in about 1859. George married a woman from Pennsylvania called Sadie ID 4716, and they had at least five children:

  William E. Clautice ID 4717, born about 1900. William married a woman named Mary, but I haven't pursued this line any further.
  Laura V. Clautice ID 4718, born about 1902.
  Earl L. Clautice ID 4719, born about 1904.
  Albert H. Clautice ID 4720, born about 1908.
  Leroy M. Clautice ID 4721, born about 1913.

William Henry Gonce & Alice Elizabeth Clautice

By the time of the 1880 Census, my great-grandfather William Henry Gonce ID 32, born 15 January 1857, had already married[286] Alice Clautice and the two of them were living with William's parents (my 2nd great-grandparents) John and Catharine Gonce at 60 Etting Street[287]. This address, shown in the map to the right, was renumbered in 1887 to 1228 Etting Street.

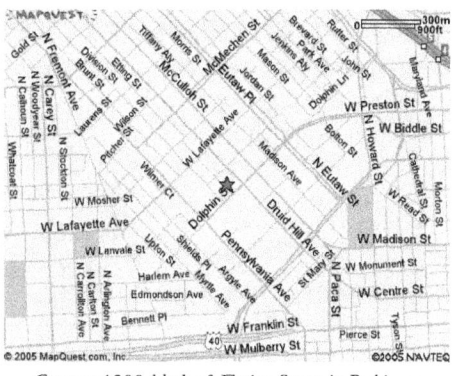

Current 1200 block of Etting Street in Baltimore

---

[285] Lyman is a relatively unusual name that also appears as a middle name in the next generation of the Gonce family. See, for instance, Edward Lyman Gonce in the section "Children and Grandchildren of William Henry Gonce & Alice Clautice" beginning on page 107. There may likely be some meaning there, but it isn't apparent to me.

[286] William and Alice seem to have been married sometime in 1877, but I was unable to confirm this.

[287] This is important to note and clarify, since the 1880 census makes it appear as if Alice Gonce is actually John and Catherine's daughter, rather than their daughter-in-law. See Church of Latter Day Saints Series mdt9, Roll 505, Page 480 (there is a copy of this census sheet on page 84)

William Henry Gonce

Alice Elizabeth Clautice

William and Alice's first child, George E. Gonce [ID 151], was born on 22 January 1879, but he was not listed on the 1880[288] census for some reason (another mystery to be solved). Between then and 1900, William and Alice had eight more children, all of whom are listed on page 107.

Segment from 1900 U.S. Census page showing William and Alice Gonce and their family of eleven. My grandfather Charles Gonce was four years old and Alice's uncle Frank was living with them as well.

---

[288] See an image of the relevant 1880 census sheet on page 84..

A segment from the 1900 U.S. Census[289] pictured above shows the family, along with Frank Clautice, Alice's uncle, who was then living with them. In 1880, William and his younger brother Thomas were both plumbers, but some time before 1900, William Gonce began working for the railroad and was a baggage agent/handler by the time of the census.

His oldest son George was working as an electrician by this time. One has to suspect from the number of errors in birth dates that "Uncle Frank" may have been the respondent when this census was taken. The birth dates were incorrect for Laura (1882 vs. 1883), William Henry Jr. (1886 vs. 1887), John (May vs. April), my grandfather Charles (April vs. May), and Raymond (1898 vs. 1900).

from page 713 of the 1906 Baltimore City Directory

Many of the Gonces can be seen on page 713 of the 1906 Baltimore City Directory shown above – my great-grandfather [ID 32] is the second of the "Gonce, Wm H." listings, and his recently widowed mother Catherine can also be seen as the first entry.[290]

By 1910, William had become the Stable Master for a local transfer company[291].

By 1920, the local delivery and transfer aspects of the transportation industry were in

An Aside:

In 1904, in the same general time frame during which William Henry moved from the railroad to the cartage business, only 700 heavy trucks were built in the United States. That number had grown to 1000 annually by 1907, 6000 by 1910, and 25,000 by 1914.

During and after World War I, several advances were made: pneumatic tires replaced the previously common full rubber versions. Electric starters, power brakes, 4, 6, and 8 cylinder engines, closed cabs, and electric lighting followed. The first modern semi-trailer trucks also appeared. Touring car builders such as Ford and Renault entered the heavy truck market.

the midst of a rapid and irreversible shift from the horse to the internal combustion engine. This would shortly have a negative impact on my great-

---

[289] National Archives Series t623, Roll 607, Page 3b.

[290] The other entries are for George E. Gonce [ID 2609], his oldest brother; John Thomas Gonce [ID 3458], George's son; his youngest brother Louis A. Gonce [ID 1580]; his younger brother Thomas S. Gonce [ID 1579]; his nephew William Howard Gonce [ID 2285] (Thomas' son). Following my 2nd great-grandfather in the list is his cousin (another of George's sons) William Henry Gonce [ID 2982].

[291] National Archives Series t624, Roll 551, Page 128b. A Transfer Company moves long-haul freight between railroad docks and local trucking company terminals for local pickup and delivery. During this period, very few motorized vehicles were in use for such operations because they didn't yet have the power and hauling capacity of horse drawn wagons. The family was then living at 117 Holden Avenue.

grandfather William's employment, but provide a ground-floor opportunity for his son (and my grandfather) Charles.

My great-grandmother Alice, not yet 55, died on 4 July 1912 of a carcinoma of the stomach (see her death certificate on page 106). She was buried in lot P-352 of Holy Redeemer Cemetery (see page 105). Following Alice's death, William moved in with his son Edward and daughter-in-law Mary Ruth.

The 1920 Census[292] shows that William was still a stable foreman, and still living with Edward and Mary Ruth at 203 Oakland Avenue; by this time, Edward and Ruth had four children.

Lantern used by William Henry Gonce during his late-life stint at the Railroad

During the 1920s, Edward's family continued to grow. William's daughter Grace, who had married Alfred P. Wills, an English Immigrant who had arrived in 1889[293], became a widow. Because of these circumstances, William moved in with Grace, and lived with her for the remainder of his life.

At the time of the 1930 census, he was still living with his daughter Grace at 2412 Arlington Avenue; by this time, he was 73 years old. Horse transportation had virtually disappeared and, with it, his job, but he found other employment as a corporate messenger.

William eventually worked for the railroad again – as a signalman. Various family members of my mother's generation remember him wearing his railroad uniform to and from work[294]. Two of his signal lanterns are still in the family. One is displayed in the home of one of his grandson's widow. The other, shown in the illustration to the left, is in the home of his great-granddaughter, whose daughter kindly provided me with this picture.

---

[292] National Archives Series t625, Roll 668, Page 7a
[293] National Archives Series t626, Roll 869, Page 85; Alfred became a naturalized citizen in 1894.
[294] Coincidentally, according to the 1870 U.S. Census (NARC Series m593 Roll 575 Page 277), William Gantz (born in 1845 in Pennsylvania, and not a relative of ours) had earlier worked in Baltimore as a railroad conductor. Care should be taken when reviewing railroad records to avoid confusing the two.

OUR GONCE ANCESTORS

Grave Markers for William Henry and Alice Gonce

William Henry Gonce, Sr. passed away on Thursday 27 June 1935 at age 78, and was buried next to his wife Alice in Holy Redeemer Cemetery. Their headstones (by the road that parallels Moravia Avenue) are shown on the left.

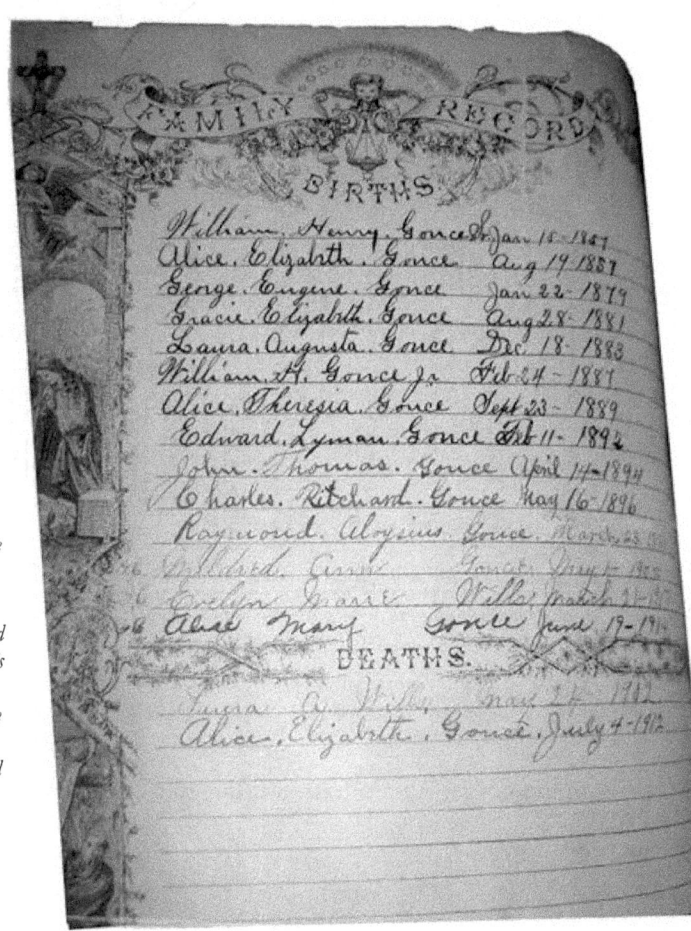

Page from William Henry Gonce's Bible showing his family.

Note that the three births after Raymond are William Henry's grandchildren, and the deaths listed here are his daughter Laura Augusta and his wife Alice.

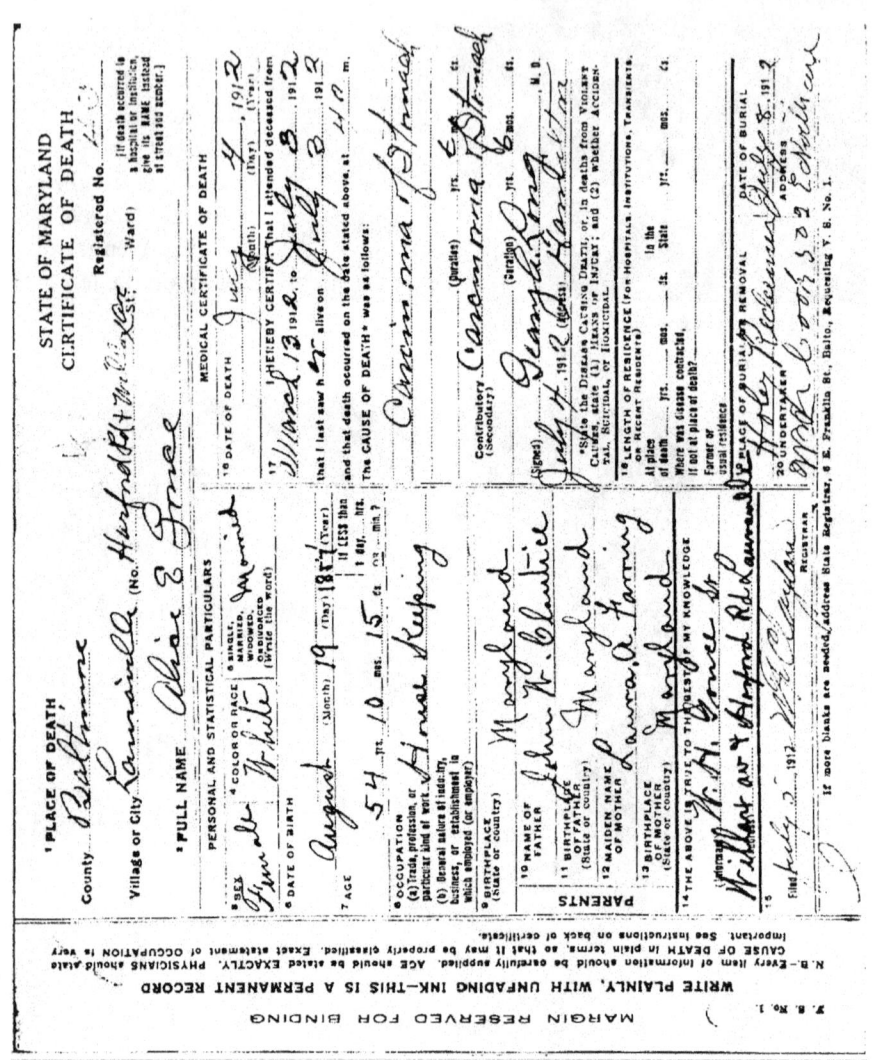

Death Certificate of Alice Elizabeth Clautice Gonce

My great-grandmother Alice's death was due to a carcinoma of the stomach.

Children and Grandchildren of William Henry Gonce & Alice Clautice

The births of each of William Henry's children, along with three of his grandchildren, are recorded in his bible. An image of the "Births" page of this bible is provided on the facing page.

- George Eugene Gonce [ID 151], born 22 January 1879, and his wife Bertha Ellen Clautice[295] [ID 647] had two daughters, neither of whom married:

    Beatrice W. Gonce [ID 700], born 2 October 1914; Beatrice never married.

    Mildred Gonce [ID 701], born 23 April 1920; Mildred never married.

- Grace Elizabeth Gonce [ID 152] (August 1881 – 6 April 1962) married her brother-in-law Alfred P. Wills [ID 146] on 17 January 1906 (after the death of his wife, Grace's younger sister Laura); their children are:

    Evelyn Marie Wills [ID 702], born 21 March 1907, married Thompson A. Wallace [ID 576] and had one son, Austin Wallace [ID 705].

    W. A. Geary Wills [ID 575], (1910 – 18 February 1990), married Catherine [ID 574], but had no children as far as I can determine.

    Paul Melvin Wills [ID 704], born about 1914; I have located no information about him.

- Laura Augusta Gonce [ID 154], born 18 December 1883, died during childbirth on 24 May 1902 with her firstborn; her husband Alfred P. Wills [ID 146] then married her older sister Grace.

- William Henry Gonce, Jr. [ID 697] (24 February 1887 – 1954), known as "Willie," was a machinist. He and his wife Caroline (known as Carrie) Enis [ID 646] had five children:

    Bernard A. Gonce [ID 1311] (1911 – May 1960) and his wife Clara [ID 3310] had no children that I am aware of.

    Alice Mary Gonce [ID 1312], born 19 June 1914, married Charles Murphy [ID 2526] and had two sons, Charles and Craig.

    Charles Joseph Gonce [ID 1313], called Buck, was born on 23 April 1918. Buck had one son with his first wife Nancy [ID 2419], and nine children with his second wife Marjorie [ID 2530]. Buck died on 6 August 1997.

    Regina M. Gonce [ID 1314] was born about 1923; Regina never married.

    Dorothy E. Gonce [ID 1315], was born about 1926 and never married.

---

[295] Bertha is the daughter of John F. Clautice [ID 2335], my great-grandmother's first cousin. See the section "Children and grandchildren of John W. Clautice & Elizabeth Goodwin" on page 98.

- Alice Theresa Gonce ID 153 (23 September 1889 – June 1973) married George Louis Gordon ID 147, and had three children:

    Alvin Eugene Gordon ID 253 (2 November 1918 – 1 February 1980) married Marian Katherine Wyatt ID 2253 and had five children.

    Mary Eileen (Eileen) Gordon ID 252 (31 October 1923 – 23 October 2007) had one child with George Herak ID 2250. After George's death during World War II, she married Donald Francis Gumaer ID 265 and had five more children.

Alice Theresa Gonce Gordon

    Alice Juanita Gordon ID 2252 was born 28 August 1932 and married Michael Linehan ID 2254. Alice and Michael had four children.

    Alice and her husband George moved to Spokane, and this branch of the family now lives in the northwestern United States, mostly in the state of Washington.

- Edward Lyman Gonce ID 155 (11 February 1892 – 23 May 1977) married Mary Ruth O'Donnell ID 643 and, before Ruth's death, had eight children.

    Thomas Norman (Norman) Gonce ID 648, was born about 1912.

    Dorothy Gonce ID 649 was born in about 1916.

    Edward Lyman Gonce ID 34 was born in July of 1918 and died about a month after birth.

    Lyman N. Gonce ID 3450 was born 24 October 1919.

    Edward G. Gonce ID 159 was born about 1922 and married Mary ID 160; I have located no information about Edward and Mary.

    Vernon Gonce ID 35 was stillborn on 3 October 1925.

    William Carl Gonce ID 156 was married with one son.

    Mildred Gonce ID 158 was born after 1930; she married John H. Chester ID 157.

    Edward Lyman Gonce remarried another woman named Ruth ID 644, but they had no children that I'm aware of.

- John Thomas Gonce ID 150 (14 April 1894 – 27 June 1978) and his wife Anna ID 645 had two children:

    Andrew I. Gonce ID 654 was born about 1917; I have located no information about him.

Margaret M. Gonce ^{ID 653}, born about 1923, married Karl Schwarz ^{ID 652} and had one daughter.

- Charles Richard Gonce ^{ID 43}, my maternal grandfather and our direct ancestor, will be discussed in more detail below.
- Raymond Aloysius Gonce ^{ID 36} (23 March 1898 – 15 November 1968) married Edna I. Sparr ^{ID 31} and had two daughters:

  Geraldine Gonce ^{ID 706}, born about 1919

  Beatrice Gonce ^{ID 650}, born after 1930

There is another child's birth recorded in William Henry Gonce's bible, that of Mildred Ann Gonce, born on 1 May 1905. Because of her year of birth, she is almost certainly a grandchild, but I have found no other records concerning her. Her date of birth and surname would suggest that she is most likely the first child of William Henry Gonce, Jr., and that she died before the 1910 census, but this isn't certain.

7th Generation: Charles Richard Gonce & Anna Gertrude Hulshoff

My great-grandmother Mary Regina Kerchner & Our Kerchner Ancestors

The history of the Kerchner family can be found in two books written by Fr. Frank Kunkel, one focused on the Kerns and Kunkels [296], and another on the Kerns and Kerchners [297]. This history will not therefore be repeated in any detail here, but the following will provide a brief summary.

My 6th great-grandparents Johannes Michael Kerchner ^{ID 1178}, born 15 September 1709, and his wife Gertrude Groos ^{ID 1179}, born 5 August 1717, are the earliest Kerchner ancestors I have identified.

Their son was my 5th great-grandfather Francis Caspar Kerchner ^{ID 107}, born 2 January 1750, and his wife Anna Katherina Rauch ^{ID 1169}, daughter of Andreas Rauch ^{ID 1174} and Margaret Hoskin ^{ID 1175}.

Caspar and Anna's son, my 4th great-grandfather Paul Kerchner ^{ID 82} (19 January 1782 – 14 September 1856) married Maria Rosina Mussig ^{ID 83} (12 July 1778 – 16 April 1853) on 16 February 1802 in Baden Germany.

Paul and Rosina's son, my 3rd great-grandfather Michael Anthony Kerchner ^{ID 100} (10 January 1804 – 13 March 1857) married Anna Maria Kern ^{ID 91} (21 January 1806 – 5 May 1879) on 12 February 1828 in Freudenberg, Duchy of

---

[296] "John Nepomucene Kunkel and his wife Mary Rosina Kerchner - A Short Sketch of their Lives," self-published in 1939 by Rev. Frank Kunkel, SS (S7). I have reproduced this document along with commentary, an index, cross reference to my own data set, and corrections, in an appendix to the book "Our Hulshoff and Kerchner Ancestors."

[297] "John Dominic Kern and Margaret Vaeth Kern - A Family Record" self-published 13 August 1941 by Rev. Frank Kunkel, SS (S13). This document is also reproduced as an appendix to the book "Our Hulshoff and Kerchner Ancestors."

Baden, Germany. Michael was the first of the Kerchners to bring his family to the United States; details of this are given in the appendix to "Our Hulshoff and Kerchner Ancestors" mentioned earlier.

Although his two oldest brothers came to this country with their parents, my 2nd great-grandfather Ferdinand Kerchner [ID 38] (11 July 1835 - 1 June 1918) was born in the United States. He married Anna B. Linnenkemper [ID 39] (21 January 1839 - 26 November 1914) just before the Civil War. Their daughter Mary Regina (Jennie) Kerchner [ID 8] (20 April 1873 - 21 April 1940) is discussed below.

Anna Gertrude Hulshoff & Her Family

I have discussed the history of the Hulshoff family in great detail in a separate book[298], so detailed information on the Hulshoff family will not be repeated here.

My grandmother Anna Gertrude Hulshoff [ID 44], born on Wednesday September 30, 1896, was the first of eight children of Herman [ID 7] and Jennie (Mary Regina) Kerchner Hulshoff [ID 8]. Grandmom was known as "Gert" by her family.

Mary Regina (Jennie) Kerchner

Some time in 1939, Jennie suffered a serious stroke and was confined to her bed. It is said that Herman sat by her bedside almost constantly, although she was apparently uncommunicative.

Herman passed away on the 19th of February in 1940 at age 69; shortly afterwards, on the 21st of April, Jennie, then 67 years old, died as well.

Herman and Jennie (Kerchner) Hulshoff at their home at 602 Springhill Terrace (later Springfield Avenue) in Baltimore.

Herman and Jennie were both buried in the Hulshoff lot[299] at Holy Redeemer Cemetery.

---

[298] The aforementioned "Our Hulshoff and Kerchner Ancestors," covering our Hulshoff ancestors from 1665 into the twentieth century.

[299] Plot C-111. The tall monument, located at one of the highest points in the cemetery, very near Belair Road, can be seen from most other points in the cemetery.

Charles Gonce & Gertrude Hulshoff – The Great War (World War I)

As mentioned earlier, my grandfather Charles Gonce was born on Saturday May 16, 1896. Little is known about his childhood, but evidence suggests he was mechanically minded and became an automobile mechanic in his teens.

On 28 June 1914, when Granddad had just turned eighteen, Archduke Francis Ferdinand, the presumptive heir to the crown of the Austro-Hungarian Empire, was assassinated in Sarajevo. By 1916, the resulting "world war" (now known as World War I) had spread across Europe, involving England, Russia, and several other countries not at that time usually associated with Europe. There were a significant number of Americans participating as volunteers with the French and English forces in a variety of roles, but up until late 1916, the United States had limited its official participation to providing supplies and materiel to support the western allies.

This changed on 6 April 1917, when the United States declared war on Germany, and began preparing to send troops to Europe to support the Allies. The Selective Service Act of 1917 was passed, and a schedule for registration was published. On June 5th, Granddad and his older brother William Henry Gonce, Jr. registered for the draft in accordance with that law. Their remaining brothers registered later.

5 June 1917 World War I Draft Card for Charles Gonce

At the time the draft began, Charles was already working as an automobile mechanic for the Winton Auto Company on Charles Street in Baltimore. Charles was 21 at the time of his registration, and still living with his father at 4526 Arlington Avenue in the Lauraville section of Baltimore. He became engaged to Anna Gertrude Hulshoff around this time, but had to postpone the marriage because of his military service.

Charles was inducted into the army on 24 May 1918 right after his twenty-first birthday, and assigned as a Wagoner (possibly due to his experience as an automobile mechanic) to Company A of the 310th Machine Gun Battalion at Camp Meade in Maryland, but remained there only until July 8th, when he and his unit were sent to France[300].

---

[300] Most information about his military service is from "Maryland Military Men 1917-1918," an on-line database based on "Maryland in the World War, 1917-1919; Military and Naval Service Records, Vol. I-II," published by Twentieth Century Press, 1933. (S44)

Charles' letter to his fiancé Gertrude of June 20th, which seems to have been written over several days, is shown below:

Letter from Charles Gonce to Gertrude Hulshoff while he was stationed at Camp Meade, MD, preparing for overseas deployment.

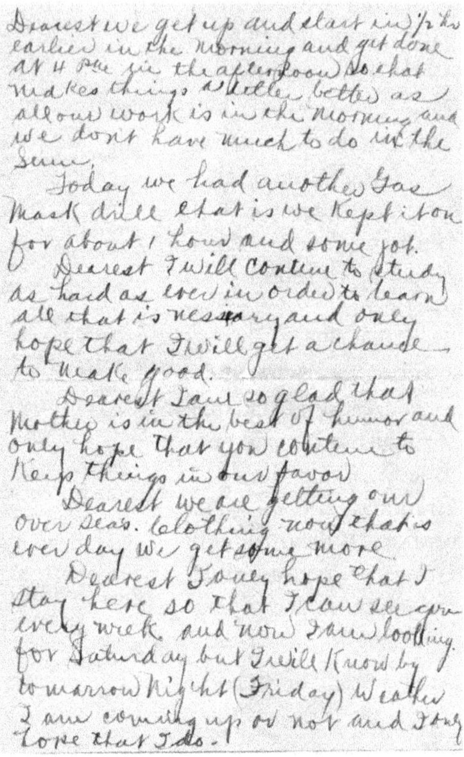

The letter is dated Thursday 20 June 1918.

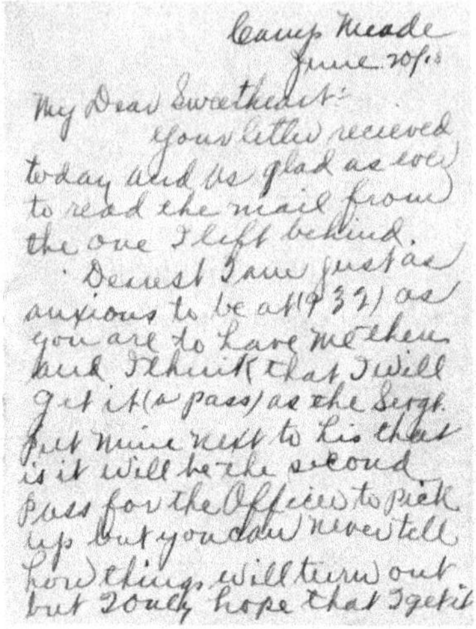

My transcription of this letter, which (hopefully) reproduces the typos exactly as written, is shown on the facing page:

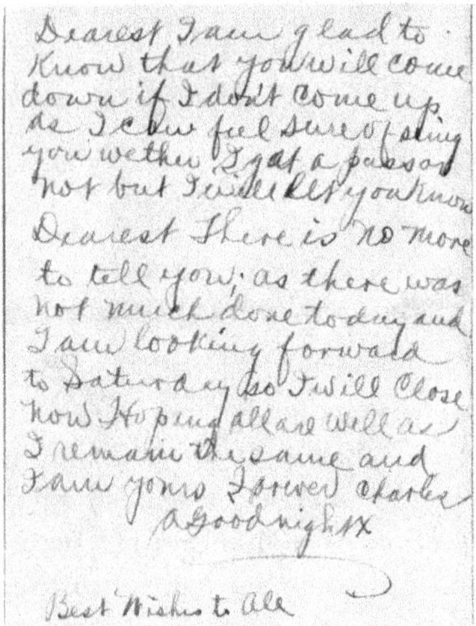

OUR GONCE ANCESTORS

Camp Meade[301]
June 20/18

My Dear Sweetheart:

Your letter received today and as glad as ever to read the mail from the one I left behind.

Dearest I am just as anxious to be at (932)[302] *as you are to have me there and I think that I will get it (a pass) as the Sergt. put mine next to his that is it will be the second pass for the Officer to pick up but you can never tell how things will turn out but I only hope that I get it.*

Dearest we get up and start in ½ hr earlier in the morning and get done at 4 pm in the afternoon so that makes things a little better as all our work is in the morning and we don't have much to do in the Sun.

Today we had another Gas Mask drill that is we kept it on for about 1 hour and some job.

Dearest I will continue to study as hard as ever in order to learn all that is nessiary and only hope that I will get a chance to make good.

Dearest I am so glad that Mother is in the best of humor and only hope that you continue to keep things in our favor.

Dearest we are getting our oversea's clothing now that is ever day we get some more.

Dearest I only hope that I stay here so that I can see you every week and now I am looking for Saturday but will know by tomorrow night (Friday) Weather I am coming up or not and I only hope that I do.

Dearest I am glad to know that you will come down if I don't come up as I can feel sure of seeing you wether I get a pass or not but I will let you know.

Dearest there is no more to tell you; as there was not much done today and I am looking forward to Saturday so I will close now. Hoping all are well as I remain the same and I am yours forever   Charles

    A Goodnight X

Best Wishes to All

I haven't encountered any information to suggest how Charles and Gert came to meet each other. They weren't neighbors, and don't appear to have attended the same church. However it occurred, though, there are hints in this letter that Grandmom was encouraging Granddad to "better himself" ("*I will continue to study as hard as ever in order to learn all that is nessiary and only hope that I will get a chance to make good.*"), and that her mother Jennie was

---

[301] Camp Meade, a little southwest of Baltimore, is now known as Ft. Meade.

[302] This refers to Gertrude's address at 932 East Biddle Street in Baltimore.

perhaps not yet totally on-board with the idea of Charles as good "husband-material" ("*I am so glad that Mother[303] is in the best of humor and only hope that you continue to keep things in our favor.*"). In the end, however, he seemed to have proven himself sufficiently.

The picture on the right dates from this short training period in 1918. His fiancé Gertrude's last visit with him at Camp Meade before his departure was on the July 4th holiday. The next day, he wrote the following letter to his future mother-in-law:

My Grandfather Charles Richard Gonce in 1918

"*Dearest Mother: Just a few lines to tell you how sorrow (sic) I am and how disappointed I am not being able to get home to accept the one that you have given me before I go over, but I only hope that when I come home I will have a chance to be married and things will be as good as when I left and as I cannot get a pass because we are going to leave almost any day, but I don't know how soon so I would advise that you and Gertrude put your name on all mail that you send me so it can be returned if I don't get it.*

"*I certainly was heartbroken last night to have Gertrude leave me for the last time as I did not want to tell her but that fellow by the name of Leonheart came over and started to tell me all about what was going on, as though I did not know but I did not want Gertrude to know it on account of coming home alone and I knew how she would feel as I know how I feel myself and I know that you feel the same way as I know how you have things planned and it being my fault I don't know to tell you how sorrow (sic) I am that I can't get home if its only for a hour, but I hope and will expect another chance when I get home and that I will always be remembered in your prayers and I am going to confession and Holy Communion today and will keep the same thing up as long as I am away and will be the same when I come home as I was when I left.*

"*Now I am going to close as I can't write any more so I remain as ever your expected Son, Charles.*

"*Remember me to everyone at home.*

---

[303] Granddad's own mother Alice Elizabeth (Clautice) Gonce had died six years earlier, so it wasn't that unusual that he would have used the term "mother" for Jennie Hulshoff.

"I will send you a card when I leave this camp. Try to keep Gertrude from worrying as I know she will and that will worry me as long as I am away.

Charles"

Letter from Charles Gonce to his future mother-in-law Jennie Hulshoff sent on 5 July 1918, just three days before his departure to France during World War I.

Letter dated 5 July 1918 from Charles R. Gonce to Jennie Hulshoff and transcribed above.

■ 115 ■

Although I have no direct evidence, it is almost certain that Charles and his unit traveled to France on the troop ship Leviathan[304] – a former German luxury passenger liner seized at Hoboken, New Jersey by the United States government when war was declared on Germany in April 1917.

The U.S.S. Leviathan in its "Dazzle Camouflage"
Photo is NH-51396 in the United States Naval Archives.

During the 310th's initial stint in the Argonne forest, sniper fire from retreating German stragglers was a continuing distraction. After his return, Granddad related the following story of an encounter with one of these, whom they had discovered hiding in a box in a tree, to the local newspaper:

> *"We* (Granddad, his sergeant, and another soldier) *went after the 'boche'*[305] *just like a hunter would go after a coon. We pestered him a few times and soon had him yelling 'kamerad.' He then bobbed out in the uniform of a poilu*[306]*. He couldn't talk French and he couldn't talk English, so we just threatened to pump some hot lead in him unless he told us where his sniping partner was. He came across, pointing to a spot in the ground that we had suspected. This one was all fixed up in an American uniform."* [307]

On October 15th 1918, Granddad was assigned (still as a Wagoner) to the 9th BN, 154th Dep Brigade in the Avocourt Sector of the Meuse-Argonne in support of a major offensive in that area. A few weeks later, during the third (pursuit) phase of the battle on November 5th, Granddad's unit was in the Troyan Sector heading towards Verdun when an exploding shell seriously wounded him in the foot, blowing out his Achilles Tendon. My mother's brother Charles related that his father had also been exposed to mustard gas on at least one occasion.

---

[304] Because a picture of the Leviathan hung in the hallway of their house for many years, some family stories relate that he returned home on the Leviathan, but this was actually the ship he departed on.

[305] Boche is a French word for Cabbage, often used as an insult (e.g. cabbage-head); this was picked up by the GIs as a slang term for Germans (similar to the use of "Kraut" in World War II, which also refers to the German love of cabbage).

[306] Poilu was an old French word that meant "hairy." This was an allied nickname for the free French soldiers.

[307] See a copy of the whole article reproduced on page 122.

OUR GONCE ANCESTORS

Mollie Zang [ID 567], Grandmom's cousin[308], was credited with saving Granddad from losing his lower leg when she providentially ran across him in the field hospital, recognized him as her cousin's fiancée, and dissuaded the doctors from amputating until she had a chance to apply maggots (used at the time[309] to remove gangrenous flesh) and tend to him personally. Within a few weeks, his leg and foot had healed sufficiently for him to be transferred back to the United States. Molly eventually suffered from post-traumatic stress disorder resulting from her experiences in the war, and never fully recovered.

More details of the Meuse-Argonne offensive, during which 117,000 US troops were casualties, are given in "World War I – Day by Day," by Ian Westwell[310]. Granddad's combat service had ended less than six months after arriving in France.

Serbian Medal of the Order of St. Sava

Although Granddad obviously served in a combat role, there is some indication that he also did relief work while in France. His military records have a notation that he was awarded the Order of St Sava. Since this award was instituted in 1883 by King Milan 1 of Serbia for services rendered in the field of science, arts and letters, and since there is no evidence that Charles was ever in Serbia, I first assumed the entry was in error. Further research, however, showed that quite a few allied military men were awarded the medal for relief work (including transportation) during World War I, regardless of where such work was performed. Therefore, it is quite possible that he may have received this award in addition to the Purple Heart[311] granted by the United States in 1932.

On Christmas day of 1918, after sending his fiancée Gertrude a cable to let her know he was coming back to the United States, Charles left Brest, France on the USS Northern Pacific; he was one of 2,508 passengers, virtually all military. At 2:20am on New Year's Day, as the ship was approaching New York in a driving rain, it ran aground off Fire Island. Having been wounded, Granddad was one of the first few hundred to be rescued, and he arrived at

---

[308] Mollie was the daughter of Mary Catherine Kerchner [ID 565], who was Jennie Kerchner Hulshoff's older sister.

[309] Although maggots fell out of favor in medical circles in the decades following World War I, their use has been steadily increasing in recent years; apparently they work just as well and there are far fewer deleterious side effects from maggots than from the drugs that replaced them.

[310] ISBN 0-7603-0938-8; by MBI Publishing Company; 729 Prospect Avenue; Osceola, WI 54020-0001

[311] Purple Hearts were not issued during the period of World War I, but when they were reestablished in 1932, the awards were granted retroactively to those wounded in that conflict from 5 April 1917 on.

1759 – 1983 History

the 3rd Debarkation Hospital in New York City later that same day. It would be several days before the remaining passengers and crew were removed. Pictures of the Northern Pacific during rescue operations are shown below.

Photo # NH 1023   SC-291 debarking wounded troops from grounded USS Northern Pacific, January 1919

Photographs from the U.S. Naval Photographic Archives of the Submarine Chaser (SC-291) and the troop transport USS Northern Pacific connected by a Breeches Buoy being used to offload wounded soldiers (including Charles Gonce) from the grounded Northern Pacific off Fire Island, NY, on 1 January 1919

Photo # NH 44758   Breeches buoy used to rescue men from stranded USS Northern Pacific, January 1919

Closer view of a Breeches buoy set up on the shore. Other photos of the rescue can be seen on page 9.

When word reached Baltimore that the ship had arrived, Grandmom, chaperoned by her Aunt Anna Gertrude Kerchner [ID 40], and three of Granddad's brothers William[ID697], Raymond[ID36] and Edward[ID155], traveled to New York City to meet him. Grandmom and Granddad were married at Saint Patrick's Cathedral in New York City on Wednesday, January 8, 1919.[312]

---

[312] The marriage was reported in the Baltimore papers at the time (some clippings are shown below).

Charles' brothers gave him a gold Hamilton watch as a wedding gift, and he wore this until his death.

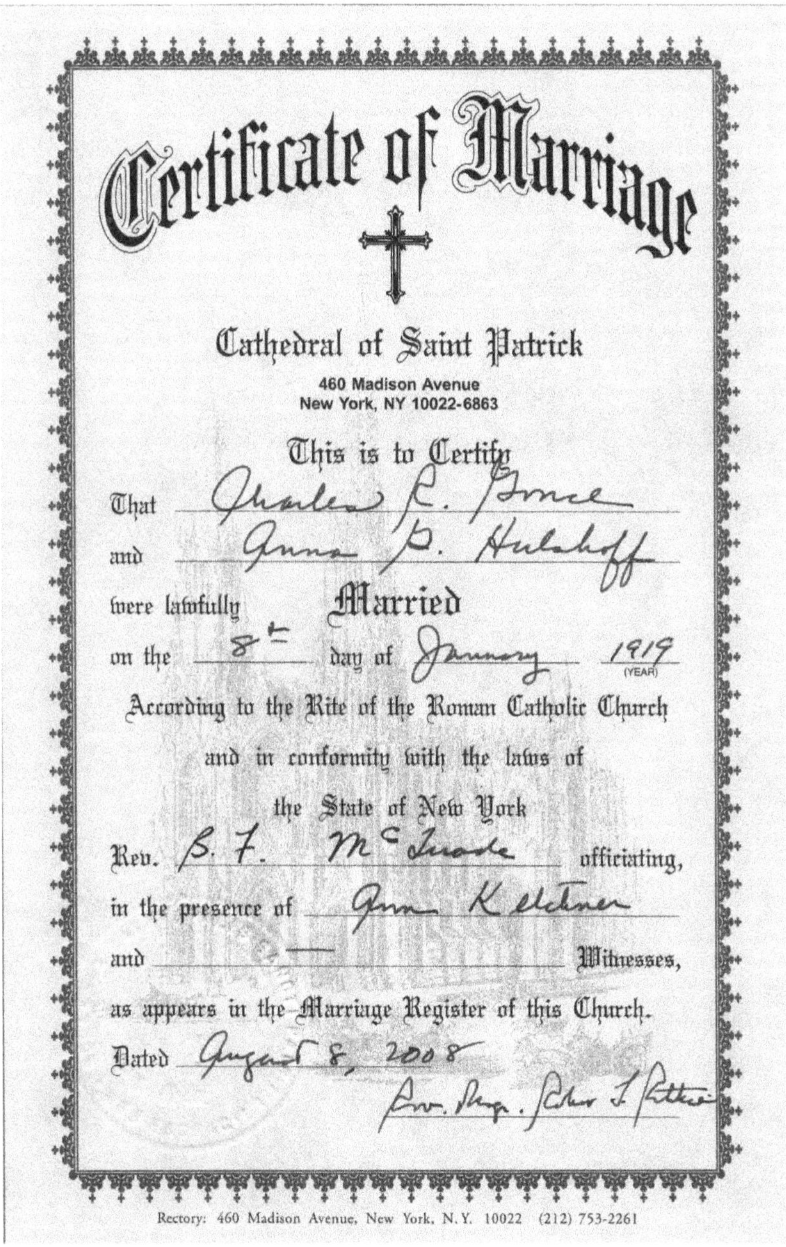

Certificate of Marriage ✠

Cathedral of Saint Patrick
460 Madison Avenue
New York, NY 10022-6863

This is to Certify

That *Charles R. Gonce*

and *Gertrude D. Hulshoff*

were lawfully **Married**

on the 8th day of *January* 1919 (YEAR)

According to the Rite of the Roman Catholic Church and in conformity with the laws of the State of New York

Rev. *B. F. McQuade* officiating,

in the presence of *Ann Kellner*

and ——— Witnesses,

as appears in the Marriage Register of this Church.

Dated *August 8, 2008*

Rectory: 460 Madison Avenue, New York, N.Y. 10022 (212) 753-2261

Marriage Certificate for my maternal grandparents Charles Gonce and Gertrude Hulshoff supplied by the Pastor of St. Patrick's Cathedral in New York, New York. The location of their original Marriage Certificate is unknown.

Charles and Gertrude on their wedding day in New York City

Charles R. Gonce, standing at top left. This photograph was taken at Camp Meade, Maryland in the spring of 1919 while Granddad was near the end of his physical rehabilitation from the results of his service in France during the "Great War" (World War I).

WOUNDED AND HAPPY

Private Charles R. Gonce Came On Stranded Transport Northern Pacific.

SWEETHEART HASTENS TO HIM

Man Gets Furlough From Hospital And They're Married In New York

Private Charles R. Gonce, a wounded member of the Three Hundred and Tenth Machine Gun Battalion, is happy today at his new home, 932 East Biddle street, with a rare collection of war trophies and a bride.

He is more happy than the usual chap who went through the war, because fate seemed to threaten his marriage from the time he entered the service until the American transport, on which he was within reach of happiness. He thought the ship was very near several times while en route to New York, but being shipwrecked he had not counted upon. He began to think that fate was determined not to let him see Miss Gertrude Hulshoff, 932 East Biddle street, who had promised to wait for him.

Meets Him in New York Hospital.

Miss Hulshoff knew that her sweetheart was on the Northern Pacific, for he had cabled her before leaving Brest. As soon as she heard that they were landing the wounded and returning soldiers Miss Hulshoff, her aunt, Miss Anna Kerchner, and Private Gonce's three brothers hurried to the hospital at New York where her sweetheart had been sent after his removal from the ship.

When she got to the hospital she had trouble getting in. The military police held her party up for several hours. At last the "M. P.'s" began winking at each other and let her see her here. This was Wednesday. It was a happy reunion. The pair looked for the very biggest church in New York city and found it—St. Patrick's Cathedral—and it was not very long before Father McQuade was "tying the knot."

Gonce secured a five-day furlough from the hospital, and is now home with his happy bride and all of his souvenirs, one of which, a camouflaged Hun helmet, can be seen in the front window, peacefully holding flowers. Gonce has some lively adventures to tell about. The Argonne forest was his toughest experience. He was constantly under fire from snipers. With his sergeant and another private he captured two of these. One of them had been located in a box in a tree.

Boches in Allied Uniforms.

"We went after the 'boche' just like a hunter would go after a coon. We peppered him a few times and soon had him yelling 'kamerad.' Then he bobbed out in the uniform of a poilu. He couldn't talk French and he couldn't talk English, so we just threatened to pump some hot lead in him unless he told us where his sniping partner was. He came across, pointing to a spot in the ground that we had suspected. This one was all fixed up in an American uniform.

Gonce went to Camp Meade in May, 1918, and was sent to France in July. His company was in the big American drive that reduced the St. Mihiel salient. Speaking of his experience on the stranded Northern Pacific, he said that there was quite a little fear among the men, but that no one became panicky. He said the wounded were well cared for.

BRINGS BRIDE BACK

Wounded Soldier On "North Pacific" Marries In New York.

When Wagoner Charles R. Gonce of the Three Hundred and Tenth Machine Gun Company, after having been badly wounded on the Verdun front and also undergone the strain as a passenger aboard the North Pacific when that ship was stranded on Fire Island, returned to Baltimore yesterday afternoon, he brought with him a bride.

His relatives and friends gave him a big reception at the home of the bride's parents, 932 East Biddle street. The bride was formerly Miss Gertrude Hulshoff, daughter of Mr. and Mrs. Herman Holshoff. She with her aunt, Mrs. Minnie Kerchner, and three brothers of the soldier-groom, went to New York last week to visit Gonce, who was then a patient at Debarkation Hospital.

The brothers, William H. Gonce, Jr., Ray A. and Edward L. Gonce, and the bride's aunt returned to Baltimore on Tuesday, while Miss Hulshoff remained to be near her wounded sweetheart.

"Boche," French for cabbage (or cabbage-head), was slang for a German.

"Poilu," was an old French word meaning hairy, and was a World War I slang term used by GIs for the French soldiers.

"Salient" is used here in the military meaning; a military position that projects into or across the enemy lines.

Newspaper clippings after Charles Gonce's return to Baltimore after World War I

Charles Gonce & Gertrude Hulshoff – After the Great War

Charles and Gertrude returned to Baltimore when he was transferred to the Camp Meade Base Hospital for rehabilitation on January 24th. On April 29th, after a short furlough, he finally returned to the 154th (by then also back at Camp Meade), and was discharged from there on May 6th.

Charles returned to work in the Winton automobile garage, where he shortly became the Garage Foreman. Both now 23 years old, Charles and Gertrude moved out of the Hulshoff house and rented space in the house next door at 918 E. Chase Street from Mrs. Hintenach. Their first child, my mother Rosalie Gertrude Gonce [ID 242], was born on Friday the 26th of December, just about a year after their marriage[313].

Charles and Gertrude Gonce – Spring 1920

Rosalie's birth at their home on Chase Street was attended both by Dr. James Fenton, and by Mary Zang, a nurse who was Gertrude's first cousin and the sister of Molly, who had saved Charles' leg while they were both serving in France.

Because of his profession, Granddad was one of the few people in their circle who owned an automobile and he used to take his family on long driving excursions, even when his children were very young.

The car that figured the most in the memories of Charles and Gertrude's children was his Winton 6, and the acquisition of the car itself was an excuse for a cross-country trip.

Gertrude holding Rosalie – Spring 1920

---

[313] For those who keep track of such things, my Mother weighed 7.5 pounds at her 10:45am birth.

In July of 1920, when my Mother Rosalie was about seven months old, Grandmom and Granddad headed out with their new daughter to Cleveland, Ohio on a Pullman train car to pick up a new Model 6 from the Winton Motor Carriage Company's factory there. From Cleveland, they took a roundabout road trip back to Baltimore – spending the night in Pittsburgh, and visiting Harpers Ferry, Gettysburg, and Philadelphia along the way home to Baltimore.

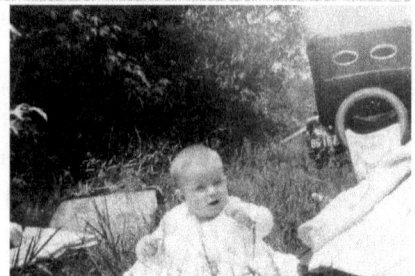

Rosalie Gonce during July 5, 1920 picnic while on her first road trip.

Their second child, Mary Regina (Jean) [ID 248], was born 24 May 1921. At about this time, Charles moved from servicing automobiles to selling them.

In July of 1921, with their second child (my Aunt Jean) barely two months old, my grandparents and their two daughters headed off to Atlantic City, where they stayed for four days. This was to become a recurring summer trip for the next several years.

In April 1923, with another child on the way, the Gonce family moved into their new home at 613 Springhill Terrace (later named Springfield Avenue), just down the street from Gertrude's parents[314], who had moved there a little earlier. The price of their home was about $5,250; the Hulshoffs had paid $5,159.86 for their very similar home. The new homes on Springfield Avenue were contemporary versions of the classic Baltimore row house; 613 can be seen in the photograph on page 135. My grandmother continued to live in this house for over fifty years.

The couple's first son, Charles Richard [ID 243], was born on 26 October 1923. Shortly after this, in 1924, my Grandfather became Sales Manager of the Winton dealership.

In the ensuing years, Granddad would take his children along with their friends and cousins in the relatively large Winton on various day trips. Although the Winton had jump seats, Granddad liked to maximize the passenger-carrying capacity by means of boards spread across these so more kids could ride along.

Granddad in his 1920 Winton 6 – passengers unidentified

---

[314] The Hulshoff house was located at 602 Springhill Terrace, just across from Blessed Sacrament Church.

OUR GONCE ANCESTORS

Segment of the 1920 U.S. Census Page showing 918 East Chase Street, where Charles and Gertrude Gonce were tenants of the widowed Mrs. Hintenach and her daughter. Their first daughter Rosalie was only about a month old when this census was taken. Taken from National Archives Series t625, Roll 662, Page 162

Segment of the 1930 U.S. Census page showing 613 Springfield Avenue. Charles and Gertrude Gonce now had all four of their children, as well as Gertrude's Aunt Annie living with them. Taken from National Archives Series t626, Roll 869, Page 125

Segments of the 1920 and 1930 Census Sheets for Springfield Avenue

■ 125 ■

1759 – 1983 History

My grandfather with his daughters Ro and Jean (above) and son Charles (below) at Atlantic City, New Jersey in 1924.

last child, another son, George Joseph ID 245.

The pictures on the left show Granddad with his children on the New Jersey beach during one of their summer trips in about 1924.

With the proliferation of new automotive brands after the war, the industry was beginning to enter an inevitable shakeout period. Mergers, acquisitions, and corporate failures began occurring much more frequently. In 1925, the Winton automotive company ceased independent operations[315], and their localced as existing stock was sold.

Charles' reputation was such, however, that he was almost immediately hired as Sales Manager for the Franklin dealership.

On 4 March 1927, Charles and Gertrude had their

Franklin Model 9-B Sedan

Granddad sold and serviced these cars from late 1925 until September 1930

Gertrude's Aunt Annie[316] (the chaperone during the trip to New York for her wedding) had earlier lived a few doors up the street with a widower named Mrs. Mullen, the grandmother of Caroline Keller, one of my Mom's childhood friends, but in the late 1920s, she moved in with Charles and Gertrude's family. See the census form for 1930, an extract of which is

---

[315] General Motors acquired the Cleveland plant, which continued to produce the well-respected Winton engines for various General Motors cars.

[316] Anna Gertrude Kerchner ID 40, her mother's older sister, for whom Grandmom was named.

shown earlier. Aunt Annie's move would eventually have significant impacts on the family.

Aunt Annie's personality is quite difficult to discern – those who remember her and who have spoken about her seem to have strong opinions that, unfortunately, differ widely. My mother, for instance, has nothing good to say about her, while her brother Charles was very attached to Aunt Annie. The only semi-independent view I have encountered was based on her periodic role as a chaperone for her Hulshoff nieces during various trips and vacations they took. In the summer of 1920, when Gertrude's younger sister Rose turned eighteen, Aunt Annie accompanied her on a vacation to Niagara Falls. During this trip, and apparently in spite of Aunt Annie's best efforts, Rose met a man there named Frank Easter from Philadelphia, who would eventually become her husband after they had corresponded for quite some time. Years later, in 1939, while they were still raising two teens[317] themselves, Frank and Rose took in two sons of a friend of theirs who had died. Ed Wasser[318], one of these brothers, relates that Frank Easter's description of Aunt Annie was of a very strict, unpleasant, and controlling woman.

The 1929 Stock Market Crash

The 1929 stock market collapse and subsequent depression had more of an immediate impact on Gertrude's parents[319] than it did on Charles and Gertrude – at least for the moment.

In the years leading up to the crash, the Franklin Automobile Company had invested heavily in the design and production of a new twelve-cylinder model; production and marketing of the vehicle began in late 1929. In addition to what the automotive press regarded as inferior handling (which might have been overcome with further development), the intended market for what was designed to be a high-end car shrunk rapidly as the depression began to take hold. In 1930, the total sales for the new model were just slightly over six thousand across the country, resulting in

Jean (standing), Rosalie and Charles (on pony) in May of 1925

---

[317] Donald and Mary Easter. Several photos of Rose and Frank are included in the Appendix on page 243.
[318] Ed, now in his nineties, lives in Philadelphia and still drives.
[319] See my book "Our Hulshoff and Kerchner Ancestors" for further information.

Franklin having to report losses that year exceeding four million dollars[320].

Of course, this sharp decline in sales was reflected in the commissions of those who sold the Franklin. Once again, Charles was offered, and soon accepted, an offer with a company that sold a more mainstream vehicle.

In 1930, Charles became the Sales Manager for Kolpack & Mitchell, the Baltimore dealer for the Peerless Car Company. The announcement of his appointment is shown in the newspaper clipping to the right[321].

A Peerless advertisement from just before this period is shown on the following page.

During this period, Gertrude's Aunt Annie Kerchner, whose personality was apparently a whole lot more forceful than either Charles' or her own, began to insinuate herself more aggressively into the running of the household. What transpired with Aunt Annie and my grandparents in the next few years is somewhat unclear, but here is what I suspect took place based on stories passed down by various family members.

Kolpack And Mitchell Name Sales Manager

CHARLES R. GONCE
The appointment of Mr. Gonce as sales manager of Kolpack & Mitchell, Peerless distributors, was announced today by Walter A. Kolpack.

Charles and Gertrude's Separation

It was mentioned earlier that there seemed to be indications that at least some of the Kerchners may not have been pleased with Gertrude's choice of a husband. Whether related to his service in World War I (as my Mother suggests) or not, Charles seems to have begun drinking more than Aunt Annie approved of, although I've encountered no evidence that this led to any specific difficulties with his employment or marriage.

For whatever effects the alcohol consumption did have, Aunt Annie's disapproval seems to have been based on her moral perceptions rather than on any legal[322] strictures. Having insinuated herself into a dominant position in the household by this time, Aunt Annie either forced Charles out of the household or somehow compelled her niece Gertrude to do so.

---

[320] Franklin's losses continued to mount, and their annual operating loss exceeded $800,000 by 1933; the company filed for bankruptcy by the spring of 1934 and never recovered.

[321] This announcement is from the Baltimore Sun of 14 September 1930.

[322] Although Prohibition went into effect in 1920, and wasn't repealed until 1933, most histories of this era suggest that alcohol was readily available and that its use during this period was quite common and some sources suggest that it actually increased.

Peerless Motor Company Ad from 1928 – Charles Gonce became Sales Manager for this Company in 1930.

A Visit to the Beach in about 1931

Back Row: Anna Gertrude Gonce [ID 44], Anita Foley (neighbor), Charles Richard Gonce [ID 43]. Middle Row: Charles Richard Gonce, Jr. [ID 243], Regina (Jean) Gonce [ID 248], Catherine Foley (neighbor), Rosalie (Ro) Gonce [ID 242]. Front Row: George Gonce [ID 245].

There is undoubtedly more to the story of their separation, since there are obvious questions for which no one seems to have (or be willing to share) any answers. Why, for instance, did Gertrude acquiesce to her husband being forced out of the household? She always had photographs and other mementos of her husband Charles prominently displayed in her household, and, by all accounts, she was devastated at the news of his death.

There also seems to be no explanation why Charles didn't simply evict Aunt Annie from the household long before her interference in his life reached this point. My mother simply repeats that neither of her parents "had the nerve to stand up to Aunt Annie," and that "Aunt Annie was pure evil."

Both of Gertrude's parents (who, as mentioned earlier, lived just up the street at 602 Springfield) were still alive at this time[323], so it can be assumed that neither of them saw fit to intervene. Sometime in what seems to have been in the latter part of 1934 therefore, Granddad resigned from Kolpack & Mitchell and left in the Winton with a friend of his[324] to visit his older sister Alice and her family in Worley, Idaho.

Granddad's departure caused mixed reactions among his children, as not only the financial situation, but also the day-to-day priorities and pecking order within the household changed. From an economic perspective, although Aunt Annie worked at one of the Arundel Ice Cream shops that her family controlled, Charles' leaving his job to go to Idaho meant that the overall household income dropped substantially. Forcing his departure, if that is actually what happened, would seem to make little sense at least from a financial perspective, and this seems to be yet another indication that we likely don't know the full story behind Granddad's departure.

With Charles gone, my grandmother Gertrude also began working at an Arundel store, but in order to insure

The Arundel Ice Cream Company

"The Arundel," as everyone in the family referred to it, was a soda shop and ice cream chain founded by George Fisher, whose sister Caroline ID 579 *(Carrie) married Gertrude's uncle John J. Kerchner* ID 108*. Eventually the Kerchners managed the business.*

Wartime (1943) newspaper ad for "delicious and nutritious" Arundel Ice Cream

---

[323] Gertrude's father Herman Hulshoff eventually died on 19 February 1940; her mother Jennie Hulshoff, Aunt Annie's older sister, died on 21 April 1940.
[324] This was likely Charlie Burke, who appears in several photographs of my grandfather taken while he was in Idaho. No one seems to be aware of who exactly he was or why he would have been free to take off for an extended trip, although this was in the midst of the great depression.

that an adult remained at home, she and Aunt Annie worked different shifts[325].

Possibly due to his father William Henry [ID 32] Gonce's death in June of 1935, Charles returned to Baltimore after spending several months in Idaho. He began living at 3330 Chesterfield Avenue in the Lauraville neighborhood of Baltimore. My mother is aware of at least one attempt he made to visit the household after this, but with Gertrude away at work, Aunt Annie turned him away and wouldn't permit him to talk to her or any of her siblings.

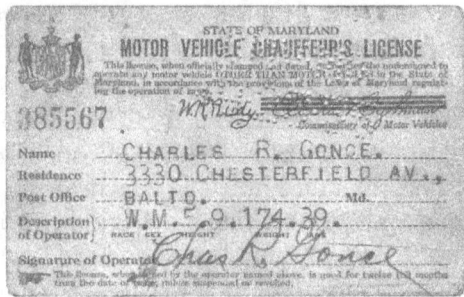

1935 Driver's License of Charles R. Gonce

After Granddad's return from Idaho, the Winton 6 was relegated to a vacant lot behind the house at 613 Springfield Avenue, where it served as part of a "Cops and Robbers" playground of sorts for the neighborhood boys, including the Gonce boys Charles and George. Charles eventually removed the Winton's "Waltham 8-Day Clock" from the car and later had it mounted separately as a memento, which is still in his family's possession.

Charles' daughters did apparently have some subsequent contact with their father. My mother recalled that he sometimes "ran into" her and her sister Jean while they walked home from Seton High School[326]. Since I have not been able to determine where (or if) Granddad was working after his return, it isn't clear how providential these meetings might have been. These encounters certainly took place during the 1935-1936 school year when my Mother was a sophomore and Aunt Jean was a freshman.

Charles and Gertrude remained in contact, and in October of 1935 he arranged to pick up Grandmom in his new 1935 Dodge sedan, so she could accompany him while he took their youngest son George, then about 9 years old, to attend the 1936 Automobile Show at the Fifth Regiment Armory in downtown Baltimore.

The headline entertainment at the auto show was Paul Whiteman[327] and his orchestra. After some time, the

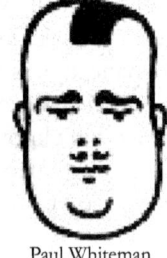

Paul Whiteman

---

[325] and, as far as my mother recalls, at different stores.

[326] They were always given money to take the Number 8 Streetcar, which ran on Greenmount Avenue but, as many teenagers did, when the weather permitted, the sisters often walked the 1.8 miles home in order to save the money for their own uses.

[327] Paul Whiteman (1890-1967) was a well-known and popular band-leader as well as host of the "Old Gold – Paul Whiteman Hour" on the CBS Radio Network. He is also remembered for commissioning some of George Gershwin's works – most notably the Rhapsody in Blue, which was orchestrated by

bandleader had become quite inebriated and began to toss wads of paper money into the crowd from an upper balcony, precipitating an immediate rush of patrons to the area where it was landing. My Uncle George, like most eight-year-olds would, began to run towards the drop zone as well, but Granddad immediately grabbed him by the collar – explaining that he was more likely to be crushed by the crowd than to come away wealthy.

It was quite snowy that night, and while driving Gertrude and his son George home, they were sideswiped on their right rear fender, and ended up sliding sideways for a time along Belair Road – an adventure that Uncle George remembers clearly.

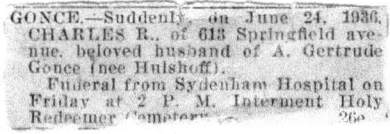

Notice of Charles R. Gonce's Death

On 24 June 1936, when he was barely forty years old, Granddad collapsed while walking near the corner of Belair Road and Erdman Avenue in Baltimore – just a few blocks from his Chesterfield Avenue address. He was taken to nearby Sydenham Hospital, where (according to the stories my mother relates) the people in the emergency room simply assumed he was some inebriated derelict picked up on the street, and didn't spend much time with him. Word was somehow sent to Gertrude that he had been taken there.

When Grandmom arrived at the hospital and asked where she should go to see him, she was told that "his body was being brought down," and this was the way she was notified that he had died. It turned out that he had actually died from spinal meningitis, something that probably couldn't have been mitigated anyway in 1936, but Grandmom was very upset at the initial assumptions[328] made by the hospital. The gold Hamilton watch, given to him by his brothers for his wedding, and which he was assumed to be wearing that day as usual, was missing. It also became apparent to her that another woman[329] was with him when he died.

Because of the meningitis, Granddad's body was laid out in a marble case with a sealed glass top, and his funeral was held at Sydenham Hospital rather than in a church; Fr. George Larkin (a family friend for whom Uncle George was named) conducted the service.

Ferde Grofé, the orchestra's pianist at the time. Grofé later became famous in his own right as a composer (e.g. Grand Canyon Suite, Niagara Suite, etc.) Whiteman was certainly an appropriate choice to perform at a car show, since he was a certified car buff himself. In 1929, he even arranged for the purchase of an automobile for each of the twenty-four members of his band. Not known for missing an opportunity to market himself, each of the cars had a spare tire cover with a caricature of his own head (see above) that had become the band's trademark.

[328] This is my mother's recollection: my grandmother's reported annoyance at the hospital's assumptions seems somewhat at odds with the idea that she knew he had a serious drinking problem.

[329] Uncle George doesn't know if or how this woman figured into my grandparents' separation, but the circumstances I've been able to dig out suggest that this relationship, whatever it may have been, came well after they separated.

Charles was buried in the plot belonging to Gertrude's maternal Kerchner grandparents Ferdinand ^{ID 38} and Anna ^{ID 39} at Holy Redeemer Cemetery. Given the separation from Gertrude, and the apparent ongoing tension with the Kerchners, and the fact that there were still open graves in his parents' plot in the same cemetery, make this choice interesting[330].

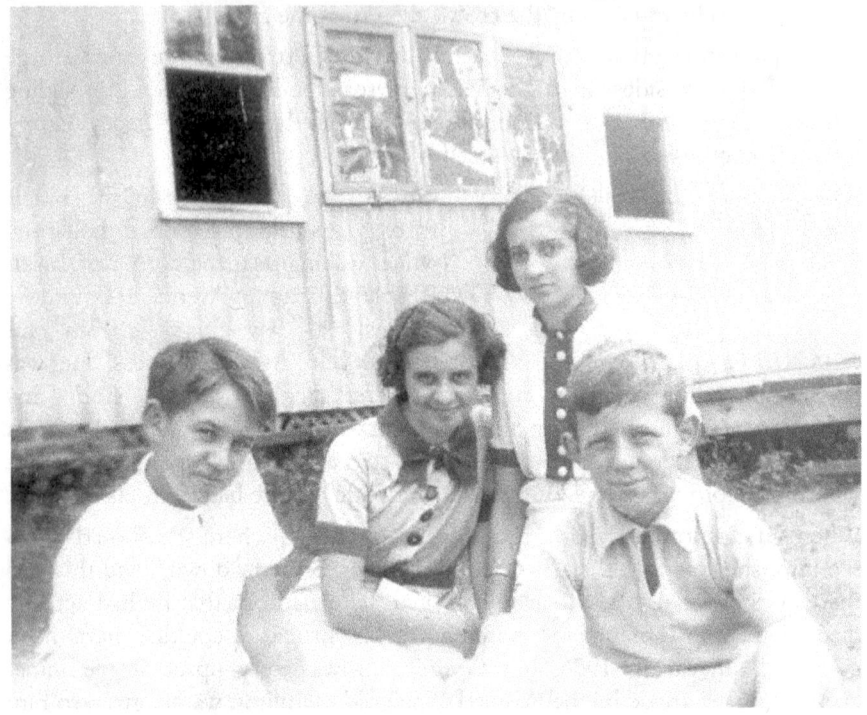

Charles and Gertrude Gonce's Children:
Charles ^{ID 243}, Rosalie ^{ID 242}, Jean ^{ID 248} and George ^{ID 245} in about 1935.

At the time of her father's death, my mother Rosalie was sixteen – and about to become a High School Junior[331]; her younger siblings were fifteen, twelve, and nine. My grandmother Gertrude, only thirty-nine, was now a widow in the midst of the great depression with four children to support. If she had considered taking her job with the Arundel to be an interim measure, reality now dictated that she become a full-time employee, and Grandmom continued working for the Arundel until she retired.

---

[330] According to Uncle George, Granddad was buried with the Kerchners only because that was the only plot Grandmom had access to (apparently she wasn't on good terms with the Gonces after she allowed Aunt Annie to kick him out – go figure!). His original stone was exactly like those of the other Kerchners buried there, and said simply "Husband." Uncle George replaced it (see a photograph on page 136) with the present stone when Grandmom died, and still has the original stone at the Ritchie Highway funeral home. There was another stone there for Grandmom that said "Wife," but Grandmom had always said that she would rather have something that said "Mother."

[331] She graduated from Seton High School on 13 June 1937.

In the latter part of the decade, the potential longer-term effects of the depression became very apparent when the house next door to the Gonces[332] was sold for an amount that was less than the remaining amount on the mortgage, causing enough stress that Grandmom's children remember the incident clearly.

Rosalie outside the Gonce home at 613 Springfield Avenue in 1939

The four children were all married by the autumn of 1945[333] and, once the last of them had left the household, Aunt Annie moved back to her old neighborhood near Asquith Street. As with much of what is known about Aunt Annie, her departure seems hard to understand ...

My Grandmother continued living on the first floor of the house on Springfield Avenue, and rented out the upstairs to a succession of women. Aunt Annie died in February 1950, and was buried in the same lot at Holy Redeemer that Charles had been buried in fourteen years earlier.

When my generation attended grammar school at the Blessed Sacrament Parish School on Old York Road in the 1950s, Grandmom worked the evening/night shift; my sister, several cousins and I would go around the corner to "Grandmom Gonce's house" almost every day for lunch. Daily hot lunches and homemade desserts were the good side of having a grandmother who lived so close to our school. The bad side, beyond the occasional appearance of lentil soup or sour beef for lunch[334], was that she could look right out on the school yard from her house, and our parents received almost immediate notification if we neglected to wear our hats, or engaged in any other unacceptable behavior.

There were, of course, some interesting benefits to having a grandmother who worked in an ice cream store. Being given a chocolate milk shake still in its tin mixing-cup when we occasionally drove out to take her home in the evenings certainly counted as one of these.

---

[332] The house at 615 Springfield Avenue.

[333] The youngest, George, had just married on June 29th of that year.

[334] I have a suspicion, however preposterous, that some of my cousins actually liked this stuff.

Whether or not this was related to her earlier experiences with Aunt Annie and Granddad is unclear, but although we all "knew" that she enjoyed a glass of beer in the evenings, she was very reluctant to do this openly. When we drove her home in the evenings, she would often have my Dad stop to buy her a pack of "ponies" and insisted that he had to bring them out to the car in brown paper sacks in order to prevent anyone from observing them.

Grandmom finally retired and, as the neighborhood began to deteriorate in the early seventies with the changing demographics, her children cajoled her into moving into an apartment that was better suited for someone her age, and in a nicer neighborhood. In 2004, when I drove through the Springfield Avenue neighborhood, it appeared to have largely returned to a more civilized state, although Blessed Sacrament Church still had bullet-proof glass doors over its original wooden ones, suggesting there were still some concerns.

Gertrude Gonce, May 1957.

As Grandmom became more debilitated with diabetes and hip problems, she moved in with Aunt Jean (her daughter) and Uncle Bob[335] until living with them was no longer feasible. She spent her last years at Stella Maris Hospice, where she died in July of 1983 at age 86.

Charles and Gertrude's Memorial Marker at Holy Redeemer Cemetery, Section V, Lot 70

Grandmom is buried with Granddad in section V-70 at Holy Redeemer Cemetery in Baltimore, MD.

I have no idea how many descendants my 6th great-grandparents Justice and Magdalene Gonce have, nor does there seem to be any practical way to determine that number, but my grandparents Charles Richard and Anna Gertrude Gonce alone have at least ninety as of this writing.

---

[335] Robert D. Iglehart ID 249

OUR GONCE ANCESTORS

8th Generation: Children of Charles Richard Gonce & Anna Gertrude Hulshoff

For privacy reasons, Charles and Gertrude's grandchildren are not listed by name as I've done with earlier generations, nor are their children (the eighth generation of Justice and Magdalin Gonce's descendants) discussed in any detail. Minimal information about this generation is given in the diagram "Four Generations of Gonces from John Thomas to Rosalie" on page 241.

The picture above shows Gertrude (seated) in 1980 with her four children (left-to-right): Jean, Charles, George, and Rosalie standing behind her.

9th Generation:

... to be continued[336]. Even in the age where many of Justice Gonce's descendants have their own web sites and Facebook pages, I'll still invoke traditional privacy concerns to avoid continuing this book any further. There are seventeen members of the ninth generation who are grandchildren of Charles and Gertrude Gonce.

---

[336] ...but not any time in the near future and not likely by me. The 9th generation is my own generation.

10th Generation:

Privacy considerations aside, it is nonetheless difficult to avoid showing some pictures of my Grandmother Anna Gertrude Gonce with three of her many 10th generation great-grandchildren – each of these three now have multiple children of their own.

Some of the 10th Generation: Anna Gertrude Gonce with a few of her great-grandchildren (Rosalie's three oldest grandchildren) at my Aunt Jean Iglehart's house in Bel Air, Maryland; August of 1977

APPENDIX I

The Gonce Migrations to Tennessee and Alabama
and an Introduction to the "Southern Branch" of
the Gonce family.

*Signature of Rudolph Gonce [ID 2578], son of Justice and Magdalen Gonce and father of the first
Gonces to migrate to Tennessee. Taken from Delaware Estate Bond dated 4 November 1783*

The Gonce Family Southern Migrations

The "Southern Branch" of the Gonce Family

What I refer to as the "Southern Branch" of the Gonce Family began with migrations, first to Tennessee, and shortly thereafter to Alabama, of some early Gonces. Although they are not the focus of this book, most Gonces in the southern United States are descended from these pioneer migrants.

The Tennessee Migration

Rudolph Gonce [ID2578], the oldest known son of Justice [ID2577] and Magdalen [ID2858] Gonce, died in Delaware on 29 April 1790. He and his wife Polly (the Widow McDade) Gonce [ID2581] had at least two sons – the twin boys Isaac [ID2583] and Abraham [ID2584] Gonce, as well as at least three (and possibly four) daughters. Polly also had at least two sons, Jeremiah and Hugh McDade, from her previous marriage.

In about 1797, Rudolph's children and their families left Delaware to join thousands of other families on the trek down what was often called the "Great Road"[337] to Tennessee. I have no information as to why they undertook this journey, but it is interesting to note that, after several fits and starts, Tennessee had finally become a State in 1796, meaning that both opportunities as well as a relative level of security were now available in what was then fairly unpopulated territory. The table below lists those believed to have been part of this migration – the beginning of the "Southern Branch" of the Gonce family.

Parents and their Children who traveled to Tennessee	Notes & Comments
Isaac[338] (Ikie) Gonce [ID 2583] (26 JUL 1770 – 4 DEC 1853), Rudolph's son Frances (Frankie) Wilson [ID 2589] (4 AUG 1778 – 18 JUL 1842), Isaac's wife No children: Isaac and Frankie's first child Elizabeth (Bettie) Gonce [ID 2658] wasn't born until 10 MAY 1798 in Tennessee.	Before his later move to Alabama, Isaac sold land near Clinch Mountain in Hawkins County, which he purchased soon after his arrival in Tennessee.

---

[337] In her book "Leaves from our Family Tree," Mettie Marie Taylor Barton says Isaac's family came to Tennessee via the "Great Road." Although no sources are given for anything in her book, and some of her early history is improbable, we know Isaac departed and arrived. Because history tells us that the "Great Road" was the major (and until considerably later, the only) migratory route to Tennessee at the time, I consider her assertion to be reliable.

[338] W.H. Watterson (citation at the end of this appendix) doesn't mention Isaac, saying "Abraham, Lydia, Sarah and Margaret came to this county after they were married and had each one or more children. At what time exactly they came, I don't know, but sometime between 1792 and 1797." The structure of the sentence could be read to suggest that they each had children before the migration, but I don't believe that was the writer's intent, and it apparently isn't true. Each of them were married before the migration, however.

APPENDIX I – GONCE FAMILY SOUTHERN MIGRATIONS

Abraham (Abie) Gonce [ID 2584] (26 JUL 1770 – abt 1851), Rudolph's son Polly Vance [ID 2590] (1774 – bef 1850), Abraham's wife Abraham and Polly's first child Margaret E. Gonce [ID 3557] was born around the time of the migration to Tennessee, but exact dates aren't known for either event.	Abraham purchased 150 acres north of Clinch Mountain in Hawkins County Tennessee on 7 MAY 1799 for $200. Abraham and Polly's remaining children are all known to have been born in Tennessee.
Lydia Gonce [ID 2586] (abt 1771 – bef 1850), Rudolph's third child Thomas Sprowl [ID 2592], Lydia's husband No children: Lydia and Thomas' first child Thomas Sprowl, Jr. [ID 3863] wasn't born until 1798 in Tennessee.	
Margaret Gonce [ID 2585] (15 FEB 1772 – 6 APR 1841), Rudolph's 4th child Benjamin Hutchisson [ID 2591] (5 OCT 1765 – 12 JAN 1852) Benjamin's only child by his deceased first wife was Mary Vance (Polly) Hutchisson [ID 3860] (6 NOV 1789 – abt 1868); Polly would have been about 7 or 8 years old when the family migrated to Tennessee. Margaret's children Elizabeth Hutchisson [ID 3595] (24 SEP 1793 – 20 JAN 1847) and Sarah Hutchisson [ID 3597] (6 MAY 1795 – 4 JUL 1855) also traveled to Tennessee in the migration. Because the date of the migration is not known for sure, Margaret's third child Joseph Hutchisson [ID 3766] (22 APR 1797 – 9 MAY 1882) may also have been born before the migration.	Benjamin purchased 100 acres in Stanly Valley (NE of Rogersville) Tennessee on 1 MAY 1802 for $200. Benjamin and Margaret's first children were the twins Jemimah [ID 3593] and Keziah [ID 3594] Hutchisson, who died as infants in April 1792 before the family migrated to Tennessee.
Sarah Gonce [ID 2588] (1777 - aft 1860), Rudolph's youngest daughter Aaron Wells [ID 2594] (– bef 1830), Sarah's husband Sarah and Aaron's first child Jeremiah Wells [ID 3861] was born in 1790, and was aged 6 or 7 during the migration to Tennessee.	The only other child I am aware of is their son Isaac Wells [ID 3862], who wasn't born until 10 DEC 1798 in Tennessee.

The majority of the Great Road followed an old and well-established American Indian route called the "Great Warrior Path," which went west from the banks of the Delaware River near present day Philadelphia, southwest through northern Maryland, and then more or less south to what is now Roanoke, Virginia – at the time called Big Lick[339]. The map below shows the route from the Maryland-Delaware border to northeast Tennessee.

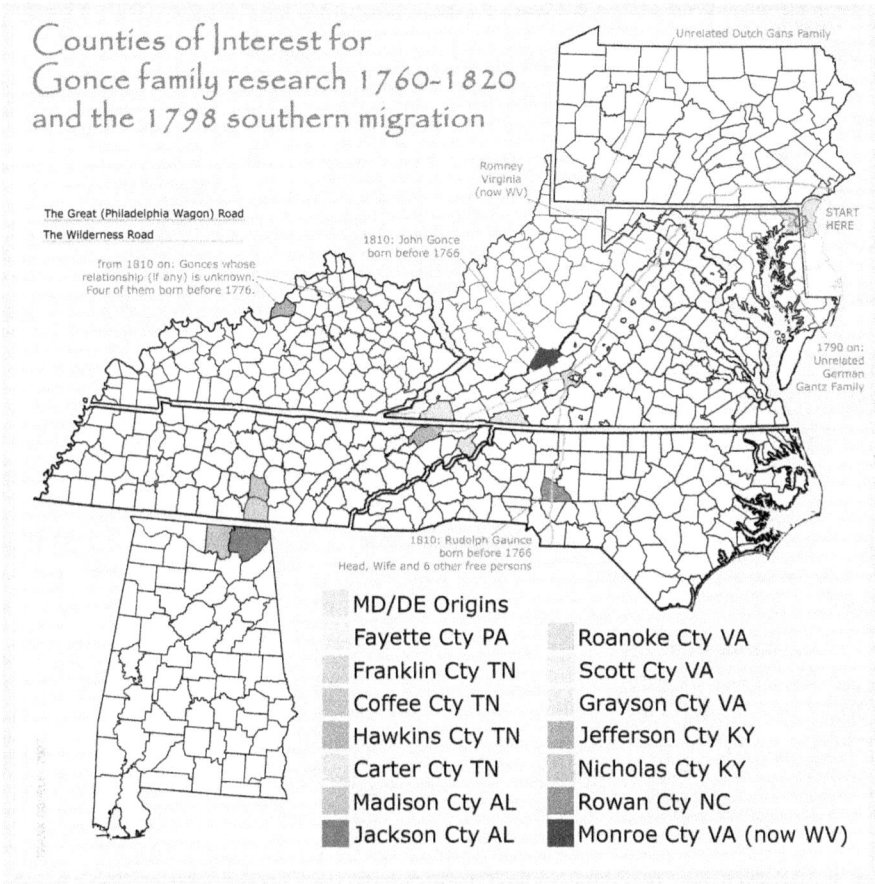

The "Southern Branch" of the Gonce family began with a migration of Rudolph Gonce's children and their families to Tennessee in about 1797. The map above shows the locations where different Gonces (as well as other families that are sometimes confused with the Gonces) lived at the time, and the migration routes the Gonces traveled.

The first part of the Great Road was the "Great Philadelphia Wagon Road." The 1744 Treaty of Lancaster[340] called for a road to be constructed from Philadelphia through the Shenandoah Valley. Work on this began in late

---

[339] It was called that because of the Salt Licks in the area, which attracted a large variety of animals. It was renamed Roanoke in 1882 in order (I suspect) to confuse young pupils studying the original, more famous, Roanoke Island.

[340] The 1744 treaty with the Six Nations (Mohawk, Oneida, Onondaga, Cayuga and Seneca) acquired land that permitted opening the "frontier," which at that time meant the territory now encompassing West Virginia and Virginia.

APPENDIX I – GONCE FAMILY SOUTHERN MIGRATIONS

summer of 1745 and, by the time of the American Revolution, the Great Road was approximately seven hundred miles long.

The road progressed through Lancaster, Pennsylvania, across the Susquehanna River, through York and Gettysburg, and continued south into Washington County, Maryland, to the town of Hagerstown.

It isn't known, and will likely prove difficult or impossible to establish, whether the Gonces joined the Great Road by traveling north to Philadelphia or by traveling west across northern Maryland. I tend to believe the latter, since it is much more direct, and there were ample locations and means for the family to cross the Susquehanna River, which was the only major obstacle between eastern Maryland and Hagerstown.

From Hagerstown, the original Great Warrior Path continued south through what is now eastern West Virginia and into Virginia, generally following the route of modern-day Interstate 81 to Roanoke which, as noted above, was then known by its original name of Big Lick.

Even in the late pre-revolutionary period, historical reports indicate that traffic, from pedestrians, small carts, and large Conestoga Wagons, was very heavy on this route. By the time Rudolph's children and their families traveled through Virginia, merchants along the route between Hagerstown and Big Lick were able to provide not only necessities, but a number of luxuries as well.

Circumstances changed beyond Big Lick, however. Another road, called the Carolina Road, continued south, and was reasonably civilized, but the Great Road continued west (still more or less along the path of modern day Interstate 81) into less settled areas. This is the section of the route, also known as the "Wilderness Road," that led to Tennessee and through the Cumberland Gap into Kentucky.

When following the Gonce's route on a modern day map, continue tracing Interstate 81 into Tennessee, but then switch almost immediately to what is now US Route 11W through Rogersville[341], located in Hawkins County. The Wilderness Trail continued on to about Mooresville before turning back northward, generally following the path now taken by Route 25E into the southwestern tip of Virginia, then through the Cumberland Gap into Kentucky.

The family stopped in Hawkins County, Tennessee, and set up new households there. Isaac and Abraham both purchased land near Clinch Mountain beside Richardson Creek in Hawkins County, Tennessee. Margaret's husband Benjamin Hutchisson purchased 100 acres in Stanley Valley (northeast of Rogersville). Some of the Gonce family still lives in

---

[341] Rogersville was named after the Irishman Joe Rogers (21 Aug 1764 – Nov 1838), who ran the first hotel in the area. He was the brother of George Rogers, whose son William Leroy Rogers later married Isaac's oldest daughter Elizabeth (Betty) Gonce.

Hawkins County today, and there is a Gonce Cemetery in Gonce Hollow founded by Hezekiah Davis Gonce ID 3021, Abraham's grandson, in 1878.

Rudolph's step-sons Jerry and Hugh McDade apparently didn't travel south; according to Hutchisson, they both settled in Pennsylvania. It also isn't clear if Rudolph's remaining daughter[342] Mary Vance Gonce ID 2587 and her husband James C. Larkin ID 2595 traveled with the rest of her siblings, although it seems likely that she did, since she is reported to have remarried a man named John Fry in Kentucky after James Larkin died in the early 1800s.

Earlier Exposure to the Great Road

Isaac, Abraham, and the others may have been given some advance knowledge of the areas to the south by their Uncle Abraham ID 2579, Justice and Magdalen's second known son. The evidence is circumstantial, but it seems very likely that this is the same Abraham who served in the Virginia Militia[343] under British Captain James Morrison in "Dunmore's War of 1774" although, along with 14 others of the 58 men in the company, he is said to have "deserted" (see below). It seems reasonable to assume that he must have been at least fifteen years old at this time, making his birth year no later than 1759, and more likely closer to 1750. Thus, he would have been in the same generation as our Rudolph, Abraham and Daniel.

This same Abraham was also on a list of those paid off in 1775 at Romney, Virginia[344] after this conflict, and the author of one book states: "most of these troops joined the Army of the Revolution after they were paid off."[345] This leads me to the conclusion that the term "desertion" may represent a British perspective on someone who decided to join the local militia, soon to become "the rebels."

It is interesting to note, however, that, although his brothers appear in Delaware records earlier, Abraham doesn't appear until August of 1778. This is yet another reason I suspect that this could very well be the same Abraham that is the son of Justice and Magdalen Gonce, but I have been unable to locate enough information to confirm this for certain.

The main location of the fighting during Dunmore's War took place in and around Fort Fincastle (later Ft. Henry), which was a little west of Big Lick, the major crossroads of the "Big Road." Anyone recruited to serve in this conflict would certainly have become familiar with the route. Romney, where he was paid off once leaving the 9th Virginia Regiment of the Continental

---

[342] If she was actually his and/or Polly's daughter, which seems to be the subject of some speculation.

[343] See "Historical Register of Virginians in the Revolution 1775-1783" by John H. Gwathmey; Genealogical Publishing Company; Baltimore, MD. 1938, 1979. Copyright © 1938 John H. Gwathmey (renewed 1966). (S73); page 137 and 140.

[344] ibid; page 314

[345] Virginia Soldiers of the American Revolution; compiled by Hamilton J. Eckenrode; copyrighted and published in 1989 by the Virginia State Library and Archives (S75); page 184. ISBN: 0-88490-164-5

Line, is located in present day West Virginia just south of the Maryland border and, again, quite near another section of the "Great Road."

The Alabama Migration

In 1818[346], after about twenty-one years in northern Tennessee, Isaac, his family, and a number of neighbors and relatives traveled on flatboats to an area called Pleasant Grove[347] around the border of Franklin County Tennessee and Jackson County Alabama[348]. By this time, Isaac and Frankie had added five more daughters and a son to their family; their first daughter Elizabeth (now Rogers), who had recently become widowed, and her son George Rogers ID 3849, about three years old, joined them on the trip south. Before departing Hawkins County, Isaac sold his land to Elizabeth's father-in-law George (her deceased husband William Leroy Rogers ID 2674 was George's son), John Briscoe and Larkin Willis. The latter is probably not related to the Willis brothers who later married Lara Athens ID 3091 and Anne Muriel ID 3112, daughters of Hezekiah Davis Gonce ID 3038, since Hezekiah's family had already returned to Maryland by the time they married.

As with the earlier migration, I'm unaware of any information that would suggest why the move took place but, in a similar pattern to the first, Alabama had become a State in 1819. Isaac received title to about 80 acres of government land on 10 May 1831. His son Randolph ID 2659 received title to an additional 80 acres shortly thereafter, on 15 June 1831. There is still a Gonce family presence in this area (which includes the town of Gonce, AL) as well, and there is another Gonce Cemetery just over the Tennessee border.

The table below lists the participants in the second migration from northern Tennessee to southern Tennessee and northern Alabama.

Parents and Children	Notes & Comments
Isaac (Ikie) Gonce ID 2583 (26 JUL 1770 – 4 DEC 1853), age 48	Isaac sold his land to his daughter Elizabeth's father-in-law and two others.
Frances (Frankie) Wilson ID 2589 (4 AUG 1778 – 18 JUL 1842), age 40	
Elizabeth (Bettie) Gonce Rogers ID 2658 (now a widow), age 20	The following children were born in Alabama after the second migration.
	Lydia C. Gonce ID 2666 (abt 1820 - abt 1851)
Elizabeth's son George	Kiziah Gonce ID 2667 (1822 - abt 1848)

---

[346] The year is given in a letter from William Leroy Rogers ID 3851 (b. 14 MAY 1838) of Cleburne TX to his grandson W.B. Rogers, dated 15 July 1922. His grandson was marrying a girl named Rogers, and William Leroy was giving a family history to assure W.B. that he and his fiancé were not related.

[347] "The Roots and Branches of Jacob (Jake) Newton Williams and Sallie Elizabeth Allison" by Betty Williams Houston; pages 97 & 98 "The Gonce Family" contributed by Eliza B. Woodall; 1984 (out of print)

[348] The area they settled was literally on the border; the home called Kinderhook, built in 1875 by John Wisdom Gonce ID 2836, supposedly had the border running through the middle of the house.

OUR GONCE ANCESTORS

Rogers ID 3849 (b 24 OCT 1815), age 3 Randolph Gonce ID 2659 (11 JUN 1800 - 13 JAN 1848), age 18 Margaret (Peggy) Gonce ID 2660 (5 FEB 1802 – 1883), age 16 Frances (Fannie) Gonce ID 2661 (1804 TN –), age 14 Ann Gonce ID 2662 (1806 – 1843), age 12 Sarah Gonce ID 2663 (1808 –), age 10 Wilson Gonce ID 2664 (1810 –), age 8 Mary Gonce ID 2665 (1812 –), age 6	In his 1922 letter referenced above, William Leroy Rogers ID 3851 refers to "7 other daughters and 2 sons" in addition to his grandmother Betty and father George, but I have only been able to identify five of the daughters.

James Matthews and his Wife
    eight children, including two daughters listed below and
    James B. Matthews ID 2701 (26 DEC 1795 - 16 OCT 1853)
	The child James B. Matthews later married Elizabeth Gonce Rogers on 29 DEC 1818.

[???] Matthews (daughter of James above) and her husband Michael Looney	Moses, Michael and Isom Looney were brothers from Botecourt County VA. Moses remained in Tennessee. Michael Looney and his wife apparently had no children.
[???] Matthews (daughter of James above) and her husband Absalom Stubblefield three children	
Isom Looney and his Wife several grown children	Brother of Michael above.
James Arnold and his Wife six children	
John Stewart and his Wife three children	
Drury Rice and his Wife Abigail Steward	

APPENDIX I – GONCE FAMILY SOUTHERN MIGRATIONS

six children	
John Matthews and his Wife	Brother of James; who settled on Little Coon.
six children	

Later migrations spread the Gonce name from Tennessee to Missouri (1852 and 1867) and Texas (1858 and 1875). My book "Abraham Rudolph Gonce – Missouri Pioneer," ISBN 978-0-61591-44-8, covers a few of these relatives.

Early 1831 Alabama Land Purchase Deeds for Isaac Gonce and his oldest son Randolph

Note that these deeds are both signed by President Andrew Jackson.

■ 148 ■

Gonce Reverse Migrations

Interestingly, members of some later generations of the Gonce branch that originally migrated to Tennessee in the period following the American Revolution managed to make their way back to Delaware and Maryland, although it seems doubtful they were aware that they were "returning."

Earl "Woodie" Gonce

Woodie Gonce [ID 4477], whose full name was Woodrow T. Gonce, died on April 29, 2000 in Kent County, Delaware – very close to the location from which his ancestors had lived two hundred years earlier. His obituary in the local newspaper, shown to the right, might lead one to the assumption that he was a descendant of the mid-Atlantic branch of the Gonce family, but his story is more interesting.

Woodie, born on 4 March 1918, is actually a 2nd great-grandson of Isaac "Ikie" Gonce [ID 2583], who lived from 26 July 1770 to 4 December 1853, and was one of the original group that left for Tennessee back in the late eighteenth century. Ikie moved his family, including Woodie's then 18 year old great-grandfather Randolph Gonce [ID 2659], south to northern Alabama in 1818.

Isaac's grandson Randolph Madison Gonce [ID 2693] (7 October 1840 - 26

> The News Journal
> Wilmington, Delaware
> May 1, 2000
> Obituary
>
> Earl W. "Woodie" Gonce, age 83, of Townsend, died Saturday in the Kent General Hospital. Mr. Gonce operated a Dairy Farm near Townsend and also was involved with Race Horses, his favorite being "Lucky Ron Ron." He was a member of the US Trotting Association and also enjoyed Coon Hunting. His wife, Virginia Frances Gonce, died in 1994. He is survived by 1 son, [living – name removed] of Dover; 4 daughters, [living] of Smyrna, [living] of Orange Park, FL, [living] of Sharpetown, MD and [living] of Troy, PA; 2 brothers, [living] Gonce of Townsend and [living] Gonce of Dover; 1 sister, [living] of Clayton; 12 grandchildren and 7 great-grandchildren.
>
> Services will be held on Wed. at 11 a.m. in the Daniels & Hutchison Funeral Home, 212 N. Broad St., Middletown. Viewing will be Tuesday evening from 7-9 p.m. at the Funeral Home. Burial will be in Dulaneys Church Cemetery, Clayton.
>
> Copyright (c) The News Journal.

December 1907), was still living in Alabama just across the Tennessee border, when the Civil War broke out. He joined Company I of the 17th Tennessee Regiment as a Confederate soldier in April of 1861 and served through the end of the Civil War. Randolph Madison Gonce is also mentioned on page 175 (Other Gonces in the American Civil War) of this book.

Isaac's great-grandson (Randolph Madison's son) William T. (Will) Gonce [ID 3561] (abt 1879 - 14 November 1928), a fourth generation Alabama resident, eventually migrated west, living in Texas and eventually becoming an oil field manager in Oklahoma. Woodie was the second child of Will Gonce and his wife Ophelia [ID 4475] and, for reasons I haven't yet determined, settled in Delaware after his military service in World War II.

APPENDIX I – GONCE FAMILY SOUTHERN MIGRATIONS

Hugh Bernard Gonce; Pilot Officer of the Royal Air Force

Woody's older brother Hugh Bernard Gonce [ID 4476], Will and Ophelia's first child, also served in World War II, but had actually joined that conflict prior to official American involvement. Hugh had been trained as a pilot, and joined the volunteers of England's Royal Air Force, where he was a "Pilot Officer"[349] commanding a bomber flight crew in the 156th Squadron.

On 16 April 1943, while on a bombing run in their Avro Lancaster Bomber[350] to attack Pilzen, Hugh and the six men in his multi-national crew were shot down and crashed in the area of Aigny, France. Hugh's burial took place in Marne, France, and his tombstone is shown to the right.

Hugh Gonce is mentioned, not only because his is an interesting story, but because I have encountered at least one web posting[351] suggesting that he was actually English, and thus offering additional support for the idea that the Gonces might have an English origin. His quintessentially British name "Hugh Bernard" only adds to the believability of this speculation.

But – Hugh Bernard Gonce was clearly an American descendant of Justice Gonce, and he appears in Oklahoma with Woodie and their parents at 325 East Iowa St; Walter City, Cotton County, Oklahoma on both the 1920[352] and 1930[353] United States censuses.

Tombstone of Plt.Off. Hugh Bernard Gonce in the Chalons-en-Champagne East Communal Cemetery, Marne, France

Hezekiah Davis Gonce

Isaac's twin brother Abraham (Abie) Gonce [ID 2584] was, of course, another of the original group that migrated to Tennessee, but his descendants remained in the same northeastern area of the state for several generations.

So far as I can determine, Abie's son Vance Gonce [ID 2881] and Vance's son William D. Gonce [ID 3020] never left the area. William D. Gonce, by the way, is

---

[349] "Pilot Officer" is often abbreviated Plt.Off. in English records; his RAF service number was 146157.
[350] The plane's ID number, for those who care about such things, was W4930. The web sites
http://olivier.housseaux.free.fr/AVIONS/W4930/equipage.htm and
http://www.weltkriegsopfer.de/_Neuheiten_2.html?sold=1&dat=1222207201 contain information on Plt.Off. Gonce's mission.
[351] Although there are several, it appears as if most are repetitions of the same source speculation.
[352] NARC Microfilm Series t625 Roll 1459 Page 16b
[353] NARC Microfilm Series t626 Roll 1896 Page 2b

an older brother of the infamous Abraham Rudolph "Doc" Gonce, about whom I have written elsewhere. William is buried at the Gonce Hollow Cemetery discussed on page 195.

Hezekiah Davis Gonce [ID 3038] (24 October 1869 - 10 May 1941), known as "Car," was the third child of William D. Gonce and his second wife Vianna Anderson [ID 3029].

After living in Tennessee for most of his life[354], Hezekiah and his wife Martha Maryland Collins [ID 3088] moved with several of their children[355] back to Maryland in 1920, at which time they were living in Oakland Mills (Howard County), Maryland.

The reason for their move is a mystery, and it apparently didn't work out the way they expected. On page 56 of his book[356], Arch Heck quotes Hezekiah's daughter Annie [ID 3112] as saying:

> "...They were prosperous as farmers and merchants in Tennessee ... To their everlasting regret they moved to Maryland March 25, 1920 and settled here in Howard County on a large dairy farm. It was too late in life for them to uproot and settle in a new territory. They never adjusted themselves to their new surroundings, the people, or their habits."

As with Hugh Gonce discussed above, I have as yet uncovered no explanation for why Hezekiah and his family moved to Maryland[357]. Many of his descendants still live in the Maryland area, however, often resulting in quite a bit of confusion when attempting to determine whether or how the many Gonces in the mid-Atlantic region are related.[358]

---

[354] He appears there in every census from 1870 through 1920.

[355] At least two of their daughters had already been married, and their son Walter Lee Gonce permanently returned to Tennessee in late 1933.

[356] "Descendants of Hezekiah Davis I" Arch O. Heck; Columbus Ohio, 1965. Annie Gonce Kepding's letter was written to Professor Heck on July 5, 1962.

[357] It would indicate a lack of attention on my part not to point out the coincidence of "Maryland" being part of Martha's name. Unfortunately this seems to be just a coincidence and nothing more.

[358] For the record, I am fairly certain that all Gonces in the United States are related in some fashion.

APPENDIX II

Location of my 4th great-grandparents Samuel Comegys and Rachel Vansant in 1820

Location of Samuel Comegys in 1820

This discusses my selection of the appropriate census page for Samuel Comegys [ID 2508] and his wife Rachel Vansant Comegys [ID 2509] in the 1820 census.

The name Samuel Comegys was quite common in both Kent and Cecil County Maryland during the revolutionary period and early nineteenth century. For the most part, the various counts and age groupings allow us to select the appropriate census form[359], but in the year 1820, it happens that there are two viable possibilities: one in Kent County, and one in Cecil County. The two counties are close enough that back and forth migration between them was common. During this time period, the Kent County Quaker community served both counties, and the Presbyterian Church in Cecil County also served both Counties.

The choice, therefore, is not obvious, so the following tables will present the counts for each of these census listings along with the pros and cons for the selection of each.

First is the Kent County listing[360]:

1820 United States Census Listing for "Sam'l Comegys" in Kent County, MD	
1820 Census Counts	Comments (my assumptions)
1 Free White Male, age 26-44:	born 1776-1794 – Samuel Comegys, head of household.
1 Free White Female, age 18-26:	born 1794-1802 – presumably the wife of Samuel
1 Free White Female, age 10-15:	born 1805-1810 – presumably a daughter who would have appeared in the 1810 census
1 Free White Female, age <10:	born 1811-1820 – presumably another daughter that would not have appeared on the 1810 census
No Other Entries on Line:	(no slave ownership)

Our Samuel was born in about 1784. His wife Rachel was born in about 1791, which doesn't fit precisely, but the older daughter matches Catharine Comegys, who was born in 1808. If this were the correct listing, it would indicate that Samuel and Rachel had another daughter between the 1810 and 1820 census counts.

Next is my transcription of the Cecil County listing[361], an image of which appears below:

---

[359] Recall that, in censuses prior to 1850, only the names of the head of household were given on the form.
[360] National Archives Microfilm Series m033 Roll 44 Page 126
[361] National Archives Microfilm Series m033 Roll 45 Page 143

Appendix II – Location of Samuel Comegys and Rachel Vansant in 1820

1820 United States Census Listing for "Sam'l Comegys" in Cecil County, MD	
1820 Census Counts	**Comments (my assumptions)**
1 Free White Male, age 26-44:	born 1776-1794 – Samuel Comegys, head of household.
1 Free White Female, age 18-26:	born 1794-1802 – presumably the wife of Samuel
1 Free White Female, age 10-15:	born 1805-1810 – presumably a daughter who would have appeared in the 1810 census
2 Free White Males, age <10:	born 1811-1820 – presumably two younger sons that would not have appeared on the 1810 census
No Other Entries on Line:	(no slave ownership)

Pros and Cons for Selecting the Samuel Comegys in Kent County

Kent County seems to be the obvious choice, since Samuel's forebears had all lived there. He himself had started his family there and appeared in the 1810 census in Kent County.

Samuel was the oldest son and likely to have inherited father Jesse's land in Kent County. On the other hand, it isn't clear that Jesse inherited any of his own father's land and, although his older brother Edward had left land to Jesse in his Will, Jesse predeceased him.

Pros and Cons for Selecting the Samuel Comegys in Cecil County

Samuel and Rachel's daughter Catharine married George Gonce of Cecil County on April 2nd, 1823. As described earlier, I suspect that George was living with his grandfather George Hedney. In the 1820 census[362], the Samuel Comegys of Cecil County had a neighbor called George "Hadley"[363] who might actually be George Hedney – see the image below.

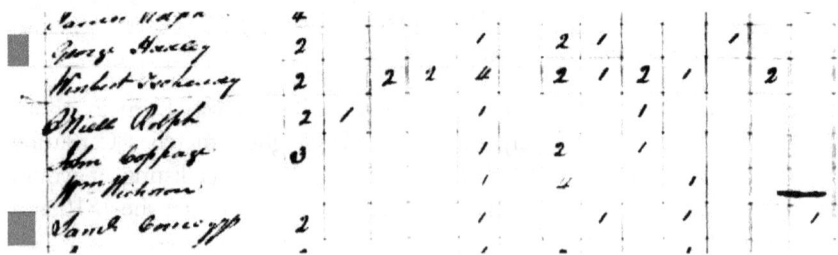

Extract of 1820 US Census Sheet *m033r0045p143* (Cecil County MD) showing lines 32-37

My transcription of the entry for "George Hadley" is shown below:

---

[362] National Archives Microfilm Series m033 Roll 45 Page 143.

[363] This transcription of the original is from the Ancestry.com index; since I haven't found other listings for "George Hadley," the suspicion that this might be our ancestor George Hedney seems warranted.

1820 United States Census Listing for "George Hadley" in Cecil County, MD	
1820 Census Counts	Comments (my assumptions)
1 Free White Male, age 26-44:	born 1776-1794 – possibly George Hedney [2595], died about 1825 **Possibly Our Direct Ancestor**
1 Free White Female, age 26-44:	born 1776-1794 – possibly wife of George above. **Possibly Our Direct Ancestor**
1 Free White Female, age 10-15:	born 1805-1810 –
2 Free White Males, age <10:	born 1811-1820 –
2 White Females, age <10:	born 1805-1810 –
No Other Entries on Line:	(no slave ownership)

Whether or not this is actually George Hedney's household, it is clear that neither George Gonce, who would then have been about 24 years old, nor his younger brother John, were living there in 1820.

Since the two counties are close enough, and our ancestors George Gonce and Catharine Comegys could have easily become acquainted through their church, I believe (at least for the moment) that the Kent County Samuel is likely our ancestor.

APPENDIX III

Birth Year of my 3rd great-grandfather George Gonce

Birth Year of George Gonce

Synopsis of Sources for George Gonce's Date of Birth

It was mentioned earlier that my 3rd great-grandfather George's birth date is uncertain. There are, as we shall see, at least six sources available that give an indication of his birth year, and two of these provide an actual date as well:

These are summarized in the table below and, as can be seen, are inconsistent:

Tombstone of George Gonce

Source	Data Provided	Implied YOB	Date of Birth
Tombstone[364] *(from referenced transcription – tombstone is now illegible)*	"Died June 26, 1860 Aged 68 yrs. 8 Mos. & 14 days"	1791	12 OCT 1791 *(see math below)*
Published Data Compilations[365]	"Gonce, George b. 12 Oct 1791 and d. 26 Jun 1860"	1791	12 OCT 1791 *(stated explicitly)*
1830 U.S. Census[366]	Age Bracket 30-39	1791 to 1800	
1840 U.S. Census[367]	Age Bracket 40-49	1791 to 1800	
1850 U.S. Census[368]	Age 56	About 1794	
1860 U.S. Census[369]	Age 60	About 1800	
George W. Gonce[370] Bible	"B 11/12/1791"	1791	12 NOV 1791

---

[364] The transcription of the tombstone is from "Tombstone and Family Records of Cecil County, Maryland; Volume II" (S156); compiled by Leone R. (Mrs. W. H.) Terrell, Chapter Chair, Daughters of the American Revolution; Elk Chapter. St. Stephen's Protestant Episcopal Church Cemetery is located at 14 Glebe Road in Earleville, Maryland just north of the intersection with Crystal Beach Road.
[365] "Inhabitants of Cecil County Maryland. 1774-1800", compiled by Henry C. Peden, page 103 (S140)
[366] National Archives Series m019, Roll 56, page 5. (S80) See document image on page 67.
[367] National Archives Series m704, Roll 163, page 206. (S81) See document image on page 60.
[368] National Archives Series m432, Roll 290, page 59. (S53) See document image on page 68.
[369] National Archives Series m653, Roll 472, page 44. (S17) See document image on page 63.
[370] This is George Washington Gonce ID 2520, the third child of George Gonce and Catharine Comegys. The transcription of the bible entries was made by John E. Gonce ID 2624 of Charleston, Maryland in November of 1993.

Appendix III – Birth Year of George Gonce of Cecil County, MD

1860	06	26	Date of Death...
–68			...aged 68 years
1792	06	26	
	–8		...aged 8 months
1791	10	26	
		–14	...aged 14 days
1791	10	12	i.e. 12 Oct 1791

George's Birth Date Calculation

Based on the transcription of his tombstone in the St. Stephen's Protestant Episcopal Church Cemetery, his date of birth can be calculated as shown on the right to be 12 October 1791. While this would seem to be supported by the date of birth given in Henry Peden's compilation[371], and only a month off from that recorded in his son George's bible, a date in 1791 would seem to be implausible if not impossible, since his parents would have only been about twelve years old at the time he was born.

Mr. Peden claims to have used the Parish Registers rather than the DAR transcriptions as his source, but without knowing what sources the DAR relied on, I don't know if these two can really be considered alternate sources. As of October 2008, the Parish Registers no longer seem to be present at St. Stephens, and no one there currently knew what had become of them.

The U.S. Censuses for 1830 and 1840 don't provide much help, since they encompass the entire range of dates we are considering, but neither of the two later censuses (1850 and 1860) tend to support the 1791 date.

His son George W. Gonce's bible has the notation "George Gonce; B 11-12-1791; married 04-03-1823; Catherine Comegys; B 8-(illegible)-1810."

It is perhaps presumptuous to question so many sources but, since a birth year of 1791 seems impossible, I suspect his age may have been misread due to the stone's deterioration, and that George's age at death was more likely 63[372]. This would make his date of birth 12 October 1796, which is two weeks before his parents' wedding date of 26 October 1796. Although this is still inconvenient for their reputation[373], it seems to be more plausible.

---

[371] "Inhabitants of Cecil County Maryland. 1774-1800" by Henry C. Peden, published 1993, Family Line Publications; Westminster, MD, page 103. This is located in the University of Baltimore; Baltimore MD Library; Call Number F187 .C3 P135 1993. (S140)

[372] Assuming the "8" was read incorrectly, the only other digit that seems reasonable would be a faded "3."

[373] Actually, it was not uncommon in these days for marriages to be "made official" some time after the families were started. The reason is simply that those who might officiate were in short supply and weren't always available. In the Middle Neck Hundred of Cecil County, there were only thirty families recorded in 1790, a low population density even for that period. The nearest church, where George was eventually buried, was in North Sassafras Hundred to the south.

APPENDIX IV

Birth Year of my 3rd great-grandmother Catherine Comegys

Birth Year of Catherine Comegys

My 3rd great-grandmother Catherine "Kitty" Comegys Gonce passed away in 1858. Kitty is buried in St. Stephens Protestant Episcopal Church Cemetery in Earleville, Maryland. The inscription on her tombstone, as transcribed by the church custodian some years back, is:

"In memory of Catharine A. wife of George Gonce who departed this life July 26, 1858 Aged 19 Yrs. 11 mos. & 11 days." [374].

Synopsis of Sources for her Date of Birth

It was mentioned earlier that Kitty's birth date is uncertain. There are at least five sources available that give an indication of her birth year, one of which is the inscription just mentioned. These are summarized in the table below:

Source	Data Provided	Implied YOB	Date of Birth
Tombstone transcription *(see above – actual inscription now worn and illegible)*	"… departed this life July 26, 1858 Aged 19 Yrs. 11 mos. & 11 days."		15 AUG 1838 or 1808 *(see math below)*
1810 U.S. Census[375]	Age Bracket less than 10	1801 to 1810	
1820 U.S. Census[376]	Age Bracket 10-15	1805 to 1810	
1830 U.S. Census[377]	Age Bracket 20-29	1801 to 1810	
1840 U.S. Census[378]	Age Bracket 30-39	1801 to 1810	
1850 U.S. Census[379]	Age 46	About 1804	
George Gonce[380] Bible	"B 8-*(illegible)*-1810"	1810	?? AUG 1810

---

[374] Yes, the book really says "19 Yrs.", remarkable for someone who bore at least nine children. The tombstone transcription is from "Tombstone and Family Records of Cecil County, Maryland; Volume II" (S156); compiled by Leone R. (Mrs. W. H.) Terrell, Chapter Chair, Daughters of the American Revolution; Elk Chapter. St. Stephen's Protestant Episcopal Church Cemetery is located at 14 Glebe Road in Earleville, Maryland just north of the intersection with Crystal Beach Road.

[375] National Archives Series m252, Roll 14, page 906. (S78)

[376] National Archives Series m033, Roll 45, page 143. (S79) See the discussion of her family's location in 1820 on page 155.

[377] National Archives Series m019, Roll 56, page 5. (S80) See the document image on page 56.

[378] National Archives Series m704, Roll 163, page 206. (S81) See the document image on page 60.

[379] National Archives Series m432, Roll 290, page 59. (S53) See the document image on page 68.

[380] This is George Washington Gonce [ID 2520], the third child of George Gonce and Catharine Comegys. The transcription of the bible entries was made by John E. Gonce [ID 2624] of Charleston, Maryland in November of 1993.

APPENDIX IV – BIRTH YEAR OF CATHERINE COMEGYS OF CECIL COUNTY, MD

```
 1858   07   26  Date of Death...        1858   07   26  Date of Death...
 -19                ...aged 19 years      -49                ...aged 49 years
 1839   07   26                           1809   07   26
        -11         ...aged 11 months            -11         ...aged 11 months
 1838   08   26                           1808   08   26
             -11   ...aged 11 Days                    -11   ...aged 11 days
 1838   08   15    i.e. 15 Aug 1838       1808   08   15    i.e. 15 Aug 1808
```

Catherine's Birth Date Calculation based on the tombstone transcription given in S156, showing her age at death as 19.

Catherine's Birth Date Calculation, assuming the transcribed "19" for her age in years is actually "49" (see text).

Simple math based on the tombstone inscription gives us a birth date of 15 August 1838 (see the calculation above left), which is obviously incorrect.

Because the tombstone is completely faded[381], it seems possible that the "19" could actually have been some other number with a straight line, such as "4" or "7." "5" or "9" are also possible, but seem less likely. An age of 79 seems highly unlikely, so assuming she was actually 49 at the time of her death, her birth date would have been 15 August 1808 (see the calculation above right), which more closely matches the other sources shown.

Unless and until some better source appears, I am accepting 15 August 1808 as Kitty's birth date.

St. Stephens Episcopal Church

The place where George and Kitty Gonce were married and buried was originally built in 1735 and later rebuilt in 1824. This modern photograph shows the church as it was after being rebuilt again in the 1870-1873 time period. The cemetery can be seen on the right.

---

[381] Emily Manlove of St. Stephens' Church reports that, as of late October 2008, the tombstones for Catharine and George Gonce were "intact, but not legible." She further reported that, when a diagram of the churchyard was made in 2001, the recorder marked Catharine's age as "19/79? Yrs" and couldn't make out the months or days.

Appendix V

Birth Year of my 2nd great-grandmother Catharine Ann Sullivan

Birth Year of Catharine Ann Sullivan

Synopsis of Sources for Catharine Ann Sullivan's Date of Birth

We have several sources for Catharine's year of birth. Unfortunately, the years they give vary from 1825 to 1834, so we need to make some inferences to eliminate some of them. The following table outlines these sources:

Year	Based On	My Comments
1829 or early 1830	1830 U.S. Census[382] (Philadelphia, PA)	Without specific names on this undated census form, it isn't certain that this is actually Catharine and her parents Eugene (shown as "Eugine") and Mary, but it seems to be a likely match for what we know of their family, since there is no indication that they had a daughter before Catharine. There is an as yet unidentified Lillie Sullivan buried in lot T-295 at New Cathedral Cemetery[383], however, which could be an earlier daughter of Eugene's who died young.
? – ?	1840 U.S. Census	Not Located. Locating this might resolve the question of whether Catharine is the newborn female in the 1830 census, or whether that infant is Lillie, and Catharine was actually a second child, perhaps born in 1831 or 1832.[384]
1825	1850 U.S. Census[385] (Cecil County, MD)	The census taker in Cecil County recorded Catharine's age as 24 on August 22nd of that year while the Gonces were visiting John's sister Margaret and her husband George Moore. It is possible that John and Catharine didn't wish to let on to John's Cecil County relatives how young Catharine actually was when they were married. Possibly George or Margaret responded and simply guessed.
1829	1850 U.S. Census[386] (Baltimore, MD)	Catharine's age was recorded as 20 in Baltimore on October 7th of that year. Since John and Catharine were staying with Catharine's parents at the time, there would have been no point in attempting to hide her actual age.

---

[382] National Archives Microfilm Series m019 Roll 159 Page 465
[383] See the appendix "Cemetery Mysteries – Section T Lot 295" on page 183 for more information.
[384] See research ID 56 in the appendix "Suggestions for Further Research" on page 267.
[385] National Archives Microfilm Series m432 Roll 290 Page 61
[386] National Archives Microfilm Series m432 Roll 284 Page 189

APPENDIX V – BIRTH YEAR OF CATHARINE ANN SULLIVAN

? – ?	1860 U.S. Census	Not Located.
1829	1870 U.S. Census[387] (Baltimore, MD)	Catharine's age was given as 40 when the census was taken on August 10th of that year.
1832	1880 U.S. Census[388] (Baltimore, MD)	Catharine's age was given as 47 when the census was taken on June 2nd of that year.
? – ?	1890 U.S. Census (Veterans Schedules)	Not Located. The 1890 census is known to have been destroyed, but although the 1890 Veterans Schedule from 1890 for Maryland supposedly survived, neither John nor Catharine's name appears in the segments I located.
1834 (Nov)	1900 U.S. Census[389] (Baltimore, MD)	On June 3rd of 1900, Catharine's age was reported as 65 and her month and year of birth were given as November 1834.
1832	9 MAR 1905 Widow's Pension Application	On her application for a Widow's Pension, Catharine stated that she was age 72.
? – ?	1910 U.S. Census	Not Located. Catharine is not living with her sons George, William, or Thomas, and her daughter Mary died in 1909. Her other children haven't yet been found in 1910.
1832	Cemetery Headstone – Lot T-295[390]	The headstone at New Cathedral Cemetery in Baltimore seems to have been made and placed on the lot well after the deaths of my 2nd great-grandparents, and without being recorded in the cemetery records. See Appendix VII beginning on page 183.

Since the date of Catharine Ann Sullivan's marriage to John T. Gonce, 12 January 1847, seems to be well documented[391], one possible way to eliminate some of the suspected years of birth would be to determine what Catharine's age at marriage would have been if she had been married in each of the years suggested.

These ages at marriage are calculated in the following table:

---

[387] National Archives Microfilm Series m593 Roll 580 Page 565

[388] National Archives Microfilm Series mdt9 Roll 505 Page 480

[389] National Archives Microfilm Series t623 Roll 616 Page 179 (segment shown on page 85)

[390] See the photograph of this headstone on page 86 and in Appendix VII.

[391] Documentation included in Civil War Pension Records, specifically page 10 (applicant questionnaire of 4 June 1898) and page 75 (11 March 1905 letter from church validating marriage). In her widow's pension affidavit, Catharine also states on page 68, dated 11 March 1905, that she had been married for 58 years.

Catharine's Age at Marriage Based on Suspected Years of Birth					
Suspected Year of	1825	1829	1830	1832	1834
Marriage date: - birth year: - birth month: - birth day:	1847 01 12 -1825 22 01 12 -11 21 02 12 -07 21 02 05	1847 01 12 -1829 18 01 12 -11 17 02 12 -07 17 02 05	1847 01 12 -1830 17 01 12 -11 16 02 12 -07 16 02 05	1847 01 12 -1832 15 01 12 -11 14 02 12 -07 14 02 05	1847 01 12 -1834 13 01 12 -11 12 02 12 -07 12 02 05
Resulting Age at Marriage:	Just over 21 Unlikely	Just over 17 Most Likely	Just over 15 Doubtful	Just over 14 Very Doubtful	Just over 12 Very Doubtful
Number of Sources:	1	3	0	3	1

All of the available censuses through 1870 seem to suggest that Catharine's year of birth is 1829. My assumption therefore, is that 1829 is Catharine's most likely year of birth unless it can be shown otherwise, in which case it seems unlikely that it would be any later than 1831.

The slowing of the aging process in someone's later years (e.g. Catharine was 40 years old in 1870, but had only reached 47 years old by 1880 and 65 in 1900) isn't an unknown phenomenon when looking at census records, so it is easy to discount the discrepancies in 1880 and 1900. In any case, if she had been born in 1832 or 1834, her likely age at her marriage in January 1847 would more likely have resulted in John's arrest than a quiet marriage.

1832 is barely plausible given that she would have been 14 at the time of her marriage, but it seems more likely to me that this represents an educated guess (and without the benefits of marriage mathematics) on the part of whichever descendant ordered and placed the tombstone, and supported by the age she reported in 1880 and subsequent years. The possibility remains, however, that whoever did this may have had access to information or documentation I haven't yet discovered.

APPENDIX VI

Gonces in the American Civil War

 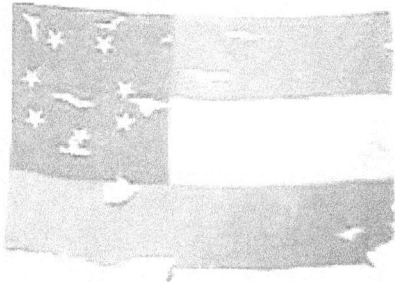

Gonces in the American Civil War

My 2nd great-grandfather John Thomas Gonce's service in the Civil War is discussed in the main body of this book beginning on page 72. This appendix discusses the service of others in our extended family.

I know of no photographs of my 2nd great-grandfather John Thomas Gonce*, but these photos show two of his compatriots from Company B of the 6th Regiment, Maryland Infantry.

These men were certainly acquaintances of John's.

* ...but see the photograph of the unidentified Civil War soldier on page 246

Private Thomas Moffitt, who died at the Prisoner-of-War camp in Andersonville on 13 June 1864. Like many others, he suffered from what is noted in the records as "chronic diarrhea" – what we now call dysentery[392].

Pvt Moffitt was buried at Andersonville in Grave number 1898.

Private Wesley Pierce, mustered out of service in 1865 due to an unspecified disability.

Pvt. Pierce is wearing a first-issue dress uniform and holding an Austrian Lorenz musket with attached bayonet at his side. On the pedestal to his left can be seen his "Hardee Hat" with the Company B insignia.

Like most soldiers of Company B, Private Pierce was recruited from and lived in Cecil County, Maryland, although he was originally born in Pennsylvania in 1839.

Other Gonces in the American Civil War

Like many families, the Gonces had sons, brothers, and cousins who fought on both sides of the Civil War. It is unlikely, however, that any of these other participants knew or had ever heard of John Thomas Gonce[393]. The following, derived from a variety of sources, is a list of Gonces other than my 2nd great-grandfather known to have served in the Civil War, and my best guess at identifying their place in the Gonce Family Tree:

---

[392] Andersonville Prisoners of War; The Generations Network, Provo, Utah; page 18 [3]; page 229 [5].
[393] ... except, of course, for his younger brother George – the first in the following list.

APPENDIX VI – GONCES IN THE AMERICAN CIVIL WAR

George Washington Gonce ID 2520 (30 JUN 1828 – 15 AUG 1902) served in Company H of the 6th Regiment in the Union Army. George was John Thomas Gonce's younger brother. His name was often spelled "Gans" in the surviving records.

John Anderson Gonce ID 3154 (12 FEB 1844 – 24 FEB 1886) was in the Union Army as a Private in the 9th Regiment of the Michigan Infantry. At the time of the 1860 census, John was a sixteen year-old living in Tennessee[394], so if he went out of his way to join the Union army, he must have been a committed abolitionist. After the conflict, he remained in the north, settling in Illinois[395], and later moving to Texas. Like all of the Civil War veterans listed here, John Anderson Gonce is a 3rd cousin of our John Thomas Gonce. John Anderson Gonce was the sixth child of John Rudolph Gonce ID 2880, and a grandson of Abraham Gonce ID 2584, one of the twin sons of Rudolph Gonce who first migrated to Tennessee.

William V. Gonce ID 3153 (1838 -) was one of two Gonces known to have died in the Civil War. William, a Private, served in the 60th and 129th Regiments of the Ohio Infantry on the Union forces. William was John Anderson Gonce's older brother – the second child of John R. Gonce. William was John Thomas Gonce's third cousin.

Thomas Allibone Robaris Gonce ID 2604 (21 DEC 1839 - aft 9 SEP 1861), younger brother of John Thomas and George Washington Gonce, was drafted at a relatively late period in the war (June 1864) but, as far as I can determine, never saw action.

Randolph Madison Gonce ID 2693 (7 OCT 1840 - 26 DEC 1907) of Alabama served in Company I of the 17th Regiment, Confederate Tennessee Infantry[396]. He is the son of Randolph Gonce ID 2659 and the grandson of Isaac Gonce ID 2583, one of Rudolph Gonce's children who made the original journey to the south. Randolph was discharged as a Corporal.

Markiel W. Gonce ID 4051 was in Company H of the 16th Regiment of the Confederate Missouri Infantry. He is the third child of Wilson Gonce ID 2664, who himself served in the Creek Indian Wars in 1815 and moved to Missouri; Markiel would, therefore, be a first cousin of Randolph Madison Gonce above. He is *not*, as stated in one source, Marion Wilson Gonce ID 2739, who wasn't born until 11 August 1865. Markiel entered Confederate service as a 1st Lieutenant, but was discharged as a Private, a reduction in rank for which I've found no explanation, although it may be related to his status as a prisoner-of-war. He was captured on 4 July 1863 at Helena, Arkansas, and sent to Overton Military Hospital in Memphis Tennessee. A notation on the POW commissioned officer roster says "transferred to Prov. Man. Memphis

---

[394] National Archives Microfilm Series m653 Roll 1241 Page 251.
[395] National Archives Microfilm Series m593 Roll 233 Page 494b.
[396] Randolph's enlistment record is shown on page 54 of the "Gonce & Wynne Genealogy."

Sep 28, 1862 (1041W).[397]" Several other prisoners at the same location were released after taking an oath of loyalty, but Markiel was "Sent to New Orleans Jan 9th 1865."[398] at Fort Warren, Boston Harbor. The records aren't explicit, but it appears that he died there. Markiel was John Thomas Gonce's third cousin.

Jefferson Gonce ID 3025 (about 1840 -) served in the 28th Tennessee Cavalry. Like John Thomas Gonce, Jefferson's surname is also spelled in different ways in his military records, being variously Gonce or Gaunce. The name on what I believe is his pension card is Thomas Gonce. I believe he is the eleventh child of Vance Gonce ID 2881 and grandson of Abraham Gonce ID 2584, one of the twin sons of Rudolph Gonce who first migrated to Tennessee. He is therefore John Thomas Gonce's third cousin.

Thomas Jefferson Gonce ID unk served in what appears to be the 38th Missouri Infantry (the handwriting is very poor). He received a pension as an invalid on 9 August 1920 at which time he was living in Arkansas. I have no idea how he is related to our family at this time, nor why he would qualify for a U.S. Pension[399]. This cannot be the Thomas Jefferson Gonce ID 3535 who was the son of the infamous Abraham Rudolph "Doc" Gonce ID 2883, since he wasn't born until 3 January 1866. It is possible, however, that he is the same individual listed as "Jefferson Gonce" above, particularly since that "Jefferson" was also known as "Thomas."

A. J. Gonce ID unk a Private in Company F[400] of a unit I can't determine, was captured at Fredericksburg, Maryland on 3 May 1863 (The most well-known "Battle of Fredericksburg" took place in December of 1862, so this was apparently in a later encounter.) The only Gonce I can locate with these initials is Arthur Jennings Gonce (7 Aug 1899 – 1 Jan 1969), but his line doesn't have an earlier Arthur Jennings of the right age that I can determine.

Isaac Gonce ID 3155? a "citizen detainee"[401] who was treated as a Union prisoner-of-war. He was captured on 24 April 1862 with the McDonnough Regiment of Missouri at McDonnough. Isaac was then hospitalized with Variola and died of smallpox in the hospital at St. Louis, Missouri on 24 January 1863. I have been unable to identify him; the only likely candidate seems to be the twelve-year-old tenth child ID 3155 of John R. Gonce ID 2880 (unlikely, since John's other sons were Union Soldiers).

Mary Gonce ID unk was another civilian detainee held at the Union Prisoner of War Hospital in Nashville, Tennessee[402]. Notations in the POW roster

---

[397] The "1862" seems legible enough, but should probably read "1863."
[398] National Archives Microfilm Series m598, Pages 80 and 82.
[399] The little research I've done indicates that Confederate Veterans did not qualify for U.S. Pensions, but he may have later served in some other conflict.
[400] National Archives Microfilm Series m598, Page 144.
[401] National Archives Microfilm Series m598, Pages 10, 28, and 72.
[402] National Archives Microfilm Series m598, Page 2.

there say that Mary was released on 8 April 1864 by order of the Provost Marshall at the expiration of her sentence, but doesn't suggest what she had done to merit confinement. Under "rank," Mary and a few others in similar circumstances are listed simply as "citizen." I have no idea who this, although Mary Gonce ID 3320, "Doc" Gonce's wife[403] at that time, may be a possibility.

Civil War Miscellany – George Gonce's Sons

LOCAL AFFAIRS.

Draft of the 100 *Days Men*.—1st district, Wm. Booker, C. C. Carpenter, T. A. R. Gonce, Francis King, Z. P. Lusby, Benj'n. Lovridge, Barney McCafferty, Nath'nl. McDaniel, John Lotheri, Daniel Pennington, Charles Pope, E. DeK. Richardson, Lee Sooy, G. T. Walmsley.

4th—Wm. Armstrong, G. R. Fulton, Jas. T. Garrett, George C. Gallaher, John Howard, Samuel McDaniel, John M'Allister, Jacob T. Markee, Jas. Radcliff, Alfred P. Simpers, Joseph Scott, Jas. Sterling. One volunteer credited to this district.

6th District,—Lloyd Balderson, Robt. D. Cather, Eli Conlson, Joseph Dennison, Henry Harrison, Henry Maxwell, Allen McKenney, Ellis P. Passmore, Wm. Sharpless, Stephen J. Woodrow, J. R. Whiteside, Jas. H. Wicks.

7th District.—George Bowen, J. M. Bullock, W. Boyd, S. P. Broughton, Aquilla M. Carroll, Hugh Crawford (dead), G. W. Gordon, John S. Gillespie, Hugh Glacken, Dr. W. W. Long, Daniel McGonegal, John Mauldin, Wm. Snyder, John Thompson.

8th District.—J. Blackburn, J. P. Dorrickson, George A. Ewing, C. C. Lecount, N. Montgomery, H. T. Smith.

9th District.—Jonathan Brown, W. W. Cameron, W. H. Harris, Jacob W. McCardell, T. W. Nowland, Caleb E. Williams.

The 2d, 3d, and 5th districts filled by volunteers.

The draft took place at the headquarters of Gen. Berry, in Baltimore, on Wednesday.

2 July 1864 Cecil Democrat

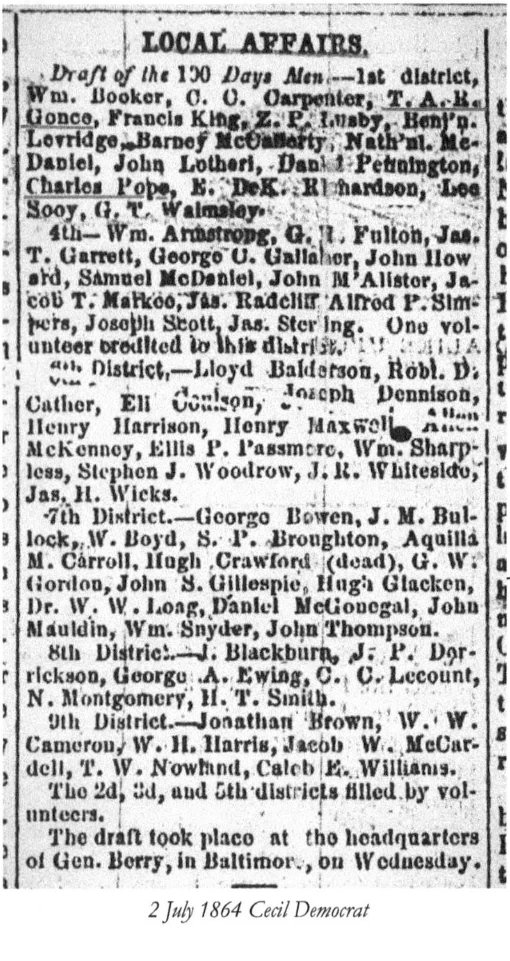

The Cecil Democrat of July 2, 1864, records the drafting of my 2nd great-grand-uncle Thomas Allibone Robaris Gonce, who would have been twenty-four years old at the time. Note that this draft of Cecil County males took place in Baltimore. Drafts were not conducted by draft boards (as in the 20th Century), but by the commanding General of the territory from which both volunteers and draftees were drawn.

Several muster rolls for our ancestor John Thomas Gonce are shown below in order to illustrate the many ways his name was spelled by the company clerks of the 6th Regiment of the Maryland Infantry.

[403] I've written a short biography of "Doc" Gonce and his wives ("Abraham Rudolph Gonce – Missouri Pioneer," ISBN 978-06159-12448), and can't account for his first wife Mary's whereabouts in this general time frame. She doesn't really seem a likely candidate to me, however.

OUR GONCE ANCESTORS

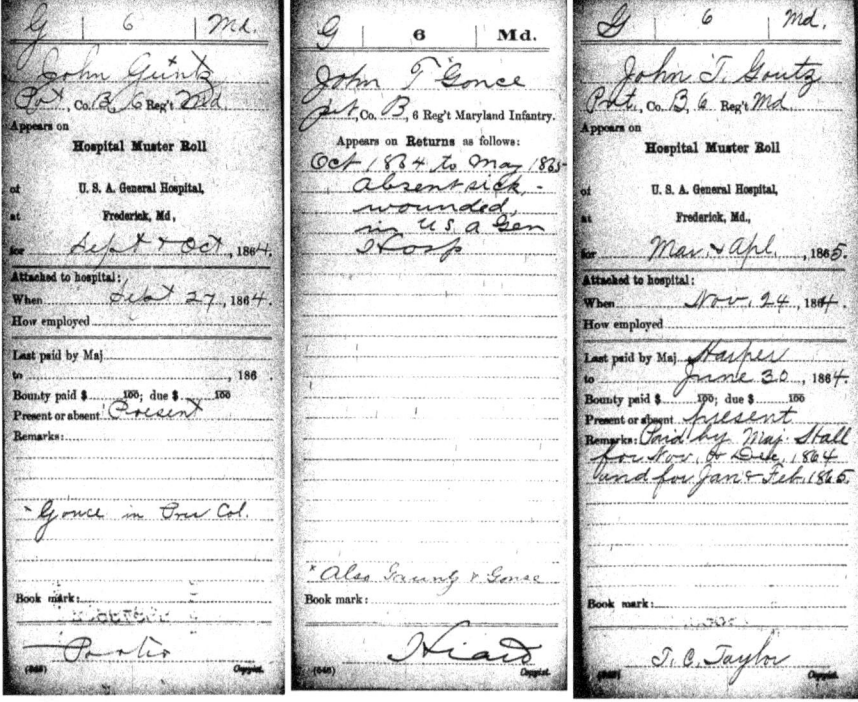

Hospital Muster: Sep/Oct 1864
Guntz and Gonce

Company B Absentee: Oct 1864
Gonce, Gauntz and Ganse

Hospital Muster: Mar/Apr 1865
Gontz

In the first muster roll (far left) from October 1864, we see John's surname spelled both "Guntz" and "Gonce." In the second (center), also from October 1864, we see "Gonce," "Gauntz" and "Ganse." On the far right, the spelling is given as "Gontz."

Left: Colonel John W. Horn, Commanding Officer of Union forces during the Battle of Opequon, also known as the Third Winchester.

Col. Horn was severely wounded during this battle.

Col Horn was John Thomas Gonce's Commanding Officer in the Battle of Opequon.

Command Staff of the 6th Maryland

■ 179 ■

APPENDIX VI – GONCES IN THE AMERICAN CIVIL WAR

Memorial to the 6th Maryland Infantry Regiment

The Sixth Maryland Infantry Regiment Monument

The Sixth Maryland Infantry Regiment Monument was erected in Pamplin Historical Park at Petersburg, Virginia on April 2011 on the spot where my 2nd great-grandfather John Thomas Gonce's unit spearheaded the Sixth Army Corps assault during the early morning hours of April 2, 1865. The Sixth was among the first Union regiments to break the Confederate main line. Fortunately or unfortunately, John Thomas Gonce was severely wounded in the Battle of Opequon the previous fall (September 1864).

The granite monument with its bronze tablet was designed by Gary Casteel, a renowned Civil War sculptor.

Appendix VII

New Cathedral Cemetery Mysteries – Section T Lot 295

Other Gonce Cemeteries of Interest

Cemetery Mysteries – Section T Lot 295

My 2nd great-grandfather John Thomas Gonce ID 1576 was the first Gonce known to have become a Catholic – prompted by his January 1847 marriage to the Irish Catharine Ann Sullivan in Baltimore.

After determining that John and Catharine are both buried in Section T, Lot 295 of New Cathedral Cemetery in Baltimore, Maryland, I obtained the records for the plot. It quickly became apparent that there were quite a number of people buried in the plot, and that these records presented more questions than answers. This appendix will discuss what I've learned about the residents of this large Sullivan-Gonce-McKenna-Butts plot; because many of the names of those buried here remain unidentified, this information is provided as a starting point for others who may wish to do further research into what are likely other Gonce relatives.

It will be helpful to begin by discussing a little of the history of New Cathedral Cemetery, shown in the picture below.

There was, of course, an "Old" Cathedral Cemetery, although it was obviously not referred to that way. In 1814, the trustees of St. Peter's church in Baltimore, which was at the time the seat of the Catholic Church[404] in the United States, purchased six acres of land (later expanded to thirteen) in downtown Baltimore[405] to build an independent religious cemetery for Baltimore's Catholic population.

---
[404] This was *not* a Cathedral, nor was there an actual Archbishop in the United States yet.

APPENDIX VII – NEW CATHEDRAL CEMETERY MYSTERIES

Both Baltimore and its Catholic population grew significantly over the next fifty years and in the meantime Baltimore had become the first Catholic Archdiocese in the new world. The famous architect Benjamin Latrobe[406] had begun planning the *Cathedral of the Assumption of the Blessed Mary* as early as 1806 and, by 1821, it was the new center of the Catholic Church in the United States.

In the early 1860s, it became apparent that a new cemetery needed to be built. In 1869, much of the land comprising the current New Cathedral Cemetery at Old Frederick Road and Edmonson Avenue was acquired. It was originally named "Bonnie Brae" (Scottish for "Beautiful Slope") Cemetery. At around the same time, it was decided that the original cemetery would be closed and all of the existing bodies re-interred at Bonnie Brae. After 1871, no more burials were performed at the old cemetery.

Beginning in 1877, and continuing over the course of the next thirteen years, the remains of those buried in the "Old Cathedral Cemetery" were moved. For reasons I haven't been able to determine, very few of the headstones from the old cemetery were moved along with the remains. On October 11th of 1887, fourteen bodies were moved from the lot owned by Eugean[407] Sullivan $^{ID\ 2599}$, who turned out to be my 3rd great-grandfather[408], to his replacement lot in section T of New Cathedral Cemetery. Eugean, who had already died by this time, was one of those re-interred that October.

While examining the cemetery records, I was surprised to find that there were twenty-five people buried in lot 295[409] – the original fourteen that had been relocated, as well as eleven more (including my 2nd great-grandparents John and Catharine) that had been buried between 1888 and 1941. A photograph of the cemetery record is shown on the next page, followed by a literal transcription[410] of the lower portion of the page.

---

[405] The cemetery was bounded by Winchester Street on the north, Fremont Street on the east, Riggs Avenue (Tenant Street at the time) on the south, and Whatcoat Street (formerly Calhoun Street) on the west.
[406] Benjamin Latrobe (1764-1820) immigrated from France in 1796 and designed (among other things) the U.S. Capitol Building. He also worked closely with Thomas Jefferson on a number of government buildings in Virginia.
[407] Although this is an unusual spelling, it appears this way consistently in other references I have subsequently located, and is therefore assumed to be correct.
[408] Eugean's daughter Catharine Ann $^{ID\ 1577}$ married my great-great grandfather John T. Gonce.
[409] A map and instructions for locating the gravesite are provided below.
[410] The original spellings have been retained.

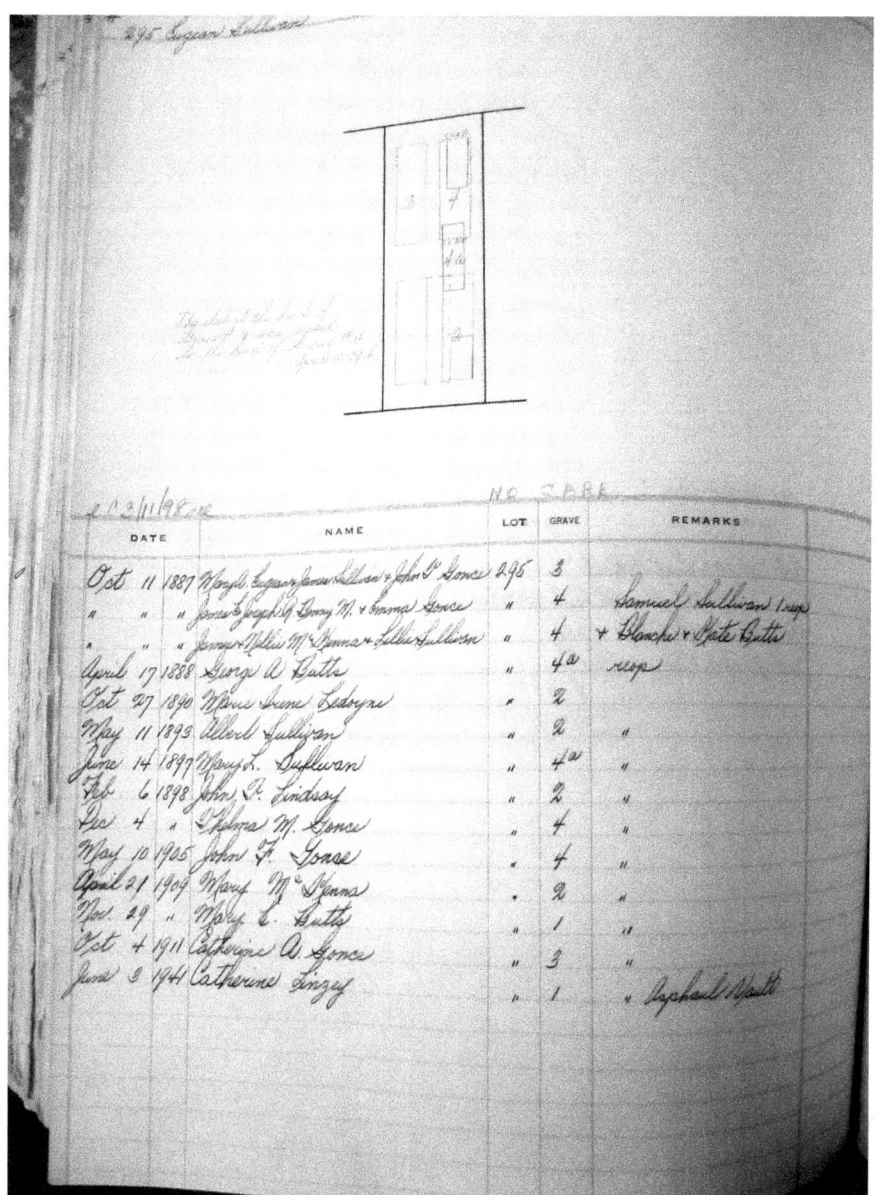

New Cathedral Record Book Page for Section T – Lot 295. The plot owner's name can be seen on upper left.

APPENDIX VII – NEW CATHEDRAL CEMETERY MYSTERIES

A Transcription of the names in the record is provided in the table below:

Date	Name	Lot	Grave	Remarks
Oct 11 1887	Mary A, Eugean & James Sullivan & John T Gonce	295	3	
" " "	James F, Joseph R, Benny M & Emma Gonce	"	4	Samuel Sullivan 1 reop
" " "	James & Nellie McKenna & Lillie Sullivan	"	4	& Blanche & Kate Butts
April 17 1888	George A Butts	"	4a	reop
Oct 27 1890	Marie Irene Ledoyne	"	2	
May 11 1893	Albert Sullivan	"	3	"
June 14 1897	Mary L. Sullivan	"	4a	"
Feb 6 1898	John T. Lindsay	"	2	"
Dec 4 1898	Thelma M. Gonce	"	4	"
May 10 1905	John T. Gonce	"	4	"
April 21 1909	Mary McKenna	"	2	"
Nov 29 1909	Mary E. Butts	"	1	"
Oct 4 1911	Catherine A. Gonce	"	3	"
Jun 3 1941	Catherine Linzey	"	1	" Asphaul Vault [sic]

Since we know for certain that some of these are relatives, it is reasonable to assume that all of them are related in some way, or are at least closely connected, to either the Sullivans or Gonces. It therefore seems useful from a genealogical standpoint to attempt to identify these people, and this appendix is a first attempt at doing so.

A significant point of interest is that the records available in the cemetery's front office indicated there were no monuments or markers on the plot, so we were given very specific instructions on how to identify the plot from other headstones in the area.

When we visited the plot, however, we found that there was indeed a single stone for John T. Gonce and his wife Catharine (sic) Ann.

The condition of the stone is quite good compared to others from the early twentieth century, suggesting that it may have been placed at a later date, but there is nothing to substantiate this. Also, note that Catharine's name on the stone is spelled with the second vowel "a" rather than the more typical "e."

Headstone on Lot 295

The Occupants of Lot 295

The following will discuss each of the names listed as being buried in Lot 295, and what we know about them. For convenience, the names of those re-interred on 11 October 1887 will be given in alphabetical order by surname; the remainder will then be given in chronological order by their burial dates.

Reburials at New Cathedral Cemetery (in alphabetical order)

Name Reburial Date ID Number	Comments about the person
Butts, Blanche Reburied: 11 Oct 1887 ID # 4141	In addition to the four Butts names interred in Lot 295, there was a couple (William $^{ID\ 4135}$ and Mary $^{ID\ 4136}$ Butts) living with my 2nd great-grandfather John T. Gonce and his wife in 1870[411] – another indication that there is some connection to the Gonces. William H. Butts and Myrtle G. Butts were living with John R. and Catharine Linzey (youngest daughter of John T. Gonce) from at least 1889 through 1905[412], but there is no indication of what their relationship was. Unfortunately, however, I have found no information on any Blanche Butts.
Butts, Kate Reburied: 11 Oct 1887 ID # 4142	See the note under Blanche Butts above. I also have no information on any Kate Butts.
Gonce, Benny M. Reburied: 11 Oct 1887 ID # 2974	Benedict and Benjamin appear frequently as given names in the Gonce family, but this particular one is not any of those I have so far identified, since he must have died prior to 1870 in order to have been moved from the old cemetery, and most likely lived in Baltimore. I believe therefore that Benny is likely one of the four children of John and Catharine Gonce who did not survive to adulthood. In the 1900 U.S. Census[413], Catharine is listed as "Mother of 10, 6 living." I suspect Benny was born in about 1854[414], making him the third of the four and fifth child overall.
Gonce, Emma Reburied: 11 Oct 1887	I believe Emma is also one, and the youngest, of the four children of John Thomas and Catharine Gonce who did

---

[411] See an image of this census showing the Gonce and Butts neighbors on page 81.
[412] This information was obtained from various documents in John T. Gonce's Civil War pension records.
[413] National Archives Microfilm Series t623, Roll 616, Page 179. (S19) (Segment shown on page 85)
[414] The birth year estimates for James F., Joseph R., Benny M. and Emma Gonce are based on known gaps in the birth years of John and Catharine's surviving children, and the assumption that their years of birth and death correspond to the order in which they are listed in the burial record. The further assumption, of course, is that they died as infants in the order they were born. Location of the family in the 1860 Census might clarify this, but I have so far been unable to locate them. The number of bodies (25), however, supports the notion that many must be infants.

APPENDIX VII – NEW CATHEDRAL CEMETERY MYSTERIES

Name Reburial Date ID Number	Comments about the person
ID # 3596	not survive to adulthood. I suspect Emma was born in about 1855. She would have been the sixth child born to Catharine. She might also be the unidentified female child of George Gonce shown in the 1830 and 1840 U.S. Censuses but, given her burial in Baltimore, this seems very unlikely.
Gonce, James F. Reburied: 11 Oct 1887 ID # 2973	I believe James is the first of the four children of John Thomas and Catharine Gonce who did not survive to adulthood. I suspect James was born in about 1848.
Gonce, John T. Reburied: 11 Oct 1887 ID # 2628	This is one of two people named John T. Gonce interred here, and this one must have died prior to 1870 in order to have been moved from the old cemetery. My speculation is that he may have been the younger sibling of my 3rd great-grandfather George Gonce, and therefore an uncle of George's son, the other John T. Gonce [ID 1576]. Based on the Baltimore City Directories, there were no Gonces in that city until my 2nd great-grandfather John T. Gonce appeared for the first time in 1853. Directories were not published during the Civil War (1861 – 1863). The difficulty with this attribution is that, from all known records, John T. Gonce [ID 2628] lived in Maryland (Kent and Cecil Counties) and Delaware (New Castle), not Baltimore.
Gonce, Joseph R. Reburied: 11 Oct 1887 ID # 2639	I believe Joseph is the second of the four children of John Thomas and Catharine Gonce who did not survive to adulthood. I suspect Joseph was born in about 1850.
McKenna, James Reburied: 11 Oct 1887 ID # 2866	I believe this is T. James McKenna, who became the husband of Mary Ann Sullivan, sister of Catherine Ann Sullivan and thus the brother-in-law of John T. Gonce. Alternatively, this could just as easily be James' father, who was also named James.
McKenna, Nellie Reburied: 11 Oct 1887 ID # 2987	I believe this is likely the mother of James McKenna above.
Sullivan, Eugean Reburied: 11 Oct 1887 ID # 2599	Eugean (and the name is consistently spelled this way) was my 3rd great-grandfather and the original owner of lot T-295. He is the father of Catharine Ann Sullivan, who married John T. Gonce and became the mother of William Henry Gonce and grandmother of Charles R. Gonce.
Sullivan, James Reburied: 11 Oct 1887 ID # 2971	James is possibly a sibling of Catharine Ann and Mary Ann who died at a rather young age, but it is doubtful that he is a sibling of their father Eugean, since obituaries for Eugean's brother Daniel (that mention Eugean) don't mention him. It's also possible, but unlikely, that he may be

Name Reburial Date ID Number	Comments about the person
	Eugean's father.
Sullivan, Lillie Reburied: 11 Oct 1887 ID # 4146	Lillie is possibly a sibling of Catharine Ann and Mary Ann who died at a rather young age, but it is doubtful that she is a sibling of their father Eugean, since obituaries for Eugean's brother Daniel (that mention Eugean) don't mention her. It is also possible that she may be Eugean's mother.
Sullivan, Mary A. Reburied: 11 Oct 1887 ID # 2600	I believe this is Mary Ann O'Brien, wife of Eugean Sullivan, mother of Catharine Ann Sullivan, mother-in-law of John T. Gonce, and my 3rd great-grandmother. She likely died before 1859, since she is not listed on the records of her daughter Mary Ann's marriage to James McKenna.
Sullivan, Samuel Reburied: 11 Oct 1887 ID # 4147	Samuel is possibly a sibling of Catharine Ann and Mary Ann who died at a rather young age, but it is doubtful that he is a sibling of their father Eugean, since obituaries for Eugean's brother Daniel (that mention Eugean) don't mention him. It is also possible that he may be Eugean's father.

"New" Burials at the cemetery (in chronological order by burial date)

Name Original Burial Date ID Number	Comments about the person
Butts, George A. Buried: 17 Apr 1888 ID # 2633	See the note under Blanche Butts above. I also have no information on any George Butts.
Ledoyne, Marie Irene Buried: 27 Oct 1890 ID # 4149	I have no idea who this is, and can find no records of anyone with the surname Ledoyne or a given name of Marie Irene.
Sullivan, Albert Buried: 11 May 1893 ID # 4144	Albert is possibly a sibling of Catharine Ann and Mary Ann Sullivan, but there is no evidence directly linking them.
Sullivan, Mary L. Buried: 14 Jun 1897 ID # 4148	Because of the first name, it doesn't seem likely that Mary is a sibling of Catharine Ann and Mary Ann Sullivan; she might be the wife of Albert Sullivan, but I haven't located any wedding announcement to confirm this.
Lindsay, John T. Buried: 6 Feb 1898 ID # 2626	This is the husband of Catherine Ann (Kate) Gonce, youngest child of John T. Gonce and Catharine Ann Sullivan. His surname is probably misspelled, since all records signed by his wife used the spelling "Linzey."
Gonce, Thelma M. Buried: 4 Dec 1898	Although possible that Thelma is a sibling of George Gonce (or at least from that generation), it seems unlikely

APPENDIX VII – NEW CATHEDRAL CEMETERY MYSTERIES

Name Original Burial Date ID Number	Comments about the person
ID # 2645	since she would have been in her nineties when she died if that were the case. I can find no record of any child of the next generation named Thelma and, again, her date of death would not be a nice fit with any of that generation. The only speculation that can't be immediately dismissed, therefore, is that she was a Gonce by marriage. In that case, the only likely candidate would be John T. Gonce's younger brother Thomas but, since his burial location is unknown (and it would be reasonable to expect he would be at New Cathedral also if they were married), this identification is speculative at best. It is also possible that this is one of John T. Gonce's children who died before the 1900 Census, when his wife Catharine reported that she was "mother of ten, six living."
Gonce, John T. Buried: 10 May 1905 ID # 1576	This is my 2nd great-grandfather – the father of William Henry Gonce and grandfather of Charles R. Gonce.
McKenna, Mary Buried: 21 Apr 1909 ID # 2865	This is Mary Ann Sullivan, sister-in-law of John T. Gonce and daughter of Eugean Sullivan.
Butts, Mary E. Buried: 29 Nov 1909 ID # 2972	The death date seems to suggest that this was the Mary Butts who, with her husband William, was living with my 2nd great-grandfather John T. Gonce and his wife at the time of the 1870 U.S. Census (see page 81). That begs the question of where William is buried however.
Gonce, Catherine A. Buried: 4 Oct 1911 ID # 1577	This is my 2nd great-grandmother – the wife of John T. Gonce, mother of William Henry Gonce and grandmother of Charles R. Gonce. Note that the spelling "Catharine" appears on her headstone and her husband's pension records in the National Archives.
Linzey, Catharine Buried: 3 Jun 1941 ID # 1581	This is Catharine (known as Kate) Gonce, youngest child of John T. Gonce and Catharine Ann Sullivan. She would be William Henry Gonce's sister and Charles R. Gonce's aunt. The name "Linzey" seems to be the correct spelling (rather than "Lindsay," as shown for her husband above).

Other Mysteries to be Unraveled

- Who put up the tombstone for John Thomas and Catharine Ann and when was it placed? The records originally indicated that there was no stone at all on the plot[415], and the stone doesn't appear to date from as far back as 1911 – the year that Catharine died.
- The New Cathedral Cemetery ledger book, old as it appears, can't be original, can it? An examination of the handwriting on the record book page that is presented on page 185 would seem to indicate that the same person wrote all the entries even though the entries on the page cover a span of 54 years.
- Who is Marie Irene Ledoyne? This is the only instance of the surname Ledoyne I have encountered while researching the Gonce family.
- Who are the Butts family and what is their relationship to the Gonces or Sullivans?
    - George A. Butts was the first person to be originally[416] buried in the plot on 17 April 1888, so there must have been some family connection earlier than that date.
    - On 18 June 1889, both John R. Linzey and William H. Butts listed their addresses as 1112 Etting Street when they signed an affidavit in support of John T. Gonce's Pension renewal application. John Linzey was John T. Gonce's son-in-law – the husband of Catharine Gonce. At the time, the John T. Gonce and his wife lived at 1228 Etting Street.
    - On 9 March 1905, Myrtle G. Butts lived at 910 N. Calhoun St. and Catharine A. Linzey lived at 912 N. Calhoun St. when they witnessed Catharine Gonce's signature on her application for a Widow's Pension[417]. Catharine Gonce was then age 72. All indications suggest that Myrtle G. Butts was the wife of William H. Butts, but this isn't certain.
    - In 1870, a William Butts and his wife Mary E. Butts were living with my 2nd great-grandfather John T. Gonce ID 1576 and his family in the 20th ward of Baltimore City[418].
    - Mary E. Gonce ID 2610 (John T. Gonce's daughter) and Mary E. Butts were both age 17 on the 1870 census, but appeared as separate names in same household, so are likely *not* the same person. Otherwise, it might be assumed that the Mary

---
[415] Notations were made on the cemetery records after we showed our photographs to the management.
[416] i.e. ignoring those who were re-interred from the old cemetery.
[417] Her husband John had just died the previous day, so this payment must have been quite important.
[418] National Archives Series m593 Roll 580 Page 565. See page 81 for an image of part of this census page.

who married William Butts was John Thomas Gonce's daughter.
- o The only record of a William H. Butts I have located is the seven-year-old son of Mary C. Butts of Hagerstown from the 1870 Census[419]. There are a significant number of Butts living in Baltimore in the latter part of the nineteenth century, but there are also some in Anne Arundel County and in New Jersey, although none of the first names I've found match those listed above.

- If the John T. Gonce who was reburied in this cemetery is indeed the son of Rudolph Gonce and younger brother of George Gonce, it would have to be assumed that he moved to Baltimore and converted to Catholicism[420] at some point, since the Gonces up to and including George seem to have been Episcopalians and Methodists. My 2nd great-grandfather John Thomas Gonce [ID 1576] who was buried in 1905 was the first of the Gonces known to have converted to Catholicism, prompted by his marriage to his Irish wife. I consider the identity of the "reburied" John still a mystery to be solved.

---

[419] National Archives Series m593 Roll 596 Page 126.
[420] There is no evidence at all to suggest that he did either.

Locating the Grave Site at New Cathedral Cemetery

The entrance to New Cathedral Cemetery in Baltimore, Maryland, is located at 4300 Old Frederick Road between the intersections with Augusta Avenue and North Athol Avenue.

A map showing the location of Section T within the cemetery is given below:

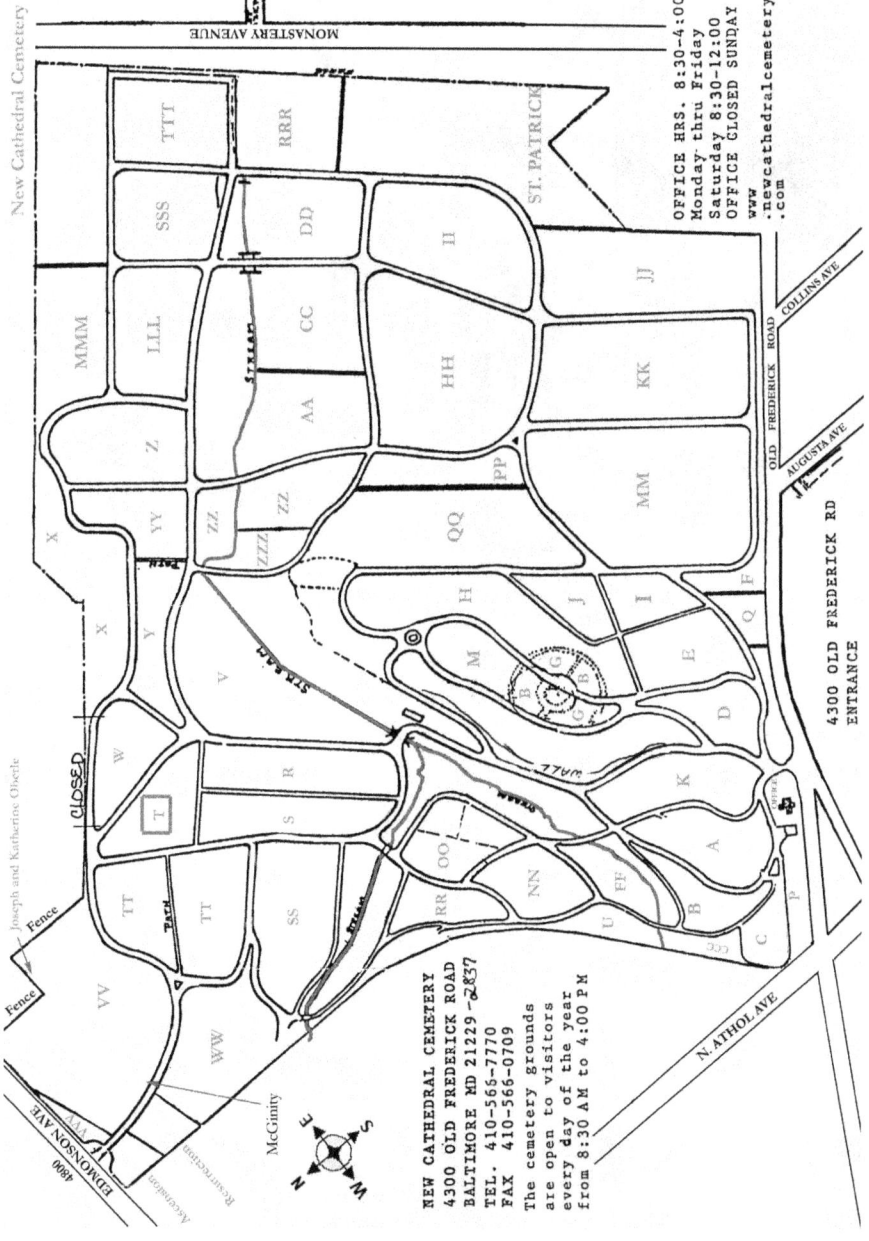

When driving north on the road running between sections T and TT, the plot itself, as shown in the picture below, is just to the east of the road.

My daughter pointing to the only headstone on Lot 295
(taken from west side of section T driving north).

Lot T-295 comprises the entire area between the stone and the obelisk on the far right of the photo.

In the picture, my daughter and the white arrow point to the tombstone illustrated earlier, which is the only marker on the plot.

The plot itself, as near as I can determine from the cemetery records, comprises the entire area outlined by the white borders.

Gonce Cemeteries of Interest

Although primarily of interest to our distant relatives from the "Southern Branch" of the Gonce family, the fact that these relatives were pioneers led to the perpetuation of "Gonce" as a place name in several locations.

Gonce Cemetery – Gonce Hollow Road – Gonce Hollow (Eidson), Tennessee

In Hawkins County, located in northeastern Tennessee, quite close to where the original children of Rudolph Gonce settled, is an early cemetery founded by Hezekiah Gonce.

One of the tombstones from this fenced-in, well-maintained cemetery is shown to the left. Hezekiah Davis Gonce [ID 3021], listed as H. D. Gonce, is buried in this plot along with his wife Chaney Anderson [ID 3093].

Hezekiah, by the way, is an older brother of Abraham Rudolph "Doc" Gonce, about whom I've written another book referenced earlier. He is not the same Hezekiah, known as "Car," who moved his family back to Maryland.

APPENDIX VII – NEW CATHEDRAL CEMETERY MYSTERIES

Gonce Cemetery, Franklin County, Tennessee

Another Gonce Cemetery is located on the original Anderson farm in far southern Tennessee, just north of the Alabama border, but serving the town of Gonce. The town, named after its founders, is at the junction of Sinking Cove Road and Round Cove Road, both of which leave Tennessee separately but intersect just over the Alabama border.

Sarah Anderson ID 2835 married Lemuel Wilson Gonce ID 2834 (shown as L.W. Gonce in the middle of the front monument shown on the left).

Sarah is a first cousin of the Chaney Anderson mentioned on the previous page.

Appendix VIII

Descendants of Justice Gonce – Eight Generations

Descendants of Justice Gonce

The table below lists eight generations of the family of Justice and Magdalen Gonce. The number preceding each line identifies the generation, and the number at the end of each line is the person's identification number in my genealogical database that is used to reference documents and other material relating to that person. The "a" number preceding the identification number is the Ahnentafel Number showing my direct line to Justice Gonce.

> A Note about Ahnentafel Numbers ...
>
> *The Ahnentafel (literally, "Ancestor Table) numbering scheme was developed by German genealogists to permit easy identification of particular ancestors in an ancestry tree relative to the person creating the tree. Essentially, the person creating the tree (in this case, me) would be assigned the arbitrary number a1. My father would then be number a2 (my number 1 multiplied by 2), and my mother would be number a3 (my father's number plus 1).*
>
> *My paternal grandparents would be a4 (2 x 2) and a5 (4 + 1), and my maternal grandparents would be a6 (3 x 2) and a7 (6 + 1) and so forth. My four great-grandparents would be 8 & 9, 10 & 11, 12 & 13, and 14 & 15. Anyone's father can be found by doubling his or her Ahnentafel number and adding 1 to that to obtain their mother's number.*

1. Justice GONCE (d.1782)a384 id 2577
...++ spouse: Magdalen UNKF[421] (d.1782)...a385 id 2858

(Rudolph is the progenitor of the Southern Branch – Tennessee, Missouri, Texas)
......2. RUDOLPH GONCE (b.1743;d.1790) – first son of Justice Gonce........id 2578
......++ spouse: Polly MCDADE (b.1738;m.1768;d.1791)....................................id 2581
..........3. Isaac GONCE (b.1770;d.1853)..id 2583
..........++ spouse: Frances WILSON (b.1775;m.1796;d.1842)............................id 2589
..............4. Elizabeth GONCE (b.1798;d.1873)..id 2658
..............++ spouse: William Leroy ROGERS (m.1814;d.1816)........................id 2674
..................5. George ROGERS (b.1815)..id 3849
..................++ spouse: Eliza MCCRARY (b.1831)..id 3850
......................6. William Leroy ROGERS (b.1838)...id 3851
..............++ spouse: James B. MATTHEWS (m.1818).......................................id 2701
..............4. Randolph GONCE (b.1800;d.1848)...id 2659
..............++ spouse: Elizabeth TALLEY (b.1805;m.1823;d.1864)......................id 2670

---

[421] The designations UNKF and UNKM represent "Unknown Female" and "Unknown Male" respectively, and are used in cases where I have not been able to determine the actual name.

..............5. Sarah GONCE (b.1823) ⁴²²..id 2685
..............++ spouse: Johnson HACKWORTH..............................id 2694
..............5. Isaac GONCE (b.1825;d.1825)......................................id 2686
..............5. Frances Ann GONCE (b.1826).....................................id 2687
..............++ spouse: Jackson WIMBERLEY (b.1816;d.1872)...........id 2699
..................6. Elizabeth Jane WIMBERLY (b.1847).......................id 3668
..............5. Polina GONCE (b.1829;d.1831)...................................id 2688
..............5. Margaret GONCE (b.1831;d.1855)..............................id 2689
..............++ spouse: Newton HACKWORTH (b.1825;d.1906)........id 2695
..................6. Elizabeth HACKWORTH (b.1849)..........................id 3548
..............5. Wilson Thomas GONCE (b.1833;d.1869)....................id 2690
..............++ spouse: Mary Jane HACKWORTH (b.1835;m.1859;d.1924)........id 2696
..................6. William Randolph GONCE (b.1860;d.1941)..........id 2736
..................++ spouse: Sarah Helen RIDDLE (b.1871)................id 2742
......................7. George W. GONCE (b.1900).............................id 3482
......................7. William R. GONCE , Jr. (b.1901;d.1990)............id 3483
......................++ spouse: Nell B. UNKF (b.1909;d.1990)............id 3676
..........................8. Doris GONCE..id 3671
..........................++ spouse: ?Male? CLAYTON........................id 3679
..........................8. Billie GONCE...id 3672
..........................++ spouse: ?Male? DANIEL............................id 3678
......................7. Mary Helen GONCE (b.1904)..........................id 3484
......................++ spouse: ?Male? HILL (d.1990).......................id 3677
......................7. Sally Ray GONCE (b.1906;d.1981)...................id 3485
......................7. Dora G. GONCE (b.1909)................................id 3486
..................6. Joseph Austin GONCE (b.1862;d.1862)..................id 2737
..................6. Elizabeth P. Eudora GONCE (b.1863;d.1942).........id 2738
..................++ spouse: Rufus W. HOLDER (b.1857;d.1931)........id 2743
..................6. Marion Wilson GONCE (b.1865;d.1929)...............id 2739
..................++ spouse: Nancy Elizabeth WYNNE (b.1876;m.1898;d.1959)....id 2744
......................7. Zadalee GONCE (b.1899;d.1980)......................id 2792
......................++ spouse: Robert Harlan RUSSELL (b.1896)........id 2818
..........................8. June Jeanette RUSSELL (b.1925;d.1981)........id 2820
..........................8. Zada Jane RUSSELL (b.1932).......................id 2821
..........................++ spouse: Jack KERN (d.2004).......................id 3632
..........................8. Joel Harlan RUSSELL (b.1932).....................id 2822
..........................++ spouse: Festus DEAL (b.1887).....................id 2819
......................7. Mary Verda GONCE (b.1902;d.1902)................id 2793
......................7. Sarah Wynne GONCE (b.1903;d.1987)..............id 2794

---

⁴²² Interestingly, five of Randolph and Elizabeth Gonce's children (generation 5) married children of Austin and Elizabeth Hackworth; this area of northern Alabama was not highly populated at the time.

................++ spouse: Paschal Clayton SHELTON (b.1903;m.1925)............id 2823
....................8. Paschal Clayton SHELTON , Jr. (b.1930)................................id 2824
................++ spouse: BeverlyJo BLAKE (b.1936).......................................id 3722
....................7. Wilson Floyd GONCE (b.1906;d.1990).............................id 2795
................++ spouse: Kitty Hayden SMITH (b.1909;m.1930;d.1963)...........id 2825
................++ spouse: Lottie Ora LOWRY (b.1917;m.1964;d.2000)..............id 2826
....................7. William Alley GONCE (b.1908;d.1933)................................id 2796
....................7. Oran Randolph GONCE (b.1910;d.1935).............................id 2797
....................7. Ollie Austin GONCE (b.1910;d.1995)..................................id 2798
................++ spouse: Gretchen Jane GONCE (b.1911;m.1935;d.1955).....id 2838
........................8. Crisler GONCE...id 2839
................++ spouse: Samuel SHELBY...id 3634
........................8. Randolph Oran GONCE..id 2840
................++ spouse: Linda RAY...id 2849
........................8. Oliva GONCE (b.1941;d.1941)..id 2841
........................8. Terrill GONCE...id 2842
........................8. Wilson GONCE..id 2843
........................8. Colleen GONCE..id 2844
................++ spouse: Unknown WHITVER..id 3635
........................8. Wenda GONCE...id 2845
................++ spouse: Unknown LOVELACE...id 3636
........................8. Jennie GONCE..id 2846
................++ spouse: Unknown GORE..id 3637
................++ spouse: Mabel L. HACKWORTH (b.1908;m.1958;d.1996)..id 2847
....................7. Albert Marion GONCE (b.1913;d.2006)............................id 2799
................++ spouse: Bertha Carol RUSSELL (b.1915;m.1934)................id 2802
........................8. Barbara Elizabeth GONCE (b.1935)..................................id 2805
................++ spouse: Gerald Michael CLEPPER (b.1937;m.1957)...........id 2808
........................8. Bertha Carolyn GONCE (b.1936)......................................id 2806
................++ spouse: William Wayne LEROY (b.1931)..............................id 2809
........................8. Donald Marion GONCE (b.1938;d.2008)..........................id 2807
................++ spouse: Nancye GUYTON (b.1940;m.[Div]).......................id 2810
....................7. Cleo Jeanette GONCE (b.1915;d.2002)..............................id 2800
................++ spouse: Lon Hoover SHELTON (b.1913;m.1937)..................id 2828
........................8. Norma Jeanette SHELTON (b.1941)..................................id 2829
................++ spouse: James Terrell BELL (b.1940)...................................id 3638
........................8. Sharon Aurora SHELTON (b.1944)...................................id 2830
................++ spouse: George Harlan Woodard MCDONALD (b.1945) id 3654
........................8. Linda Arnan SHELTON (b.1946)..id 2831
................++ spouse: Joseph Lynn BARNES , III (b.1942).......................id 3662
................++ spouse: Lynn Dickson MCGILL (b.1941)............................id 3667

..................7. Nancy Elizabeth GONCE (b.1921;d.2007)................................id 2801
..................++ spouse: James Howard GONCE , MD (b.1921)....................id 2851
..................8. Richard GONCE...id 2852
..................8. Charles GONCE..id 2853
..............6. John Mack GONCE (b.1867;d.1945)......................................id 2740
..............++ spouse: Myrtle BEAN (b.1868;d.1914)...............................id 2745
..................7. Lou Eva GONCE (b.1890;d.1893)....................................id 3669
..................7. Buford Vance GONCE (b.1892;d.1959)...........................id 3299
..................7. Mary Eunice GONCE (b.1895;d.1972)............................id 3300
..................++ spouse: ?Male? HUMBLE..id 3633
..................7. Virgil GONCE (b.1897;d.1982)...id 3301
..................++ spouse: Estelle M. UNKF (b.1902;d.1991)......................id 3306
..................7. Mansel Mack GONCE (b.1899;d.1977)............................id 2850
..................++ spouse: UNKNOWN
..................8. James Howard GONCE , MD (b.1921)............................id 2851
..................++ spouse: Nancy Elizabeth GONCE (b.1921;d.2007)...........id 2801
..................7. Lemuel B. GONCE (b.1901;d.1913)................................id 3302
..................7. Dora Ona GONCE (b.1904)..id 3303
..................7. Amanda Esther GONCE (b.1906;d.1908)........................id 3670
..............6. Thomas Newton GONCE (b.1869)..id 2741
..............++ spouse: Nannie Shipp GRIMMETT....................................id 3723
............5. Elizabeth Ann GONCE (b.1835;d.1917).....................................id 2691
............++ spouse: Jasper HACKWORTH (m.1853)..................................id 2697
............5. Lydia Clementine GONCE (b.1838)..id 2692
............++ spouse: Marion HACKWORTH (m.1853).................................id 2698
............5. Randolph Madison GONCE (b.1840;d.1907)............................id 2693
............++ spouse: Mary Ann Lowry ALLISON (b.1842;d.1895)...................id 2700
..............6. Cynthia Elizabeth GONCE (b.1868;d.1900)............................id 3307
..............6. Lowrey W. GONCE (b.1871)...id 3560
..............6. William T. GONCE (b.1878)...id 3561
..............++ spouse: Ophelia E. UNKF (b.1889).......................................id 4475
..................7. Hugh Bernard GONCE (b.1914;d.1943)...........................id 4476
..................7. Woodrow T. GONCE (b.1918;d.2000).............................id 4477
..................++ spouse: Virginia Frances UNKF (b.1919;d.1994)..............id 4512
..................8. Linda Marie GONCE (b.1940;d.2001)..............................id 4513
..................8. David F. GONCE..id 4514
..................8. Sandy L. GONCE..id 4515
..................++ spouse: UnkM ROBBINS..id 4518
..................8. Cynthia S. GONCE...id 4516
..................++ spouse: UnkM BENNETT..id 4519
..................8. Ester Virginia GONCE..id 4517

................++ spouse: UnkM HAGER..id 4520
................7. Kenneth W. GONCE (b.1923)...id 4478
................7. Paul S. GONCE (b.1931;d.2008)....................................id 4509
................7. Austin R. GONCE (b.1935;d.2005)................................id 4510
................7. Jean GONCE..id 4511
..............6. Alina M. GONCE (b.1880)..id 3562
..........4. Margaret GONCE (b.1802;d.1883)...id 2660
..........++ spouse: Anthony STEWART (b.1797;m.1831;d.1864)...........id 2671
............5. Lemuel Wilson GONCE (b.1821;d.1857)............................id 2834
............++ spouse: Sarah ANDERSON (b.1830;m.1848;d.1850)..........id 2835
..............6. John Wisdom GONCE (b.1849;d.1943)............................id 2836
..............++ spouse: Jane Julia LOVELL (b.1852;m.1870;d.1940)......id 3445
................7. Gertrude Inez GONCE (b.1871;d.1958)........................id 3571
................++ spouse: Charles Willard TAYLOR (b.1872;d.1951).......id 3584
..................8. Cecil TAYLOR (b.1899;d.1899)..................................id 3585
..................8. Mettie Marie TAYLOR (b.1901).................................id 3586
..................++ spouse: William Henderson BARTON (b.1896;m.1923)....id 3588
..................8. John Gonce TAYLOR (b.1905;d.1906).......................id 3587
................7. Maude Irene GONCE (b.1873;d.1915).........................id 3572
................++ spouse: Jake MATTHEWS (b.1869;d.1910)...................id 3674
................7. John Lemieul GONCE (b.1875;d.1961)........................id 3529
................++ spouse: Margaret PHILLIPS (b.1886;m.1907;d.1941)....id 3530
..................8. Lillian GONCE (b.1909)..id 3531
..................++ spouse: Doran RUSSELL (b.1911;m.1941)..................id 3577
................7. Dora GONCE (b.1877;d.1962)......................................id 3573
................++ spouse: Luke R. LEA (b.1874)......................................id 3675
................7. Albert Anderson GONCE (b.1879;d.1971)....................id 2837
................++ spouse: Alyne SETLIFF (b.1890;m.1908;d.1946)..........id 3298
..................8. John W. GONCE (b.1910;d.1996)...............................id 3293
..................8. Gretchen Jane GONCE (b.1911;d.1955)....................id 2838
..................++ spouse: Ollie Austin GONCE (b.1910;m.1935;d.1995).......id 2798
..................8. Albert Anderson GONCE (b.1913;d.1993)................id 3294
..................8. Catherine M. GONCE (b.1918).................................id 3295
..................8. Elizabeth A. GONCE (b.1922;d.1946)........................id 3296
..................8. Edward Arthur GONCE (b.1922)..............................id 3297
..................++ spouse: Dorothy Faye POWERS (b.1922;m.1946)........id 4147
................7. William GONCE (b.1880)..id 3574
................7. Frank L. GONCE (b.1881;d.1969).................................id 3575
................++ spouse: Hattie KERLEY (b.1888;d.1949)......................id 3589
..................8. Francis GONCE..id 3590
..................8. Virginia GONCE..id 3591

...............7. Charles Wisdom GONCE (b.1884;d.1913)...............................id 3447
...............7. Edward Everitt GONCE (b.1886;d.1903)...............................id 3576
...............7. Elmore S. GONCE (b.1889;d.1950)......................................id 3444
...............++ spouse: Annie G. BUCKNER (b.1891;d.1964).....................id 3487
.................8. Elmore S. GONCE , Jr. (b.1918;d.1986).............................id 3488
...............7. Carl GONCE (b.1892;d.1928)...id 3448
...............++ spouse: Sudie BUCKNER (b.1891).....................................id 3475
...............7. Helen GONCE (b.1894;d.1968)..id 3446
...............++ spouse: William Edgar LUTHER (b.1893;d.1956)..............id 3673
..........4. Frances GONCE (b.1804)...id 2661
..........++ spouse: Thomas Reid SHIPP (b.1791;m.1826).........................id 2675
..........4. Ann GONCE (b.1806;d.1843)..id 2662
..........++ spouse: Robert MCKINNEY (b.1807)......................................id 2676
..........4. Sarah GONCE (b.1808)..id 2663
..........++ spouse: Roland CHILDS..id 2677
..........4. Mary GONCE (b.1812)...id 2665
..........++ spouse: John R. WILKINSON...id 2679
..........4. Wilson GONCE (b.1810)...id 2664
..........++ spouse: Malinda RICE (b.1820)..id 2678
...............5. John R GONCE (b.1838)...id 4049
...............5. Isaac GONCE (b.1840)...id 4050
...............5. Markiel W. GONCE (b.1843)...id 4051
...............5. Nancy GONCE (b.1844)...id 4052
...............5. Franky A. GONCE (b.1845)...id 4053
...............5. Malinda F. GONCE (b.1847)...id 4054
...............5. Fielding GONCE (b.1849)...id 4055
...............++ spouse: Mary OILAR (b.1848;m.1871)...............................id 4004
..................6. California GONCE (b.1872)...id 4005
..................6. Frances GONCE (b.1873)..id 4006
..........4. Lydia C. GONCE (b.1820;d.1851)..id 2666
..........++ spouse: Benjamin Bledsoe STEWART (b.1810;m.1846;d.1859).......id 2673
..........4. Kiziah GONCE (b.1822;d.1848)...id 2667
..........++ spouse: John B. ROGERS..id 2682
......3. Abraham GONCE (b.1770;d.1851)...id 2584
........++ spouse: Polly VANCE (b.1774;m.1792;d.1850)............................id 2590
..........4. Margaret GONCE (b.1798;d.1857)..id 3557
..........4. Abraham GONCE (b.1800;d.1851)..id 3117
..........++ spouse: Celia UNKF (b.1800;d.1867).......................................id 4124
...............5. John R. M. GONCE (b.1824;d.1857)....................................id 3558
...............++ spouse: Louisa W. RADCLIFF..id 4601
..................6. Frances M. GONCE (b.1842;d.1845).................................id 4608

................6. Celia M. J. GONCE (b.1846;d.1846)..id 4609
................6. George W. GONCE (b.1846)..id 4610
................++ spouse: Lucinda LEEMAN (b.1852)...id 4611
..................7. Samuel C. GONCE...id 4612
..................7. Oscar Theron GONCE (b.1874;d.1927)..id 4613
..................++ spouse: Mary Elizabeth ABNEY (b.1880;m.1900;d.1914).....id 4614
....................8. Shirley GONCE..id 4617
....................8. Herschel W. GONCE (b.1903;d.1966)..id 4618
....................++ spouse: Georgeann HISEY (b.1911;m.1936;d.1983)..........id 4619
....................8. Lee GONCE...id 4637
....................8. Margarete GONCE (b.1908)..id 4638
..................7. Fanny GONCE (b.1878)..id 4627
..................7. John William GONCE (b.1879;d.1920)...id 4633
..................++ spouse: Edna Belle SWINK (b.1884;m.1912;d.1948)...............id 4641
....................8. Charles W. GONCE...id 4628
..................7. Margaret GONCE (b.1882)...id 4634
..................7. Celia GONCE (b.1885)...id 4635
..................7. Bertie GONCE (b.1890)..id 4636
................5. UnkF GONCE (b.1821)...id 4602
................5. UnkM GONCE (b.1826;d.1840)...id 4603
................5. UnkM GONCE (b.1831)..id 4604
................5. UnkF GONCE (b.1835)...id 4605
................5. UnkF GONCE (b.1836)...id 4606
................5. UnkF GONCE (b.1837)...id 4607
............4. Vance GONCE (b.1802;d.1871)...id 2881
............++ spouse: Martha Patsy DAVIS (b.1804;m.1824;d.1880).......................id 2882
..............5. Elizabeth GONCE (b.1824;d.1927)..id 3019
..............++ spouse: Pat BRAY (b.1855)...id 3871
................6. Paralee BRAY (b.1875;d.1903)..id 3872
................++ spouse: App P. DAVIS (b.1869;m.1895;d.1938)...........................id 3873
..............++ spouse: McClellan PEARSON (m.1860)...id 3129
..............5. William D. GONCE (b.1825;d.1877)...id 3020
..............++ spouse: Vianna ANDERSON (b.1840;m.1862;d.1913)....................id 3029
................6. Jefferson GONCE (b.1867;d.1957)..id 3035
................++ spouse: Sarah E. COBB (b.1864;m.1891).....................................id 3092
..................7. Nellie GONCE (b.1905)..id 3099
..................7. Daisy GONCE (b.1907)..id 4193
................++ spouse: Mary BURTON (b.1887)...id 3878
................++ spouse: Almeida WINSTEAD (b.1892)...id 3103
..................7. Ulis GONCE (b.1911)...id 3100
..................7. Glennie Estelle GONCE (b.1912)..id 3101

................++ spouse: George Barnett MARKHAM (b.1903;m.1927).........id 3910
....................8. Anna Rae MARKHAM..id 3911
....................8. J.C. MARKHAM (b.1932)..id 3912
....................8. Johnnie Ruth MARKHAM (b.1934)...............................id 3913
................7. Sarah Mae GONCE (b.1915)...id 3102
................++ spouse: Clay LAWSON (m.1929)....................................id 3915
................++ spouse: Taylor STAPLETON (m.1914)............................id 4521
................++ spouse: Wiley CHANDLER (m.1919)..............................id 4522
................7. Hazle GONCE (b.1919)...id 3104
................7. Olivia GONCE (b.1920)...id 3110
................++ spouse: Emory DRINNON..id 3914
................7. Vernell GONCE (b.1922)..id 3111
................++ spouse: Emory LAWSON..id 3916
............6. Amos Newton GONCE (b.1868;d.1922)...............................id 3036
............++ spouse: Margaret Paralee BROOKS (b.1874;m.1891;d.1941)...id 3037
................7. Arthur Davis GONCE (b.1892;d.1955)..............................id 3048
................++ spouse: Cornelia HARTLEY (m.1919).............................id 3900
....................8. Ralph William GONCE (b.1920;d.1955).......................id 3901
....................++ spouse: Irma Cebil DEBORD....................................id 3961
................7. William Tyler GONCE (b.1894;d.1903).............................id 3083
................++ spouse: Bobbie UNKF (b.1903).......................................id 3109
................7. Hugh Edward GONCE (b.1897;d.1930)............................id 3084
................7. Elizabeth GONCE (b.1903;d.1995)...................................id 3049
................7. Nancy Cornelia GONCE (b.1907)....................................id 3106
................++ spouse: Henry Clay GONCE (b.1907;d.1995)..................id 3881
................7. Stella Mae GONCE (b.1909;d.1978).................................id 3075
................++ spouse: Coy Hillary WILSON (b.1908;m.1928;d.1976)..........id 3074
....................8. Henry Clay WILSON (b.1929;d.1929)..........................id 3076
....................8. Reba Odell WILSON (b.1932;d.1994)..........................id 3078
....................++ spouse: Coy Wayne HURD (b.1925;d.1998)..............id 3077
....................8. Danna Rae WILSON (b.1934;d.1934).........................id 3079
....................8. Hope Sharon WILSON..id 3904
....................8. Coy Alfred WILSON..id 3905
....................8. Edward Melville WILSON...id 3906
....................8. Wilma Deon WILSON (b.1940)..................................id 3907
....................8. Janice Anne WILSON (b.1945)...................................id 3908
....................8. Roger Lee WILSON (b.1950)......................................id 3909
................7. Minnie Mabel GONCE (b.1914;d.1974)...........................id 3050
............6. Hezekiah Davis GONCE (b.1869;d.1941).............................id 3038
............++ spouse: Martha Maryland COLLINS (b.1869;m.1893;d.1941). id 3088
................7. Beulah Beatrice GONCE (b.1894;d.1973).........................id 3089

..............++ spouse: Nicholas MABE (b.1890;d.1961)...........................id 3875
..................8. Jessie Lema MABE...id 3876
..................7. William King GONCE (b.1896;d.1965)..........................id 3090
..................7. Lara Athens GONCE (b.1898;d.1926).............................id 3091
..............++ spouse: Charles Mack WILLIS (b.1896;m.1917;d.1923).........id 3292
..................8. John Carr WILLIS (b.1918;d.1930).................................id 3556
..................7. Anne Muriel GONCE (b.1904)..id 3112
..............++ spouse: James Albert KEPDING............................id 3917
..............++ spouse: UNKNOWN
..................8. Charles Truman WILLIS (b.1920;d.1940)........................id 3116
..................7. Walter Lee GONCE (b.1906;d.2004)...............................id 3113
..............++ spouse: Lizzie Kathleen BUTTRY (b.1900)..........................id 3918
..................8. Lowell Ellsworth GONCE (b.1936).................................id 3919
..................7. John Clayton GONCE (b.1909;d.1997).............................id 3114
..............++ spouse: Catherine Agnes BLUM (b.1915;m.1932;d.2002).......id 3311
..................8. John Clayton GONCE , Jr. (b.1933)..................................id 3312
..............++ spouse: Virginia Lee DUVALL (b.1935;m.1954;d.2002)....id 3314
..................8. Margaret Jean GONCE (b.1947)......................................id 3313
..............++ spouse: Frank CRUM...id 3315
..................7. Vick GONCE (b.1911)...id 3978
..................7. Mabe GONCE (b.1912)..id 3979
..................7. James Pryor GONCE (b.1913;d.1983)...............................id 3115
..............++ spouse: Willie Beatrice BAKER (b.1914;d.1990)....................id 3920
..................8. William Pryor GONCE (b.1934;d.1978)...........................id 3921
..............++ spouse: Doris Evelyn BROOKE (b.1927;d.2004)..................id 3322
..................8. Diane Mae GONCE (b.1939)...id 3922
..............++ spouse: Harold J ASCHENBRENNER (b.1937;m.1960)..id 3965
..................8. Martha Gale GONCE (b.1940)..id 3923
..............++ spouse: Harold Eugene OWNES (b.1934).........................id 3966
..................8. Robert Lee GONCE (b.1941)...id 3924
..................8. Linda Patricia GONCE (b.1943).......................................id 3925
..................8. Charles Gary GONCE (b.1949).......................................id 3926
............6. James Madison GONCE (b.1872;d.1911).................................id 3039
..............++ spouse: Ida M. SHROPSHIRE (b.1876;m.1893;d.1914)...........id 3080
..................7. Bessie Juliet GONCE (b.1894)...id 3085
..............++ spouse: John Jay LAWSON (b.1889)....................................id 3927
..................8. Nora Belle LAWSON (b.1915).......................................id 3928
..................8. Ruby Lee LAWSON (b.1918)...id 3929
..................8. Carl Doty LAWSON (b.1921)...id 3930
..................8. Elmer Harold LAWSON (b.1924)....................................id 3931
..................8. Omer Gene LAWSON (b.1927).......................................id 3932

............7. Mary Kyle GONCE (b.1897)..id 3086
..................++ spouse: Worth Herbert ADAIR (b.1891;m.1916)..................id 3933
....................8. Ida Mae ADAIR (b.1919)..id 3934
....................8. Verda Alice ADAIR (b.1929)......................................id 3935
............7. Ethel Lee GONCE (b.1899)..id 3087
............7. Leonidas Tyler GONCE (b.1902;d.1988)................................id 3879
..................++ spouse: Evelyn Almetta SHETTLEY (b.1906;m.1924)...........id 3936
....................8. Naomi Bertha GONCE (b.1926)..................................id 3937
........................++ spouse: Leonard Marion SCOTT (b.1925)..................id 3968
....................8. Edna Hortense GONCE (b.1931).................................id 3938
........................++ spouse: Curtis Richard CHASTAIN (b.1931)...............id 3969
........................++ spouse: Beulah Opal LITTLE................................id 4028
....................8. Ray L. GONCE (b.1935;d.1966).................................id 4027
....................8. Robert Franklin GONCE (b.1936)...............................id 3939
........................++ spouse: Rachel Blythe CARROL (b.1937)..................id 3970
....................8. Thomas Howard GONCE (b.1940)...............................id 3940
........................++ spouse: Sharon Elsie HORNE (b.1943)....................id 3971
....................8. Glenda Faye GONCE (b.1943)..................................id 3941
........................++ spouse: Claude Haskell RAUCH , I (b.1939)..............id 3972
....................8. Leonidas Tyler GONCE , Jr (b.1945)..........................id 3942
............7. Bertha Alice GONCE (b.1904)...id 3880
..................++ spouse: John Lemmy MORRIS (b.1907).........................id 3943
....................8. Vera Evelyn MORRIS..id 3944
....................8. Juanita Ruth MORRIS..id 3945
............7. Henry Clay GONCE (b.1907;d.1995)....................................id 3881
..................++ spouse: Nancy Cornelia GONCE (b.1907)........................id 3106
............7. Edna Leila GONCE (b.1910;d.1910)....................................id 3882
........6. Aaron GONCE (b.1877)..id 3082
............++ spouse: Catherine BEGLEY (m.1854)..................................id 3130
........6. Amelia Jane GONCE (b.1856;d.1937).....................................id 3030
............++ spouse: Robert Newton SHAW (d.1904)..............................id 3877
............7. John SHAW..id 3980
............7. William SHAW..id 3981
............7. Annah SHAW...id 3982
............7. Jesse SHAW...id 3983
............7. David SHAW..id 3984
............7. Joseph SHAW...id 3985
............7. Asa SHAW..id 3986
............7. James SHAW..id 3987
............7. Harvey SHAW..id 3988
............7. Isaac SHAW...id 3989

...............7. Samuel SHAW	id 3990
...............7. Homer SHAW	id 3991
...............7. George Lee SHAW (b.1899)	id 3992
...............7. Geneva SHAW	id 3993
.............6. Pleasant GONCE (b.1858)	id 3031
.............6. Harvey Vance GONCE (b.1860;d.1941)	id 3032
...............++ spouse: Martha Matilda VAUGHN (b.1874;m.1890;d.1958)	id 3033
...............7. Nora Ethel GONCE (b.1891;d.1910)	id 3041
...............++ spouse: Lee MABE (b.1887;m.1910)	id 3040
...............7. Arlie Vance GONCE (b.1892;d.1985)	id 3042
...............++ spouse: Marie Molly QUENY (m.1910;d.1917)	id 3051
...............8. Edna GONCE	id 3946
...............++ spouse: Steven STARBUCK	id 3947
...............++ spouse: Nona Bell RUSSELL (b.1908;m.1926;d.1995)	id 3052
...............8. Mildred Marie GONCE (b.1928)	id 3139
...............++ spouse: Samuel DAVIS (b.1918;m.1948)	id 3143
...............8. Arlie Vance GONCE (b.1930;d.1998)	id 3054
...............++ spouse: Sybil GOLDSMITH (b.1933;m.1954;d.2006)	id 3144
...............8. Ray GONCE (b.1932;d.1999)	id 3140
...............++ spouse: Barbara Ruth THOMPSON (b.1936;m.1956)	id 3145
...............++ spouse: Shirley UNKF (m.1966)	id 3693
...............8. Elmer Lee GONCE (b.1934)	id 3141
...............++ spouse: Mary Christine WILSON (m.1954)	id 3146
...............8. William Harvey GONCE (b.1936)	id 3142
...............++ spouse: Hazel Judith GIBBS (m.1959)	id 3147
...............8. Betty Ann GONCE (b.1938)	id 3055
...............++ spouse: Glenn R. JOYNER (b.1938;m.1956)	id 3148
...............8. James Edward GONCE (b.1939)	id 3056
...............++ spouse: Betty UNKF (m.1961)	id 3149
...............8. Charles Edward GONCE (b.1946)	id 3057
...............++ spouse: Joetta R. UNKF (b.1956)	id 3058
...............8. Evelyn Jean GONCE (b.1948)	id 3138
...............8. Gerald Wayne GONCE (b.1953)	id 3059
...............++ spouse: Bernice OWENS	id 3150
...............7. James Edward GONCE (b.1895)	id 3043
...............++ spouse: Helen UNDERWOOD (b.1900;m.1920;d.1942)	id 3883
...............8. Helen Ruth GONCE (b.1923)	id 3884
...............8. James Edward GONCE , II (b.1927;d.2002)	id 3724
...............++ spouse: Betty Enline ASHWORTH (b.1929)	id 3725
...............++ spouse: Monta Bri... THOMPSON (b.1897;m.1944;d.1947)	id 3137
...............7. Kate Maryland GONCE (b.1898)	id 3044

Descendants of Justice Gonce – Nine Generations

```
................++ spouse: Tona LAWSON..................................................id 3081
.................8. Martha LAWSON......................................................id 3886
.................8. Gertie LAWSON.......................................................id 3887
..............7. Geneva Alice GONCE (b.1900)..........................................id 3046
................++ spouse: Bailey JOHNSON (b.1895;m.1921)..........................id 3045
.................8. Carl Acree JOHNSON.................................................id 3888
.................8. Clyde Bailey JOHNSON...............................................id 3889
.................8. Versenoia Vereena JOHNSON.........................................id 3890
..............7. George Bert GONCE (b.1904;d.1986)...................................id 3097
................++ spouse: Birdie GORDON..............................................id 3891
..............7. Marion Elizabeth GONCE (b.1907;d.1936).............................id 3047
..............7. Bonnie Ruby GONCE (b.1912)..........................................id 3098
...........6. William M. GONCE (b.1864;d.1941)......................................id 3034
.............++ spouse: Rose Lee HILL (b.1890;m.1905;d.1928).......................id 3053
..............7. Dewey Lee GONCE (b.1907)............................................id 3060
................++ spouse: Allie Lou Esther SHETLEY (b.1915;m.1939)...............id 3892
.................8. William Benjamin Lee GONCE (b.1941)............................id 3893
.................8. Ronnie Ray GONCE (b.1946)........................................id 3894
..............7. Foster Brown GONCE (b.1908).........................................id 3061
................++ spouse: Mary Belle WOOD (b.1919;m.1936)........................id 3895
.................8. Leonard Paul GONCE (b.1938;d.2004)..............................id 3896
..................++ spouse: Gladys Marie HUCKABY (b.1938;m.1960)................id 3959
.................8. Donald Reeve GONCE (b.1940)......................................id 3897
..................++ spouse: Marlene Delores HOUSER (b.1943;m.1961).............id 3960
.................8. Lee Roy GONCE (b.1941)............................................id 3898
.................8. Joel Dwight GONCE (b.1949).......................................id 3899
..............7. Edith GONCE (b.1910).................................................id 3063
................++ spouse: ?Male? ROBINSON (d.1930).................................id 3062
.................8. Mildred Herdesne ROBINSON (b.1927).............................id 3069
..............7. Fred GONCE (b.1915)...................................................id 3064
..............7. James Earl GONCE (b.1920)............................................id 3065
................++ spouse: Nina Evelyn RUTLEDGE (b.1923)..........................id 3122
.................8. James Earl GONCE , Jr. (b.1944)..................................id 3125
.................8. Charles Edward GONCE (b.1946)...................................id 3123
..................++ spouse: Priscilla HUFF...........................................id 3124
.................8. Bobby Gail GONCE (b.1955)........................................id 3126
.........5. Margaret GONCE (b.1826)...................................................id 3131
...........++ spouse: John FROST......................................................id 3132
.........5. Hezekiah Davis GONCE (b.1829)............................................id 3021
...........++ spouse: Permelia UNKF (b.1832).........................................id 3474
............6. Mary Ann GONCE (b.1858;d.1900).......................................id 3118
```

................++ spouse: ?Male? ROBINSON................	id 3119
................7. Hezekiah D. ROBINSON (b.1879)................	id 3094
................7. Paralee ROBINSON (b.1880)................	id 3095
................7. Hassie ROBINSON (b.1892)................	id 3096
................6. Enoch GONCE (b.1860)................	id 3476
................++ spouse: Chaney ANDERSON (b.1844)................	id 3093
................6. Chaney GONCE................	id 3105
................++ spouse: Victory RINGLEY................	id 3108
................++ spouse: Chaney ANDERSON (b.1844)................	id 3093
................5. Abraham Rudolph GONCE (b.1831;d.1912) [423]................	id 2883
................++ spouse: Sarah Nancy FRAIZER................	id 2884
................++ spouse: Charity Elizabeth WIGGINS (m.1893)................	id 3473
................++ spouse: Mary A. FRAZIER (b.1831;m.1850)................	id 3320
................6. William McClellan GONCE (b.1851;d.1930)................	id 3480
................++ spouse: Martha Ann SIMS (b.1850;d.1945)................	id 3481
................7. James McClellan GONCE (b.1871;d.1947)................	id 3680
................++ spouse: Violet Evelyn NOE (b.1867;m.1897;d.1935)................	id 3681
................8. Martha N. GONCE (b.1897;d.1897)................	id 4021
................8. Leonard Loran GONCE (b.1899;d.1983)................	id 3814
................++ spouse: Lena L PARK (b.1907;m.1926;d.1994)................	id 4026
................8. Wealtha E. GONCE (b.1901;d.1993)................	id 4009
................++ spouse: Austin M. MAPLES (b.1890;m.1924;d.1969)................	id 4040
................++ spouse: Ida Lucinda TENNIS (b.1874;d.1955)................	id 4048
................7. Carl Abraham GONCE (b.1873;d.1946)................	id 3682
................++ spouse: Mary Matilda SANDERS (b.1876;m.1898)................	id 3817
................8. Homer Benjamin GONCE (b.1898;d.1940)................	id 3818
................8. Nora D. GONCE (b.1902)................	id 3819
................8. Lonnie L. GONCE (b.1908)................	id 3820
................++ spouse: Opal WALKER (b.1851)................	id 4192
................8. Roy E. GONCE (b.1909;d.1981)................	id 3821
................8. Raymond Sims GONCE (b.1912;d.1912)................	id 4018
................8. Infant GONCE (b.1914;d.1914)................	id 4019
................8. Infant Female GONCE (b.1915;d.1915)................	id 4020
................7. Clemons GONCE (b.1875)................	id 4140
................7. Albert Anderson GONCE (b.1878)................	id 3683
................++ spouse: Minnie Elizabeth UNKF (b.1868;m.1902)................	id 4198
................7. Winfred Pendleton GONCE (b.1883;d.1912)................	id 3684
................++ spouse: Cathrine Lottie SANDERS (b.1887;m.1903)................	id 3685
................8. Infant Male Twin GONCE (b.1904;d.1904)................	id 4016

---

[423] See my book "Abraham Rudolph Gonce – Missouri Pioneer," ISBN 978-06159-12448, for details of "Doc" Gonce's fascinating life.

………………………8. Infant Male Twin GONCE (b.1904;d.1904)………………………id 4017
………………………8. Elsie GONCE (b.1908)………………………………………id 3823
………………………8. Mildred GONCE (b.1910;d.1980)……………………………id 3824
……………………7. Fred Harrison GONCE (b.1885)………………………………id 3686
…………………++ spouse: Rosa M. SANDERS (b.1885;m.1905)………………id 3687
………………………8. Humbert A GONCE (b.1906;d.1975)…………………………id 3825
………………………8. Loral E. GONCE (b.1908;d.1982) [424]………………………id 3826
…………………++ spouse: Leta Belle BURGOON (b.1916;m.1930;d.2000)…id 3831
…………………++ spouse: Dorothy R. TAYLOR (m.1930)……………………id 4537
………………………8. Ralph R GONCE (b.1910;d.1969)……………………………id 3827
………………………8. Martha E GONCE (b.1914)……………………………………id 3828
………………………8. Ruby G GONCE (b.1915)………………………………………id 3829
………………………8. Onis H GONCE (b.1919;d.1920)……………………………id 3830
………………………8. Truman GONCE (b.1922)………………………………………id 4166
……………………7. Cleveland Elias GONCE (b.1887;d.1963)…………………id 3521
…………………++ spouse: Nettie Margaret RAY (b.1890;m.1908)……………id 3522
………………………8. Clyde Sherman GONCE (b.1910;d.1912)…………………id 4015
………………………8. Marie L. GONCE (b.1913)……………………………………id 3523
………………………8. Howard A. GONCE (b.1916;d.1977)………………………id 3524
…………………++ spouse: UNKNOWN
………………………8. Earl Willard GONCE (b.1920;d.1991)………………………id 3525
…………………++ spouse: Betty Lou NIDAY……………………………………id 4144
………………………8. Anna Marie GONCE………………………………………………id 4186
………………………8. Warren C. GONCE (b.1924)…………………………………id 3526
………………………8. Helen L. GONCE (b.1926)……………………………………id 3527
………………………8. Carl GONCE (b.1927)……………………………………………id 3692
……………………7. Doshia Anna GONCE (b.1890;d.1971)……………………id 3690
…………………++ spouse: George Thurston PENDLETON (b.1885;m.1907). id 3689
………………………8. Ethel F. PENDLETON (b.1908)……………………………id 3822
……………………7. William Wilbern GONCE (b.1892;d.1976)………………id 3691
…………………++ spouse: Blanche UNKF (b.1897;d.1924)……………………id 4505
………………………8. Elias Cleveland GONCE (b.1917)…………………………id 4506
………………………8. Wilma F. GONCE (b.1919)……………………………………id 4507
………………………8. Walter Wilbern GONCE………………………………………id 4008
…………………++ spouse: Eunice UNKF (b.1906;d.1978)……………………id 4544
………………6. Arthur Davis GONCE (b.1854;d.1916)……………………………id 3318
…………………++ spouse: Susan PRUITT (d.1880)………………………………id 4125

---

[424] Fain T. Gonce and his brother Richard, both sons of Loral and Dorothy Taylor Gonce, were participants in the United Coin Machine Robbery featured on the America's Most Wanted television show. Their stories are given in an appendix to my book "Abraham Rudolph Gonce – Missouri Pioneer," ISBN 978-06159-12448.

...........7. Minnie B. GONCE (b.1876;d.1956)..id 3565
...........++ spouse: John L. YOUNGER..id 4135
...........8. Winford Amus GONCE (b.1900;d.1974)...................................id 4129
...........++ spouse: Henrietta L. COFFMAN (b.1907;d.2003)..............id 4134
...........++ spouse: Sara Etta RUSSELL (b.1869;m.1885;d.1951)...............id 3319
...........7. John Walter GONCE (b.1885;d.1887)..id 4126
...........7. Frances Susan GONCE (b.1886;d.1963)....................................id 3566
...........7. Iva Ann GONCE (b.1888;d.1975)...id 3567
...........++ spouse: Sherman A. REEVES (b.1887).....................................id 4056
...........7. William Charles GONCE (b.1891;d.1961).................................id 3550
...........7. Lola Jane GONCE (b.1892;d.1976)...id 3568
...........++ spouse: Riley ANDERSON (b.1889)...id 4182
...........7. Lilburn Thomas GONCE (b.1895;d.1980).................................id 3513
...........++ spouse: Melvira TYLER..id 4146
...........8. Lilburn T. GONCE , Jr. (b.1921;d.1973)....................................id 3510
...........++ spouse: Gertrude MORMOYLE...id 3511
...........7. Albert Thompson GONCE (b.1897;d.1967)..............................id 3570
...........++ spouse: Abbie REED..id 4183
...........7. Arthur Jennings GONCE (b.1899;d.1969)................................id 3317
...........++ spouse: Clare Merle YOUNGER (b.1900)................................id 4136
...........7. James Bartley GONCE (b.1902;d.1953)....................................id 4127
...........++ spouse: Mary Elizab... YOUNGER (b.1904;m.1922;d.1992) id 4151
...........8. James Bartley GONCE , Jr...id 4153
...........8. John GONCE..id 4154
...........8. Avon GONCE (b.1925)..id 4155
...........8. William David GONCE (b.1928)..id 4152
...........8. Sarah GONCE...id 4156
...........8. Mary GONCE..id 4157
...........7. Ida Edna GONCE (b.1904;d.1951)...id 4128
...........++ spouse: Louis Albert WANKLE (d.1988).................................id 4184
...........7. Ruby GONCE (b.1907;d.1983)...id 3569
...........7. Ela GONCE (b.1909)...id 4199
.........6. Nancy GONCE (b.1856)..id 3848
.........6. Martha E. GONCE (b.1856)..id 3532
...........++ spouse: Robert SMITH (m.1877)...id 4158
.........6. Mary Ellen GONCE (b.1861;d.1930)...id 3533
...........++ spouse: Lafayette James CHRISMAN (b.1854;m.1876;d.1926) id 4088
.........6. Alice GONCE (b.1864)..id 3534
...........++ spouse: F.M. BROCK (m.1884)..id 4159
...........++ spouse: John W. HUFF (m.1890)...id 4160
.........6. Thomas Jefferson GONCE (b.1866;d.1946)..................................id 3535

................++ spouse: Elzada PENNINGTON (b.1882;d.1967)......................id 4162
....................7. Oman B. GONCE (b.1910)..id 4163
....................7. Dreyfus GONCE (b.1913)...id 4164
....................7. Guthrie Delmas GONCE (b.1919;d.1985).......................id 4165
................6. Laura A. GONCE (b.1869;d.1880)...id 3536
................6. Benjamin Franklin GONCE (b.1872;d.1949).........................id 3688
................++ spouse: Mary O. MCCUBBIN (b.1877;d.1957)....................id 4090
....................7. Emma GONCE (b.1906;d.1910)..id 4091
....................7. Otis D. GONCE (b.1907;d.1926)...id 4092
....................7. Lawrence F. GONCE (b.1909;d.1974)..................................id 4093
....................++ spouse: Margaret SMITHEE..id 4115
........................8. William GONCE (b.1930)..id 4118
........................8. Jewell Ray GONCE (b.1930)...id 4119
........................8. Raymond GONCE (b.1930)...id 4120
........................8. Eugene GONCE (b.1930)...id 4121
........................8. Mary GONCE (b.1930)..id 4122
........................8. Joyce GONCE (b.1930)...id 4123
........................8. Lawrence GONCE , Jr. (b.1939;d.2001)..........................id 4116
........................++ spouse: Lawanna MARCHBANKS..................................id 4117
....................7. Emma C GONCE (b.1912)..id 4508
................++ spouse: Martha Ann KEITHLEY (b.1858;m.1877;d.1899)..........id 4007
................6. Rolyn GONCE (b.1877;d.1938)...id 4161
................++ spouse: Minnie WHITE (m.1920)..id 4181
................6. Lester Olonzo GONCE (b.1882;d.1957)...id 4073
................++ spouse: Sarah Jane BRIGHT (b.1885;m.1903;d.1946)................id 4094
....................7. Thelma Irene GONCE (b.1904;d.1939)..................................id 4095
....................7. Forrest GONCE (b.1906;d.1982)..id 4096
....................7. Vollie Vernon GONCE (b.1908;d.1951).................................id 4097
....................++ spouse: Kathleen Louise CHAPMAN (b.1924;d.1951).........id 4524
........................8. Katherine GONCE..id 4525
........................8. Theresa GONCE..id 4526
........................8. Sandra Jane GONCE..id 4527
........................++ spouse: Jerry Wayne ROBERTS (m.1966)........................id 4535
........................8. Georgia Irene GONCE...id 4528
....................7. Chet Lester GONCE (b.1912;d.1992) [425]...............................id 4098
....................++ spouse: Erma Dean RUFF (b.1915;m.1935;d.1984)................id 4473
........................8. Sherman Bret GONCE (b.1934)..id 4474

---

[425] Although he lived his adult life as a broadcast pioneer and later a well-respected businessman, Chet and his older brother Forrest were infamous in their youth as the "Baby Bandits" of Colorado. Their story is told as an appendix to my book "Abraham Rudolph Gonce – Missouri Pioneer," ISBN 978-06159-12448.

................8. Lester GONCE (b.1938;d.1938)..id 4531
................8. Sandra Jane GONCE (appears twice)...................................id 4527
................8. Georgia Irene GONCE (appears twice)..................................id 4528
...............++ spouse: Velma G. KIMBROUGH (b.1911;m.1991;d.2004)...id 4523
...............7. Infant GONCE (b.1918;d.1918)...id 4542
...............7. Marion GONCE (b.1915;d.1920)...id 4099
............6. Anna Belle GONCE (b.1885;d.1957)..id 4172
............++ spouse: Susan T. HARGROVE (b.1879;m.1896;d.1911)...........id 3998
............6. Aria Edith GONCE (b.1896)...id 3999
............++ spouse: John Clinton AUSTIN (b.1879;d.1938).........................id 4100
...............7. Infant AUSTIN...id 4101
...............7. Infant AUSTIN...id 4102
...............7. Robert Vernon AUSTIN (b.1912;d.1979).......................................id 4103
...............7. Mildred C. AUSTIN (b.1913)...id 4104
...............7. Virgil L. AUSTIN (b.1915)..id 4105
...............7. Delbert W. AUSTIN (b.1917)...id 4106
...............7. Thelma V. AUSTIN (b.1918)..id 4107
............6. Cora B. GONCE (b.1899)...id 4000
............++ spouse: Levi BLEVINS..id 4089
............6. James Tilford GONCE (b.1900;d.1942)...id 4001
............++ spouse: Ruth UNKF (b.1909)..id 4044
...............7. Randolph T. GONCE...id 4045
............6. Myrtle GONCE (b.1903)..id 4002
............6. Nora GONCE (b.1907)...id 4003
.........5. Infant Female GONCE (b.1832;d.1845)..id 4029
.........5. Louisa Jane GONCE (b.1834)...id 3022
.........++ spouse: George W DEBORD (m.1862)...id 3866
............6. G.W. Theodore DEBORD (b.1863)..id 3867
............6. Martha Ann DEBORD (b.1864)...id 3868
............++ spouse: Samuel GREENE...id 3874
............6. Susan Alice DEBORD (b.1866;d.1946)...id 3869
............++ spouse: William VAUGHN (m.1882)...id 3870
.........5. Martha GONCE (b.1836;d.1880)...id 3023
.........++ spouse: John MANIS (m.1856)..id 3286
.........5. Cinda GONCE (b.1838;d.1850)..id 4600
.........5. Nancy A. GONCE (b.1839)..id 3024
.........++ spouse: Pleasant MANIS (m.1866)...id 3287
.........++ spouse: Gilbert MANIS (m.1859)...id 3559
.........5. Jefferson GONCE (b.1840)...id 3025
.........5. Melinda GONCE (b.1841;d.1875)..id 3026
.........++ spouse: Powell MANIS..id 3428

..............5. Lucinda GONCE (b.1842)..id 3027
...........4. John Rudolph GONCE (b.1805;d.1880)....................................id 2880
...........++ spouse: Sarah Ellen UNKF (b.1870;d.1936)...........................id 3427
..............5. UnkF GONCE (b.1829)..id 4626
..............5. Lorinda GONCE (b.1869)..id 3309
..............5. Lassie GONCE (b.1874)...id 3406
...........++ spouse: Eliza UNKF (b.1814)..id 3152
..............5. Mary GONCE (b.1835)...id 3403
..............5. William V. GONCE (b.1838;d.1861)....................................id 3153
..............5. Ellisa GONCE (b.1840)..id 3308
..............5. Martha GONCE (b.1841)...id 3489
..............5. Mahala GONCE (b.1842)..id 3404
...............++ spouse: John CASH...id 4195
..............5. John Anderson GONCE (b.1844;d.1886)...........................id 3154
...............++ spouse: Catherine UNKF (b.1837)..................................id 3549
.................6. James GONCE (b.1859)..id 3449
...............++ spouse: Nancy Catherine SNYDER (b.1851;d.1937).......id 3383
.................6. Lee Cester GONCE (b.1873;d.1961).............................id 3409
.................++ spouse: Rosa Adele CRANFORD (b.1876;d.1956)........id 3415
....................7. Otto GONCE (b.1896;d.1954)....................................id 3420
....................7. Hattie GONCE (b.1897)...id 4479
....................7. Roy Lee GONCE (b.1899;d.1976)..............................id 3416
....................++ spouse: Eva GARVIS...id 3425
........................8. Roy Lee GONCE (b.1927;d.1989).........................id 3426
........................++ spouse: Velma Lanell SMITH................................id 3421
....................7. Mary GONCE (b.1902)...id 4480
....................7. Clarence GONCE (b.1903;d.1971).............................id 4481
....................++ spouse: Eutie MITCHELL (b.1906;d.1985)................id 4486
....................7. Doney GONCE (b.1906)...id 4482
....................7. Ruby GONCE (b.1908)...id 4483
....................7. Charlie Rufus GONCE (b.1909).................................id 3417
....................7. Johnny B. GONCE (b.1911;d.1990)...........................id 3419
....................++ spouse: Elizabeth TIPTON.......................................id 3423
........................8. Jackie Holt GONCE (b.1938).................................id 3424
........................++ spouse: Ella L WILLIS (m.1978)............................id 3837
....................7. Elmer C. GONCE (b.1916;d.1920).............................id 3418
....................7. Edgar Lee GONCE (b.1917;d.1918)...........................id 3726
....................7. Raymond L. GONCE (b.1918;d.1923).......................id 3727
.................6. Charley GONCE (b.1878;d.1936)...................................id 3384
.................6. James Rufus GONCE (b.1880;d.1948)..........................id 3385
.................++ spouse: Achid P. UNKF (b.1882).................................id 3502

................7. Noel A. GONCE (b.1903;d.1926)..id 3503
................7. Gladys GONCE (b.1906)...id 3504
................7. James Monroe GONCE (b.1908;d.1990).....................................id 3505
................7. Inez L. GONCE (b.1911)..id 3517
................7. Bernice H. GONCE (b.1912)..id 3518
................7. Helen GONCE (b.1916)...id 3519
................7. infant GONCE (d.1918)...id 3728
................7. infant GONCE (d.1919)...id 3729
................7. infant of J.R. GONCE (b.1920;d.1920)......................................id 3501
................7. James Rufus GONCE , Jr. (b.1921;d.1990)................................id 3506
................++ spouse: Anita Jewel WILCOXSON (b.1921;d.2003).............id 3507
................8. Tandy Ken GONCE (b.1943)..id 3508
................8. Dana Jerrel GONCE (b.1948)...id 3509
................++ spouse: James E. CRAFT (m.1974)...id 3520
................++ spouse: George R. WILLIAMS , Jr. (m.1969)..........................id 3813
................++ spouse: John Frederick GRIBI (m.1979)................................id 4532
................8. Jay R. GONCE (b.1949)...id 3730
................++ spouse: Sandra Lynn BRAND (m.1969)................................id 3731
................++ spouse: Virginia M. KINNEY (m.1978)...................................id 3810
................++ spouse: Jill M. SPEAR (m.1984)...id 3811
................++ spouse: Lisa J. MARSH (m.1991)...id 3812
............6. Rosalia GONCE (b.1880)...id 3386
............6. Mary Emma GONCE (b.1883)..id 3410
............++ spouse: James Thomas LEWIS (b.1883;d.1945).........................id 3411
................7. Jim LEWIS..id 3412
................7. Mary Laura LEWIS..id 3413
................7. Nora LEWIS..id 3414
............5. Isabella GONCE (b.1846)..id 3490
............5. Dialtha GONCE (b.1849)..id 3491
............5. Sarah GONCE (b.1849)...id 3405
............++ spouse: Joel W. CASH..id 4196
............5. Isaac L. GONCE (b.1851)..id 3155
............++ spouse: Julia E. CARTER (m.1868)..id 4194
............++ spouse: Mary UNKF (b.1852)...id 3564
............++ spouse: Cora E. UNKF (b.1865)..id 4137
................6. Rudolph Edward GONCE (b.1894)...id 4138
................6. Vallie L GONCE (b.1897)...id 4139
............5. Emma GONCE (b.1854;d.1920)..id 3156
............++ spouse: Thomas SNIDER..id 3809
............5. Louis Cleveland GONCE (b.1856;d.1924)....................................id 3157
............++ spouse: Sarah Frances STEWMAN (b.1863;m.1881;d.1918).......id 3158

................6. Laura Jossie GONCE (b.1881)..id 3159
................6. Mattie GONCE (b.1884;d.1960)..id 3160
................++ spouse: John Osburn KIMBRELL..id 3241
....................7. William Rose KIMBRELL (b.1906;d.1960)................................id 3242
........................++ spouse: Annie May NEILL (b.1912)................................id 3243
........................8. Wanda Lou KIMBRELL..id 3245
............................++ spouse: ?Male? WALKER..id 3244
................6. Bert Rudolph GONCE (b.1886;d.1942)................................id 3161
................++ spouse: Callie BUTCHER (b.1881;d.1957)................................id 3407
....................7. William GONCE (d.1943)..id 3408
....................7. Milford Rudolph GONCE (b.1912;d.1975)................id 4148
........................++ spouse: Callie Jane HOLDER (b.1913;d.2000)................id 4149
........................8. Wilburn Lee GONCE (b.1942)................................id 4150
....................7. Elizabeth GONCE (b.1914)..id 4167
................6. Mollie GONCE (b.1888)..id 3162
................6. Thomas GONCE (b.1890)..id 3163
................6. Ada GONCE (b.1893;d.1980)..id 3164
................6. Ida GONCE (b.1893;d.1985)..id 3165
................6. Ruth GONCE (b.1896)..id 3166
................6. Gertrude GONCE (b.1898)..id 3167
................6. Ollie Better Check GONCE (b.1901;d.1951)................id 3168
................++ spouse: Nettie Ellen REYNOLDS (b.1908;m.1924;d.1942).....id 3171
....................7. Ollie David GONCE (b.1925;d.1974)................id 3176
........................++ spouse: Elise Louise MOORE (b.1925;m.1949)................id 3185
........................8. Charles Wayne GONCE (b.1951;d.1989)................id 3181
............................++ spouse: Sandra K. MOONEY (b.1956;m.1971)................id 3183
............................++ spouse: Sharon Marie JONES (m.1982)................id 3184
........................8. Benny Dale GONCE (b.1956)................................id 3182
............................++ spouse: Marion Gabriele OPITZ (m.1984)................id 3194
....................7. Arvle Cleveland GONCE (b.1927;d.1991)................id 3177
........................++ spouse: Wilma Viola YATES (b.1930;m.1947;d.2000)............id 3186
........................8. Arvle Cleveland GONCE (b.1948)................................id 3188
............................++ spouse: Winnie L. PARSONS (m.1982)................id 3195
........................8. Donald Cleveland GONCE (b.1949;d.2001)................id 3189
............................++ spouse: Devora Ann BURRIS (m.1973)................id 3196
........................8. Shirley Arlene GONCE (b.1951)................................id 3190
............................++ spouse: James Harold REEL................................id 3197
........................8. David Glen GONCE (b.1955)................................id 3191
............................++ spouse: Mary Ann WOOD (m.1974)................id 3204
....................7. Better Check GONCE , Jr. (b.1928;d.1973)................id 3178
........................++ spouse: Frances Lee YOUNGER (b.1932;m.1950;d.1973)....id 3187

..................8. Michael Allen GONCE (b.1954)...id 3192
..................++ spouse: Jackie Sue WILLIAMS (m.1978).........................id 3206
..................++ spouse: Pamela Ann COLE (m.1982)................................id 3207
..................++ spouse: Deborah J. HALL (m.1974)..................................id 3205
..................8. Roland Lynn GONCE (b.1957)..id 3193
..................++ spouse: Yvonne Suzette PANCAKE (m.1978)...................id 3217
............7. Clayton Allen GONCE (b.1929;d.1954)............................id 3179
............++ spouse: Hilda HOUSERY (b.1928)..................................id 3390
............8. Clayton Allen GONCE (b.1951;d.1951).........................id 4599
............8. Hilda June GONCE (b.1952)..id 3391
............7. Juanita Mae GONCE (b.1933;d.2002).............................id 3180
............++ spouse: Henry Louis JERNIGAN (m.1949)......................id 3220
............8. Brenda June JERNIGAN (b.1950)...................................id 3221
............8. Kenny Louis JERNIGAN (b.1951)...................................id 3222
............8. Ricky Lenn JERNIGAN (b.1952)....................................id 3223
............8. Samuel Clay JERNIGAN (b.1954)...................................id 3224
............8. Henry Lawrence JERNIGAN (b.1956)............................id 3225
............8. Belinda Jean JERNIGAN (b.1957)..................................id 3226
............++ spouse: Don G. JAMES (m.1981)...................................id 3227
............7. Adrian Houston GONCE (b.1937;d.2008)........................id 3267
............++ spouse: Verta Arlene ROBERTS (b.1938;m.1955)............id 3268
............8. Mickey Dale GONCE (b.1955;d.1955)............................id 3269
............8. Clayton Kevin GONCE (b.1956)....................................id 3270
............++ spouse: Victoria Annette WALLS (b.1957;m.1975).........id 3272
............++ spouse: Marilyn M. THOMPSON (m.2002)......................id 3273
............8. Darlene GONCE (b.1964)...id 3376
............++ spouse: Mike MCCORMICK (b.1963;m.1982)................id 3377
............++ spouse: Greg NORRIS (b.1965;m.1989).........................id 3378
............8. Donna Ray GONCE (b.1968)..id 3271
............++ spouse: Gertrude REYNOLDS (d.1983).........................id 3175
............7. Nettie Pearl GONCE (b.1945)...id 3397
............7. Eddie Earl GONCE (b.1945)...id 3398
............++ spouse: Lurena Lee CRAWFORD (m.1968)....................id 3399
............8. Eddie Allen GONCE..id 3400
............++ spouse: Mendy DRERUP (m.1994)................................id 3402
............8. John Wesley GONCE..id 3401
......6. Warner Franklin GONCE (b.1904;d.1960).................................id 3291
......++ spouse: Lena Matilda PAULSON (b.1905;m.1925;d.1987)........id 3327
............7. Worney Cleveland GONCE (b.1926;d.1973)....................id 3328
............++ spouse: Ruth Lorraine PINNICK...................................id 3350
............8. Ruth Ann PINNICK (b.1947;d.1983)..............................id 3351

...................++ spouse: Charles Ray GONCE (b.1945)..................................id 3337
...................8. Norma Sarah PINNICK (b.1948)..id 3352
...................8. Floyd Elmore PINNICK (b.1954)...id 3353
...................++ spouse: Wilma OLSEN (m.1947).......................................id 3363
...................++ spouse: Marilynn UNKF (m.1962)....................................id 3364
...............7. Louis Franklin GONCE (b.1928;d.2004)..................................id 3329
...................++ spouse: Lucille VALENTINE (b.1931;d.2006)....................id 3339
...............7. Anna Geraldine GONCE (b.1930)...id 3330
...................++ spouse: J.C. JAMES..id 3365
...................8. Barbara Ann JAMES (b.1947)..id 3367
...................8. Kathy JAMES (b.1948;d.1948)..id 3368
...................8. Shirley Jean JAMES (b.1951)...id 3369
...................++ spouse: J.R. BLASSINGAME...id 3366
...............7. Jerry Garland GONCE (b.1932;d.1963)...................................id 3331
...................++ spouse: Ollie Margaret WILDER (m.1954)........................id 3340
...................8. Michael Dean GONCE (b.1956)..id 3343
...................++ spouse: Pamela K. NELSON (m.1974)..............................id 3841
...................++ spouse: Bari D. JOHNSON (m.1991).................................id 3842
...................++ spouse: Clessie Pauline LYNCH.......................................id 3341
...................8. Jerry Garland GONCE , Jr. (b.1957)....................................id 3344
...................++ spouse: Mary Lou MCKINNERNEY (b.1937;m.1958).........id 3342
...................8. Jerry Garland GONCE , Jr. (b.1959)....................................id 3345
...................8. Fred Cisroe GONCE (b.1960)..id 3346
...................++ spouse: Sheri G. MERRILL (m.1981)..................................id 3843
...................++ spouse: Leslie A. PRICE (m.1994)......................................id 3844
...................++ spouse: Victoria V. BOGDANOVICH (m.2001)..................id 3845
...................8. Christine Lavelle GONCE (b.1961)......................................id 3347
...................++ spouse: Stevie R BAREFOOT (m.1977).............................id 3846
...................++ spouse: Jay C DRENNAN (m.1984)...................................id 3847
...............7. Thelma Marie GONCE (b.1934)..id 3332
...................++ spouse: George Franklin ARNOLD (b.1927).......................id 3348
...................8. George Franklin ARNOLD , Jr. (b.1952)..............................id 3370
...................8. Susan Marie ARNOLD (b.1955)...id 3371
...................8. Thelma Darlene ARNOLD (b.1956)....................................id 3372
...................8. Edward Lewis ARNOLD (b.1960).......................................id 3373
...................8. Christine Dianne ARNOLD (b.1962)...................................id 3374
...............7. Mary Ruth GONCE (b.1935;d.1937)..id 3333
...............7. Nancy Lucille GONCE (b.1937)..id 3334
...............7. Worney Franklin GONCE , Jr. (b.1942).....................................id 3335
...................++ spouse: Lesley VIRGINIA..id 3349
...............7. Lena Elaine GONCE (b.1943)...id 3336

................++ spouse: Ronald Lee LOVELL (b.1942)...................................id 4033
....................8. Ronald Dean LOVELL (b.1960;d.1961)......................id 4035
....................8. Linda Elizabeth LOVELL (b.1962)..............................id 4036
................++ spouse: Andy NOTTINGHAM...id 4039
....................8. Rebecca Lucille LOVELL (b.1964)..............................id 4037
................++ spouse: Richard William ROY (m.1983)........................id 4202
....................8. Rhonda Lee LOVELL (b.1970)...................................id 4038
................++ spouse: ?Male? VANEK..id 4204
................++ spouse: Floyd E. BOYKIN..id 4034
................7. Charles Ray GONCE (b.1945)...id 3337
............++ spouse: Ruth Ann PINNICK (b.1947;d.1983)......................id 3351
................8. Sheila Ann GONCE (b.1964)...id 3354
............++ spouse: Ricky MORGAN..id 3498
................8. Charla Jean GONCE (b.1965)..id 3355
............++ spouse: Abraham P. GARZA (m.1984).................................id 3492
............++ spouse: Larry W. TEAGUE (m.1988)....................................id 3494
............++ spouse: Mark S. DVORAK (b.1968;m.1998).........................id 3497
................8. Charles Ray GONCE , Jr. (b.1966)...................................id 3356
............++ spouse: Cammie D. AUTREY (m.1989)................................id 3375
............++ spouse: Jennifer Jo LEE..id 3359
................8. Stephen Louis GONCE (b.1971)......................................id 3357
............++ spouse: Kim BUSICK (b.1967)..id 3361
................8. Sharon Matilda GONCE (b.1976)....................................id 3358
............++ spouse: Erik Wade RADLE (m.[Div])..................................id 4206
............++ spouse: Jerry Bob BOMAR (m.2000)..................................id 4208
............7. Linda Joyce GONCE (b.1949)...id 3338
........3. Lydia GONCE (b.1771;d.1850)..id 2586
........++ spouse: Thomas SPROWL (m.1792)..id 2592
............4. Thomas SPROWL , Jr. (b.1798)..id 3863
............4. John SPROWL..id 3864
........3. Margaret GONCE (b.1772;d.1841)...id 2585
........++ spouse: Benjamin HUTCHISSON (b.1765;m.1790;d.1852)...............id 2591
............4. Jemima HUTCHISSON (b.1792;d.1792)..............................id 3593
............4. Keziah HUTCHISSON (b.1792;d.1792)................................id 3594
............4. Elizabeth HUTCHISSON (b.1793;d.1847)............................id 3595
............4. Sarah HUTCHISSON (b.1795;d.1855).................................id 3597
............4. Joseph HUTCHISSON (b.1797;d.1882)...............................id 3766
............4. Lydia HUTCHISSON (b.1799;d.1876).................................id 3767
............4. Benjamin HUTCHISSON (b.1801;d.1813)...........................id 3782
............4. Rebecca HUTCHISSON (b.1803;d.1899).............................id 3783
............4. John HUTCHISSON (b.1805;d.1894)...................................id 3852

DESCENDANTS OF JUSTICE GONCE – NINE GENERATIONS

............++ spouse: Rachel MCKIRGAN (b.1805;m.1829;d.1883)......................id 3853
...............5. William W HUTCHISSON (b.1834;d.1918).................................id 3854
...............++ spouse: Hester Ann WILKINS (b.1835;m.1858;d.1884)..............id 3855
..................6. Harry HUTCHISSON (b.1869;d.1947)....................................id 3856
.....................++ spouse: Anna Bertha MERRICK (b.1871;m.1898;d.1930)........id 3857
.......................7. Lawrence Elmer HUTCHISSON (b.1902)...........................id 3858
...........4. William HUTCHISSON (b.1808;d.1865).......................................id 3784
...........4. Rudolph HUTCHISSON (b.1810;d.1872).....................................id 2872
...........4. Eleanor Ingram HUTCHISSON (b.1812;d.1864)............................id 3785
...........4. Margaret HUTCHISSON (b.1815;d.1840)....................................id 3786
........3. Mary Vance GONCE (b.1774)..id 2587
........++ spouse: James C. LARKIN (m.1794;d.1810)..................................id 2593
...........4. Abram G. LARKINS (b.1825;d.1860)...id 4629
...........++ spouse: Lucretia UNKF (b.1827)..id 4632
..............5. Mary J. LARKINS (b.1847)..id 4630
..............5. Frances LARKINS (b.1849)...id 4631
........3. Sarah GONCE (b.1777;d.1860)..id 2588
........++ spouse: Aaron WELLS (m.1792;d.1830).......................................id 2594
...........4. Jeremiah WELLS (b.1794)...id 3861
...........4. Isaac WELLS (b.1798)..id 3862

(Abraham is possibly the progenitor of a Kentucky Branch of the Gonce Family)
......2. ABRAHAM GONCE (b.1748) [426] – second son of Justice Gonce........id 2579

(Daniel is the progenitor of the Mid-Atlantic Branch – Maryland and Delaware)
......2. DANIEL GONCE (b.1758;d.1782) – third son of Justice Gonce.a192 id 2580
......++ spouse: Mary LOWERY (b.1760;m.1778)..a193 id 2582
.........3. Rudolph GONCE (b.1779,d.1804)...a96 id 2596
.........++ spouse: Elizabeth HEDNEY (b.1780;m.1796;d.1800)...............a97 id 2597
............4. George GONCE (b.1796;d.1860)...a48 id 2511
............++ spouse: Catherine A. COMEGYS (b.1808;m.1823;d.1858)....a49 id 2510
...............5. John Thomas GONCE (b.1823;d.1905)...................................a24 id 1576
...............++ sp: Catharine Ann SULLIVAN (b.1831;m.1847;d.1911)....a25 id 1577
..................6. George E. GONCE (b.1847;d.1926).....................................id 2609
..................++ spouse: Mary Elizabeth UNKF (b.1849;d.1943)....................id 2631
.....................7. William H. GONCE (b.1869;d.1913)..................................id 2982
.....................++ spouse: Mary C. UNKF (b.1868;m.1895)..........................id 2983

---

[426] I have not yet identified any descendants of Abraham, the middle of the three sons of Justice and Magdalen Gonce. There are, however, a number of Gonces who appear in Kentucky starting in the late eighteenth and early nineteenth centuries. Whether these are Abraham's descendants or part of the Gans family from Pennsylvania is unclear.

................7. John Thomas GONCE (b.1875;d.1926)......................................id 3458
................++ spouse: Julia May APPLER (b.1877;d.1962).........................id 3459
................8. Evelyn M. GONCE (b.1900)...id 3461
................++ spouse: Leo M. GERY (b.1899)...id 3460
............7. Gery C. GONCE (b.1888)..id 2985
............++ spouse: George H. SMITH (b.1883;m.1908)..........................id 2984
............8. Dorothy SMITH (b.1918)...id 2996
............7. Albert GONCE (b.1889;d.1901)...id 2632
........6. James E. GONCE (d.1861)..id 2973
........6. Joseph R. GONCE (d.1871)...id 2639
........6. Mary E. GONCE (b.1852;d.1909)..id 2610
........6. Benny M. GONCE (d.1861)...id 2974
........6. Emma GONCE (b.1855)..id 3596
........6. William Henry GONCE , Sr. (b.1857;d.1935).........................a12 id 32
........++ spouse: Alice Eliz. CLAUTICE (b.1857;m.1877;d.1912)....a13 id 33
............7. George Eugene GONCE (b.1879)...id 151
............++ spouse: Bertha Ellen CLAUTICE (b.1882;m.1904;d.1970).....id 647
................8. Beatrice W. GONCE (b.1914;d.1990)..................................id 700
................8. Mildred Emily GONCE (b.1920;d.1998)............................id 701
............7. Grace Elizabeth GONCE (b.1881;d.1962)................................id 152
............++ spouse: Alfred P. WILLS (b.1874;m.1906;d.1930)...................id 146
................8. W. A. Geary WILLS (b.1910;d.1990)...................................id 575
................++ spouse: Catherine M. UNKF (d.1924)................................id 574
................8. Evelyn Marie WILLS (b.1907)..id 702
................++ spouse: Thompson A. WALLACE (b.1906;d.1993).............id 576
................8. Paul Melvin WILLS (b.1914)..id 704
............7. Laura Augusta GONCE (b.1883;d.1902)..................................id 154
............++ spouse: Alfred P. WILLS (b.1874;m.1901;d.1930)..................id 146
............7. William Henry GONCE , Jr. (b.1887;d.1954)...........................id 697
............++ spouse: Caroline ENIS (b.1889;d.1978)..................................id 646
................8. Bernard A. GONCE (b.1911)..id 1311
................++ spouse: Clara R. UNKF (b.1914;d.2000).............................id 3310
................8. Alice Mary GONCE (b.1914)..id 1312
................++ spouse: Charles MURPHY...id 2526
................8. Charles Joseph GONCE (b.1918;d.1997).............................id 1313
................++ spouse: Nancy UNKF (m.[Div])..id 2419
................++ spouse: Marjorie Darlene DAGUE.....................................id 2530
................8. Regina M. GONCE (b.1923)..id 1314
................8. Dorothy E. GONCE (b.1926)...id 1315
............7. Alice Theresa GONCE (b.1889;d.1973)....................................id 153
............++ spouse: George Louis GORDON (b.1866;d.1964).................id 147

..................8. Alvin Eugene GORDON (b.1918;d.1980)..................id 253
..................++ spouse: Marian Katherine WYATT..................id 2253
..................8. Mary Eileen GORDON (b.1923;d.2007)..................id 252
..................++ spouse: Donald Fran... GUMAER (b.1922;m.1949;d.1983)..id 265
..................++ spouse: George HERAK (m.1942;d.1944)..................id 2250
..................8. Alice Juanita GORDON (b.1932)..................id 2252
..................++ spouse: Michael LINEHAN (b.1921;d.1960)..................id 2254
............7. Edward Lyman GONCE (b.1892;d.1977)..................id 155
..................++ spouse: Ruth UNKF (b.1898)..................id 644
..................++ spouse: Mary Ruth O'DONNELL (m.1903)..................id 643
..................8. Thomas Norman GONCE (b.1912)..................id 648
..................8. Dorothy GONCE (b.1916)..................id 649
..................8. Edward Lyman GONCE (b.1918;d.1918)..................id 34
..................8. Lyman N. GONCE (b.1919;d.1981)..................id 3450
..................8. Edward G. GONCE (b.1922)..................id 159
..................++ spouse: Mary UNKF..................id 160
..................8. Vernon GONCE (b.1925;d.1925)..................id 35
..................8. William Carl GONCE..................id 156
..................8. Mildred GONCE (b.1930)..................id 158
..................++ spouse: John H. CHESTER..................id 157
............7. John Thomas GONCE (b.1894;d.1978)..................id 150
..................++ spouse: Anna M. UNKF (b.1898;d.1981)..................id 645
..................8. Andrew I. GONCE (b.1916;d.1981)..................id 654
..................8. Margaret M. GONCE (b.1923)..................id 653
..................++ spouse: Karl SCHWARZ (d.2006)..................id 652
............7. <u>Charles Richard GONCE</u> (b.1896;d.1936)..................a6 id 43
..................++ sp: <u>Anna Gertrude HULSHOFF</u> (b.1896;m.1919;d.1983) a7 id 44
..................8. <u>Rosalie Gertrude GONCE</u> (b.1919)..................a3 id 242
..................++ sp: <u>Cornelius Fr OBERLE</u> (b.1917;m.1941;d.2004).....a2 id 196
..................8. Mary Regina GONCE (b.1921;d.2011)..................id 248
..................++ spouse: Henry Otis COOPER (m.[Div];d.1975)..................id 247
..................++ spouse: Robert D. IGLEHART (b.1911;m.1955;d.1996).....id 249
..................8. Charles Richard GONCE (b.1923;d.2007)..................id 243
..................++ spouse: Dorothy M. DUNN (b.1923;m.1944;d.2007)..........id 244
..................8. George Joseph GONCE (b.1927)..................id 245
..................++ spouse: Marguerite MORTILLARO (b.1924;m.1945)..........id 246
............7. Raymond Aloysius GONCE (b.1898;d.1968)..................id 36
..................++ spouse: Edna I. SPARR (b.1900;m.1917;d.1968)..................id 31
..................8. Geraldine GONCE (b.1919)..................id 706
..................8. Beatrice GONCE (b.1930)..................id 650
........6. Thomas S. GONCE (b.1859;d.1931)..................id 1579

................++ spouse: Agnes O. UNKF (b.1859;d.1948).....................................id 2284
................7. William Howard GONCE (b.1886;d.1919)..id 2285
................++ spouse: Mary Elizab SUDSBURG (b.1886;m.1909;d.1956). .id 2286
....................8. Margaret Frances GONCE (b.1910;d.1994)..........................id 2287
....................8. William Paul GONCE (b.1912;d.1987)....................................id 2288
....................++ spouse: Margaret E. UNKF (b.1912;d.2004)....................id 2297
....................8. Dorothy E. GONCE (b.1916)..id 2295
....................++ spouse: Charles Lee ANDERSON (b.1912)........................id 2302
....................8. Edythe V. GONCE (b.1918;d.2002)......................................id 2296
....................++ spouse: Richard GRASON , IV (b.1914;d.1998)................id 2307
................7. Rae O. GONCE (b.1890)..id 2291
................7. Howard Thomas GONCE (b.1892;d.1951)................................id 2292
....................++ spouse: Sarah E. YOUNGHEIN (b.1893;d.1940)..................id 2768
....................++ spouse: Anna L. UNKF (m.1941)...id 3290
................7. Mary E. GONCE (b.1896)...id 2293
................7. Albert E. GONCE (b.1903)..id 2294
............6. Louis A. GONCE (b.1866;d.1920)..id 1580
................++ spouse: Mary E. UNKF (b.1871;m.1890).....................................id 2280
................7. Catherine M. GONCE (b.1891;d.1970)..id 2281
................7. Edith GONCE (b.1893)...id 2282
................7. Louis Augustus GONCE (b.1896;d.1979).....................................id 2283
....................++ spouse: Pauline M. UNKF (b.1901)...id 2727
....................8. Louis Augustus GONCE , Jr. (b.1920;d.1979)........................id 2728
....................8. Charles GONCE (b.1922;d.1985)..id 2729
....................8. Pauline GONCE (b.1924)...id 2730
....................8. Mary GONCE (b.1928)..id 2731
................7. Ellen GONCE (b.1899)..id 2734
....................++ spouse: Frank BENNY (b.1892)..id 2735
................7. Walter E. GONCE (b.1904)...id 2732
................7. Carl E. GONCE (b.1911;d.1992)...id 2733
............6. Catherine A. GONCE (b.1868;d.1941)...id 1581
................++ spouse: John T. LINDSAY (b.1853;d.1898).................................id 2626
................7. Mary E. LINDSAY (b.1893)...id 2627
........5. Margaret Ann GONCE (b.1825;d.1860)..id 2519
............++ spouse: George MOORE (b.1817;m.1846)..id 2521
............6. George MOORE (b.1846)..id 2523
........5. George Washington GONCE (b.1828;d.1902).......................................id 2520
............++ spouse: Emmaline Jane COX (b.1824;m.1850;d.1884)..................id 2522
............6. George Rudolphis GONCE (b.1852;d.1913)....................................id 2709
................++ spouse: Susan Casander MANON (b.1858;m.1879;d.1917).......id 2710
................7. Willie Mae GONCE (b.1880;d.1929)..id 3789

................++ spouse: John Thomas ALGARD (m.1903)........................id 3790
................++ spouse: Ed ORMESBE..id 3791
................7. Thomas Allibone GONCE (b.1882;d.1952)........................id 2711
................++ spouse: Ellenora M. WORRILOW (b.1879;m.1905;d.1943). id 2721
................8. Joseph Earl GONCE (b.1906;d.1978)...............................id 2722
................++ spouse: Mary Louise PRYOR (b.1910;d.1947)....................id 3798
................++ spouse: Florence Lillian PRYOR (b.1916;d.1982)................id 3799
................8. Alverta G. GONCE (b.1908;d.1982)..................................id 2909
................++ spouse: ?Male? SCHIRLING..id 2908
................8. Mary A. GONCE (b.1909;d.1961)......................................id 2723
................8. George M. GONCE (b.1911;d.1985).................................id 2910
................++ spouse: Ruthie CONWAY..id 2911
................8. Wilna G. GONCE (b.1914;d.1974)....................................id 2913
................++ spouse: James Marple DENNISON (b.1909;d.1997).........id 2912
................8. Robert W. GONCE (b.1917;d.1978).................................id 2914
................8. Percy Ellis GONCE (b.1922;d.1973).................................id 2915
................++ spouse: Dorothy Lena SIMPERS (b.1931;m.1957;d.2004) id 2922
................7. George Washington GONCE (b.1884;d.1952)....................id 2712
................++ spouse: Ethel CARL (m.1907)..id 3792
................7. Sara Emily GONCE (b.1886;d.1959)................................id 2713
................++ spouse: Charles ROTHERMEL (m.1907).........................id 3793
................7. Mary Elizabeth GONCE (b.1888;d.1975)..........................id 2714
................++ spouse: Edward RUTTER (m.1917)..................................id 3794
................7. Samuel Uhler GONCE (b.1890;d.1940)............................id 2715
................++ spouse: Bertha Jane WILSON (b.1891;m.1918;d.1932).........id 2726
................8. Samuel Uhler GONCE , Jr. (b.1926;d.1995)......................id 2920
................++ spouse: Doris B. COALE (b.1927)....................................id 2921
................7. Susan Cleveland GONCE (b.1892;d.1970).......................id 2716
................++ spouse: Hugh LAZELERE (m.1912)................................id 3795
................7. Josephine GONCE (b.1894;d.1904).................................id 2717
................7. Annie Elsie GONCE (b.1900)...id 2718
................++ spouse: Lawrence RUPP...id 3796
................++ spouse: Colman PHILLIPS..id 3797
................6. Samuel GONCE (b.1855)...id 2525
................6. William T. GONCE (b.1856)..id 2524
................++ spouse: Henrietta UNKF (b.1858;m.1885).......................id 2641
................7. James GONCE (b.1886)...id 2642
................7. Emily GONCE (b.1888)...id 2643
................5. Mary Matilda GONCE (b.1829;d.1861)............................id 2601
................++ spouse: Charles ROBERTS (m.1861)................................id 2611
................6. Thomas Allibone ROBERTS (b.1857)...............................id 4645

................++ spouse: Laura UNKF (b.1857)..id 4646
................6. Margaret ROBERTS...id 2644
................5. Augusta GONCE (b.1834;d.1861)...id 2605
................++ spouse: Edward LEE (b.1823;m.1851)..id 2656
................6. Ann LEE (b.1853)..id 3834
................6. Charles LEE (b.1855)..id 3835
................6. Edward LEE (b.1858)..id 3836
................5. Benedict Rudolph GONCE (b.1836)..id 2602
................++ spouse: Margaret J. UNKF (b.1837;d.1910)......................................id 2603
................6. Benjamin F. GONCE (b.1864)..id 2648
................++ spouse: Annie UNKF (b.1866)...id 2649
....................7. Lenore GONCE (b.1884)..id 2650
....................7. Mary O. GONCE (b.1889)...id 2651
....................7. Margaret GONCE (b.1894)...id 2652
....................7. Julia GONCE (b.1899)..id 2653
................6. Frank R. GONCE (b.1863)..id 2614
................++ spouse: Annie K. UNKF (b.1878)..id 2615
....................7. Benedict Jones GONCE (b.1897;d.1978)..id 2616
................6. William Robert GONCE (b.1863;d.1934)...id 2654
................++ spouse: Annie H. UNKF (b.1878)...id 2655
................6. Mary E. GONCE (b.1866)..id 2704
................++ spouse: James BALEY (b.1860)...id 2703
....................7. Martha BALEY (b.1888)...id 2705
....................7. Arthur BALEY (b.1891)..id 2706
....................7. Beaulah BALEY (b.1893)..id 2707
....................7. Edna V. BALEY (b.1909)..id 2708
................6. Georgiana GONCE (b.1867)..id 2874
................6. Martina GONCE (b.1869)..id 2875
................6. Walter GONCE (b.1875)..id 2876
................++ spouse: Margaret UNKF (b.1884;m.1902;d.1922)...........................id 2898
....................7. Benjamin J. GONCE (b.1896;d.1978)..id 2899
....................++ spouse: Margaret A. UNKF (b.1901)..id 2900
........................8. Vernon GONCE (b.1919;d.1980)...id 2901
....................7. Walter C. GONCE , Jr. (b.1906;d.1977)...id 2902
....................++ spouse: Helen UNKF (b.1905)..id 2903
....................7. James A. GONCE (b.1909;d.1910)...id 2904
....................7. Benton GONCE (b.1919;d.1930)..id 2905
....................7. Burton Lewis GONCE (b.1921;d.1987)..id 2906
....................++ spouse: Alvira Jean UNKF (b.1923;d.1996)..................................id 4174
........................8. Paula J. GONCE (b.1875)...id 4175
........................8. Burton Lewis GONCE , Jr. (b.1940;d.2001)..............................id 4504

................7. Catherine GONCE (b.1922)................id 2907
............5. Thomas Allibone Robaris GONCE (b.1839;d.1861)................id 2604
............5. Laura Ellen GONCE (b.1843;d.1875)................id 2606
............++ spouse: Charles POPE (b.1833;d.1880)................id 2988
............6. John T. POPE (b.1862)................id 2989
............6. Charles W. POPE (b.1864)................id 2990
............6. Evalina E. POPE (b.1869)................id 2991
............6. Annie POPE (b.1871)................id 2992
............6. Susan POPE (b.1875)................id 2993
............6. Dennis POPE (b.1875)................id 2994
............5. James Allibone GONCE (b.1844;d.1920)................id 2607
............++ spouse: Sarah J. HILL (b.1850)................id 2608
............6. William H. GONCE (b.1870)................id 2867
................++ spouse: Lida UNKF (b.1875;d.1920)................id 4074
................7. Ola GONCE (b.1894)................id 4075
................7. Elwood GONCE (b.1895)................id 4076
................7. Edna E. GONCE (b.1902)................id 4077
................7. Elia GONCE (b.1903)................id 4078
................7. Roy GONCE (b.1905)................id 4079
................7. Grover GONCE (b.1907)................id 4080
................7. Riley GONCE (b.1908)................id 4081
................7. Edward GONCE (b.1909)................id 4082
................7. Ruth GONCE (b.1913)................id 4057
................7. Alvin E GONCE (b.1914;d.1988)................id 4058
................++ spouse: Frances H. UNKF (b.1918;d.1997)................id 4176
................7. Estella GONCE (b.1916)................id 4059
................7. Mildred GONCE (b.1917)................id 4060
............6. Benjamin GONCE (b.1871)................id 2868
............6. Sarah GONCE (b.1871)................id 2869
............6. Richard GONCE (b.1873;d.1955)................id 2995
........4. John T. GONCE (b.1800;d.1871)................id 2628
........++ spouse: Susan UNKF (b.1803;m.1825)................id 2629
............5. John R. GONCE (b.1831;d.1870)................id 2612
............++ spouse: Sarah Elizabeth ALRICH (b.1836;m.1858;d.1929)................id 2613
............6. John Eugene GONCE (b.1859)................id 2617
................++ spouse: Eliza BRATTON (b.1864;m.1892;d.1920)................id 2618
................7. John Eugene GONCE , II (b.1892)................id 2619
................++ spouse: Louise ALLYN (m.1927)................id 2623
................8. John Eugene GONCE , III (b.1929)................id 2624
................8. Allyn GONCE (b.1932)................id 2625
................7. Robert Levis GONCE (b.1900;d.1968)................id 2620

..................++ spouse: Mary Ann BRATTON (b.1889;m.1921;d.1969)...........id 2646
.................6. Mary Alrich GONCE (b.1861;d.1942)...id 2621
.................++ spouse: John H. FRAZER (b.1865)..id 2622
..............5. Susannah GONCE (b.1835)..id 2630
.........++ spouse: Ann COX (m.1801)..id 2598
............4. Elizabeth GONCE (b.1802)..id 4751

None of the ninth (of which I am a part), tenth, eleventh and twelfth generations of American Gonces have been listed for privacy reasons, and it should be noted that a few of those in the eighth generation listed here are still alive.

APPENDIX IX

Ancestors of Rosalie Gonce Oberle, Mary Regina Gonce Iglehart, Charles R. Gonce, Jr. and George J. Gonce, Sr.

(includes direct line ancestry charts as well)

Ancestors of Rosalie Gonce & her Siblings

The table below lists the known ancestors of Rosalie Gertrude Gonce Oberle[427], daughter of Charles Richard Gonce and Anna Gertrude Hulshoff. The number preceding each line identifies the generation relative to Rosalie, who is considered generation 1 in this table (start with the line containing Rosalie's name on the next page). Her paternal ancestors are listed above her in the table, and her maternal line is listed below her. Her father Charles Richard Gonce, for instance, can be found by locating generation 2 above, and her mother Anna Gertrude Hulshoff by finding generation 2 below. Her grandparents all are numbered 3, her great-grandparents are numbered 4, etc. The number at the end of each line is the person's identification number in my genealogical database that is used to reference documents and other material relating to that person. The "a" number preceding the identification number is my Ahnentafel Number[428].

```
...............8. Justice GONCE (d.1782)..................................a384 id 2577
.............7. Daniel GONCE (b.1758;m.1778;d.1782).........a192 id 2580
...............8. Magdalen UNKF (d.1782)...............................a385 id 2858
..........6. Rudolph GONCE (b.1779;m.1796)........................a96 id 2596
...............8. John LOWERY (d.1780)..................................a386 id 3516
.............7. Mary LOWERY (b.1760)..................................a193 id 2582
...............8. ?Female? UNKF............................................a387 id 3592
........5. George GONCE (b.1796;m.1823;d.1860)................a48 id 2511
.............7. George HEDNEY (d.1825)................................a194 id 2595
..........6. Elizabeth HEDNEY (b.1780;d.1800)....................a97 id 2597
.....4. John Thomas GONCE (b.1823;m.1847;d.1905).........a24 id 1576
.....................11. Cornelius COMEN GYSEN (b.1610)...........a3136 id 4546
................10. Cornelius COMEGYS (b.1630;m.1688;d.1709). a1568 id 2431
.....................11. Jannegan JANS.......................................a3137 id 4547
................9. Edward COMEGYS (b.1689;m.1717;d.1761)...........a784 id 2443
................10. Rebecca SMITH (d.1735).........................a1569 id 2436
............8. Edward COMEGYS, II (b.1718;m.1737)..........a392 id 2552
............9. Mary HARWOOD..........................................a785 id 2548
.........7. Jesse COMEGYS (b.1747;m.1770;d.1801).........a196 id 2564
............8. Mary THRAUL................................................a393 id 2560
```

---

[427] If it is not obvious, this table is identical to what would be created for any of her siblings Mary Regina Iglehart, Charles Richard Gonce, Jr., or George Joseph Gonce.

[428] That is, an Ahnentafel number based on me as number 1, my father as number 2, and my mother Rosalie Gonce as number 3. See an explanation of Ahnentafel numbers on page 199.

.................6. Samuel COMEGYS (b.1784;m.1807;d.1841)..........................a98 id 2508
.................7. Mary UNKF (d.1801)...a197 id 2570
...............5. Catherine A. COMEGYS (b.1808;d.1858)...................................a49 id 2510
.................................13. Harmens VANSANT (d.1643)...............a12672 id 4568
..............................12. C'stoffel VANSANT (b.1618;m.1643;d.1655)...a6336 id 4563
..........................11. Garret Stoffelse VANSANT (b.1644;d.1706). a3168 id 4545
.............................13. Ger. JANSZEN (b.1592;m.1616;d.1634).a12674 id 4566
............................12. Moedertien GERRITS (b.1623;d.1644).......a6337 id 4564
.................................13. Vroutgen PIETERS (d.1643)..................a12675 id 4567
...........................10. Christoffel VANSANT (b.1670;d.1749).............a1584 id 4552
..............................12. Cornelis VAN WESTEN (b.1630)...............a6338 id 4571
............................11. Elizabeth GERRITTSE (b.1647).......................a3169 id 4562
..............................12. Josyntje VER HAGEN.................................a6339 id 4572
......................9. Joshua VANSANT (b.1703;d.1771)........................a792 id 3751
...........................11. Hendrick COURSON...................................a3170 id 4593
.........................10. Rachel COURSON.......................................a1585 id 3748
.........................11. Aeltje GERRITSEN......................................a3171 id 4594
....................8. John R. VANSANT (b.1731;m.1769;d.1773).................a396 id 2498
......................9. Catherine JOHNSTON..a793 id 4579
..................7. John VANSANT , Jr. (m.1788).................................a198 id 3769
...............6. Rachel VANSANT (b.1792;d.1841).............................a99 id 2509
........3. William Henry GONCE , Sr. (b.1857;m.1877;d.1935)..........................a12 id 32
...............6. ?Male? SULLIVAN...a100 id 2969
.............5. Eugean SULLIVAN (b.1805;d.1871)................................a50 id 2599
............4. Catharine Ann SULLIVAN (b.1831;d.1911)..........................a25 id 1577
.............5. Mary A. O'BRIEN (b.1805;d.1871).................................a51 id 2600
......2. Charles Richard GONCE (b.1896;m.1919;d.1936)..........................a6 id 43
.................6. John Peter CLAUTICE (b.1768;m.1795;d.1825)................a104 id 2330
..............5. John W. CLAUTICE (b.1805;d.1870)..............................a52 id 2320
.................6. Anne Marie UnkF (b.1774;d.1840)..............................a105 id 4647
...........4. John W. CLAUTICE (b.1831;m.1854;d.1907)..............................a26 id 2322
.................6. Lloyd GOODWIN (b.1771)....................................a106 id 4656
............5. Elizabeth GOODWIN (b.1815;d.1880)............................a53 id 2321
........3. Alice Elizabeth CLAUTICE (b.1857;d.1912)............................a13 id 33
.................6. John B. FARRING (b.1766;d1839)..............................a108 id 4648
.............5. Augustus FARRING (b.1795).....................................a54 id 3514
.................6. Eliza UnkF (b.1765;d1839).....................................a109 id 4665
...........4. Laura Ann FARRING (b.1836;d.1883)...............................a27 id 2328
..............5. Hellen Clouse (b.1797;d.1860)...................................a55 id 3515
1. **Rosalie Gertrude GONCE** (b.1919) (also M.R., C.R. & G.J. Gonce)........a3 id 242
......................8. Joannes David HULSHOFF (b.1667;m.1697;d.1717)..a448 id 1602

................7. Joannes Henricus HULSHOFF (b.1704;m.1732;d.1757) a224 id 1606
..................9. Johann THOBEN (b.1645)..a898 id 1660
................8. Anna Margareta THOBEN (b.1665).............................a449 id 1603
..................9. Wibbeke STRAHTMANS (b.1649)........................a899 id 1661
..............6. Joannes Gerhardus HULSHOFF (b.1742;m.1784;d.1820). a112 id 1626
................8. Heinrich Albers LUERS...a450 id 2980
..............7. Anna Margahreta LUERS (b.1710;d.1771)...................a225 id 1610
................8. Gertrud Tole THOBEN...a451 id 2981
............5. Joannes Gerard HULSHOFF (b.1786;m.1830)..............................a56 id 665
..............6. Anna Maria Gertrud KRUSE (d.1820)........................a113 id 1631
..........4. John Gerhart HULSHOFF (b.1831;d.1916)........................a28 id 12
................6. Victor JANSSENS (b.1755;d.1820).............................a114 id 2384
............5. Dorothea Antoinette JANSSENS (b.1798;d.1876)..................a57 id 13
................6. Anna Catharina MEYER..a115 id 2385
........3. Herman R. HULSHOFF (b.1869;d.1940)...............................a14 id 7
..........4. Elisabethe UNKF (b.1829;d.1907).....................................a29 id 10
......2. Anna Gertrude HULSHOFF (b.1896;d.1983)..............................a7 id 44
................8. Johannes Michael KERCHNER (b.1709)..................a480 id 1178
..............7. Francis Caspar KERCHNER (b.1750)............................a240 id 107
................8. Gertrude GROOS (b.1717)...a481 id 1179
..............6. Paul KERCHNER (b.1782;m.1802;d.1856)....................a120 id 82
................8. Andreas RAUCH..a482 id 1174
..............7. Anna Katharina RAUCH (b.1756)................................a241 id 1169
................8. Margaret HOSKIN...a483 id 1175
............5. Michael Anthony KERCHNER (b.1804;m.1828;d.1857)............a60 id 100
................8. Johann MÜSSIG...a484 id 1171
..............7. Anton MÜSSIG (b.1741)..a242 id 1170
................6. Maria Rosina MUSSIG (b.1778;d.1853)........................a121 id 83
................8. Michael ARNOLD..a486 id 1172
..............7. Maria Anna ARNOLD...a243 id 1173
..........4. Ferdinand KERCHNER (b.1835;m.1860;d.1918)..........................a30 id 38
..............6. John Dominic KERN , Sr. (b.1781;m.1805;d.1826)..............a122 id 84
............5. Anna Maria KERN (b.1806;d.1879).....................................a61 id 91
..............6. Margaret VAETH (b.1780;d.1820)..................................a123 id 85
........3. Mary Regina KERCHNER (b.1873;d.1940).............................a15 id 8
..............6. ?Male? LINNENKEMPER...a124 id 87
............5. Henry LINNENKEMPER (b.1806).......................................a62 id 98
..............6. Mary Rosina UNKF...a125 id 88
..........4. Anna B. LINNENKEMPER (b.1839;d.1914)...........................a31 id 39
............5. Annie UNKF (b.1805)...a63 id 99

Ancestors of Rosalie Gonce and her Siblings

Five Generations of Comegys from Cornelius to Samuel

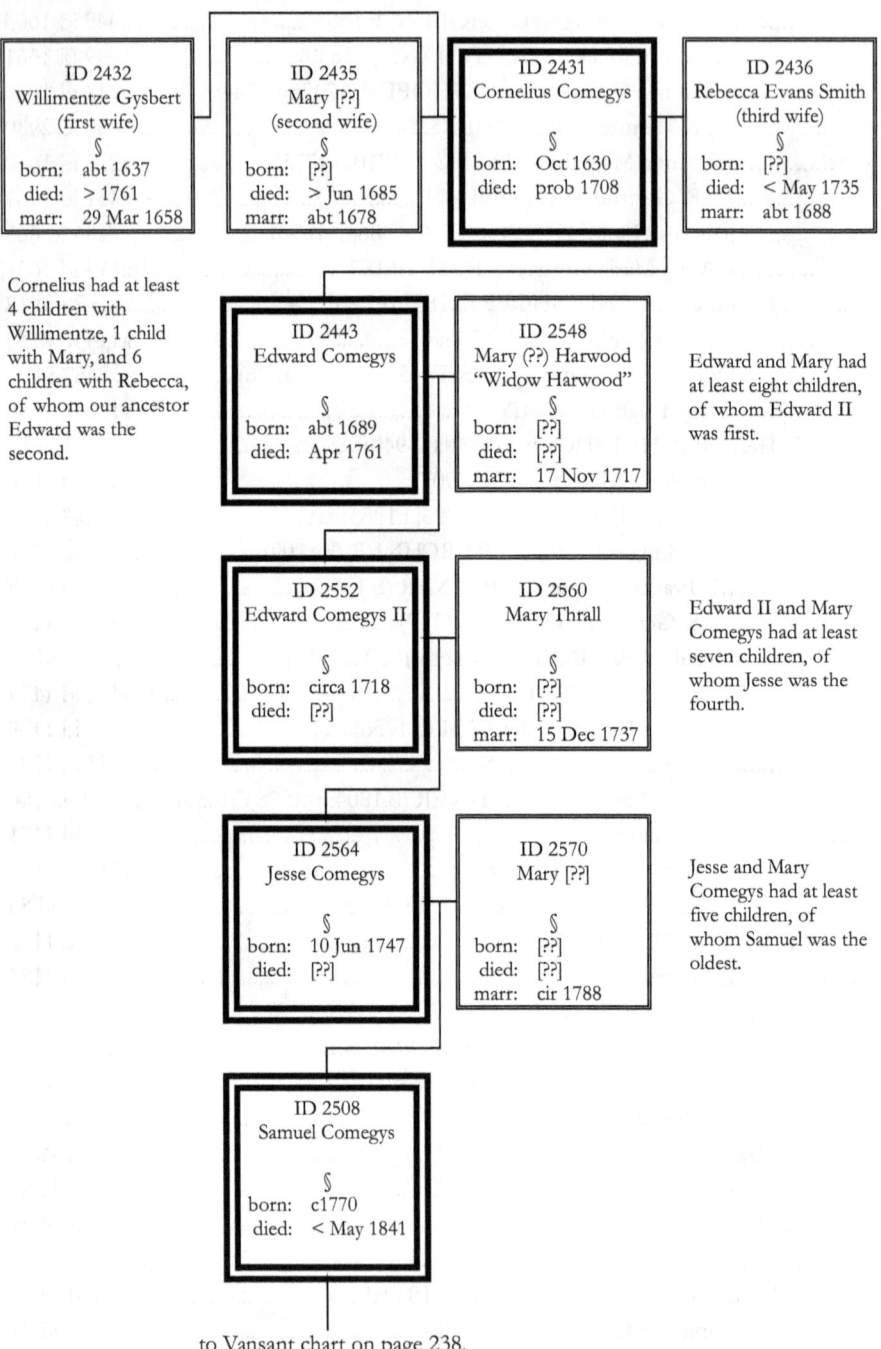

to Vansant chart on page 238.

OUR GONCE ANCESTORS

Five Generations of Vansants from Harmens to Joshua

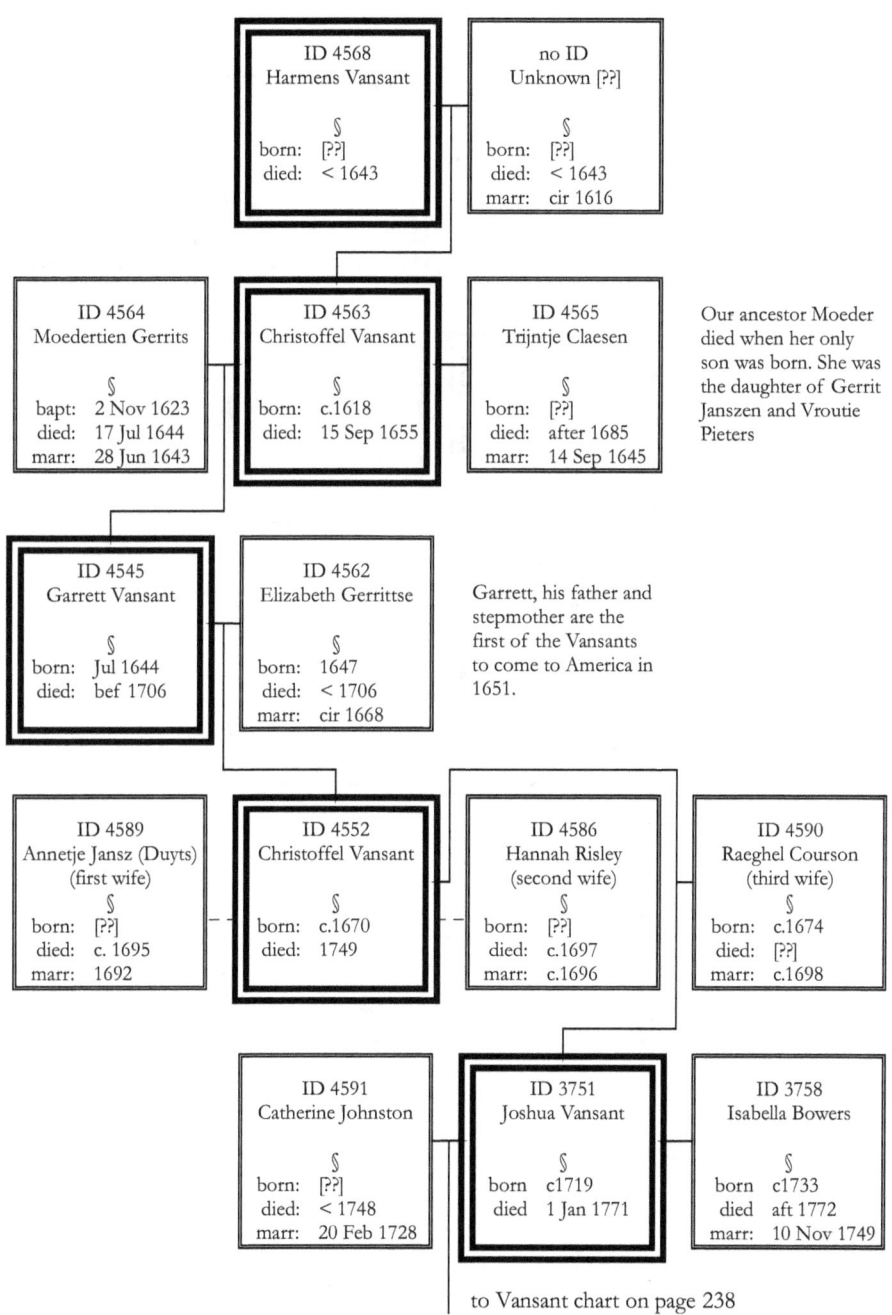

to Vansant chart on page 238

ANCESTORS OF ROSALIE GONCE AND HER SIBLINGS
Four Generations of Vansants from Joshua to Rachel

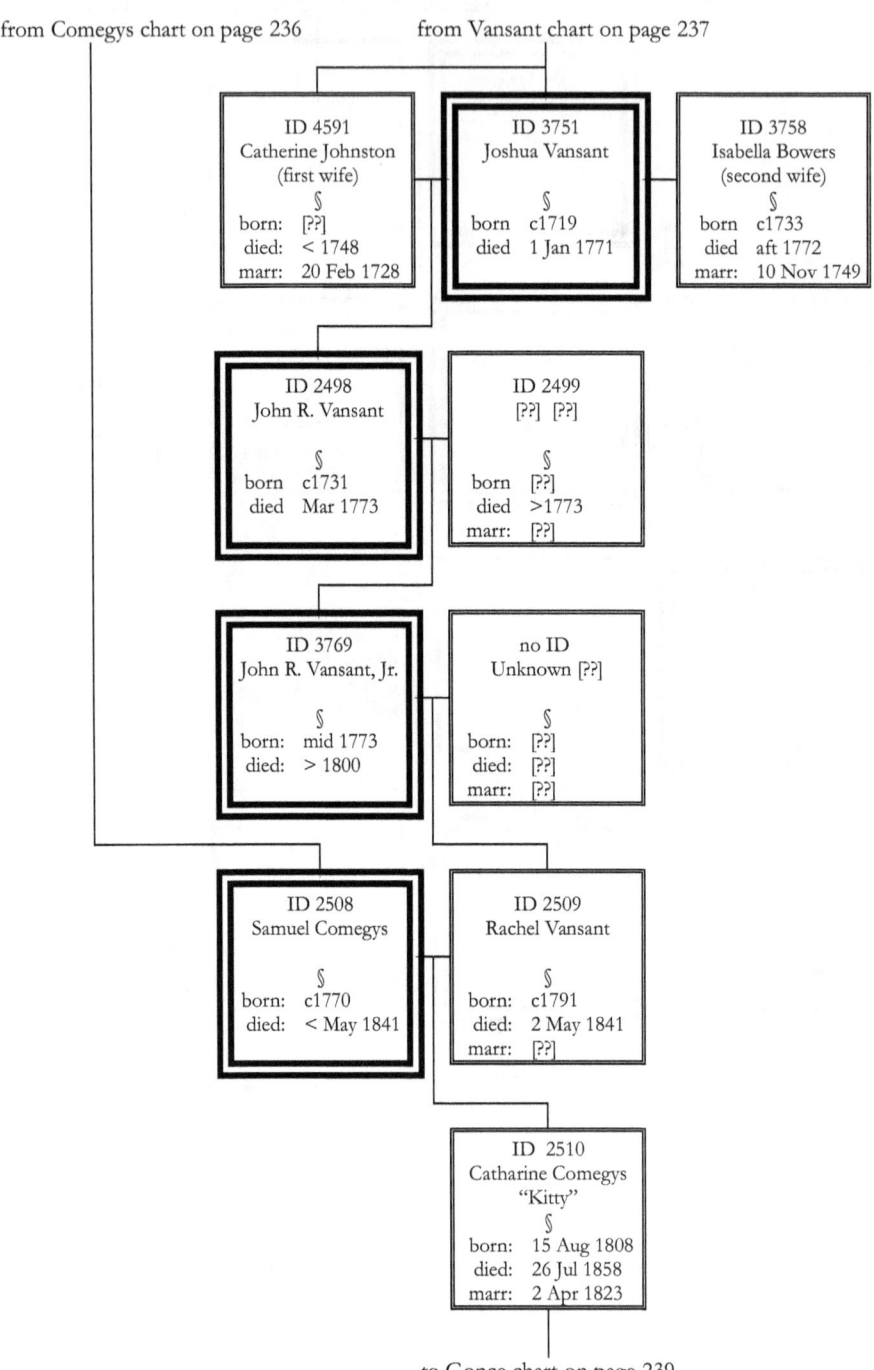

Five Generations of Gonces from Justice to John Thomas

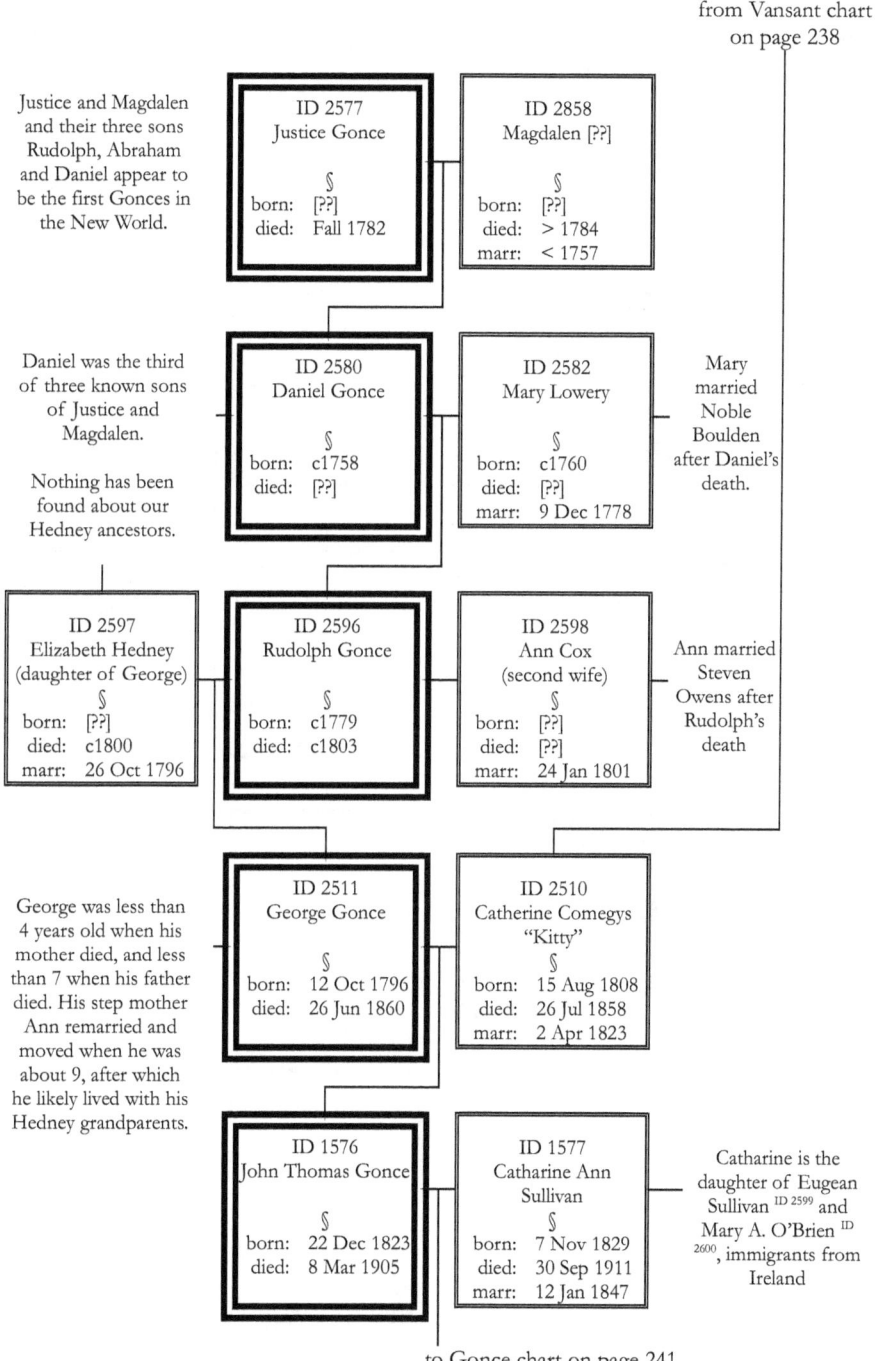

Ancestors of Rosalie Gonce and her Siblings

Four Generations of Clautices from John P. to Alice E. (with Farrings & Goodwins)

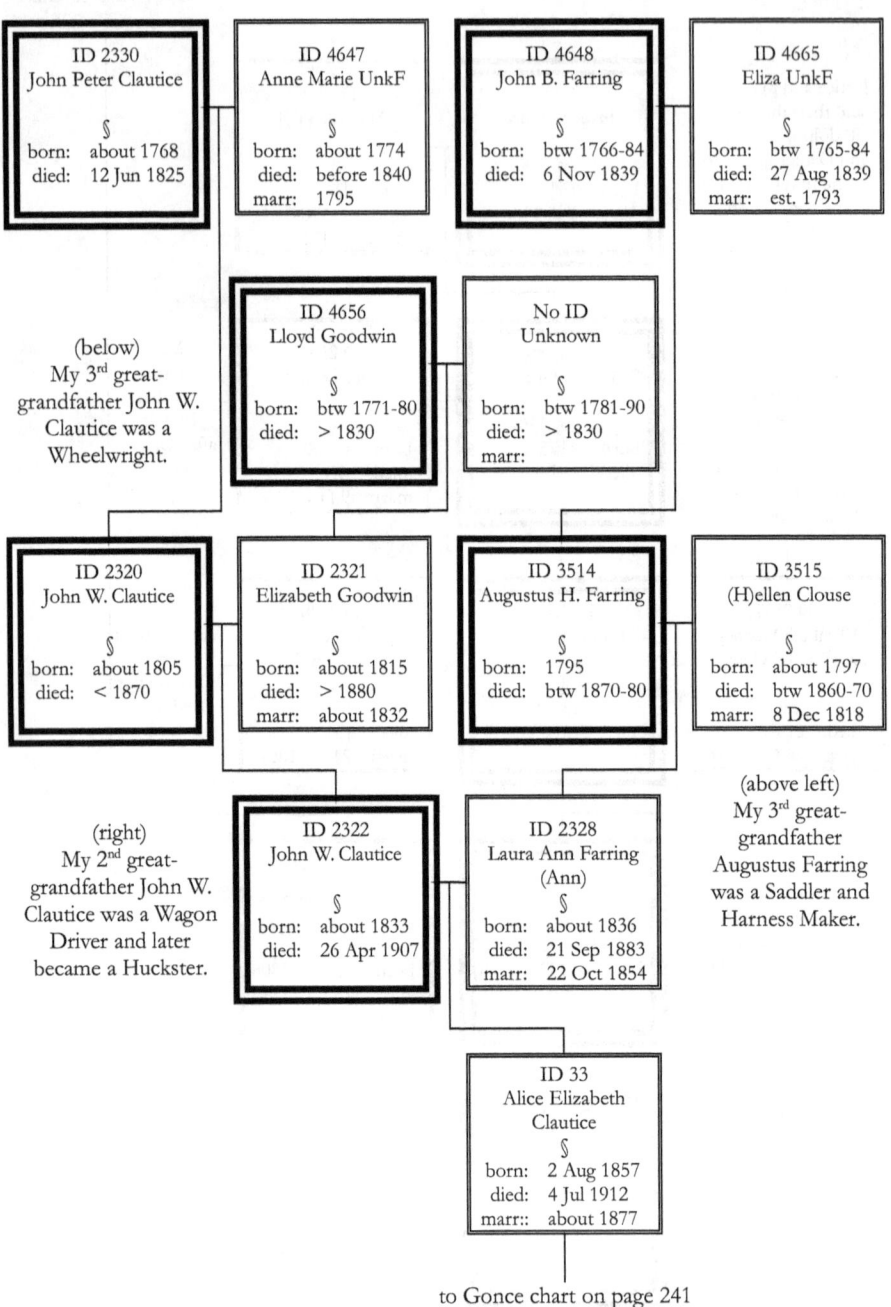

OUR GONCE ANCESTORS

Four Generations of Gonces from John Thomas to Rosalie, Jean, Charles & George

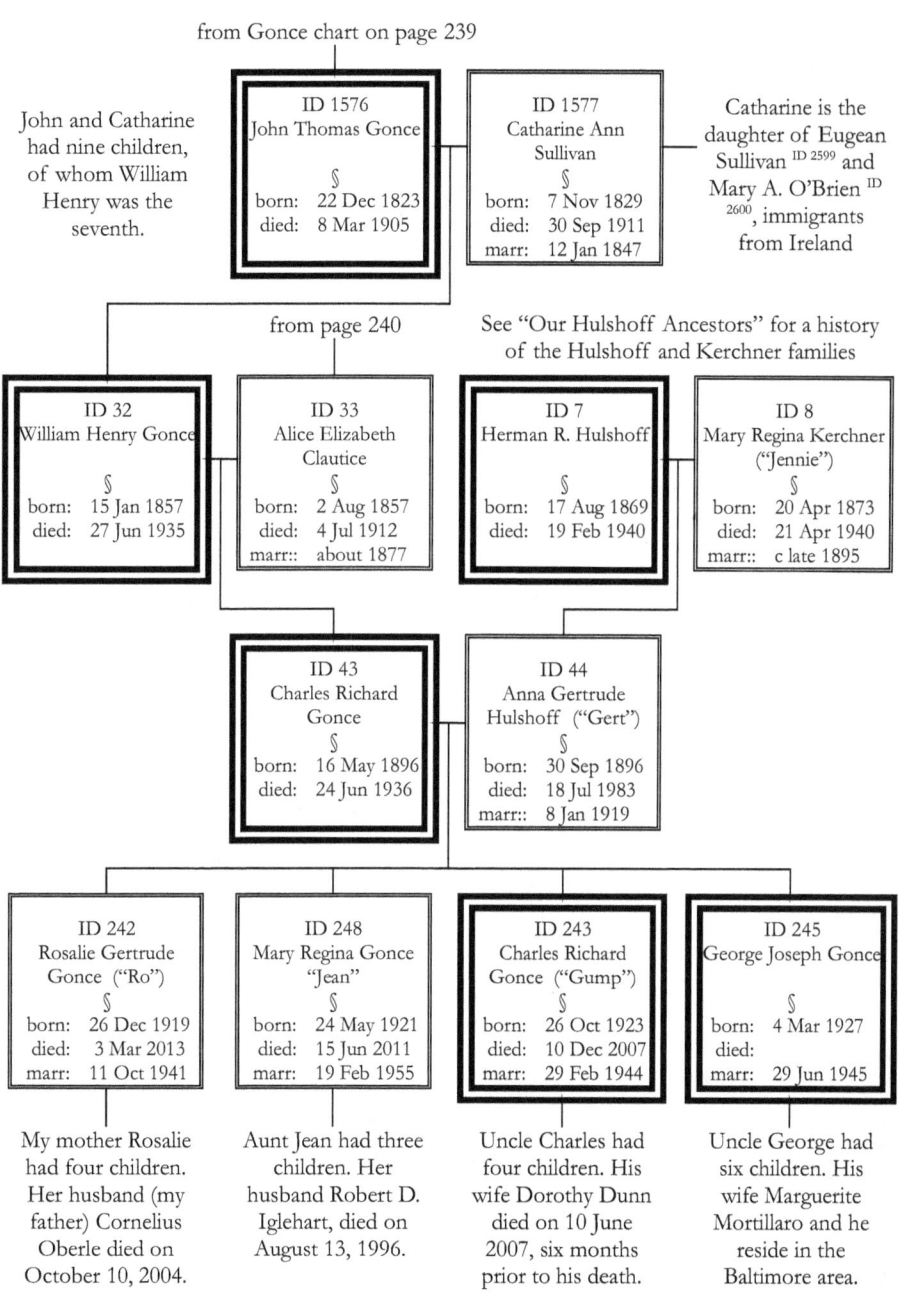

APPENDIX X

Gonce Ancestors Photo Album

A selection of photos of our Gonce-side ancestors dating from about 1862 to 1945.

In some cases where only a year or an estimated year (rather than a full date) is given, it should be considered an estimate. These estimates are based on comparisons with other photographs, known dates of certain events, and so forth. If anyone has other opinions, or is in possession of similar photographs with dates marked on them, I would appreciate hearing from them.

Anna Maria Kern [ID 91], who lived from 21 January 1806 to 5 May 1879, is the earliest of our Gonce-side ancestors for whom any picture survives. Anna was the wife of Michael Anthony Kerchner [ID 100]. Anna Maria is mentioned on page 109. Anna and Michael are my third great-grandparents.

Pictured below are Anna Linnenkemper [ID 39], who lived from 21 January 1839 to 26 November 1914, and her husband Ferdinand Kerchner [ID 38], who lived from 11 July 1835 to 1 June 1918. Ferdinand was the son of Anna Maria Kern Kerchner shown on the left. My second great-grandparents Ferdinand and Anna are mentioned on page 110.

Anna Maria Kern [ID 91] (Circa 1870 – from Fr. Frank Kunkel's Kern-Kerchner-Kunkel Books)

Circa 1905: Left: Anna Linnenkemper Kerchner [ID 39] and Ferdinand Kerchner [ID 38] – Right: Anna alone.

APPENDIX X – GONCE ANCESTORS PHOTO ALBUM

This is the oldest photograph (a ferrotype) of what is likely a Gonce-Side ancestor (although not necessarily a Gonce himself) that I am aware of. The details of the uniform are too distorted to be able to identify for certain whether he was a Union or Confederate soldier.

No Hulshoffs served during the Civil War, but John Thomas Gonce served in the Union Army. Although "Uncle Willie" Kerchner served in the U.S. Army under then Col. Robert E. Lee, and was known to be a confederate supporter, I haven't located any evidence that he ever joined or served in the Confederate army.

Although it is difficult to be certain, this man's general build doesn't seem to match the description of John Thomas Gonce (see page 72 & ff).

Circa 1862: Unidentified, but likely related, soldier during the Civil War

The first of our Hulshoff ancestors to come to the United States was my second great-grandfather Johann Gerhardt Hulshoff [ID 12], who lived from 9 February 1831 to 23 February 1916.

This photograph, taken just over a year before his death was included in the 50th anniversary booklet issued by the German Fire Insurance Company of Baltimore; Johann was a prominent businessman and had been elected a director of that company in January of 1880.

Our Hulshoff ancestors are discussed more fully in my book "Our Hulshoff and Kerchner Ancestors"; see footnote Error: Reference source not found on page 110 for further information.

17 March 1915 Johann Gerhardt Hulshoff [ID 12].

Page 110 shows a photo of Mary Regina (Jennie) Kerchner [ID 8], taken at her wedding in 1895; this photo is of her husband Herman Hulshoff [ID 7] taken at the same time.

My great-grandfather Herman, who lived from 17 August 1869 to 19 February 1940, was the son of Johann Gerhardt Hulshoff [ID 12], shown on the previous page.

1895 Wedding Photo of Herman Hulshoff [ID 7].

Anna Gertrude Hulshoff [ID 44], circa 1916

This photo of Anna Gertrude Hulshoff (later Gonce) [ID 44], dating from about 1916 is the earliest known photo of Herman and Jennie Hulshoff's oldest daughter. The person with her doesn't appear to be her eventual husband Charles R. Gonce, but that isn't certain.

Early pictures of Charles and Gert are shown on pages 114, 120, 121, with more on pages 123 and the following.

Photographs of Charles' parents William Henry Gonce [ID 32] (15 January 1857 - 27 June 1935) and Alice Elizabeth Clautice Gonce [ID 33] (2 August 1857 - 4 July 1912) are shown on page 102, and are the earliest known photographs of any ancestors with the Gonce surname I am aware of.

Charles and Gertrude Gonce's first child was Rosalie, born 19 December 1919; the photo of her on the left dates from 1920.

Rosalie is shown above in 1921 with her mother's younger sister Mary Agnes Hulshoff [ID 67] (Aunt Ag), then about 10 years old.

Left: Rosalie Gonce in December 1920; Right: Rosalie with her Aunt Agnes Hulshoff [ID 67] in 1921.

Left: Second Gonce child Regina (Jean) Gonce [ID 248] in 1923 — Right: Jean with Ro [ID 242] later that year.

Summer 1923
Back Row from Left to Right: Unidentified Female, Unidentified Female, Unidentified Adult Female, Unidentified Adult Male, Charles R. Gonce [ID 43]
Fron Row Left to Right: Unidentified Child, Rosalie Gonce [ID 242]*, and another unidentified child.*

1923: Ro Gonce at an unknown location   *Circa 1924: Jean and Ro Gonce on the beach*

Later, on 26 October 1923, Charles and Gertrude's third child (and first son) Charles, Jr. was born.

APPENDIX X – GONCE ANCESTORS PHOTO ALBUM

Circa 1924: Rosalie [ID 242] and Regina [ID 248] with their Hulshoff Grandmother Jenny [ID 8]

These 1924 and 1925 photos show Charles, Jr. [ID 243] alone and with his Hulshoff Grandmother Jennie [ID 8]

Summer 1924
From Left to Right: Charles Gonce, Jr. [ID 243], *Charles Gonce* [ID 43], *Rose Hulshoff Easter* [ID 127], *Donald Easter* [ID 130], *Rosalie Gonce* [ID 242], *Jean Gonce* [ID 248], *and Frank Easter* [ID 126].

Gonce Girls First Communion Photos: Left: Rosalie (27 MAY 1927); Right: Jean (19 JUN 1929)

APPENDIX X – GONCE ANCESTORS PHOTO ALBUM

27 May 1927: Charles Gonce

August 1927: Ro, George and Jean on the beach

The Gonce Kids with their Hulshoff grandparents, aunts and uncle circa 1928 (probably Easter, 8 April)
Front Row Left to Right: Charles, George (head only), Jean and Rosalie
Back Row Left to Right: Dorothy (Aunt Dot) [ID 11], Mary Agnes (Aunt Ag) [ID 67], Clara Rosalia (Aunt Rose) [ID 127], Jennie (Grandmother) [ID 8], Herman (Grandfather) [ID 7], and Gerard (Uncle Jerry) [ID 3].

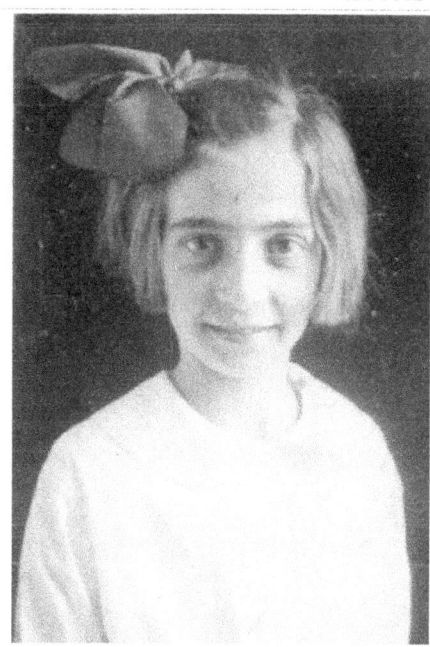

School Photos from September 1930 (Blessed Sacrament School): Left: Ro (Grade 6); Right: Jean (Grade 4)

Rosalie's Grammar School Graduation (13 June 1933 with her youngest brother George [ID 245])

Charles Gonce [ID 243] became an altar boy at Blessed Sacrament Church in 1934

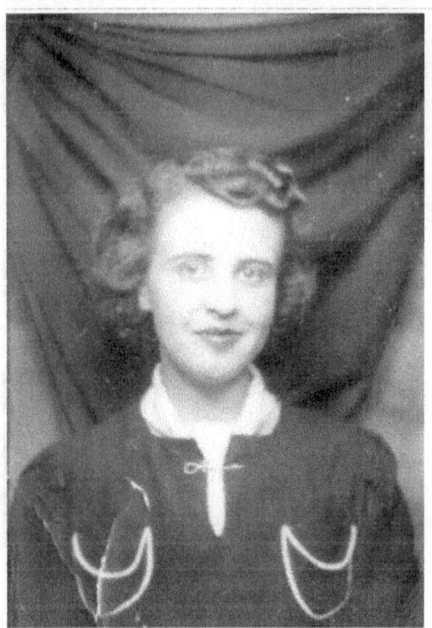 

Photos from 1936: Left: Ro (about age 17); Right: Jean (about age 15)

In 1937, Rosalie graduated from Seton High School and Charles graduated from Blessed Sacrament Grammar School.

13 June 1937: Anna Gertrude Gonce and Rosalie Gonce (Rosalie's High School Graduation from Seton)

13 June 1937: Charles Gonce's Grammar School Graduation Day from Blessed Sacrament School.

13 June 1937: Charles' older sister Jean in her Hulshoff grandparents' back yard (602 Springfield)

13 June 1937: Youngest brother George, and Rosalie's formal High School graduation picture.

APPENDIX X – GONCE ANCESTORS PHOTO ALBUM

In 1939, Jean graduated from Seton High School

Her youngest brother George with their mother's sister Dorothy Hulshoff (Aunt Dot) after the graduation.

Other Photos from Regina Gonce's Seton High School Graduation Day.

Rosalie's fiancée Cornelius Oberle [ID 196]

Charles Jr.'s fiancée Dorothy Dunn [ID 244]

11 October 1941: Rosalie's Wedding Day: Rosalie and sister Jean at 613 Springfield Avenue.

11 October 1941: Jean in Maid-of-Honor gown in backyard of 613 Springfield Avenue.

Appendix X – Gonce Ancestors Photo Album

1942: Charles Gonce Jr. before heading off to World War II.

November 1942: George Gonce ID 245 with his mother's youngest brother Gerard Hulshoff ID 3

1944: Charles ID 243 and Dorothy Gonce ID 244

1944: Charles Gonce with his wife Dorothy (left) and his mother Gertrude (right).

1945: Charles R. Gonce, Jr. ID 243, Gertrude Gonce ID 44 and Gerard Hulshoff ID 3.

29 June 1945: Marguerite Mortillaro ID 246 marries George J. Gonce ID 245.

APPENDIX XI

Suggestions for Further Research

For those who develop an interest in genealogical or historical research, these suggestions outline specific questions regarding the Baltimore Gonce line that remain unanswered, and are intended to provide some background for each, enabling the researcher to "pick up" where I "left off."

Suggestions for Further Research

ID	VALUE	RESEARCH PROJECT	PAGE
10	Interest Only	Determine the exact location of the land in St. George's Hundred in New Castle County Delaware on which Justice and Magdalen Gonce lived.	4
12	Interest Only Probability of success is very low.	Locate the graves of Justice and Magdalen Gonce, which are most likely to be in St. George's Hundred of New Castle County, Delaware. The graves are possibly located on the land they owned or farmed, but the precise location of that land hasn't been determined. The Cemeteries that have so far been searched for Gonce headstones by walk-throughs[429] are: Immanuel Protestant Church Cemetery, Old New Castle Town, DE The Glebe Cemetery (adjunct to Immanuel Protestant Church above) Unnamed Cemetery behind Gabicorta dealership, Old New Castle Town Pencader Cemetery, DE St. Georges Cemetery, St. George's Town, DE Old Swedes Church, Wilmington, DE Presbyterian Cemetery, Middletown, DE	9
14	Interest Only	Determine the exact location of the land in St. George's Hundred in New Castle County Delaware on which Rudolph Gonce and Polly McDade Gonce lived. It is likely adjacent to the land that Justice and Magdalen occupied, since they are very close together on the census page for 1782.	10
15	Interest Only	Determine the birth name of Polly ("the widow McDade") Gonce; find some record of her marriage to Mr. McDade (which probably occurred before 1769) and from that, identify his first name and the location where the marriage took place.	10
16	Interest Only Probability of success is very low.	Locate the graves of Rudolph Gonce and Polly McDade Gonce, which are most likely to be in St. George's Hundred of New Castle County, Delaware. The graves are possibly located on the land they owned or farmed, but the precise location of that land hasn't been determined. Rudolph died on 29 April 1790. Polly likely died within the next seven years before their children all left for Tennessee. See Research ID 12 above for Delaware Cemeteries searched to date.	11

---

[429] I did none of these walk-throughs personally. All were done by local volunteers who knew the area and offered their assistance. All reports are that finding legible headstones from the period in question was possible, but very unlikely. Several cemeteries from the colonial and early American period have disappeared, including at least one that was covered over to make a parking lot.

SUGGESTIONS FOR FURTHER RESEARCH

ID	VALUE	RESEARCH PROJECT	PAGE
18	Interest Only	Attempt to determine why all of Rudolph Gonce's children left Delaware to settle in Tennessee.	11
19	General Interest	Determine what became of Abraham Gonce, one of the three sons of Justice and Magdalen Gonce, and whether he had any descendants.	14
20	General Interest	Confirm or reject the hypothesis that Justice and Magdalen's middle son Abraham Gonce is the progenitor of the Gonces who began appearing in Virginia and Kentucky in the early nineteenth century.	14
21	Clarify Existing Records	Locate any marriage record for Polly McDade Gonce's sons by her first marriage. See if either Jeremiah or Hugh McDade married and/or had children before 1782, thus helping to verify the inhabitants of Rudolph's household in the Delaware census of 1782.	18
22	Confirm an Ancestor's Name	Locate a marriage for John Lowery (who died in 1780) to someone named either Ann or Jane, likely before 1750 in either Delaware or Maryland. This will determine whether it is Ann or Jane that is our ancestor, and possibly identify her surname and lead to another generation of our ancestors.	20
24	Interest Only	Locate the grave of Daniel Gonce, who died in about 1782, probably in New Castle County, Delaware. See ID 12 above for Delaware Cemeteries searched to date. It would seem to me that the probability of success is very low.	20
26	Interest Only	Locate the grave of Mary Boulden, the former Mary Lowery, who was Daniel Gonce's wife. She died after 1783 and is likely buried with her second husband Noble Boulden. Although not certain, I suspect she and Noble lived in Back Creek Township in Cecil County, Maryland.	20
28	Clarify Existing Records	Find any records for an earlier marriage of Noble Boulden, including possible death records for his first/earlier wife prior to 1783. Any records indicating any children they might have had will help interpret the 1790 census and possibly indicate whether Rudolph Gonce was living with his mother and stepfather at that time.	21
30	Biographical info for our ancestors.	Find a marriage record for George Hedney (or Headney, Headner, etc.) probably prior to 1780 (approximately when his daughter Elizabeth was born). This will possibly indicate the name of his wife and thus identify another ancestral line.	22
32	Biographical info for our ancestor George Gonce.	Locate George Hedney (or Headney, Headner, etc.) in the 1790, 1800, or 1820 U.S. Census or elsewhere, probably in Cecil County, Maryland. This will assist in determining whether or not George Gonce and his younger brother were raised by the Hedney family (their maternal grandparents) after the death of their father and remarriage and relocation of their mother.	26
34	Biographical info for our	Locate the grave of Elizabeth Hedney Gonce who died in about 1800 in Cecil County, Maryland. This might confirm her date or at least year of death. My suspicion is that she died in childbirth	24

ID	Value	Research Project	Page
	ancestor Elizabeth	with her second son John T. Gonce.	
35	Confirm an Ancestor's Name	Determine the name of John Vansant, Jr.'s [ID 3769] wife, who was the mother of my 4th great-grandmother Rachel Vansant Comegys. John Jr. and his wife were likely married in the decade of the 1790s.	44
36	Might help find John T. Gonce and family in 1860.	Locate Rachel Vansant Comegys, maybe *with* her husband Samuel Comegys in Kent County or possibly in Baltimore, in the 1830 census. Their daughter Catharine married George Gonce in 1823 and would not be listed with them in 1830. This will help track Rachel to determine the timing of her move to Baltimore. Also look for Joshua Vansant, presumably a relative of Rachel's, and likely living in Baltimore; he was the executor of Rachel's Will. Confirm that he is indeed the same Joshua who was later Mayor of Baltimore.	52
38	Might help find John T. Gonce and family in 1860.	Locate Rachel Vansant Comegys, probably *without* her husband Samuel Comegys (who likely died), possibly with a Vansant or Comegys relative in Baltimore, in the 1840 census. This will help track Rachel to determine the timing of her move to Baltimore and likely timing of John Thomas Gonce's move there as well. Also look for Joshua Vansant, presumably a relative of Rachel's, and likely living in Baltimore; he was the executor of Rachel's Will.	52 69
40	Might help find John T. Gonce and family in 1860.	Locate any record of the death of Samuel Comegys, husband of Rachel Vansant Comegys. If he died before Rachel's move to Baltimore, his death would likely be in Kent County, but if he moved with her, it would more likely be in Baltimore.	52
42	Interest Only	Locate a marriage record for Charles Roberts and Mary Gonce, probably between 1845 and 1860, and most likely in Cecil County, MD.	61
44	Interest Only	Locate a marriage record for Edward Lee and Augusta Gonce, probably between 1845 and 1860, but definitely before September 1861, and most likely in Cecil County, MD.	61 64
46	Better documentation of secondary sources.	Obtain a photograph of George and Catharine Gonce's headstones at St. Stephen's Protestant Episcopal Church in Earleville, Maryland. According to reports, the stone exists, but is close to impossible to read due to deterioration. Use of inventive side-lighting or filtering might be useful in obtaining a readable photograph.	161 165
48	Clarify some assumptions	Obtain a copy of George Gonce's Will. Will was probated 9 Sep 1861, but FHC/LDS Films available from Family History Centers apparently only go up to 1851.	63

Suggestions for Further Research

ID	Value	Research Project	Page
50	Biographical info for our direct ancestors.	Locate any immigration record for Eugean Sullivan, probably to Philadelphia (but this is based solely on where he later lived) sometime between 1805 (his estimated birth year) and 1830 (birth of his daughter Catharine in Philadelphia). He may have immigrated with his brother Daniel (and perhaps their parents and other siblings), or he may have immigrated with his wife Mary Ann O'Brien. Possibly NARC Microfilm Series m237 Roll 11, List 204, line 9, which lists a Eugene Sullivan, age 24 (ergo YOB = 1804) arriving with a Maria Sullivan (Mary A?), although the manifest clearly says "Maria"). They arrived in New York on the ship Jubilee on 12 May 1828 that had departed from Liverpool England. This needs to be examined more closely. There were other Eugene Sullivans whose arrivals are recorded, but whose details don't match up very well with what we know of our Eugene. There is, for example, a Eugene, born about 1806 (close enough), who left Cork, Ireland on the Governor Douglas and arrived in New York on 3 June 1839 (but our Sullivans were here during the 1830 census). See NARC Microfilm Series m237 Roll 38, List 333, Line 4.	66
52	Biographical info for our ancestors.	Locate any immigration record for Mary Ann O'Brien, probably to Philadelphia but possibly in the Virginia area sometime between 1805 (her estimated birth year) and 1830 (birth of her daughter Catharine in Philadelphia). She may have immigrated with her parents and perhaps other siblings, or come with her husband Eugean Sullivan. See notations under ID 50 above.	66
54	Biographical info for our ancestors.	Locate any record of a marriage for Eugean Sullivan and Mary Ann O'Brien, possibly in Philadelphia, and likely sometime between 1825 and 1830 – likely closer to 1829. This will help determine whether they immigrated separately at a younger age, or came together after getting married. Although not a likely location, Virginia records should be checked as well based on William Henry Gonce's comments on the 1900 census. (See footnote Error: Reference source not found on page 66)	66 102
56	Biographical info for our ancestors.	Locate the Sullivan family in the 1840 census. They would likely be in either Pennsylvania (where they were in 1830) or in Maryland (where they were in 1850). The table below indicates what their census line should look like based on what I know.	

See notes on research ID #56 beginning on page 268. The Sullivan family's listing in the 1840 census (re: ID 56 above) if located should look something like the following:

■ 266 ■

1840 United States Census Listing for "Eugene Sullivan?" in [MD or PA]	
1840 Census Counts	**Comments (my assumptions)**
1 Free White Male, age 30-39:	born 1801-1810 – Eugene Sullivan [2599], born ~1805, age ~35
1 Free White Female, age 30-39:	born 1801-1810 – Mary A O'Brien [2600], born ~1805, age ~35
1 Free White Female, age 5-9:	born 1836-1840 – Catharine Ann Sullivan [1577], born Nov 1831
1 Free White Male, age 15-19:	born 1836-1840 – James Sullivan [3551], born 1832, age ~8
1 Free White Female, age < 5:	born 1836-1840 – Mary Ann Sullivan [2865], born ~1840, newborn
No Other Entries on Line:	? ? ? ? ?

ID	*VALUE*	*RESEARCH PROJECT*	*PAGE*
58	Highest Priority	Locate John Thomas and Catharine Sullivan Gonce in the 1860 Census. This will help resolve a number of issues such as: when they had the children who died young, what their family looked like right before the Civil War, etc. A separate section below discusses possible avenues for exploration to determine the family's whereabouts in 1860.	72
60	High Priority	Locate John Thomas and Catharine Sullivan Gonce in the 1890 Census Veteran's Schedules. The 1890 Census was destroyed by fire, but the Veteran's Schedules for Maryland are supposed to have survived. To date, I have been unable to locate John or Catharine in any of the available indexes. This will help resolve a number of issues such as: when John became completely disabled (in the 1900 census, Catharine is listed as head-of-household even though John was still alive and living with her), and what the nature of the disability was.	
62	General Interest	George E. Gonce [ID 151], the oldest son of William Henry Gonce and Alice Elizabeth Clautice, was born on 22 January 1879, but was not listed on the 1880 census. It would be interesting to know why.	
99	Extend the History	Finally, locate any information that would suggest where the Gonce family may have come from when they arrived in the new world. Genealogy forums devoted to the Gonce name suggest many different countries of origin, but I believe most of these are insupportable. I have discussed all the speculations I am aware of in a separate document titled "Origins of the Gonce Family in America" in order to provide some support for anyone attempting to continue this research.	

Suggestions for Further Research

Notes on Research ID #56 – Location of John Thomas Gonce and Family in 1860

To date, I have not been able to locate John Thomas Gonce [ID 1576], his wife Catharine Ann Sullivan Gonce, and their 5 or possibly 6 children (4 boys and 1 or 2 girls)[430] at the time of the 1860 Census. The oldest child would have been about 13 years old, so their children could not yet have had households of their own.

In 1860, John would have been about 37 years old and Catharine about 30. They were likely living in Baltimore, since that is where they had been living prior to 1860 and the place to which John returned after his Civil War service, but it is possible they might have been in Cecil County where John was born (and where he still had many siblings and other relatives) for a variety of reasons.

Some Chronology before 1860

30 April 1841:	Grandmother Rachel Vansant's Will – John may have already moved to Baltimore
12 January 1847:	John marries Catharine Sullivan in Baltimore at bishop's residence next to Cathedral
10 February 1849:	John T. Gonce of Sassafras Neck, Cecil County sells household items, 2 bay mares, 1 bay horse to Alfred C. Nowland. It isn't clear if this is our John or one of the other John T. Gonces (although I suspect the latter).
22 August 1850:	John, Catharine, and their oldest son George were recorded in the 1850 census as living in the household of John's younger sister Margaret and her husband George Moore in Cecil County. My speculation is that they were simply visiting at the time.
7 October 1850:	Less than two months later, John, Catharine, and George were recorded in the 1850 census as living in the Sullivan (Catharine's parents) household in Baltimore.
1854	It appears that John (presumably with his family) was living on "Chase near Decker" ("Matchett's Baltimore Director 1853-54", p120)
1858	It appears that John (presumably with his family) was living at 12 Tyson (Baltimore City Directory 1858, page 133)

---

[430] See the list of their children on page 86.

The following sections discuss what would seem to be the most likely possibilities:

Possibility 1: They could have been living with John or Catharine's parents in 1860.

We know that John was living with the Sullivan family in Baltimore (his wife Catharine's parents) in 1850[431], so it is possible they were still living with them in 1860, but I haven't yet located the Sullivans in 1860 either. The table below discusses the available information regarding their parents in 1860.

1860 Location:		
With parents of John Thomas Gonce, age 37, or Catharine Ann Sullivan Gonce, age 30		
Person	Location in 1860	? Possible location of John T. Gonce and family in 1860
George Gonce ID 2520	John's father George, now a widower, is living with John's brother George W. Gonce and his family.	Definitely Not
Catherine Comegys ID 2510	John's mother Catharine died on 26 July 1858.	Definitely Not
Eugean Sullivan ID 2599	I have not been able to locate Catharine Ann's father Eugean in the 1860 U.S. Census. His death date is known to be before 1871, but may have been as early as 1860. It is possible, though it seems unlikely, that Eugean returned to Philadelphia, and was living there in 1860.	Possibly, but seems unlikely although if he was a widower, he might be living with the Gonces
Mary A. O'Brien ID 2600	I have not been able to locate Catharine Ann's mother Mary A. O'Brien in the 1860 U.S. Census either. Her death date is unknown, but since she is not listed on her daughter Mary Ann's marriage notice in November 1859, she was probably deceased before 1860.	Definitely Not

---

[431] See the 1850 census on page 68.

SUGGESTIONS FOR FURTHER RESEARCH

Possibility 2: They could have been living with John's grandparents in 1860.

1860 Location:	Grandparents of John Thomas Gonce, age 37	
Person	Location in 1860	? Possible location of John T. Gonce and family in 1860
Rudolph Gonce ID 2596	John's paternal grandfather died in about 1803	Definitely Not
Elizabeth Hedney ID 2597	John's paternal grandmother died in about 1800	Definitely Not
Samuel Comegys ID 2508	John's maternal grandfather was known to have died before May 1841, since he wasn't mentioned in his wife's Will.	Definitely Not
Rachel Vansant ID 2509	John's maternal grandmother died in May 1841. She had moved to Baltimore after her husband's death, and it is possible that John may have lived with her for a short time after moving from Cecil County himself. It isn't known if she lived alone, or in the home of one of her Vansant relatives (many of whom had moved to Baltimore) or Comegys relatives (not likely, but possible). Joshua Vansant, who was Rachel's administrator with specific responsibility for John's inheritance, is a likely choice, but I was unable to locate him in 1860.	Definitely Not, but perhaps one of her Vansant relatives may have taken in Rachel's grandson and his family.

Possibility 3: They could have been living with Catharine's grandparents in 1860.

Catharine Ann's grandparents – the Sullivans and the O'Briens – never came to America as far as I'm aware, although we haven't yet found Eugean and Mary's immigration records, so that isn't clear. It seems very unlikely, however. (see comment about Eugean and Mary's arrival on page 66)

Possibility 4: They could have been living with one of John's siblings in 1860.

We believe that, although John and Catharine were living in Baltimore in 1850, they seemed to have been present at his sister Margaret's home in Cecil County[432] when the 1850 census was taken there. So it is certainly possible that they might have returned to Cecil County for a while.

1860 Location:	With siblings of John Thomas Gonce, age 37	
Person	Location in 1860	? Possible location of John T. Gonce and family in 1860
Margaret A. Moore [ID 2519] Age in 1860: deceased	Margaret Ann [ID 2519] had died by the time of the 1860 census. Her husband George Moore, with whom John had lived or visited in 1850, was living alone with his son George. (NARC m653r0472p044)	Definitely Not
George W. Gonce [ID 2520] Age in 1860: about 32	George W. [ID 2520] was living with his wife and family in 1860, along with his father George Gonce (see above) (NARC m653r0472p044)	Definitely Not
Mary M. Roberts [ID 2601] Age in 1860: about 30	Mary Matilda [ID 2601], widow of Mary Roberts, was living with her (and John's) brother Benedict and family in 1860 (NARC m653r0472p052)	Definitely Not
Augusta Lee [ID 2605] Age in 1860: about 26	Augusta [ID 2605] was living with her husband Edward Lee, their children and Edward's mother in 1860. (NARC m653r0472p054)	Definitely Not

---

[432] Margaret was married to George Moore at that time. See page 63.

SUGGESTIONS FOR FURTHER RESEARCH

1860 Location:	With siblings of John Thomas Gonce, age 37	
Person	Location in 1860	? Possible location of John T. Gonce and family in 1860
Benedict Gonce [ID 2602] Age in 1860: about 24	Benedict [ID 2602] was living with his wife Margaret, their children, and his widowed sister Mary Roberts (see above) in 1860 (NARC m653r0472p052)	Definitely Not
Thomas A. Gonce [ID 2604] Age in 1860: about 20	Thomas Allibone Robaris [ID 2604] has not been located in 1860. He seems old enough to have been living on his own in 1860, but I have found no trace of him after 1850.	He had possibly died by this time…
Laura Ellen Pope [ID 2606] Age in 1860: about 17	Laura Ellen [ID 2606] has not been located in 1860; she married Charles Pope and was living with him in 1870, but I don't know the date of their marriage. She could conceivably have been married at age 17 but, since she is not the only child whose location is unknown in 1860, locating her might be helpful.	Possible
James A. Gonce [ID 2607] Age in 1860: about 15/16	James Allibone [ID 2607] has not been located in 1860; he married Sarah J. Hill, but I don't know the date of their marriage. Sarah's mother was living with the couple in 1870. It seems unlikely that he would have been married by age 15, so locating him might be helpful.	Possible

Possibility 5: They could have been living with one of Catharine's siblings in 1860.

1860 Location:
With siblings of Catharine A Sullivan, age 29, wife of John T Gonce

Person	Location in 1860	? Possible location of John T. Gonce and family in 1860
Samuel Sullivan [ID 3553] Age in 1860: unknown	Samuel Sullivan [ID 3553], who I'm not certain is actually one of Catharine's siblings, married Mary Renn in January 1851, but I haven't located either of them in the 1860 census. There is an unidentified Samuel Sullivan in Lot T-295 with the rest of the Sullivan/Gonce family but, if he were Catharine's brother, it seems that he would likely be older than her, and there was no male child at all in the 1840 census for Eugene Sullivan and his family.	Probably Not
James Sullivan [ID 3551] Age in 1860: about 28	James Sullivan [ID 3551], Catharine's brother, married Josephine Wilson in April 1852. He and his family were living in Baltimore in 1860.	Definitely Not
Mary A. McKenna [ID 2865] Age in 1860: about 20	Mary Ann Sullivan [ID 2865] married T. James McKenna in November 1859, but I found no census record of either of them until 1880.	Possible
Eugene Sullivan [ID 3552] Age in 1860: about 18	I haven't located Eugene in 1860	Possible
Albert Sullivan [ID 4144] Age in 1860: unknown	I haven't located Albert Sullivan [ID 4144] in 1860. Since I'm not certain he is actually one of Catharine's siblings, and he would definitely have been younger than the other siblings if he were, his household is not a likely location for the Gonces in 1860. Albert died in	Probably Not

SUGGESTIONS FOR FURTHER RESEARCH

1860 Location: With siblings of Catharine A Sullivan, age 29, wife of John T Gonce			
Person	Location in 1860		? Possible location of John T. Gonce and family in 1860
	May 1893.		

Final Note:

All of the references cited in this document were also checked for the suggested research items given above. These include:

"Inhabitants of Cecil County Maryland. 1639-1774"; Family Line Publications; Westminster, MD, 1993

"Maryland Marriages 1667-1899"; compiled by Jordan Dodd of Liahona Research.

"Cecil County, Maryland Marriage Licenses 1777-1840" at the Cecil County Historical Society

"Inhabitants of Cecil County Maryland. 1774-1800" compiled by Henry C. Peden

"Delaware Bible Records", Volume 2; Donald O. Virdin

"Index to Marriages and Deaths in the (Baltimore) Sun 1837-1850" Thomas L. Hollowak, Compiler

"Index to Marriages in the (Baltimore) Sun 1851-1860" Thomas L. Hollowak, Compiler

"Marriages, Births & Deaths - St. Stephen's Parish, Cecil County, Maryland 1687-1837"

"Maryland Marriage Evidences 1634-1718" compiled by Robert Barnes

"Maryland Marriages 1634-1777" compiled by Robert Barnes

"Maryland Marriages 1778-1800" compiled by Robert Barnes

Appendix XII

Speculations on the Pre-American Origins of the Gonce Family

Appendix

Possible Gonce Family Origins

I have traced the Gonce family back to pre-revolutionary Maryland, but have as yet been unable to determine how or from where the early Gonces arrived in this country. As anyone researching genealogy in the United States can attest, there is a dearth of information regarding the immigration of our country's pre-revolutionary inhabitants. Unless and until some more concrete data surfaces, I can only draw inferences from what little there is. The purpose of this appendix, therefore, is two-fold.

First, I will attempt to outline all of the early references that I am aware of, and see what inferences can be drawn from them. This will include references to the surnames Gans, Ganse, Gants, Gantz, Gaunce, Gonce, and Gons. I will attempt to show that there are at least three distinct and unrelated families included under these names.

Second, although there is much published[433] and unpublished[434] speculation about the original nationality of the Gonces, I am aware of no good evidence to support any of it. This appendix, therefore, will also summarize and comment on the various theories and speculations I am aware of, as well as discuss a bit of incidental information and historical background that may or may not turn out to be relevant.

To organize this collection of background, theories, guesses, and speculations, I've divided the first part of this appendix into five major sections:

- ♦ A discussion of possible arrival time windows in the context of what we know about the American pre-revolutionary period and the existence of documented references to the Gonces.
- ♦ Comments on the Gonces' probable location of entry into this country.
- ♦ A list of the various countries put forth as possible origins or at least intermediate venues of the original Gonce settler(s), along with some commentary on each. Examples of why each particular location was suggested will be given if known and where appropriate. This is the largest section of this appendix.
- ♦ A brief summary of Surname and Proper Name Etymology and common origins will be given in the hope that this might offer some clues to the family's pre-American location.
- ♦ My own tentative conclusions as to a best-guess theory, which may lead to more research by others attempting to prove or disprove any or all of these conclusions.

---

[433] I am using the term "published" to include printed books and documents as well as formal postings of genealogies (particularly Gedcom files) on the World-Wide-Web.
[434] I am using the term "unpublished" to include informal comments posted to genealogy forums on the web as well as in various written and electronic correspondence I have had over the past few years.

APPENDIX XII – ORIGINS OF THE GONCE FAMILY

Part I – Likely Timing of Gonce Immigration

It might seem that determining when the Gonce family arrived in this country would provide a clue to their country of origin. To do this is mostly an exercise in guesswork, however. Nevertheless, it seems reasonable to attempt some inferences. The obvious place to start is with eighteenth-century Maryland and Delaware – the earliest documented location of any Gonces in what would later become the United States.

By the beginning of the seventeenth century, Maryland was an established province, although the area known as Cecil County wasn't created as a separate entity until 1674[435]. Delaware, on the other hand, was under Pennsylvania's administrative control from about 1682 to 1704 and to a lesser extent from 1704 until United States independence. Delaware acted independently for the most part, but care probably needs to be taken to include "Pennsylvania records of the three Delaware counties[436]" with "Delaware records" of this period when looking for evidence of some early Gonce presence.

For general reference, maps showing the first areas where the Gonces were known to have settled are provided on pages 5 (wider view) and on page 2 of this book (more localized view). Paying close attention to the second of these maps, note that all of the areas in which we have so far found references to one or more of the Gonce family are within about a ten-mile radius; the apparent movement from state to state, then, seems to have been entirely incidental. It is only the happenstance of the odd border placement that requires us to search archives in three different states for possible evidence of our Gonce ancestors.

Maryland Records

The following published material pertaining to possibly relevant early Maryland records, listed in chronological order by the period covered, has been reviewed[437]:

- ♦ Maryland Marriages 1634-1777; Robert Barnes, Compiler; Genealogical Publishing Co., Inc. Baltimore, MD, 1975; 929.3752 BAR; ISBN: 0-8063-0700-5; LoC 75-27355 (S123)

---

[435] The area of Cecil County was taken from what was then Baltimore County; Harford County, which now sits between Baltimore and Cecil County, wasn't formed until 1773. Also see the comparative timeline beginning on page 316.

[436] The three Delaware counties are also known in some historical documents as the "three lower counties."

[437] This is not at all a comprehensive list, but contains only those sources that would appear to indicate presence or absence of any Gonces during the particular periods of interest. Additional references are cited in various sources referred to in this document, particularly those of Barbara Gonce-Clepper and Benjamin Hutchisson.

- Index of Maryland Colonial Wills 1634-1777; James M. Magruder, Jr., Compiler; 1933, 1967, 1975; Genealogical Publishing Co., Inc. Baltimore, MD.; ISBN: 0-8063-0233-X (S126)
- Inhabitants of Cecil County Maryland. 1639-1774; Family Line Publications; Westminster, MD, 1993; University of Baltimore; Baltimore MD; F187. LoC Catalog Number C3 P135 1993 (S138). This is a collection of data taken from a wide variety of extant source material, and includes (among other sources) the following:
- 1752 List of Taxables for Cecil County, Maryland
- 1759 List of Taxables for Middle Neck Hundred; Cecil County, Maryland
- 1761 List of Taxables for Middle Neck Hundred; Cecil County, Maryland
- 1766 List of Taxables for Middle Neck Hundred; Cecil County, Maryland
- 1774 List of Amerciaments (Persons owing Court Costs) (Rudulph & Abraham)
- Maryland Marriages 1667-1899; Jordan Dodd, Liahona Research, Compiler (S56)
- Early Maryland Probate Records; Calendar of Wills 1674-1774; Broderbund CD#206 (S34)
- Settlers of Maryland 1679-1783; Peter Wilson Coldham; Genealogical Publishing Co. Inc.; ISBN 0-8063-1693-4; R929.3752 (S121)
- Marriages and Deaths from the Maryland Gazette, 1727-1839; Robert Barnes, Compiler; Genealogical Publishing Co., Inc., 1979; ISBN: 0-8063-0580-0 (S69)
- Maryland Naturalization Petitions 1797-1906; National Archives Microfilm Series M1168 (25 rolls) (S52)

The first mention of the name Gonce in these sources[438] is in the 1761 list of taxables for Middle Neck Hundred, where "Justis Gonce" and "Radalph Gonce" are mentioned. These are assumed to be Justice Gonce and his son Rudolph Gonce. Assuming Rudolph was born in about 1743, he would have been about 18 at this time. The closest previous list of taxables is for 1759. Since Rudolph was only 16 at the time, we would not expect to see him on this list. We would expect to see Justice if he were there, however, but we don't. This leads to a reasonable hypothesis that the Gonces arrived in Middle Neck Hundred in about 1760. This rests, of course, on a number of assumptions:

1. That Rudolph is Justice's son.

---

[438] As far as I am aware, this is the first mention of a Gonce in any source. It is on page 48 of the noted reference.

APPENDIX XII – ORIGINS OF THE GONCE FAMILY

> This seems to be a reasonable assumption. Rudolph Gonce later became co-executor with Magdalen of Justice's estate, most likely indicating that he was the oldest son, although he could conceivably be a younger brother of Justice or some other relation.

2. The Rudolph listed in 1761 is the same Rudolph that we are presuming to be Justice's son.

> This seems to make sense, since Rudolph married Polly McDade in early 1769, and their children were born beginning with the twins Abraham and Isaac in 1770. Since Justice died in 1782, it seems reasonable that he and this Rudolph are from different generations.

Abraham joined Justice (shown as "Justis") and Rudolph on the list for 1766, which is also consistent with the view that Abraham was born a few years after Rudolph; a birth year of 1748 would make Abraham about 18 at the time of the 1766 list.

Justice appears again on the list of persons owing Cecil County court costs in 1774.

Delaware (and Pennsylvania) Records

The following published material pertaining to possibly relevant early Delaware records, listed in chronological order by the period covered, has been reviewed:

- Ship Passenger Lists; Pennsylvania and Delaware (1641-1825); Carl Boyer, 3rd; ISBN 0-936124-02-4; LDS Microfiche 6048670 (S129)
- Early Delaware Census Records 1665 – 1697; Ronald Vern Jackson & Gary Ronald Teeples, Editors; Accelerated Index Systems, Inc. ISBN: 0-89593-166-4; R929.3751/JAC (S86)
- 1671 Census of the Delaware; Peter Stebbins Craig, J.D.; Genealogical Society of Pennsylvania; No ISBN or LoC Number; Dewey 929.3749 CRAIG,P (S130)
- New Castle County Delaware Tax Lists 1738-1783: A List of the Taxable Persons and Estates in the new acquired part of St. George's Hundred; State of Delaware; Delaware State Archives (S99).

  The key here is the phrase "new acquired part." Rudolph Gonce appears in the New Castle County Tax Rolls for the St. George's Hundred in the years 1777 through 1782[439], and resided there at the time of his father Justice's Will was probated in 1783.

- Warrants and Surveys of the Province of Pennsylvania including the Three Lower Counties 1759; Allen Weinberg and Thomas E. Slattery; City of Philadelphia Department of Records, 1965; No ISBN or LoC

---

[439] The name Rudolph Gonce also appears in these lists from 1791 through 1795 but, since the Rudolph we are discussing died on 29 April 1790, I am assuming the latter listings are for his nephew (Daniel's son) Rudolph [ID 2596], my 4th great-grandfather.

Number; Dewey 929.3748 WARRANTS (S131). The "Three Lower Counties" are what eventually became the State of Delaware; New Castle County is the northernmost of these.

♦ Delaware Archives: Military and Naval Records Volume II; The Public Archives Commission of Delaware; Mercantile Printing Company, 1912. No ISBN or LoC Number; Delaware Archives Call Number R975.1. (S83)

♦ The Reconstructed Delaware State Census of 1782 (10 June 1782); Harold Bell Hancock, Editor; The Delaware Genealogical Society, 1983. (S135)

♦ Reconstructed 1790 Census of Delaware; Leon DeValinger, Jr. et al; (S58)

♦ Delaware Bible Records, Volume 2; Donald O. Virdin (S57)

♦ Delaware Estate Bonds; State of Delaware; unpublished (S85)

♦ New Castle County (DE) Will Book L; New Castle County Office; State of Delaware; unpublished (S84)

Rudolph [ID 2578] Gonce is reported to have married the widow Polly McDade [ID 2581] in Middletown[440], Delaware in very early 1769.

The Delaware Archives have reports in their Military Records that Rudolph ("could not go at this present time") and Daniel ("being ailing, I can't bear the fatigue")[441] declined service with Captain Abraham Staats in June of 1777.

In the Delaware State Census of 1782, we find the following names listed in the St. George's Hundred:

Name [442]	Males (above 18)	(below 18)	Females (above 18)	(below 18)
Rudolph Gonse	3	3	2	3
Widow Gonse	2	1	2	0

Captain Abraham Staats, by the way, is listed in this census under the Appoquinimink Hundred. Other surnames in Appoquinimink familiar to Gonce researchers include Barnett Van Horn and Nemiah Vansant, although it isn't known if or how these are connected with the Gonces.

---

[440] Family of Benjamin Hutchisson 1765-1852, 2nd Edition; Elmer Hutchisson; September 1976, page 25. Also recorded in "Maryland Marriages 1667-1899" compiled by Jordan Dodd of Liahona Research. (S56)

[441] Daniel's entry actually says "ditto." This apparently stock excuse was first listed under Garret Vansant, part of the Vansant family that later married into the Maryland Gonce line. These references are given on page 812.

[442] Yes, these are the actual headings. The census taker from Christiana Hundred, apparently realizing the silliness of what the others were doing, inserted additional columns for Males and Females age 18. The legislators' intent when calling for the census was "… distinguishing therein the number of each sex, male and female, of the age of eighteen years and upwards, and the number of each sex under that age." I am therefore assuming that the "above 18" categories include any eighteen year olds in the "Gonse" households, but this can't be certain from the headings.

Appendix XII – Origins of the Gonce Family

It therefore appears that some or all of the Gonces migrated over the Maryland border back to Delaware sometime in the period between 1770 and 1777.

Conclusion

The list of resources given above is not comprehensive, but only includes those covering the areas known to have been inhabited by one or more of the Gonces. Of course, it's logically impossible to prove a negative, but other than those specified above, none of the Maryland and Delaware sources listed contain the name Gonce or any similar name. It is thus a reasonable assumption that the Gonces did not reside in this area until about 1760, when they appeared in the Middle Neck Hundred of Cecil County, Maryland. At this time, Justice and Magdalen's oldest known son, Rudolph, would have been about seventeen, Abraham about twelve, and their youngest son, my ancestor Daniel, would have been about two.

This doesn't entirely fit with family traditions that tell of the three Gonce brothers who first came to this country, although there is nothing to say that Justice or an earlier Gonce may not have been one of three brothers. If that were true, however, it would suggest that the family actually came from elsewhere in the "Colonies."[443]

So far, unfortunately, no one I'm aware of has located any records to support or disprove this conjecture.

Part II – North American Entry Point

The reasons for Newcastle's role as an entry point into America were outlined at the beginning of this book on page 3.

While the timing of heavy immigration through Newcastle, near where the Gonces were first known to have lived, suggests that this is likely where Justice and his family entered North America, it doesn't really help to identify the Gonces' native country. As it happens, William Penn's desire to accommodate a wide variety of settlers resulted in arrivals during this period from many of the areas identified as our Gonce family's possible ancestral origins.

It seems likely, however, that the first Gonces settled in an area near where they landed.

Part III – Suggested Countries of Origin

The following subsections will comment on the countries that I have seen proposed as possible origins of the Gonce family. These countries seem to have been suggested for one or more of the following reasons:

- **Family Tradition**: Stories passed down from prior generations, but usually with no specific facts that could be used to substantiate the story.

---

[443] See the section about the American Colonies and particularly Virginia on page 291.

- **Known Immigrant Origins**: Some genealogy forum posters have made the assumption that, if we can document arrivals of some Gonces from particular countries at a later date, there is at least a possibility that the original Gonce settler(s) may have come from the same location.
- **Population Density**: Some have speculated that, if there are large concentrations of Gonces in a particular European[444] area, this may suggest that the Gonces may have originated in that area. While true enough, it is important when considering population clusters that we determine what these concentrations would have been in the appropriate time frame (e.g. the American colonial period), and not simply what they are today.
- **Copying**: There are quite a few cases where one party has offered a speculation based on some discovery, and that speculation shows up as a source reference for someone else's citation of the speculation as fact. Even if we were to accept the selection of the family's origin by popular acclamation, such repetition might be considered merely a supporting "aye" vote, but a solution based on actual evidence would seem to be more satisfying from a genealogical standpoint.

I hope to categorically discount some of these suggestions, identify those that I still consider plausible, and introduce at least one other possibility in the hopes that some readers might be able to offer other facts that will lead us to the origins of our earliest Gonce ancestors. When discussing published materials, I will mention the author if appropriate, but will not give the names of those whose unpublished speculations I've seen, since it seems unfair to treat such informal musings with the same formality or rigor as should be given to published works.

---

[444] This (and earlier allusions to Europe) might be perceived as beginning the discussion with a close-minded bias, but I have seen or heard nothing that would suggest anything else. Certainly, Asian, Indian (but see the discussion on page 294), and African origins seem too far-fetched to consider.

APPENDIX XII – ORIGINS OF THE GONCE FAMILY

For each country (or area) discussed below, I will use the following symbols to indicate my assessment based on what information I've found to date:

 The case for this country or area being either the country of origin, or at least an intermediate stop on the path from Europe to the New World, seems reasonable, even if it isn't totally convincing. There doesn't seem to be any evidence that would argue against such a theory, and further research to prove or disprove this suggestion seems warranted.

 This country (or area) cannot be dismissed out of hand as a place of origin for the Gonces, but would require more evidence to take the suggestion seriously enough to research further.

 There doesn't seem to be any reason to spend further time considering this country or area as a possible origin unless some really good new evidence surfaces to reopen the discussion.

Germany and Holland are discussed first since they are the most often suggested. Other countries I have seen proposed as being the original homeland of the Gonces are listed in alphabetical order in succeeding subsections.

| Germany | Possible Country of Origin – My Vote: |

Several authors have suggested that the Gonce family originated in Germany.

Clepper: The Gonce & Wynne Genealogy [445], written more than twenty-five years ago by a member of the "southern branch" of the Gonces, contains the history of the author's line back to Rudolph Gonce [ID 2578]. We now know that Rudolph is one of the sons of Justice and Magdalen Gonce, who lived in Middle Neck Hundred, Cecil County, Maryland and Appoquinimink Hundred, New Castle County, Delaware.

The author, my sixth cousin once removed, Barbara Gonce-Clepper, was unaware of Justice and Magdalen at the time her book was published, but mentioned two possible candidates[446] for the original Gonce settler in this country – one from Germany and one from Holland.

One possibility she mentioned is Johannes Gantz, who was a 1709 immigrant from Germany. Although the spellings Gantz and Gonce are occasionally used indiscriminately[447], comparison of early American Gonce and Gantz

---

[445] Gonce & Wynne Genealogy; Barbara Gonce Clepper; Gregath Publisher; 1986, (formerly of Cullman Alabama). (S64)

[446] It bears repeating that Barbara never stated these were Gonce ancestors; as any good researcher would, she merely presented her discoveries and speculated on whether or not they *might* be our ancestors.

[447] …as well as Gauntz, Gons, Gans, etc. My great-great grandfather John T. Gonce was listed under the name Gantz in the 1870 census, and his Civil War records sometimes have different spellings of his

records would seem to indicate clearly that the German Gantz family, which had been established in Baltimore, Maryland as early as 1750, is not related to our Gonce family. Johannes Gantz appears to be the first of the Baltimore Gantz family, and his descendants are well documented[448]. Johannes simply isn't a good candidate to be our ancestor.

Heck: On page 20 of his history[449] of the Davis family, Professor Arch Heck has this to say about Vance [ID 2881] Gonce, the second child and first son of Abraham [ID 2584] Gonce and grandson of Rudolph [ID 2578] Gonce, and the man who married Martha "Patsy" Davis:

> *"Vance was born in Germany; he and two brothers migrated to the United States as young men. Vance settled at Rogersville, Tennessee; one brother settled in New York; and the other went further south."*

Dr. Heck doesn't provide any sources for this statement, but it is clearly incorrect. In actuality, Vance was (at least) a fourth generation American born in Tennessee. His parents Abraham and Polly, along with other relatives, migrated from Delaware to Tennessee in about 1797[450]. Since Dr. Heck provides no further information about the brothers in New York or "further south," it's difficult to comment on that portion of his story. I am unaware of any evidence to support it, however, other than to note that Vance did indeed have two brothers: John Rudolph Gonce [ID 2880] and Abraham Gonce [ID 3117]. They were both born in Tennessee, as was an older sister Margaret E. Gonce [ID 3557], who later married John T. Mendenall; none of them ever went near New York that I'm aware of.

Although Dr. Heck's book is quite interesting, it seems mainly intended to document his Davis ancestors; his coverage of the Gonce family that descended from Vance and Patsy is inaccurate in several areas.

Hutchisson: Margaret Gonce, the fourth child of Rudolph and Polly Gonce, married Benjamin Hutchisson. Elmer Hutchisson's family history[451] begins with Benjamin and Margaret. On page 16 of his book, Elmer has the following to say about the Gonces:

> *"The name Gonce is undoubtedly of German origin. Since in Colonial times, spelling was often determined by the way a name sounded to the recorder, we find Gonce also spelled Gance, Gaunce, Gans, Ganz, Gantz and even Gone. There*

---

name on the same page (for an example of this, see the muster roll cards on page 179).

[448] For example, although I was unable to locate the family in U.S. Census of 1800, records exist for the Gantz family for 1790, and for 1810 through 1870, and I have found no points at which they intersect with the Gonces.

[449] The Descendants of Hezekiah Davis I; Arch Oliver Heck, PhD; Columbus Ohio, 1965. See the document "Commentary on Heck Book" for a list of errors in Dr. Heck's presentation of the Gonce line.

[450] ee the appendix "The Gonce Family Southern Migrations" on page 141 of this book for details.

[451] amily of Benjamin Hutchisson 1765-1852, 2nd Edition; Elmer Hutchisson; September 1976, page 16.

Appendix XII – Origins of the Gonce Family

are many references to Gonces (with various spellings) in Delaware, Maryland, Pennsylvania and Virginia..."

"*Rudolf Gonce. We know very little of the early life of Rudolf Gonce. He may have been born in this country or he may in the 1750's have come when many Germans landed in Philadelphia and settled in Delaware and Maryland. There is no doubt that he spent his later life in and around Middletown, Del.*"

Again, unfortunately, the author provides no sources for his assertions, so it is difficult to comment on them. I believe, however, that several assumptions he makes are unwarranted. I have seen nothing to suggest that the name Gonce is German, and much to suggest that it is not. His assertion about the variety of spellings is certainly valid, but isn't a very good reason for asserting that all the homophonic names he provides represent the same family. For the record, the data I have found strongly suggests that Gonce, Gans and Gantz are the correct spellings of three separate and distinct families, although members of each family may, at any given time, appear in historical records with any of the spellings Mr. Hutchisson mentioned.

Copying of speculation as fact is fairly rampant with regard to Rudolph Gonce. A number of Internet postings and on-line genealogies state that one of the early Gonce brothers (typically Rudolph) was born in Germany. Examination of these postings leads me to infer that, in each case, the compiler took Elmer Hutchisson's or Arch Heck's statements at face value or used Barbara Gonce-Clepper's speculations as if they were confirmed facts – something she never stated in her book. While it is difficult to state categorically that our Gonces are not from Germany, it seems to me that there is actually no evidence to suggest this.

The two areas Elsass and Lothringen, once part of Germany, and known as Alsace and Lorraine in French and sometimes mentioned as a possible origin of the Gonces, are discussed in a separate section below.

As an example of later immigration suggesting a possible country of origin, we have August Gonce or Ganser (see illustration on the right), a white male, born 1869 in Germany, who lived in New York (Manhattan), New York at the time of the 1920 U.S. Census[452], and worked as a factory engineer. August immigrated in 1893, and was naturalized in 1900. It doesn't seem likely to me that he is a Gonce at all, much less part of our family.

---

[452] National Archives Microfilm Series t625, Roll 1212, Page 108. The name appears in the two major census transcriptions as "Gonce" and "Ganser" respectively, but appears more likely to me to be "Ganser" or "Ganses."

The German names Gans, Ganz, Gantz, and Gansz, by the way, meant "one who lived at the sign of the goose; one with the qualities of a goose[453]." A Ganser, similarly, was "one who took care of, or dealt in, geese."

Holland – The Netherlands	Possible Country of Origin – My Vote:

Holland appears in two published works as a possible origin of the Gonce family.

Clepper: Barbara Gonce-Clepper mentions in her book the discovery of records indicating that a Jacob Gons (or Gans) immigrated to Pennsylvania from the Netherlands on the ship "William and Sarah" on 18 September 1727[454].

Jacob's genealogy has subsequently been documented[455] from his birth in the Netherlands to Cumberland, Pennsylvania to Winchester, Virginia and back and, I believe, demonstrates clearly that there is no connection to our Gonces. Jacob, the son of George Balthassar and Agnes Joanna Gans[456], and grandson of Johann George and Anna Catherina Hertzog[457] Ganss of Hessen, Germany[458], married Elisabeth Fleming[459], a native Virginian, while he was in Winchester, Virginia, and had at least five children between 1748 and 1758, all of whom were born in Pennsylvania. This Gans/Gons family lived in southern and western Pennsylvania, far from the coastal areas our known Gonce ancestors inhabited. The names of Jacob's children[460], their dates of birth, and their geographic location, make it reasonably certain that Jacob is not our progenitor.

---

[453] The source for this, *The New Dictionary of American Family Names*, by Elsdon C. Smith, is strangely silent on exactly what qualities these might be. The book is copyright 1956, 1973 by the publishers Harper & Row, and the ISBN is 06-013933-1.

[454] See page 31 of the aforementioned book. Barbara's source for this information is *Ship Passenger Lists of Pennsylvania and Delaware 1641-1825* compiled by Carl Boyer of Newhall California. The ISBN for this book is 0-936124-02-4, and it is also available through Mormon Family History Centers on LDS Microfiche 6048670.

[455] See LDS Ancestral File, AFN:1V76-J55

[456] ibid; AFN:1573-JFX and AFN:1V76-JDL respectively

[457] ibid; AFN:1573-JTF and AFN: 1573-J8W respectively

[458] Even though they arrived from the Netherlands, it appears that this family may actually be German in origin.

[459] ibid; AFN:1V76-J6C

[460] Joseph, born about 1748 in PA (AFN:1V76-HKG); John George, born 1744 in VA (AFN:1V76-J7K); John, born about 1756 in PA (AFN:1V76-J8R); Jacob, born about 1758 in PA (AFN:1V76-J90); and Agnes, born 1754 in VA (AFN:TQ12-N6). These birth years generally overlap, and therefore conflict with, those of Rudolph, Abraham and Daniel Gonce.

APPENDIX XII – ORIGINS OF THE GONCE FAMILY

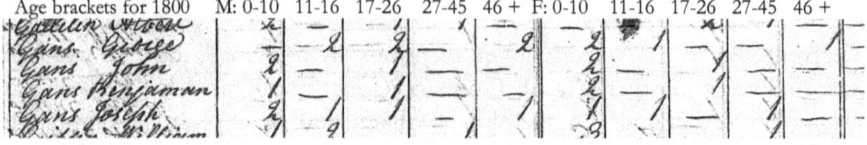

Age Brackets for the first Census in 1790: free white males over 16, free white males under 16, and free white females. 4th and 5th columns are for slave counts.

Jacob (here spelled Gants) appears in the 1790 U.S. Census in the town of *Springhill*, which is in Fayette County, Pennsylvania.

Joseph and George Gants appear on the same page. Note that names other than Gants have been removed from the illustration for clarity.

Taken from National Archives Microfilm Series m637, Roll 8, Page 572.

The 1800 U.S. Census shows various Gans families still living in Pennsylvania; the four above (George, John, Benjamin and Joseph) reside in the town of *Springhill* in Fayette County. Joseph added another boy and girl to the family between the 1790 and 1800 censuses, and Jacob apparently died in that time frame.

(Taken from National Archives Microfilm Series m032, Roll 38, Page 595)

Aside from the fact that Jacob Gans came from Holland, there are other arguments supporting the idea that the Gonces may have been Dutch. At various times between 1631 and 1664[461], the Dutch did in fact control the New Castle County area in what is now Delaware where Justice and Magdalen were known to have lived a century later. The lack of any references to the Gonce name in any extant Delaware records from the period make Dutch ancestry dubious though. For instance, Delaware census records from the period 1665-1697[462] show no Gonce or similar names, and the English had forced the Dutch out of the entire east coast by 1655.

One issue that needs to be kept in mind is that, until the eve of the American Revolution, the three counties of Delaware were under Pennsylvania's control. It is therefore possible that, if there are extant records of the Gonce family, they might be found in Pennsylvania records as well as in those of Delaware. The Gons/Gans/Gants family described above, however, does not appear to be related to either our Gonce ancestors or to the Baltimore Gantz family.

Barton: In her history of the Andersons, Gonces, and Lovells[463], another of the "southern" Gonce branches, Mettie Marie Taylor Barton opens chapter II by writing:

---

[461] See the comparative timeline beginning on page 316.

[462] Early Delaware Census Records 1665 – 1697; Ronald Vern Jackson & Gary Ronald Teeples, Editors; published by Accelerated Index Systems, Inc. (S86)

[463] "Leaves from our Family Tree," by Mettie Marie Taylor Barton published in Nashville Tennessee in 1990. Quotation is from Chapter II, Section 1, page 37.

"Joseph Gonce, first generation in America, and his wife, Sara, came from Holland by way of Alsace-Lorraine. They came to Pennsylvania, settling with the Pennsylvania Dutch or German community. Joseph became a naturalized citizen in 1818. They had two sons: Rudolph Gonce, our ancestor, was born in Pennsylvania. The name of his brother has been lost. Rudolph Gonce (second generation) and his wife, Molly, moved to Delaware."

Ms. Barton provides no source information in her book, nor is there any contact information that I could find, so it is difficult to comment on her statements. I believe, however, that she may be mistakenly referring to Joseph Gants, who can be seen in the 1790 census segment above (or, as Joseph Gans, in the 1800 census segment), although why she came to believe Rudolph was one of his sons is a mystery. Aside from listing Rudolph's wife's name as "Molly" (Rudolph Gonce's wife's name was "Polly"), I was unable to spot any later discrepancies with known records in the remainder of her clan's history though. It is also unclear why anyone would need or want to go "by way of" Alsace or Lorraine (although often grouped together[464], they are actually two separate areas) in order to get from Holland to America. While ports in Holland were relatively accessible, one would need to cross the Vosges Mountains[465] to get from Alsace to one of the French ports. Without some good sources, it is difficult to believe this account.

An important point to remember is that we know that the spelling "Gonce" was used by the family from at least the mid-eighteenth century forward. With no other indications that the Gonces may have come from Holland, I believe there is no evidence that the Gonces are of Dutch ancestry.

Alsace / Alsace-Lorraine	Possible Locale of Origin – My Vote:

First of all, it should be stated that Alsace and Lorraine (the latter more properly known as Moselle) are two separate and distinct areas. They are typically grouped not only because they share a common border, but because they have been conquered and controlled as one entity on several occasions.

Alsace is not, of course, a country, as are most other locales discussed in this appendix, but is treated separately here for two reasons:

- ♦ Family tradition in several branches of the Gonce tree suggests that our ancestors may have originated in Alsace, France.

---

[464] Likely because they were usually conquered as a pair throughout the area's history. There is a separate discussion of Alsace as a possible origin of the Gonces below.
[465] The Vosges Mountains are one of the main reasons the Alsatians were traditionally "separate" from the rest of France, just as the Rhine provided some isolation from Germany on the east.

APPENDIX XII – ORIGINS OF THE GONCE FAMILY

- ◆ The previously mentioned book by Mettie Marie Taylor Barton, "Leaves from our Family Tree," states that the original Gonce settlers "passed through" Alsace.
- ◆ The area has gone back and forth between France and Germany for hundreds of years. Alsace and Lorraine, by the way, are the French forms of the names, while Elsass and Lothringen are the German forms.

I find the idea that Alsace is where the Gonces originated doubtful for a number of reasons. Because of my Oberle family's origins in Alsace, I have examined a variety of birth, death, and marriage records from many towns across that province[466], and have never encountered the surname Gonce or anything similar enough to warrant attention. Other members of my family and I have also walked through and photographed quite a few cemeteries in Alsace without encountering the name Gonce or anything similar. The closest name I have encountered in Alsatian vital records is Gintz, but there are only five[467] of these.

In the series of twentieth-century French population density maps given on page 315, the regions marked 57 (Moselle or Lorraine), 67 (the Bas-Rhin region of Alsace) and 68 (the Haut-Rhin region of Alsace) show the number of Gonce births between 1891 and 1990. As can be seen, there have only been two Gonce births in Alsace in that entire period.

There are a few Gonces listed in modern-day telephone books for Strasbourg (in Bas-Rhin) but, since Strasbourg has become one of the major political centers of the European Union, many non-native surnames have shown up there since World War II.

While it certainly isn't possible to prove a negative (i.e. that the Gonces did *not* come from Alsace), I would need to see some compelling evidence to undertake any further research there that was directed specifically at our Gonce ancestry. Family traditions, of course, should not be dismissed lightly, since there is often some elusive grain of truth to them; I haven't yet discovered what that might be, however, but some alternative locations in France (and discussed on page 299) are intriguing possibilities.

Note that the Clautice family (see page 94), which is connected to the mid-Atlantic branch of the Gonce family through two marriages, likely originated in Alsace. Although confusion about this may have caused the tradition in the mid-Atlantic branch, it wouldn't explain the same tradition in the southern branch of the Gonce family.

---

[466] Specifically, I have pored through vital records from the mid-eighteenth to late nineteenth centuries for the following towns in Alsace: Baerenthal, Boofzheim, Engenthal-le-Bas, Friesenheim, Gambsheim, Kilstett, Muttersholtz, Obernai, Obersteigen, Osthouse, Rhinau, Uhlwiller, and Wangenbourg (Engenthal-le-Haut).

[467] There is a Valentine Gintz, born about 1650 in Weyersheim; a Gertrude Gintz, Marguerithe Gintz and Maria Gintz living in Weiterswiller; and another Marguerithe Gintz living in Lampertheim.

American Colonies (other)	Possible Intermediate Locale – My Vote:

As with all discussions of some *intermediate* stop on the path from Europe to Maryland, we are obviously dodging the real question of origin, but any such determination can go a long way towards identifying the actual European origin of the first American Gonce, so it is a useful exercise. One possibility mentioned by a few people is that Justice Gonce may have migrated to the Maryland area from some other colony in the New World. Such speculations have included both the settlement at Jamestown, as well as some later colony in Virginia, possibly Williamsburg.

Without any evidence of our ancestors' presence in either of these "famous" colonies, it is hard to consider these speculations seriously. There were only 105 settlers who remained in Jamestown, for instance, and most of them didn't survive very long. The names of these original settlers, as well as most of the crew who returned to England, are well known[468], and do not include anyone with Gonce or anything similar as a surname.[469]

There is, however, some evidence that there may have been Gonces in Virginia. There is a John Gonce listed in the 1810 Census[470] of Monroe County, Virginia who was born prior to 1765, although it isn't possible to tell from this census where he was born or the exact year. John had a wife who was born between 1765 and 1784; they had six young sons and two young daughters, all born between 1790 and 1806. Whether or how John and his family were related to our Gonces is unknown. Given that the surname appears only once per family in the 1810 Census, it is equally likely that they could be part of the Pennsylvania Gans family or the Baltimore Gantz family.

If he were in fact related to Justice Gonce, John's estimated birth year would suggest that he would either be a sibling or an older child.

… The Gonces and the Rockefellers in the New Jersey Colonies?

In a discussion of the genealogy of the well-known Rockefeller family[471], I came across evidence of an earlier mention of the name "Justice Gonce" [472]. In his Will of 6 December 1763, the beginning of which is transcribed below,

---

[468] A list can be found on-line at www.genealinks.com/states/va.htm.
[469] There is a Gonce-side ancestor who did live in Jamestown, however, but only for a short time and many years after the original colony was lost. See page 45 for details of Cornelius Comegys.
[470] National Archives Microfilm Series m252 Roll 70 Page 568. This might be read as "Gonoe" though.
[471] i.e. the Rockefellers of Standard Oil, Rockefeller Plaza and so forth. From "The Transactions of the Rockefeller Family Association … with Genealogy;" The Knickerbocker Press; New York, 1910. Copyright 1910 by Henry Oscar Rockefeller.
[472] Earlier, that is, than what I had previously uncovered – recall that this was in the 1761 List of Taxables in the Middle Neck Hundred of Cecil County Maryland. See page 4.

APPENDIX XII – ORIGINS OF THE GONCE FAMILY

Johann Pieter Rockefelder[473], mentions an earlier purchase of land from, among others, "Justice Gonce."

> ### Will Of Johann Peter Rockefeller[474]
>
> In the name of God—Amen: This sixth day of December in the year of our Lord one thousand seven hundred and sixty-three I
> 1 Peter Rockefelder of the township of Amwell, County of Hunterdon and Western Division of the Province of New Jersey
> 2 yeo^m being of perfect health and sound of mind and memory blessed be God, do, in this my time of health make this my last will and testament writing in manner and form following, viz:
> 1 Item, I give and bequeath to my son William Rockafelt all my lands or plantation lying in Amwell Township, County of Hunterdon, New Jersey purchased of William Burtis, Samuel
> 3 Green, and Justice Gonce Bounded South by Ezcal Rose's land, West by James Abits land, North by Peter Fisher's land, East by Noah Hixon's land, containing two hundred seventy and five acres of land be there more or less all the above described land with all thereunto appertaining or thereunto belonging I give to
> 1 him the said William Rockafelt and his heirs and assigns forever, except a half acre where the Burying Place is.
> … (the Will continues from this point)

NOTES ON PETER ROCKEFELLER'S WILL

1. Note the variation in surname spelling, even in this small section. Later in the Will, he also uses "Rockefelt" and "Rockerfeller."

2. This is an abbreviation for Yeoman. In this case, the term likely implies Mr. Rockefeller's middle class status as a farmer who cultivated his own land as opposed to farming on land belonging to someone else.

3. The name "Justice Gonce" is given in the original with our family's spelling.

Since the land was obviously purchased prior to 1763 when the Will was written, could this refer to our Justice Gonce, and could our ancestor possibly have come to Maryland from New Jersey after selling his land?

Tracking this "Justice" back a few years, we discover that on 7 June 1756, "John Justus Ganse," age 36, married Helena Harley, also aged 36, a daughter

---

[473] The spelling of the name varies, but Johann Pieter Rockefelder is an early ancestor of the Rockefellers –Pieter had arrived in the town of Amwell in about 1723, and he and his sons were naturalized in Perth Amboy on 20 August 1755 under the Act of 1730. (from page 42 of "A History of East Amwell 1700-1800; 1976; East Amwell Bicentennial Committee and Samuel Allinson's "Acts of the General Assembly of New Jersey").

[474] New Jersey Archives Vol 33; Abstracts of Wills; Vol 4 1761-1770; Page 360; December 6, 1763; Publication: Somerville, NJ

of Rudolph Harley. The name "Helena" doesn't seem like something that could be equivalent to "Magdalen," although the birth year of 1720 implied by the couples' ages would certainly not be inconsistent with having three sons born in approximately 1743 (Rudolph), 1748 (Abraham), and 1758 (Daniel). The late wedding date doesn't really fit well but, nonetheless, some further investigation seemed warranted, and led to the following discoveries:

Records of Mr. Gonce's original purchases of the land he sold survive: He acquired eight acres from Hans Rudolph Herli (b.1692; d.1764) on 31 July 1743 for £80. Hans' son Rudolph Herli, Jr. was a witness to the purchase.

On 23 June 1744, "Justus Gans" purchased another fifty acres from Rudolph Harley[475], Jr. (b. 14 Jun 1719). Justus' eventual bride Helena Harley, it turns out, was a daughter of the older Rudolph and sister to the younger. Justus, by the way, was a Cooper by trade while our ancestor Justice was a Farmer.

An argument could be made that Justus, if he were our ancestor, could conceivably have held these properties for over fifteen years, sold them to Peter Rockefeller, and still relocated to Cecil County, Maryland by 1760. It is interesting, however, that there are no extant records of Justus and Helena having any children, making his connection to our family quite unlikely.

On October 9, 1739, a "Justice Gons" was one of those submitting receipts for payment from the Estate of Henry Woolever on Amwell Township[476]. Tracking this "Justice" back further, "John Justus Ganze" seems to have been the son of "George Balzar Gantz," also a Cooper, and one of the area's early Dutch settlers. Justus had a brother named Jacob, who seems to be the same Jacob Gans[477] referred to earlier, whose father was called "Balthazar."

There is an 8 January 1776 record of a "John Gansel" being an ensign in the Fifth Pennsylvania Battalion[478] during the Revolutionary War. Although I am not convinced, two posted genealogies claim (albeit with no references) that this is in fact the same person as "John Justus Ganze." If this could be proven, it would positively confirm that "John Justus" is not our ancestor but, regardless, I don't think there is sufficient reason to suggest that he is.

It doesn't seem reasonable to me that the Gonces came from another area of the new world unless some better evidence or a good theory turns up to support this idea.

---

[475] There is ample evidence that Harly, Harley and Herli, are different spellings for the same family.

[476] "Documents relating to the Colonial History of the State of New Jersey; Calendar of New Jersey Wills, Administrations, etc.; Volume II – 1730-1750." Edited by A. Van Doren Honeyman; published 1918 by the Unionist-Gazette Association in Somerville, N.J.

[477] See the section "Holland – The Netherlands" on page 287.

[478] If this were the John Justus Ganze born in 1820, he would then have been about 55 years old.

APPENDIX XII – ORIGINS OF THE GONCE FAMILY

American Indian – Native American	Possible Country of Origin – My Vote:

The placement of this section near the beginning of the list of suggested origins is a fluke of the alphabet, but one comment I encountered on the Internet alluded to a possible American Indian connection, so it should be mentioned. This seems to have been suggested by the presence of the family of Peter Ka Tar Gonce in the 1860 Census[479], living in Isabella, Michigan. In addition to Peter, there is his wife Nor Ge She Go Quay Gonce, his daughter Min We Quet Gonce, age 16, and his son Paul[480] Gonce, age 6.

If indeed this is the surname Gonce and not simply the census taker's rendering of a homonym, it seems more likely the result of a traveling French-Canadian's extra-curricular activities than a connection to our family. I don't feel, therefore, that it would be worthwhile spending any time researching this line, particularly given the location. Our Gonces seemed to migrate solely to the south and west.

Belgium	Possible Country of Origin – My Vote:

A family of nine persons named Gonnz arrived in New York from Antwerp on the ship Frederick on 26 July 1843[481] – because of the source, it is assumed that this family is actually of German origin. Antwerp wasn't the most common port of departure for Germans, but it was common enough. Additionally there doesn't seem any reason to suspect that this family is related to ours, and therefore no reason to suspect that the Gonces are Belgian.

The Gonce name does exist in Belgium today: a Michel Gonce of Liège, Belgium, for instance, teaches courses on movement disorders at the European Federation of Neurological Studies in Brussels.

There are concentrations of French Gonces in Ardennes just across the border, but I'm unaware of any evidence to suggest whether the Gonces now living in France originated in Belgium or vice-versa.

---

[479] National Archives Microfilm Series m653 Roll 547 Page 22.
[480] One wonders whether the other children made fun of his odd name. Seriously, this abrupt change in naming strongly suggests the presence of missionaries at work.
[481] Germans to America; P. William Philby et al., Editors; 60 Volume Series ISBN 0-8420-2279-1, Supplemental Volume 2, page 24. This series covers immigrants of German nationality, no matter where they arrived from.

Canada	Possible Intermediate Country – My Vote:

Beverly R. Gonce, a white English-speaking male, was born in New Brunswick, Canada in 1858, and lived in Boston, Suffolk County, Massachusetts at the time of the 1900[482] and 1910[483] U.S. Censuses and in nearby Cambridge at the time of the 1920[484] U.S. Census. In 1900 and 1910, he was married, but had no children. By 1920, he was living with the family of a cousin named Wesley McSorley, most likely indicating that his wife had died between 1910 and 1920 (i.e. between the ages of 50 and 60). I know of no connection between Beverly and the Gonces of our family, none of which seem to have settled in the far northern United States. Since white, English-speaking Canadian families most likely had their origins in England, however, England should be kept in mind as a possible Gonce origin.

It should also be pointed out, however, that many "English" settlers arrived in Canada in the late eighteenth century from what had become the United States. These were Loyalists who opposed the revolution. I have found nothing to date to suggest that any of our Gonces ancestors were Loyalists, however. The presence of Gonces in Canada probably isn't, therefore, the result of northward migration.

The Canadian Census of 1881 shows a number of Gonces in the French-speaking province of Quebec, but these were all born in France in the nineteenth century. Examples include Caterine Gonce, born in 1824, Pierre Gonce, born in 1843, and Emile Gonce, born in 1852.

For the most part, Canadian immigration to the United States wasn't documented at all until the late nineteenth century, but in 1755, during the Seven Years' War, the British Governor Charles Lawrence and the Nova Scotia Council began what is now known as the *Grand Dérangement* of Acadians. These families, who had come to the area from France in the seventeenth century, were forced to either declare their allegiance to England or leave. A significant number of them fled to either Quebec or the American Colonies[485]. At least 454 of the exiled Acadians made their way to the Pennsylvania area[486], however, and the time frame of this migration fits with the 1730-1765 estimation of the Gonce's arrival in Delaware made earlier. Most of the Acadians eventually ended up in the French territory of

---

[482] National Archives Microfilm Series t623 Roll 680 Page 2a
[483] National Archives Microfilm Series t624 Roll 622 Page 1b
[484] National Archives Microfilm Series t625 Roll 708 Page 21a
[485] A good article on this subject can be found in the June 2006 issue of Family Tree Magazine beginning on page 63.
[486] "Population Distribution in Colonial America," Stella H. Sutherland, Columbia University Press, NY, 1936; reprinted 1966 by AMS Press, NY. Northwestern University Library reference 312.73/S966p, Evanston, IL, pg 155.

APPENDIX XII – ORIGINS OF THE GONCE FAMILY

Louisiana, though, so it seems doubtful (although not impossible) to me that our Gonces came to Delaware as part of the *Grand Dérangement*.

Interestingly, one of the few groups of Acadians who were unaffected by the *Grand Dérangement* were those who lived on Magdalen Island, which is located in the Gulf of St. Lawrence. This is the only instance I've found where the French use a form of this name that contains a "g."[487]

| **Croatia** | Possible Country of Origin – My Vote: |

Mike and John Gonce, white males, born 1884 and 1870 respectively in Croatia, lived in the 2nd Ward of Etna, Allegheny County, Pennsylvania at the time of the 1920 U.S. Census[488], but I have been unable to find any connection between them and our Gonce family. Both worked as mill laborers and were boarders with the family that owned the home. According to this census, John immigrated first, in 1911, and Mike immigrated in 1913. Although it seems very likely that these two were related somehow, there appear to be no other Gonces in or around Allegheny County, nor have I been able to locate either Mike or John in the 1930 census. There doesn't seem to be enough information, therefore, to suggest that these are related to our Gonce family.

Because of the late immigration dates, Mike and John, even if they were related to our family, would be at best very distant cousins with a common ancestor much farther back than we can currently trace.

| **Cuba** | Possible Intermediate Country – My Vote: |

Although there is no real reason to suggest that our Gonce ancestors may have come from Cuba, the idea that they may be Hispanic is buttressed by the number of Gonces currently living in Spanish speaking areas, one of which is Cuba.

The photographer Juan Carlos R. Gonce[489], for instance, was born in Havana, Cuba in 1963 and graduated from the San Alejandro Academy of Fine Arts in that same city in 1993.

---

[487] See a discussion of the etymology of the name Magdalen beginning on page 311.

[488] National Archives Microfilm Series t625 Roll 1512 Page 18b

[489] Juan Carlos seems like a better example of Hispanic Gonces than Jorge Gonce, an Argentine porn star most famous for appearing in "Madame Olga y sus Pupilas" ("Madame Olga and her Pupils").

Juan Carlos now lives and works primarily in Madrid, Spain, although he has had exhibitions throughout southern Europe.

The Miami Herald and El Nuevo Herald reported the death of Esther Gonce, 76, in their issues of 17 and 18 August 1994. Esther appears to have been a Cuban immigrant, and would have been born about 1918.

Madrid 4 by Juan Carlos R. Gonce
Double exposure from 2002

Nonetheless, the number of Gonces currently in Cuba isn't sufficient (Raul and Wilfredo and their wives) to suggest this as a country of origin, although it might qualify as an area some early Gonce may have passed through on the way to America, and it does lend more credence to the idea of an Hispanic origin. I believe we would need to have some specific information in order to seriously consider Cuba as an intermediate stop on some past migration.

England / Great Britain	Possible Country of Origin – My Vote:

Justice and Magdalen Gonce, as well as the three sons we know of, were certainly in this country during the transition from English rule to American independence. Could they or their forebears have come from England themselves? It certainly seems plausible. The English gained control of the Delaware area in 1664 after driving the Dutch out from Pennsylvania and New Amsterdam (which the English promptly renamed New York in honor of the Duke of York).

In the early 20th century, there were quite a few Gonces living in Camberwell, London, and Newington Hythe, Kent, both in England, but these have not yet been researched to determine their earlier origins. As mentioned earlier, Beverly R. Gonce emigrated from Canada, and his family was likely British originally. Furthermore, several people have pointed to a number of (possibly) independent Gonce arrivals in the United States from England during the latter 19th and early 20th centuries.

On 8 September 1885, for instance, forty-eight year old James Gonce arrived in New York from Liverpool and Queenstown on the ship Gallia[490]. An examination of the actual ship's manifest shows, however, that James is listed

---

[490] National Archives Microfilm Series M237 Roll 489 List 1121.

APPENDIX XII – ORIGINS OF THE GONCE FAMILY

as a U.S. Citizen, and so was probably returning to the United States, not immigrating. He appears to have been traveling alone, since there are no other Gonces on the list. I have not been able to identify any James Gonce born near 1837 with our family[491], but since he is already a U.S. citizen, he must have originated here, and this arrival cannot be taken to indicate England as the Gonce homeland.

In the 1900 U.S. Census[492], Joseph Gonce of Missouri (where there are a significant number of Justice and Magdalen Gonce's documented descendents living) states that his parents came from England (below).

His family is living at 1005 Brooklyn Street in St. Louis, Missouri.

Similarly, in the 1920 Census[493] (shown below), Richard B. Gonce, living with his mother Sarah in New Castle, Delaware, states that his father was born in England. In the 1900 census, however, Richard appears as a son of J.A.N. Gonce (James Allibone Gonce ID 2607) and Sarah J. Gonce (James' wife Sarah J. Hill ID 2608). James, the son of George Gonce ID 2511 and youngest brother of my 2nd great-grandfather John Thomas Gonce ID 1576 was certainly not born in England. Complicating this, however, is that although Richard's birth is given as February 1873 on the 1900 census[494] (which is consistent with his age being 52 in 1920), he does not appear with James and Sarah in the 1880 census, at which point he would have been about seven years old. A possible explanation may be that Richard's father was actually born in England, but that he was later adopted by the Gonces. Since he states that both his parents were born in Maryland on the 1900 and 1910[495] censuses, however, I am

---

[491] There is a James Gaunce, born in 1835, and living in Findley Township of Allegheny County, Pennsylvania at the time of the 1860 census (National Archives Microfilm Series m653 Roll 1063 Page 284). He is a day laborer though, and doesn't seem to be a likely candidate. This James is more likely part of our family that I have yet to identify.
[492] National Archives Microfilm Series t623, Roll 889, Page 8b
[493] National Archives Microfilm Series t625, Roll 202, Page 3a
[494] National Archives Series t623, Roll 156, Page 12; here he states that both parents were born in Maryland.

OUR GONCE ANCESTORS

inclined to think the reference to England on the 1920 census was simply an error.

[census record image]

Arguing against the Gonces having come to the New World from England, however, is the fact that the English kept quite detailed records of those who left for the American colonies both voluntarily and involuntarily. These records, from a variety of sources, have been collated and summarized in a series of books by Peter Wilson Coldham, and cover the period from 1607 through the American Revolution.

> The Complete Book of Emigrants 1607-1660; ISBN: 0-8063-1192-4.
> The Complete Book of Emigrants 1661-1699; ISBN: 0-8063-1282-3.
> The Complete Book of Emigrants 1700-1750; ISBN: 0-8063-1334-X.
> The Complete Book of Emigrants 1751-1776; ISBN: 0-8063-1376-5.
> Emigrants in Bondage 1614-1775; ISBN: 0-8063-1221-1.

All these volumes have been published by the Genealogical Publishing Co., Inc; Baltimore, and are readily available in many libraries. Because this series is considered very well researched and complete by all the genealogical references I have consulted, it seems unlikely that the Gonce family could have come from England during the period from 1607 to 1775 (the period in which they must have arrived) without being documented. I am therefore discounting England as a possible origin unless further information surfaces.

Lastly, as regards an English origin for the Gonce family, the Royal Air Force pilot Hugh Bernard Gonce, whose plane was shot down during World War II, is sometimes presented as a possible "English connection." Hugh, however, was a fifth generation American, and is discussed on page 150.

France   Possible Country of Origin – My Vote:

Family tradition in several branches of the Gonce line suggests that our ancestors may have originated in Alsace, France; because of its history, Alsace and Lorraine have been covered (and discounted, at least by me) in a separate section above, beginning on page 289.

---

[495] National Archives Series t624, Roll 146, Page 4b; here he also states that both parents were born in Maryland.

APPENDIX XII – ORIGINS OF THE GONCE FAMILY

It does seem possible that they could have been French, however. The largest concentration of Gonces in present-day Europe is in France, and I have found the name Gonce to be relatively common in certain French records of the seventeenth and eighteenth centuries – specifically those from the following areas:

Signy-le-Petit, *Ardennes*;	Rocroi, *Ardennes*;	Etalle, *Ardennes*;	Allier, *Auvergne*;
Aouste, *Ardennes*;	Marnieres, *Eure*; and	Cernay, *Eure-et-Loir*.	

As can be seen in the series of twentieth-century French population density maps given on page 315, the Gonce name was most prevalent in Nord (all black on the map) and the Ardennes, with a pronounced increase in the city of Paris after 1966.

It therefore seems likely that, if they were originally French, the Gonce family was more likely to have originated in the Nord or Ardennes area (part of the Champagne region by the Belgian border) than in Alsace[496], but I have as yet been unable to establish any connection between the colonial Gonce family and the "old world."

William Penn's marketing of his colonies[497], coupled with both political unrest and Catholic intolerance of religious dissenters, resulted in the exodus of significant numbers of French and others to America. Between 1562 and 1598, there were bitter wars between the Catholics and Protestants in France. Even with a Huguenot King, Henry IV, the dissension continued. Although Henry issued the Edict of Nantes in 1598, which guaranteed religious freedoms, the Catholic Church kept up the pressure, and religious strife continued, increasing steadily after Henry's death. By 1681, the persecution of Protestants was full-blown, forcing many to leave the country surreptitiously. This turned into a flood in 1685 when King Louis XIV revoked the Edict of Nantes, giving the excuse that, since there were no more Huguenots in France, the Edict had no further relevance. Although the bulk of French Protestants fled to Holland and England, some made their way to America. The timing doesn't seem quite right for our Gonce ancestor(s) to have migrated as part of this contingent, but the possibility can't be discounted entirely.

Later studies of the population of Pennsylvania and Delaware suggest that the French Catholics who emigrated to America in this time period did so through Germany and its ports, although they didn't seem to settle on the coast. Although the early Gonces may have been Huguenots or Quakers, they

---

[496] Could "Alsace" and "Ardennes," or even "Auvergne," have been confused by some long-ago (i.e. prior to the southern migration) family member?

[497] Strictly speaking, Penn was British and received his lands from the Crown, but the impression that he was a loyal Englishman is not quite accurate. He himself was a recurring prisoner of the British and a known "troublemaker." The Crown provided the lands to satisfy a debt to Penn's father, and it was his intention to accept both English and any other European victims of religious persecution into his colonies. He thus actively promoted such emigration.

were certainly Protestants, not Catholics, so the Catholic migration probably doesn't have much relevance for our search for Gonce origins.

As with other countries proposed as possible origins, there are some later Gonce immigrants that arrived from France. Louis Gonce, born approximately 1834, supposedly arrived in New York from Le Havre France on 10 December 1861 on the ship St. Genevieve, and listed his destination simply as United States of America. Examination of the actual ship's manifest, however, shows that his name was crossed off with the notation "not going."

Examples of interesting Gonces from France include "Madame Gonce," immortalized in the painting[498] (shown to the right) by the famous artist Jean Ingres. Prior to her marriage, Madame Gonce herself was an artist and a pupil of Ingres. At the time the portrait was painted, Caroline was the wife of Jean-Henri Gonce, councilor of the Rouen court in France. Rouen is on the Seine River, about seventy miles northwest of Paris, and in an area where "Gonce" is and was a relatively common name.

"Madame Gonce"

Portrait by Jean Auguste Dominique Ingres (1780-1867) of his pupil Caroline Maille (1815-1901).

Caroline Gonce, the actress and production manager, is another well-known French Gonce. She played the part of Ilse in *L'Homme de sa vie*, released in 2005, and the part of Géraldine in *Le Syndrome de Cyrano*, released in 2004. She was assistant director (*régisseur adjoint*) for the 2005 movie *Coeurs*.

Additionally, there are numerous Gonces in a variety of professions currently living in France.

The largest concentration of Gonces in present-day Europe is in France, so the country itself cannot be easily dismissed as a likely origin of our family.

---

[498] The painting is currently in the Musée Ingres in Mountauban.

Appendix XII – Origins of the Gonce Family

Hungary	Possible Country of Origin – My Vote:

Stephen Gonce, a Magyar male born 1894 in Hungary, lived in Stratford, Fairfax County, Connecticut at the time of the 1920 U.S. Census[499] with his wife and four children. According to this census, Stephen, who worked as a steel foundry forger, immigrated in 1910, and his wife Mary, also Hungarian, immigrated in 1908. Their children were all born in Connecticut between 1914 and 1919. I know of no connection between Stephen and the Gonces of our family, none of which are known to have settled in the far northern United States. I was unable to locate this family in later censuses.

It should be mentioned that Samuel Aba, King of Hungary from 1041-1044, was born in the "Castle Gonce"[500] in 1010. Although it isn't clear what that was, associating the name "Gonce" with Hungary isn't out of the question.

Ireland	Possible Country of Origin – My Vote:
	Possible Intermediate Country – My Vote:

According to the indexes for the National Archives Passenger Lists, a John Gonce, age 24 arrived in New York from Ireland on the ship Umbria on 27 April 1891[501].

The actual handwritten entry from line 543 on the passenger manifest

is shown to the right. Because I am not convinced that this actually says "Gonce" (the line above what would be the "n" is actually a descender from a character in the name above, so the name isn't Johnson either), I tend to doubt that this finding has any relevance to a search for our Gonce origins.

In the U.S. Census for 1850[502], we can find a Henry and Sarah McGonce living with their six-month old son James in Newtown, Queens, New York. Henry, 22, was a laborer who stated that he, Sarah and James were all born in Ireland, although the name itself suggests that they were originally of Scots-Irish ancestry. Although it isn't impossible that the name Gonce was

---

[499] National Archives Microfilm Series t625 Roll 178 Page 1b
[500] Castle Gonce was, at the time, in the city of Krosno, county of Abranvaj, Kingdom of Hungary.
[501] National Archives Microfilm Series m237, Roll 566, List 550, Line 543.
[502] National Archives Microfilm Series m432 Roll 583 Page 63

originally McGonce, our ancestors would certainly have had to abandon the "Mc" part before the American Revolution, so it seems very doubtful.

Because I have found nothing else whatever to suggest that the Gonces may have been Irish, an Irish origin for the Gonce family seems unlikely to me. The possibility that they might have passed through Ireland on the way from Scotland, however, is discussed under Scotland.

Italy	Possible Country of Origin – My Vote:

Joseph de Goncé, a forty-eight year old Baker from Italy, lived in Brooklyn, New York at the time of the 1910 Census[503]. His second wife Grace, also born in Italy and to whom Joseph had been married for four years, and their five[504] American-born children lived with them on Humbold Avenue. It isn't clear when Joseph immigrated, but it would have to have been before 1899 when his first child was born.

The name "de Goncé", of course, is certainly not the same as "Gonce", and if there is a connection, we need to remember that the "de" ("from") would have to have been lost to our own ancestors for at least 150 years by the time Joseph arrived from Italy. Nonetheless, it indicates that there may have been a place or locale known as "Gonce," presumably (although not necessarily) in Italy. I have yet to identify such a place, however, so can't determine whether Joseph's existence is a clue to our origins or merely an interesting but meaningless tidbit.

Mexico	Possible Country of Origin – My Vote:

Caterina Gonce, a white female, was supposedly born 1893 in Mexico, and lived in Laredo, Webb County, Texas at the time of the 1910 U.S. Census[505]. I know of no connection between her and the Gonces of our family, many of which settled in Texas after migrating from Tennessee and other states.

The first of Justice Gonce's descendants I am aware of to migrate to Texas[506] were the family of Louis Cleveland [ID 3157] and Sallie [ID 3158] Gonce, who were both born in Tennessee, but left their home in Georgia to settle in Texas in the mid-1890s. A substantial number of their descendants live in Texas, but

---

[503] National Archives Microfilm Series t624 Roll 965 Page 5a
[504] We would have to assume that at least one of these children was by his first wife.
[505] Listed in Heritage Quest Index but not located; not found at all on Ancestry database.
[506] Texas became a State on 29 December 1845, so these Gonces were not "pioneers" of Texas.

APPENDIX XII – ORIGINS OF THE GONCE FAMILY

so far, I have been unable to connect this Caterina with any of them. As far as I can determine, Caterina is not part of our family, or at least not a descendant of Justice Gonce.

Panama   Possible Country of Origin – My Vote:

The origin of this speculation was an index entry for the arrival of a James T. Gonce[507] from Cristobal (in the Panama Canal Zone) in New York on the ship Eten on 21 April 1919. An examination of the actual ship's manifest, however, indicates that James was a United States soldier from Walnut Shade, Missouri[508] who was born on 10 November 1900. He was not an immigrant, but a returning citizen. James' arrival, therefore, is no reason to suspect that the Gonces may have come from Panama.

Puerto Rico   Possible Country of Origin – My Vote:

No one I'm aware of has yet suggested Puerto Rico as a place where the original American Gonces may have come from. It seems to me however that if we consider "motive, means, and opportunity," Puerto Rico should be added to the list of suspects, at least for an intermediate origin through which a French or, more likely, Spanish colonist might have come to Delaware in the eighteenth century.

For Puerto Rico to make sense as an intermediate country of origin, we would need to establish how far back the Gonces have been living in Puerto Rico – and specifically that there were one or more Gonces in Puerto Rico in the mid eighteenth century or earlier – a difficult task given the lack of available records.

In the early 20th century, there were Gonces living in Caguas, Mayaguez, San German, and other towns in Puerto Rico, but these have not been researched to determine their earlier origins due to the difficulty in obtaining vital records from periods prior to 1917, when Puerto Rico became an unincorporated territory of the United States.

Available records of the late nineteenth and early twentieth centuries show that Gonce is not an uncommon name in Puerto Rico. There are Gonces in

---

[507] I have identified him as James Tilford Gonce [ID 4001], son of Abraham Rudolph "Doc" Gonce [ID 2883] and Susan T. Hargrove [ID 3998]. Susan was the last of "Doc" Gonce's many wives, and the one he is buried with.

[508] National Archives Microfilm Series t715, Roll 2638, Page 187, Line 8.

the Puerto Rican Censuses from 1910 onwards, and there are Puerto Rican Gonce males who registered for the military drafts in both World Wars. Importantly, it is worth noting that the early twentieth century Gonces in Puerto Rico include "White," "Mulatto," and "Black," so the intermingling of Gonces with others in that territory had to have gone on for quite some time.

But – could one or more Gonces have made it from Puerto Rico to the Delaware area in the American colonial period? Strangely enough, Puerto Rican history books suggest an interesting mechanism by which this may have been possible. Briefly, and in order to avoid discussing this possibility out of proportion to others, the Spanish who originally settled in Puerto Rico in the very early sixteenth century used the native Borinquero Indians as slaves to mine the gold found there. Most of these were wiped out after a slave rebellion in 1511, after which many Spaniards were recruited to come and mine the gold. By 1570, however, the gold had been effectively depleted, leading to a significant economic decline.

After fifty years of periodic attacks on Puerto Rico by the Dutch and English, all of which were repelled by the Spanish, Puerto Rico was virtually ignored by the mother country. Trading ships from Spain arrived only every ten to twelve years from about 1626 onward, and the local population, although forbidden to do so under threats of some fairly severe punishments from the crown, began to develop a very significant level of contraband trading with passing British and Dutch ships. It is quite conceivable, therefore, that an entrepreneurial Gonce could have gotten passage on a British freighter to their colonies on the mainland – a location that would have seemed quite attractive to someone mired in the conditions existing on the island at the time. For someone to have negotiated passage from Puerto Rico to Philadelphia (with a stop at Newcastle) on an English ship certainly isn't inconceivable. The aforementioned colonial population study[509] by Stella Sutherland mentions some known migrations from "the West Indies," which also lends credence to Puerto Rico as an intermediate origin of the Gonces.

There are a number of well-written histories that cover this era of Puerto Rican history [510] [511] [512], so the possibility that the original Gonce settler in our country may have first come from Puerto Rico is left for further exploration. See page 316 to compare Puerto Rican and Delaware histories.

---

[509] "Population Distribution in Colonial America," Stella H. Sutherland, Columbia University Press, NY, 1936; reprinted 1966 by AMS Press, NY. Northwestern University Library reference 312.73/S966p, Evanston, IL, pg 155.

[510] History of Puerto Rico: A Panorama of Its People; Fernando Picó; Markus Wiener Publishers, Princeton; Copyright © 2006 by Fernando Picó; ISBN: 1-55876-371-6

[511] Puerto Rico: A Political and Cultural History; Arturo Morales Carrión; W.W. Norton & Company, New York; Copyright © 1983 American Association for State and Local History, Nashville; ISBN: 0-393-30193-1

[512] Puerto Rico – the Trials of the Oldest Colony in the World; José Trías Monge; Copyright © 1997, Yale University Press; ISBN: 0-300-07110-8.

APPENDIX XII – ORIGINS OF THE GONCE FAMILY

Scotland Possible Country of Origin – My Vote:

Under Ireland, the nineteenth-century immigration of Henry and Sarah McGonce is mentioned. History tells us that significant numbers of English-speaking Presbyterian Scots lived in Northern Ireland for a time before making the journey to North America in the sixty years preceding the American Revolution.

The reasons for this migration[513] are beyond the scope of this book, but a good introductory discussion of these Scots-Irish immigrants can be found in Internet Genealogy Magazine, April/May 2007, beginning on page 22. This is available in many public libraries. In her study of colonial population distribution, the author Stella H. Sutherland[514] writes "…Newcastle, at which all incoming and outgoing vessels were obliged to touch, witnessed a secondary but impressive immigration of Scotch-Irish." Interestingly, this took place in the late seventeenth century – late enough that Justice's father could fit such a time frame.

For the most part, the Scotch-Irish continued to proceed westward into America, however, so if one Gonce person or family stayed behind, it would have been unusual. Not having done any further research into this, I am reserving judgment that we may actually be descended from a McGonce instead of a Gonce.

Spain Possible Country of Origin – My Vote:

There have been postings suggesting that the Gonces may have come from either Spain or, more specifically, the Basque region of Spain, which is in the far north. I have as yet been unable to locate Spanish records from the American colonial period, but a review of current day white pages shows that there are indeed a number of Gonces currently living in Spain. The only suggestion that they have been there for some time that I have found is a wedding between Juan Gonce and Agustina Ventosa on 22 June 1884 in Santa Maria, Geltru, in Barcelona[515] – too late to be of interest to us.

---

[513] Suffice it to say that, as usual, they include economic, political and religious difficulties.

[514] "Population Distribution in Colonial America," Stella H. Sutherland, Columbia University Press, NY, 1936; reprinted 1966 by AMS Press, NY. Northwestern University Library reference 312.73/S966p, Evanston, IL.

[515] Listed in the International Genealogical Index maintained by the Church of Jesus Christ of Latter Day Saints.

There are some Gonces in northern Catalonia, but only in the Girona (2 listings) and Barcelona (6 listings) provinces[516]. There is only one listing in Madrid and one in Cantabria. The largest concentration is in Sevilla (13 listings), in the south of Spain. There are no listings at all in the Basque provinces of Alava, Burgos, Guipuzcoa or Vizcaya.

The present-day distribution of Gonces in Spain doesn't immediately suggest a migration pattern between France and Spain in either direction. Nonetheless, the name seems more similar to Spanish names than French, so Spanish heritage seems a possibility worth pursuing, particularly due to the large concentrations of the name in the former Spanish-American colonies.

Sweden	Possible Country of Origin – My Vote:

In the 1870 U.S. Census[517], Charles Gonce, a single white male, reportedly born in 1849 in Sweden, lived in Tarkio Township, Atchison County, Missouri. I have been unable to identify this particular Charles Gonce but, given the location, it's difficult not to suspect that he was born in the town of Sweden, Missouri rather than the country of Sweden. This is particularly true because of the many of our distant cousins who have lived in other parts of Missouri since the mid-nineteenth century. I have been unable to find a good match for this Charles in any other records, however, so he might be a real Swede.

If the Gonces were originally from Sweden[518], the original Gonce male probably would have arrived between 1638 and 1654, but this seems very unlikely. All but the thirty Swedish settlers from that period who swore loyalty to the Dutch were sent back to Sweden when Peter Stuyvesant's forces recaptured Fort Casimir (present-day New Castle) in 1655. Coupled with the fact that I have found no records to indicate that any Gonces were present in the area before the eighteenth century, the probability that our first American Gonce ancestor arrived before that year seems extremely low.

---

[516] The source for these numbers is the Spanish on-line white pages, found at http://www.paginas-amarillas.es/. The Spanish often use two surnames, known as "Primer apllido" and "Segundo apellido," so care should be taken to search under both to locate names such as "Gonce-Matos," "Gomez-Gonce," and simply "Gonce."
[517] National Archives Microfilm Series m593 Roll 756 Page 447.
[518] Peter Minuit is best known for purchasing Manhattan Island on behalf of the Dutch West India Company, but after his falling out with the Dutch, he entered the service of Queen Christina of Sweden and led a group of fifty Swedish men in 1638 to found Fort Christina near what is now Wilmington, Delaware. Although this colony grew over the years, the Dutch recaptured the territory they had taken and shipped most of the colonists back to Sweden. Could a Gonce have been one of the thirty Swedes to remain in the Delaware area and submit to Dutch rule in 1655?

APPENDIX XII – ORIGINS OF THE GONCE FAMILY

Switzerland	Possible Country of Origin – My Vote:

Ulrich Gonce, born approximately 1838 in Switzerland, arrived in New York from Le Havre France on 4 December 1878 on the ship Canada, and listed his destination as Nebraska[519]. He was apparently traveling alone. Interestingly, there are two other people, Barthalomi Schmidt and Maria Paro[520] on the same page of the passenger manifest who listed their place of origin as "Alsace, Germany," suggesting that at least some passengers on that ship were from Alsace. See page 289.

There are a small number of Gonces in Switzerland today. Maurice Gonce, for instance, was a member of the Ecumenical Jury for the 1999 Cannes Film Festival.

There seems to be insufficient evidence to suggest a Swiss origin for the Gonce family, so I don't consider it useful to pursue this as a country of origin any further.

---

[519] National Archives Microfilm Series m237 Roll 415l Number 47 List 278

[520] They were not traveling together. Barthalomi was intending to stay in New York; Maria was going to California.

| And: Beware of False Gonces! | |

In the Ancestry.com indexes for the 1860 United States Census, there are references to Daniel and Sarah Gonce, both 77 years old (thus born in about 1783), living in Windsor County, Vermont with Stillman Yoney and his family. Since an age of 77 could make Daniel a possible (although otherwise unknown) son of our ancestor Daniel [ID 2580], and therefore a possible younger brother of our ancestor Rudolph [ID 2596] who was born in about 1779, a magnified image of that particular census page is provided here.

Magnified portion of 1860 Census Page from National Archives Microfilm Series m653 Roll 1329 Page 272

I think it likely that both "Yoney" and "Gonce" are transcription errors. The name Yoney, as seen on the first line shown above, looks more to me like "Jones," although the name transcribed as "Jared" on the fifth line indicates that the census taker's "J" was pretty traditional. The last name for Daniel and Sarah, in the tenth line, looks to me to be almost identical to what is purportedly "Yoney" in the first line, so I don't understand why they were transcribed differently.

In any case, I have a difficult time reading either of the surnames as "Gonce" but, since I have no idea what they actually are, am including this image here for whatever it might be worth.

Another point (not shown above, since the right-hand columns have been eliminated to allow the names to be more easily read) of interest is that the census form says that both Daniel and Sarah were born in New Hampshire – very improbable if they were actually related to our Gonce family.

APPENDIX XII – ORIGINS OF THE GONCE FAMILY

| CONCLUSION | Country of Origin mentioned in this Document – My Vote: |

The country where the Gonce family originated is almost certainly mentioned in this document. Based solely on data gleaned from the discussions of all the proposed countries of origin, it seems to me that the most plausible scenario is that the Gonces are of French or Hispanic origin, but may not have come from either of those locations directly to the Delaware/Maryland area. This, of course, is of little help, except to narrow down the field of search somewhat.

Part IV – Name Etymology

In some circumstances, the given names of early settlers can provide a clue as to their background, if not their actual origin, but with a sample as small as "Gonce," "Justice," and "Magdalen," this is a problematic exercise at best. For one thing, we don't know for certain if Justice was actually the first Gonce settler in America[521]; if he wasn't, his name may have been influenced as much by his parents' New World contacts as by their family's Old World traditions. Nonetheless, the following paragraphs will discuss the etymology of these names – more with an eye to being able to eliminate certain possible countries of origin than to actually pin one down.

The Surname "Gonce"   My Vote: Hispanic or French

I have found no references at all to the surname Gonce in the many books and web sites purporting to have comprehensive surname origins and meanings. It does seem clear from colonial records available that the name was clearly spelled that way as far back as the mid-eighteenth century, and should therefore be treated separately from other possible variants until there is clear evidence to suggest otherwise.

Although the name "Gonce" could be French, it certainly has more of a Hispanic feel to it. In fact, the only other word I have identified with the "-once" ending appears in the Hispanic territory of Puerto Rico, which has a region as well as a town named "Ponce."

The family of Chicago television journalists named Ponce[522] is of Hispanic descent, and pronounces their name Páuns-eh (accent on the first syllable). If the same pronunciation is applied to the similarly spelled Gonce, the resulting Gáuns-eh might well be written by a third party as "Gaunce," the most

---

[521] Although that is obviously my current belief.
[522] Phil Ponce, Anchor and Managing Editor for News at WTTW, the primary Chicago PBS station, and his two sons Dan and Anthony who are on different local network news teams. The Ponces are Mexican-American, however, not Puerto Rican.

common misspelling of the name in available Colonial records. Intriguing, certainly, but likely irrelevant.

Gonce is the 19,174th most popular last name (surname) in the United States; it falls in the 77.645th percentile[523]. Since this name has been around for at least two hundred fifty years that we know of, it doesn't seem fruitful at this point to speculate on whether it had been earlier derived from some other Hispanic name, such as Gonzales[524] or something similar.

The Given Name "Justice"   My Vote: Romantic

The name "Justice" is an Anglicized form of the Latin name Justus that is either based on the New Testament biblical name Justus, or shares a common origin. The name, which seems to have only ever been used for males, means "just" or "righteous." This suggests a Romantic origin, but since our most likely candidates (France and Spain) are both Romance countries, this name tells us nothing.

The Given Name "Magdalen"   My Vote: Likely Hispanic

We don't know if Justice Gonce met and married Magdalen in the New World or whether they arrived as a couple from the same place – and we don't know, in the latter case, whether they arrived with or without any or all of their children[525]. Looking at the etymology of Magdalen's name, therefore, might not tell us anything about Justice's origins or those of his Gonce forebears, but nonetheless might suggest something interesting about our heritage. Pay close attention to the next four boring paragraphs …

The name Magdalene is most commonly associated with the New Testament Mary Magdalene. In that context, the name simply meant "woman from Magdala." The name also exists earlier in both Hebrew and Aramaic, however. In Hebrew, it meant "woman from the tower." This is, in turn, derived from the Aramaic Maghdela, the name of a place on the Sea of Galilee referred to as "the tower[526]."

Common spellings seen in America for this name include: Madeleine, Madelena, Madelene, Magda, Magdala, Magdalen, Magdalen, Magdalena, and Magdalene.

---

[523] SourceCBN, from http://From www.placesnamed.com/g/o/gonce.asp

[524] Gonzales is a patronymic name meaning "son of Gonzalo." The given name "Gonzalo" comes from the medieval name Gundisalvus, which was the Latin form of a Germanic name composed of the elements "gund," meaning "war" and "salv" which is of unknown meaning. It has many alternate spellings (e.g. Gonzalez, Conzalez, Gonzalas, Gonzalaz, Gonsales, Goncalez, and Goncales), but I haven't ever seen Gonce listed as one.

[525] My current inclination is to believe they arrived together, and with their three sons.

[526] I'm assuming these all refer to the same location, but the sources aren't very clear on this.

APPENDIX XII – ORIGINS OF THE GONCE FAMILY

In Spain, variants commonly seen include: Madelynn, Magdalen, Magdalena, and Magdalene. One web site describing Spanish names suggests that the name means "bitter," but provides no etymological basis for this assertion[527].

The shortened form Magda appears in Slavic and some South American countries, and the forms Magdalen, Magdalena, and Magdalene appear in Czechoslovakia. These were likely the result of the influence of early missionaries but, since we're assuming our Gonce roots are neither Slavic nor Czech, it doesn't really matter.

In France, we see variants of this name such as Madelina, Madeline, and Madelon[528].

The last four paragraphs seem to have been a tedious and useless recital of name variations, but if you have been paying very close attention, you will have noted that the key difference between the French versions of the name and everyone else's[529] is that there is never a "g" in French. It's probably not possible to draw any firm conclusions from this, but it certainly argues against our Magdalen being of French origin. It seems that Magdalen is definitely a Hispanic form[530] of the name. But, then... – there is the island of Magdalen in the French-Canadian Gulf of St. Lawrence[531] to explain ...

The Given Names Rudolph, Daniel and Abraham   My Vote: Judaeo-Christian

There is probably less value in evaluating the names of the sons than there is for Magdalen's, and for much the same reasons. Based on what I believe is the likely period when Justice arrived in the country, he and Magdalen could easily have chosen these names to "fit in" with their new neighbors rather than to follow their own cultural heritage. If they arrived with the sons, all we can determine for sure is that they came from a country with Judaeo-Christian traditions. I have not yet attempted to look for religious influences, but this may be a fruitful avenue for further investigation.

Part V – Tentative Conclusions

The big conclusion is that we know very little about the arrival of Gonce family in the New World. With the information so far discovered, the best we can do is make some semi-educated guesses.

---

[527] It certainly isn't the Spanish word for "bitter" however, which is "amargo". Spanish is derived primarily from Latin, in which the word for "bitter" is "amarus." There are Moorish influences on the Spanish language, however, but I've been unable to locate any justification based on that language either.

[528] Madelon is sometimes seen in France as a male name as well.

[529] The French always seem to be contrary in one respect or another – regardless of the subject. (I'm entitled to say this, since I can document other French ancestry.)

[530] Once again, I'm perhaps being close-minded, but it doesn't seem likely that there were immigrants from the area of Czechoslovakia during the time period in question.

[531] See the discussion of *Le Grand Dérangement* under the discussion of Canada on page 295.

In deciding whether and to what degree to accept any of the origins proposed above as realistic enough to warrant further research, I've tried to consider the following:

- Is there any contemporary documentation to support the proposal?
- Does the theory fit into the historical context of the time?
- Were there known Ship and Trading Routes that support the theory?
- The theory should present no conflicts with known facts.

My own guesses as to the answers of the classic journalistic questions "who, what, where, when, why and how?" are summarized below.

Who were the first Gonces to arrive?

With the available information, it's hard to argue strongly, but I suspect that the Gonces arrived as a family, with Justice, Magdalen, and at least three sons, and that this was the first generation of Gonces in the New World. A major influence on this belief is the family tradition that there were originally three brothers who came to America. Since this tradition survives in both the Maryland and Tennessee branches of the family (which split apart in the late eighteenth century), it seems plausible that the story could have originated while the brothers or their children were still alive, thus giving it a certain level of credibility.

Where did Justice and/or his Family originate?

The style of the name Gonce suggests Hispanic origins, but population statistics suggest French origins. The French Huguenots were known to have arrived at the right time period, so France would seem to be the strongest candidate. But several other theories need to be disproved, or better evidence needs to be located, before this guess can be moved from "maybe" to "likely." The fact that they seem to have been Protestants in New Castle tends to argue against Spain or Puerto Rico, but "fitting in" was quite important in those days, so this may not mean much.

Where did Justice and/or his Family arrive?

It seems likely that Justice, along with his family, arrived at the fort in Newcastle, in what is now known as New Castle County. This is a handy and convenient guess, but it might suggest that they either knew someone already there[532], or that they wished to enter the country with a minimum of questioning from pesky customs agents. I believe there is no reason to suspect that our early Gonce immigrant ancestors were ever in what is present day Pennsylvania.

When did Justice and/or his Family arrive?

We don't know for sure when the Gonces arrived, but it seems reasonable to assume that it was between 1730 and 1760, and perhaps even between 1755

---

[532] Or possibly learned of the area and entry point from a sailor.

APPENDIX XII – ORIGINS OF THE GONCE FAMILY

and 1760. I would tend to argue this time frame unless and until some earlier evidence of their presence in this country is found.

Why did Justice and/or his Family migrate to America?

The answer to this depends primarily on where we assume they came from. They seem to have been Protestants when we first encounter them in Delaware, so religious discrimination, whether in France or Ireland, is a possibility. Economic opportunity is another possibility.

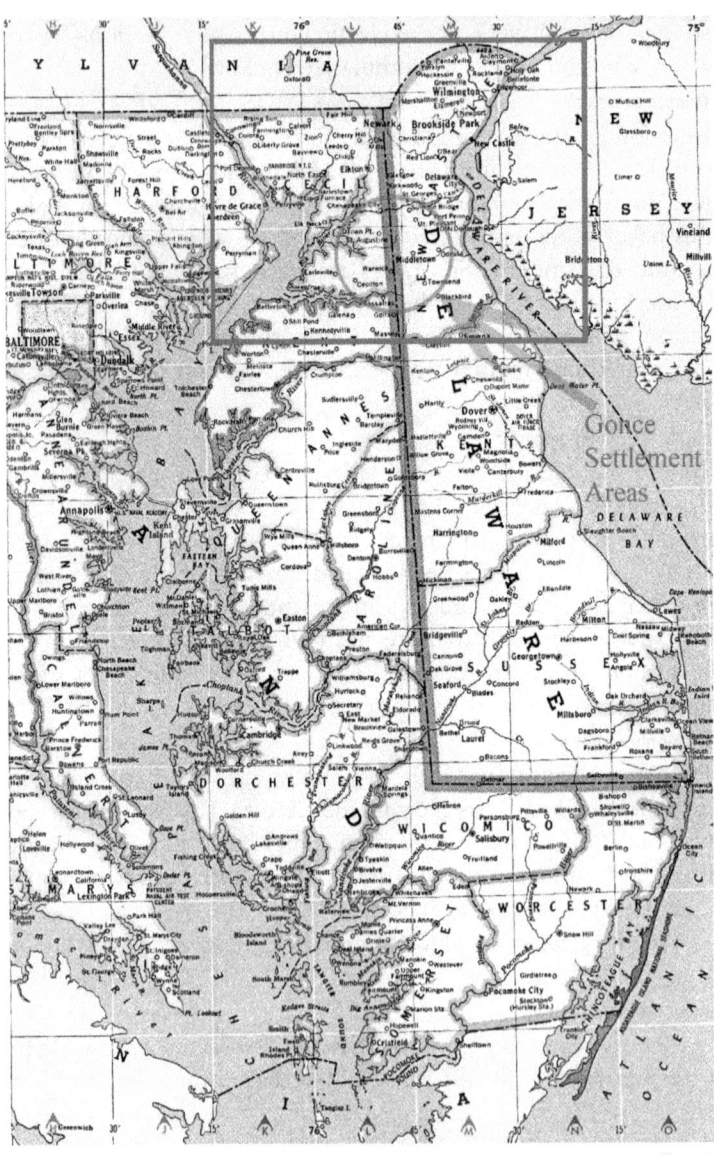

Modern map of the original areas (inner circle) where the Gonce family was first known to have settled.. The area bounded by the rectangle is shown in more detail on page 2.

Part VI – Distribution of Gonce Births in Twentieth Century France

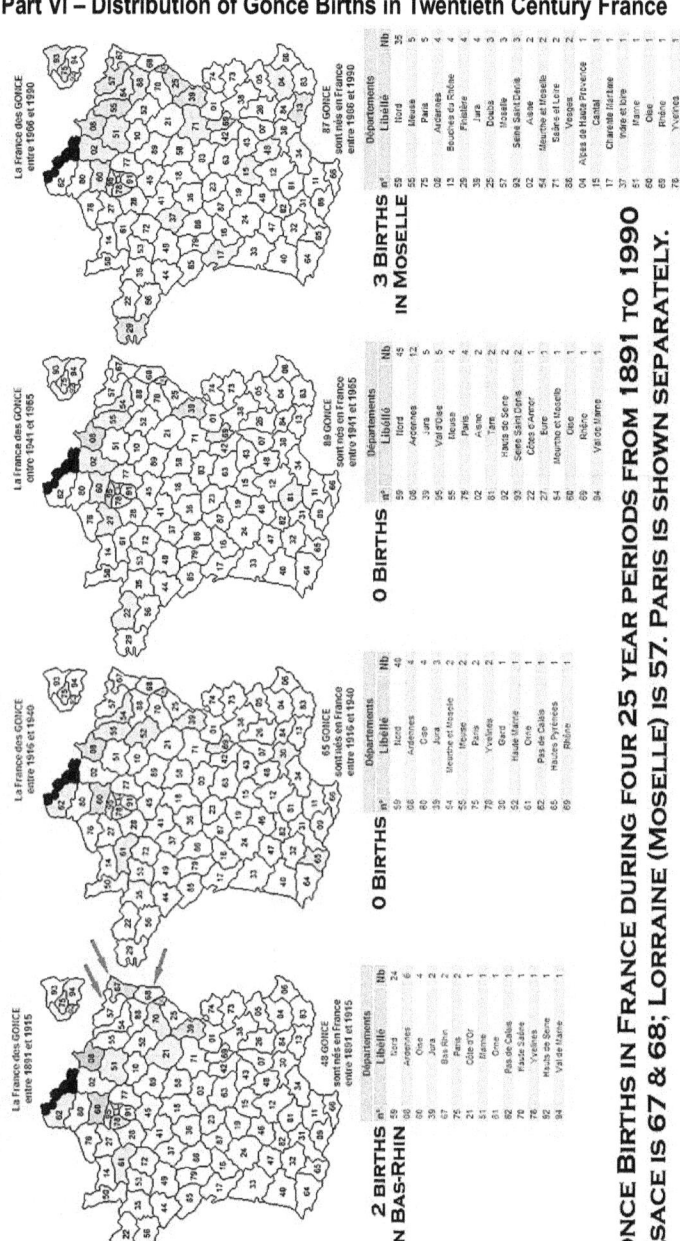

The number of Gonce births gives an indication of the distribution of the name during the four quarter-centuries depicted in the maps above. The text describes the lack of any Gonce surnames found while researching Alsatian records from about 1770 through 1860. As these maps indicate, there were only two Gonce births in the Bas-Rhin section of Alsace between 1891 and 1915, and 3 births in Moselle between 1966 and 1990. It's quite clear, however, that there has been a significant Gonce presence in the Nord region (the black area marked #5), so French ancestry can't be discounted.

Appendix XII – Origins of the Gonce Family

Part VII – Time Lines for Delaware, Scotland/Ireland, Puerto Rico, and France related to Gonce Family Events

Year Range	Events in Delaware History	Control of Delaware	Events in Scots/Irish History	Events in Puerto Rican History	Events in French History	Events in Gonce Family
1511				Uprising of Borinqueno Indian Slaves forced to mine gold for the Spaniards.		
1521				Many Spanish men arrive to mine gold. No women come with them. At this time, Puerto Rico was under the Viceroyship of New Spain/Mexico.		
1570		Various Native-American Tribes		Puerto Rican gold mines become depleted. Colony shifts to ginger exports.	1562-1598: Wars between Catholics and Protestants in France.	
1596				English under Sir Francis Drake attack Puerto Rico and control the island for a period of days.		
1598					Henry IV issues Edict of Nantes granting partial religious freedom to Protestants.	

■ 316 ■

Year Range	Events in Delaware History	Control of Delaware	Events in Scots/Irish History	Events in Puerto Rican History	Events in French History	Events in Gonce Family
1611	Captain-General Thomas West, Baron De La Warr (guess where the name Delaware comes from) and Governor of Virginia, visited the Bay and River later named for him.				Catholic discrimination against Protestants continues, increasing over the years.	
1623-1631	Dutch first visit and explore Delaware Bay					
1625		Various Native-American Tribes		Holland attacks Puerto Rico; the Dutch are repelled by the Spanish		
1626	Peter Minuit, a German, purchased Manhattan Island on behalf of the Dutch West India Company.			From this period on, trading ships arrive from Spain only every ten to twelve years. Colonists in Puerto Rico begin contraband trading with the English and Dutch.		
1631	David Pietersen De Vries of the Dutch-West India Company establish a settlement at present day Lewistown (Lewes), DE.	Dutch		"The Law restricted commerce to Seville, but smuggling was a main way of life."[533]		

---

[533] Puerto Rico – the Trials of the Oldest Colony in the World; José Trías Monge; Copyright © 1997, Yale University Press; ISBN: 0-300-07110-8.

APPENDIX XII – ORIGINS OF THE GONCE FAMILY

Year Range	Events in Delaware History	Control of Delaware	Events in Scots/Irish History	Events in Puerto Rican History	Events in French History	Events in Gonce Family
1631	Peter Minuit recalled back to Holland and discharged after differences with Dutch authorities	Dutch				
1634-1636		Dutch		King Philip IV of Spain instituted a large series of fortifications beginning with a fort at San Cristóbal to protect against privateers and pirates.		
1638	Peter Minuit, now in the service of Queen Christina, and fifty Swedish Colonists (apparently all male) establish "New Sweden." Fort Christina constructed near present-day Wilmington	Dutch/ Swedish				If Swedish, the original Gonce male probably would have arrived in this period (1638-1654), but this seems very unlikely.
1651	The Dutch under Peter Stuyvesant of New Netherlands establish Fort Casimir near present-day New Castle					
1654	The Swedes capture Fort Casimir and push out the Dutch	Swedish				

■ 318 ■

OUR GONCE ANCESTORS

Year Range	Events in Delaware History	Control of Delaware	Events in Scots/Irish History	Events in Puerto Rican History	Events in French History	Events in Gonce Family
1655	Peter Stuyvesant's forces recapture Fort Casimir and take over entire Delaware area. All but thirty Swedes return to Sweden.	Dutch				If Swedish, the original Gonce male would have had to have been one of these thirty settlers – again, very unlikely.
1664	British forces seize New Netherlands as well as the Pennsylvania and Delaware areas from the Dutch.					
1665-1697	Delaware census records from this period show no Gonce or similar names.[535]					
1681-1685		British	Scottish Presbyterians, forced to tithe to the Catholic Church, leave Ireland for England in large numbers, looking for religious tolerance.		Heavy persecution of the Huguenots by the Catholics begins in 1681. In 1685 the Edict of Nantes was formally revoked by King Louis XIV[534].	

---

[534] His stated reason was that there were no longer any Huguenots in France. Ouch.
[535] Multiple references; see above.

APPENDIX XII – ORIGINS OF THE GONCE FAMILY

Year Range	Events in Delaware History	Control of Delaware	Events in Scots-Irish History	Events in Puerto Rican History	Events in French History	Events in Gonce Family
1682	William Penn obtained a deed (by purchase) for "the territories or Three Lower Counties on the Delaware" and formally added Delaware to the British holdings.		Significant Scots-Irish Presbyterian emigration from Ireland to Pennsylvania and Delaware begins.		Significant German emigration to America in this period known to include some French[536]. Other French emigrate to Holland and England.	
1682-1704	The three-county Delaware area is under Pennsylvania rule.					
1698	I was unable to locate any Delaware area census records from this period on through the first United States census.	nominally British, but controlled exclusively by William Penn until his death on 30 July 1718.				The earliest year in which any Gonce likely arrived in the Delaware area. (see 1665 entry) If so, it would likely have been Justice's father.
1702	Many Irish Presbyterians settle under indenture arrangements.		Scots-Irish colonists established in New Castle County, Delaware.	The British attack Arecibo, but are turned back.		
1704	A separate legislature is established for the Delaware area, but it remains under Pennsylvania rule		1700-1732: Scots-Irish from Pennsylvania and Delaware) begin migrating westward as German presence increased, and inland lands became available.			

---

[536] "Population Distribution in Colonial America," Stella H. Sutherland, Columbia University Press, NY, 1936; reprinted 1966 by AMS Press, NY. Northwestern University Library reference 312.73/S966p, Evanston, IL; pp 140, 141, 156

Year Range	Events in Delaware History	Control of Delaware	Events in Scots/Irish History	Events in Puerto Rican History	Events in French History	Events in Gonce Family
1710	A separate Executive Council is established for the Delaware area					
1710-1730						Likely birth year range for Justice and Magdalen Gonce
1730-1765		continued control by William Penn and, after his death in 1718, by his successors.				Likely period when Justice Gonce arrived in the Colonies if he wasn't born here.[537]
1745-1760						Likely birth year range for Justice and Magdalens' children
1759	No Gonce land assessments in New Castle County.[538]					
1765				General O'Reilly commissioned by King Charles III of Spain to investigate and deal with contraband activity on Puerto Rico.		This is probably the last year in which any Gonce was likely to have arrived in the PA/DE area from (or by way of) Puerto Rico.

---

[537] I have found no evidence of the name Gonce in this area prior to Justice, so am assuming that he was the first immigrant. Whether he was already married when he arrived, or met Magdalen here is unknown. Family traditions differ across the branches of the Gonce family as to whether the sons were born here or arrived with their parents. See the narrative discussion of the Gonces' likely arrival time period on page 278.

[538] Warrants and Surveys of the Province of Pennsylvania including the Three Lower Counties 1759; Allen Weinberg and Thomas E. Slattery; City of Philadelphia Department of Records, 1965 (S131)

APPENDIX XII – ORIGINS OF THE GONCE FAMILY

Year Range	Events in Delaware History	Control of Delaware	Events in Scots/Irish History	Events in Puerto Rican History	Events in French History	Events in Gonce Family
1776	The three counties comprising modern day Delaware are established as the Delaware State					
1777						Gonce sons known to be in America.
1778		State of Delaware and the United States of America				Justice and Magdalen's son Daniel Gonce marries Mary Lowery on 9 DEC 1778 in Cecil County, MD[539]
1782						Likely year Justice Gonce died in New Castle County; his will was probated and Magdalen assigned as Administrator on 4 NOV 1782.

---

[539] Cecil County, Maryland is just west across the state border from New Castle County, Delaware.

Year Range	Events in Delaware History	Control of Delaware	Events in Scots/Irish History	Events in Puerto Rican History	Events in French History	Events in Gonce Family
1792	The new U.S. constitution officially establishes the State of Delaware as part of the United States of America			Spain comes under control of Napoleon Bonaparte and his French Empire. France's Caribbean interest is primarily in Mexico.		

APPENDIX XIII

Family Group Sheets: Extending the Line…

As explained elsewhere, privacy considerations have dictated that, with few exceptions, names and personal information for the descendants of my parents' generation (listed in this book as generation 9 based on their removal from Justice Gonce) are not included in this book.

For those who wish to add descendant names for use within their immediate family, the following pages provide a number of what are known in genealogical circles as **Family Group Sheets**, although I have modified them slightly to permit referencing back to one of the Gonce ancestors who is described in this book. Since the tradition of family bibles as family history archives (see the example on page 105) has faded away, recording information on these may help future descendants to more easily connect the relatives they know to those discussed in this history.

The first two sheets are for recording data about the spouse and children of *one* of the 8th generation of the American Gonces, for example Rosalie G. Gonce, M. Regina Gonce, Charles R. Gonce Jr., or George J. Gonce.

The next two sheets are for data about *one* of the 9th generation and any spouse or children that person may have; likewise, the following two sheets are for information pertaining to *one* of the 10th generation. Obviously, even for the 9th, 10th, and 11th generations alone, many more sheets would be required but, since this is impractical, these sheets should be useful as examples, and many more examples can easily be located on the internet if desired.

Family Group Record: 8th – 9th Generation

for _____ **GONCE** (from page 137)

Spouse's Name			
Spouse Born	Date	Place	
Spouse Baptized	Date	Place	
Married	Date	Place	
Spouse Died	Date	Place	
Spouse Buried	Date	Place	
Spouse's father's name			
Spouse's mother's name			

Child: **9.1**			Name	Male / Female
Born	Date	Place		
Baptized	Date	Place		
Died	Date	Place		
Buried	Date	Place		
	Continued on page		(continuation sheet if this child has its own family)	

Child: **9.2**			Name	Male / Female
Born	Date	Place		
Baptized	Date	Place		
Died	Date	Place		
Buried	Date	Place		
	Continued on page		(continuation sheet if this child has its own family)	

Child: **9.3**			Name	Male / Female
Born	Date	Place		
Baptized	Date	Place		
Died	Date	Place		
Buried	Date	Place		
	Continued on page		(continuation sheet if this child has its own family)	

Family Group Record: 8th – 9th Generation (continued)

Child: **9.4**			Name	Male
				Female
Born	Date	Place		
Baptized	Date	Place		
Died	Date	Place		
Buried	Date	Place		
	Continued on page		(continuation sheet if this child has its own family)	

Child: **9.5**			Name	Male
				Female
Born	Date	Place		
Baptized	Date	Place		
Died	Date	Place		
Buried	Date	Place		
	Continued on page		(continuation sheet if this child has its own family)	

Child: **9.6**			Name	Male
				Female
Born	Date	Place		
Baptized	Date	Place		
Died	Date	Place		
Buried	Date	Place		
	Continued on page		(continuation sheet if this child has its own family)	

Child: **9.7**			Name	Male
				Female
Born	Date	Place		
Baptized	Date	Place		
Died	Date	Place		
Buried	Date	Place		
	Continued on page		(continuation sheet if this child has its own family)	

Family Group Record: 9th – 10th Generation

for _____ (from page ___)

Spouse's Name		
Spouse Born	Date	Place
Spouse Baptized	Date	Place
Married	Date	Place
Spouse Died	Date	Place
Spouse Buried	Date	Place
Spouse's father's name		
Spouse's mother's name		

Child: **10.1**			Name	Male Female
Born	Date	Place		
Baptized	Date	Place		
Died	Date	Place		
Buried	Date	Place		
	Continued on page	(continuation sheet if this child has its own family)		

Child: **10.2**			Name	Male Female
Born	Date	Place		
Baptized	Date	Place		
Died	Date	Place		
Buried	Date	Place		
	Continued on page	(continuation sheet if this child has its own family)		

Child: **10.3**			Name	Male Female
Born	Date	Place		
Baptized	Date	Place		
Died	Date	Place		
Buried	Date	Place		
	Continued on page	(continuation sheet if this child has its own family)		

Family Group Record: 9th – 10th Generation (continued)

Child: **10.4**			Name	Male / Female
Born	Date	Place		
Baptized	Date	Place		
Died	Date	Place		
Buried	Date	Place		
	Continued on page		(continuation sheet if this child has its own family)	

Child: **10.5**			Name	Male / Female
Born	Date	Place		
Baptized	Date	Place		
Died	Date	Place		
Buried	Date	Place		
	Continued on page		(continuation sheet if this child has its own family)	

Child: **10.6**			Name	Male / Female
Born	Date	Place		
Baptized	Date	Place		
Died	Date	Place		
Buried	Date	Place		
	Continued on page		(continuation sheet if this child has its own family)	

Child: **10.7**			Name	Male / Female
Born	Date	Place		
Baptized	Date	Place		
Died	Date	Place		
Buried	Date	Place		
	Continued on page		(continuation sheet if this child has its own family)	

OUR GONCE ANCESTORS

Family Group Record: 10th – 11th Generation

for _____ (from page ___)

Spouse's Name			
Spouse Born	Date	Place	
Spouse Baptized	Date	Place	
Married	Date	Place	
Spouse Died	Date	Place	
Spouse Buried	Date	Place	
Spouse's father's name			
Spouse's mother's name			

Child: **11.1**			Name	Male Female
Born	Date	Place		
Baptized	Date	Place		
Died	Date	Place		
Buried	Date	Place		
	Continued on page	(continuation sheet if this child has its own family)		

Child: **11.2**			Name	Male Female
Born	Date	Place		
Baptized	Date	Place		
Died	Date	Place		
Buried	Date	Place		
	Continued on page	(continuation sheet if this child has its own family)		

Child: **11.3**			Name	Male Female
Born	Date	Place		
Baptized	Date	Place		
Died	Date	Place		
Buried	Date	Place		
	Continued on page	(continuation sheet if this child has its own family)		

Family Group Record: 10th – 11th Generation (continued)

Child: **11.4**			Name	Male / Female
Born	Date	Place		
Baptized	Date	Place		
Died	Date	Place		
Buried	Date	Place		
	Continued on page		(continuation sheet if this child has its own family)	

Child: **11.5**			Name	Male / Female
Born	Date	Place		
Baptized	Date	Place		
Died	Date	Place		
Buried	Date	Place		
	Continued on page		(continuation sheet if this child has its own family)	

Child: **11.6**			Name	Male / Female
Born	Date	Place		
Baptized	Date	Place		
Died	Date	Place		
Buried	Date	Place		
	Continued on page		(continuation sheet if this child has its own family)	

Child: **11.7**			Name	Male / Female
Born	Date	Place		
Baptized	Date	Place		
Died	Date	Place		
Buried	Date	Place		
	Continued on page		(continuation sheet if this child has its own family)